VITRUVIUS

THE TEN BOOKS ON ARCHITECTURE

TRANSLATED BY

MORRIS HICKY MORGAN, PH.D., LL.D.

WITH ILLUSTRATIONS AND ORIGINAL DESIGNS

PREPARED UNDER THE DIRECTION OF

HERBERT LANGFORD WARREN, A.M.

DOVER PUBLICATIONS, INC.
NEW YORK   NEW YORK

Published in the United Kingdom by Constable and Company Limited, 10 Orange Street, London W. C. 2.

This new Dover edition, first published in 1960, is an unabridged and unaltered republication of the first edition of the English translation by Morris Hicky Morgan, originally published by the Harvard University Press in 1914.

Manufactured in the United States of America

Dover Publications, Inc.
180 Varick Street
New York 14, N. Y.

PREFACE

During the last years of his life, Professor Morgan had devoted much time and energy to the preparation of a translation of Vitruvius, which he proposed to supplement with a revised text, illustrations, and notes. He had completed the translation, with the exception of the last four chapters of the tenth book, and had discussed, with Professor Warren, the illustrations intended for the first six books of the work; the notes had not been arranged or completed, though many of them were outlined in the manuscript, or the intention to insert them indicated. The several books of the translation, so far as it was completed, had been read to a little group of friends, consisting of Professors Sheldon and Kittredge, and myself, and had received our criticism, which had, at times, been utilized in the revision of the work.

After the death of Professor Morgan, in spite of my obvious incompetency from a technical point of view, I undertook, at the request of his family, to complete the translation, and to see the book through the press. I must, therefore, assume entire responsibility for the translation of the tenth book, beginning with chapter thirteen, and further responsibility for necessary changes made by me in the earlier part of the translation, changes which, in no case, affect any theory held by Professor Morgan, but which involve mainly the adoption of simpler forms of statement, or the correction of obvious oversights.

The text followed is that of Valentine Rose in his second edition (Leipzig, 1899), and the variations from this text are, with a few exceptions which are indicated in the footnotes, in the nature of a return to the consensus of the manuscript readings.

The illustrations in the first six books are believed to be substantially in accord with the wishes of Professor Morgan. The suggestions for illustrations in the later books were incomplete,

PREFACE

and did not indicate, in all cases, with sufficient definiteness to allow them to be executed, the changes from conventional plans and designs intended by the translator. It has, therefore, been decided to include in this part of the work only those illustrations which are known to have had the full approval of Professor Morgan. The one exception to this principle is the reproduction of a rough model of the Ram of Hegetor, constructed by me on the basis of the measurements given by Vitruvius and Athenaeus.

It does not seem to me necessary or even advisable to enter into a long discussion as to the date of Vitruvius, which has been assigned to various periods from the time of Augustus to the early centuries of our era. Professor Morgan, in several articles in the *Harvard Studies in Classical Philology*, and in the *Proceedings of the American Academy*, all of which have been reprinted in a volume of *Addresses and Essays* (New York, 1909), upheld the now generally accepted view that Vitruvius wrote in the time of Augustus, and furnished conclusive evidence that nothing in his language is inconsistent with this view. In revising the translation, I met with one bit of evidence for a date before the end of the reign of Nero which I have never seen adduced. In VIII, 3, 21, the kingdom of Cottius is mentioned, the name depending, it is true, on an emendation, but one which has been universally accepted since it was first proposed in 1513. The kingdom of Cottius was made into a Roman province by Nero (cf. Suetonius, *Nero*, 18), and it is inconceivable that any Roman writer subsequently referred to it as a kingdom.

It does seem necessary to add a few words about the literary merits of Vitruvius in this treatise, and about Professor Morgan's views as to the general principles to be followed in the translation.

Vitruvius was not a great literary personage, ambitious as he was to appear in that character. As Professor Morgan has aptly said, "he has all the marks of one unused to composition, to whom writing is a painful task." In his hand the measuring-rod was a far mightier implement than the pen. His turgid and pompous rhetoric displays itself in the introductions to the different books, where his exaggerated effort to introduce some semblance of style into his commonplace lectures on the noble principles which should govern the conduct of the architect, or into the prosaic lists of architects and writers on architecture, is everywhere apparent. Even in the more technical portions of his work, a like conscious effort may be detected, and, at the same time, a lack of confidence in his ability to express himself in unmistakable language. He avoids periodic sentences, uses only the simpler subjunctive constructions, repeats the antecedent in relative clauses, and, not infrequently, adopts a formal language closely akin to that of specifications and contracts, the style with which he was, naturally, most familiar. He ends each book with a brief summary, almost a formula, somewhat like a sigh of relief, in which the reader unconsciously shares. At times his meaning is ambiguous, not because of grammatical faults, which are comparatively few and unimportant, but because, when he does attempt a periodic sentence, he becomes involved, and finds it difficult to extricate himself.

Some of these peculiarities and crudities of expression Professor Morgan purposely imitated, because of his conviction that a translation should not merely reproduce the substance of a book, but should also give as clear a picture as possible of the original, of its author, and of the working of his mind. The translation is intended, then, to be faithful and exact, but it deliberately avoids any attempt to treat the language of Vitruvius as though it were Ciceronian, or to give a false impression of conspicuous literary merit in a work which is destitute of that quality. The translator had, however, the utmost confidence in the sincerity of Vitruvius and in the serious purpose of his treatise on architecture.

To those who have liberally given their advice and suggestions in response to requests from Professor Morgan, it is impossible for me to make adequate acknowledgment. Their number is so great, and my knowledge of the indebtedness in individual cases is so small, that each must be content with the thought of the full and generous acknowledgment which he would have received had Professor Morgan himself written this preface.

Personally I am under the greatest obligations to Professor H. L. Warren, who has freely given both assistance and criticism; to Professor G. L. Kittredge, who has read with me most of the proof; to the Syndics of the Harvard University Press, who have made possible the publication of the work; and to the members of the Visiting Committee of the Department of the Classics and the classmates of Professor Morgan, who have generously supplied the necessary funds for the illustrations.

ALBERT A. HOWARD.

CONTENTS

BOOK I

Preface	3
The Education of the Architect	5
The Fundamental Principles of Architecture	13
The Departments of Architecture	16
The Site of a City	17
The City Walls	21
The Directions of the Streets; with Remarks on the Winds	24
The Sites for Public Buildings	31

BOOK II

Introduction	35
The Origin of the Dwelling House	38
On the Primordial Substance according to the Physicists	42
Brick	42
Sand	44
Lime	45
Pozzolana	46
Stone	49
Methods of Building Walls	51
Timber	58
Highland and Lowland Fir	64

BOOK III

Introduction	69
On Symmetry: in Temples and in the Human Body	72
Classification of Temples	75
The Proportions of Intercolumniations and of Columns	78

CONTENTS

The Foundations and Substructures of Temples 86
Proportions of the Base, Capitals, and Entablature in the Ionic Order 90

BOOK IV

Introduction 101
The Origins of the Three Orders, and the Proportions of the Corinthian Capital 102
The Ornaments of the Orders 107
Proportions of Doric Temples 109
The Cella and Pronaos 114
How the Temple should face 116
The Doorways of Temples 117
Tuscan Temples 120
Circular Temples and Other Varieties 122
Altars 125

BOOK V

Introduction 129
The Forum and Basilica 131
The Treasury, Prison, and Senate House 137
The Theatre: its Site, Foundations, and Acoustics . . 137
Harmonics 139
Sounding Vessels in the Theatre 143
Plan of the Theatre 146
Greek Theatres 151
Acoustics of the Site of a Theatre 153
Colonnades and Walks 154
Baths 157
The Palaestra 159
Harbours, Breakwaters, and Shipyards 162

BOOK VI

Introduction 167
On Climate as determining the Style of the House . . 170
Symmetry, and Modifications in it to suit the Site . . 174

Proportions of the Principal Rooms	176
The Proper Exposures of the Different Rooms	180
How the Rooms should be suited to the Station of the Owner	181
The Farmhouse	183
The Greek House	185
On Foundations and Substructures	189

BOOK VII

Introduction	195
Floors	202
The Slaking of Lime for Stucco	204
Vaultings and Stucco Work	205
On Stucco Work in Damp Places, and on the Decoration of Dining Rooms	208
The Decadence of Fresco Painting	210
Marble for use in Stucco	213
Natural Colours	214
Cinnabar and Quicksilver	215
Cinnabar (continued)	216
Artificial Colours. Black	217
Blue. Burnt Ochre	218
White Lead, Verdigris, and Artificial Sandarach	219
Purple	219
Substitutes for Purple, Yellow Ochre, Malachite Green, and Indigo	220

BOOK VIII

Introduction	225
How to find Water	227
Rainwater	229
Various Properties of Different Waters	232
Tests of Good Water	242
Levelling and Levelling Instruments	242
Aqueducts, Wells, and Cisterns	244

CONTENTS

BOOK IX

Introduction	251
The Zodiac and the Planets	257
The Phases of the Moon	262
The Course of the Sun through the Twelve Signs	264
The Northern Constellations	265
The Southern Constellations	267
Astrology and Weather Prognostics	269
The Analemma and its Applications	270
Sundials and Water Clocks	273

BOOK X

Introduction	281
Machines and Implements	283
Hoisting Machines	285
The Elements of Motion	290
Engines for raising Water	293
Water Wheels and Water Mills	294
The Water Screw	295
The Pump of Ctesibius	297
The Water Organ	299
The Hodometer	301
Catapults or Scorpiones	303
Ballistae	305
The Stringing and Tuning of Catapults	308
Siege Machines	309
The Tortoise	311
Hegetor's Tortoise	312
Measures of Defence	315
Note on Scamilli Impares	320
Index	321

LIST OF ILLUSTRATIONS

Caryatides from Treasury of Cnidians, Delphi	6
Caryatides of Erechtheum, Athens	6
Caryatid in Villa Albani, Rome	6
Caryatides	7
Persians	9
Construction of City Walls	23
Tower of the Winds, Athens	26
Diagram of the Winds	29
Diagram of Directions of Streets	30
Vitruvius' Brick-Bond	44
Travertine Quarries, Roman Campagna	49
Example of Opus Incertum, Circular Temple, Tivoli	51
Opus Reticulatum, Thermae of Hadrian's Villa, Tivoli	52
Example of Opus Reticulatum, Doorway of Stoa Poecile, Hadrian's Villa	52
Mausoleum at Halicarnassus, restored	54
Classification of Temples according to Arrangements of Colonnades	76
Hypaethral Temple of Vitruvius compared with Parthenon and Temple of Apollo near Miletus	77
Classification of Temples according to Intercolumniation	79
Eustyle Temple of Vitruvius compared with Temple of Teos	81
Vitruvius' Rules for Diameter and Height of Columns compared with Actual Examples	83
Diminution of Columns in Relation to Dimensions of Height	85
Entasis of Columns	87
Fra Giocondo's Idea of "Scamilli Impares"	89
Ionic Order according to Vitruvius compared with Order of Mausoleum at Halicarnassus	91
Comparison of Ionic Order according to Vitruvius with Actual Examples and with Vignola's Order	95
Basilica at Pompeii	104
Corinthian Capital of Vitruvius compared with Monuments	105
Vitruvius' Doric Order compared with Temple at Cori and Theatre of Marcellus	111

LIST OF ILLUSTRATIONS

Vitruvius' Temple Plan compared with Actual Examples	115
Vitruvius' Rule for Doorways compared with Two Examples	119
Tuscan Temple according to Vitruvius	121
Circular Temple, Tivoli	123
Maison Carrée, Nîmes	123
Plan of Temple, Tivoli	123
Plan of Temple of Vesta, Rome	123
Plan of Circular Temple according to Vitruvius	124
Forum, Timgad	131
Forum, Pompeii	133
Plan of Basilica, Pompeii	134
Vitruvius' Basilica, Fano	135
Roman Theatre according to Vitruvius	147
Theatre at Aspendus	149
Theatre Portico according to Vitruvius	152
Tepidarium of Stabian Baths, Pompeii	157
Apodyterium for Women, Stabian Baths, Pompeii	157
Stabian Baths, Pompeii	158
Palaestra, Olympia, and Greek Palaestra according to Vitruvius	161
Plans of Houses, Pompeii	176
Plan of House of Silver Wedding, Pompeii	177
Plan of typical Roman House	178
Peristyle of House of the Vettii, Pompeii	179
Plan of House of the Vettii, Pómpeii	179
Plan of Villa Rustica, near Pompeii	183
Plan of Vitruvius' Greek House	186
Plan of Greek House, Delos	187
Plan of Greek House discovered at Pergamum	188
Retaining Walls	191
Construction of the Analemma	271
Construction of Water Screw	295
Water Screw	296
Hegetor's Ram and Tortoise	312

1. From sixteenth century MS.   2. From model by A. A. Howard.

VITRUVIUS
BOOK I

BOOK I

PREFACE

1. WHILE your divine intelligence and will, Imperator Caesar, were engaged in acquiring the right to command the world, and while your fellow citizens, when all their enemies had been laid low by your invincible valour, were glorying in your triumph and victory, — while all foreign nations were in subjection awaiting your beck and call, and the Roman people and senate, released from their alarm, were beginning to be guided by your most noble conceptions and policies, I hardly dared, in view of your serious employments, to publish my writings and long considered ideas on architecture, for fear of subjecting myself to your displeasure by an unseasonable interruption.

2. But when I saw that you were giving your attention not only to the welfare of society in general and to the establishment of public order, but also to the providing of public buildings intended for utilitarian purposes, so that not only should the State have been enriched with provinces by your means, but that the greatness of its power might likewise be attended with distinguished authority in its public buildings, I thought that I ought to take the first opportunity to lay before you my writings on this theme. For in the first place it was this subject which made me known to your father, to whom I was devoted on account of his great qualities. After the council of heaven gave him a place in the dwellings of immortal life and transferred your father's power to your hands, my devotion continuing unchanged as I remembered him inclined me to support you. And so with Marcus Aurelius, Publius Minidius, and Gnaeus Cornelius, I was ready to supply and repair ballistae, scorpiones, and other artillery, and I have received rewards for good service with them. After your first bestowal of these upon me, you continued to renew them on the recommendation of your sister.

3. Owing to this favour I need have no fear of want to the end of my life, and being thus laid under obligation I began to write this work for you, because I saw that you have built and are now building extensively, and that in future also you will take care that our public and private buildings shall be worthy to go down to posterity by the side of your other splendid achievements. I have drawn up definite rules to enable you, by observing them, to have personal knowledge of the quality both of existing buildings and of those which are yet to be constructed. For in the following books I have disclosed all the principles of the art.

CHAPTER I

THE EDUCATION OF THE ARCHITECT

1. THE architect should be equipped with knowledge of many branches of study and varied kinds of learning, for it is by his judgement that all work done by the other arts is put to test. This knowledge is the child of practice and theory. Practice is the continuous and regular exercise of employment where manual work is done with any necessary material according to the design of a drawing. Theory, on the other hand, is the ability to demonstrate and explain the productions of dexterity on the principles of proportion.

2. It follows, therefore, that architects who have aimed at acquiring manual skill without scholarship have never been able to reach a position of authority to correspond to their pains, while those who relied only upon theories and scholarship were obviously hunting the shadow, not the substance. But those who have a thorough knowledge of both, like men armed at all points, have the sooner attained their object and carried authority with them.

3. In all matters, but particularly in architecture, there are these two points: — the thing signified, and that which gives it its significance. That which is signified is the subject of which we may be speaking; and that which gives significance is a demonstration on scientific principles. It appears, then, that one who professes himself an architect should be well versed in both directions. He ought, therefore, to be both naturally gifted and amenable to instruction. Neither natural ability without instruction nor instruction without natural ability can make the perfect artist. Let him be educated, skilful with the pencil, instructed in geometry, know much history, have followed the philosophers with attention, understand music, have some knowledge of medi-

cine, know the opinions of the jurists, and be acquainted with astronomy and the theory of the heavens.

4. The reasons for all this are as follows. An architect ought to be an educated man so as to leave a more lasting remembrance in his treatises. Secondly, he must have a knowledge of drawing so that he can readily make sketches to show the appearance of the work which he proposes. Geometry, also, is of much assistance in architecture, and in particular it teaches us the use of the rule and compasses, by which especially we acquire readiness in making plans for buildings in their grounds, and rightly apply the square, the level, and the plummet. By means of optics, again, the light in buildings can be drawn from fixed quarters of the sky. It is true that it is by arithmetic that the total cost of buildings is calculated and measurements are computed, but difficult questions involving symmetry are solved by means of geometrical theories and methods.

5. A wide knowledge of history is requisite because, among the ornamental parts of an architect's design for a work, there are many the underlying idea of whose employment he should be able to explain to inquirers. For instance, suppose him to set up the marble statues of women in long robes, called Caryatides, to take the place of columns, with the mutules and coronas placed directly above their heads, he will give the following explanation to his questioners. Caryae, a state in Peloponnesus, sided with the Persian enemies against Greece; later the Greeks, having gloriously won their freedom by victory in the war, made common cause and declared war against the people of Caryae. They took the town, killed the men, abandoned the State to desolation, and carried off their wives into slavery, without permitting them, however, to lay aside the long robes and other marks of their rank as married women, so that they might be obliged not only to march in the triumph but to appear forever after as a type of slavery, burdened with the weight of their shame and so making atonement for their State. Hence, the architects of the time designed for public buildings statues of these women, placed so as to

CARYATID NOW IN THE VILLA ALBANI AT ROME

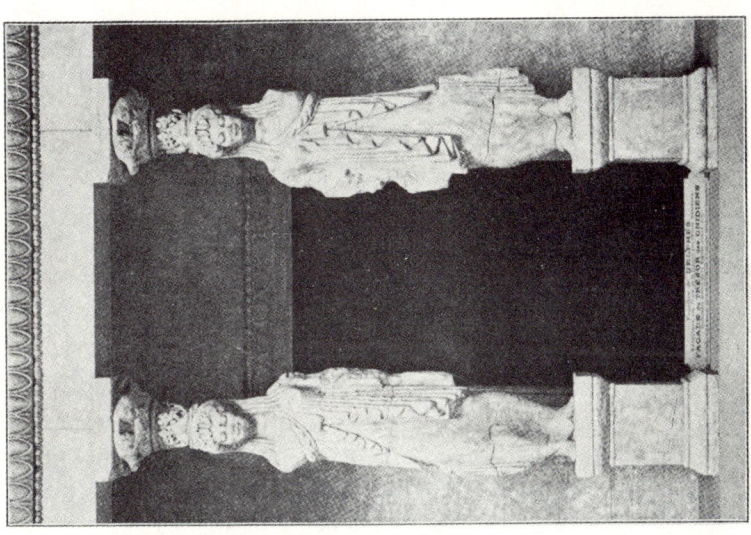

CARYATIDES FROM THE TREASURY OF THE CNIDIANS AT DELPHI

CARYATIDES OF THE ERECHTHEUM AT ATHENS

carry a load, in order that the sin and the punishment of the people of Caryae might be known and handed down even to posterity.

6. Likewise the Lacedaemonians under the leadership of Pausanias, son of Agesipolis, after conquering the Persian

CARYATIDES
(From the edition of Vitruvius by Fra Giocondo, Venice, 1511)

armies, infinite in number, with a small force at the battle of Plataea, celebrated a glorious triumph with the spoils and booty, and with the money obtained from the sale thereof built the Persian Porch, to be a monument to the renown and valour of the people and a trophy of victory for posterity. And there they set effigies of the prisoners arrayed in barbarian costume and holding up the roof, their pride punished by this deserved affront, that enemies might tremble for fear of the effects of their courage, and that their own people, looking upon this ensample of their valour and encouraged by the glory of it, might be ready to defend their independence. So from that time on, many have put up statues of Persians supporting entablatures and their ornaments, and thus from that motive have greatly enriched the diversity of their works. There are other stories of the same kind which architects ought to know.

7. As for philosophy, it makes an architect high-minded and not self-assuming, but rather renders him courteous, just, and honest without avariciousness. This is very important, for no work can be rightly done without honesty and incorruptibility. Let him not be grasping nor have his mind preoccupied with the idea of receiving perquisites, but let him with dignity keep up his position by cherishing a good reputation. These are among the precepts of philosophy. Furthermore philosophy treats of physics (in Greek φυσιολογία) where a more careful knowledge is required because the problems which come under this head are numerous and of very different kinds; as, for example, in the case of the conducting of water. For at points of intake and at curves, and at places where it is raised to a level, currents of air naturally form in one way or another; and nobody who has not learned the fundamental principles of physics from philosophy will be able to provide against the damage which they do. So the reader of Ctesibius or Archimedes and the other writers of treatises of the same class will not be able to appreciate them unless he has been trained in these subjects by the philosophers.

8. Music, also, the architect ought to understand so that he may have knowledge of the canonical and mathematical theory, and besides be able to tune ballistae, catapultae, and scorpiones to the proper key. For to the right and left in the beams are the holes in the frames through which the strings of twisted sinew are stretched by means of windlasses and bars, and these strings must not be clamped and made fast until they give the same correct note to the ear of the skilled workman. For the arms thrust

Chap. I] EDUCATION OF THE ARCHITECT 9

through those stretched strings must, on being let go, strike their blow together at the same moment; but if they are not in unison, they will prevent the course of projectiles from being straight.

PERSIANS
(From the edition of Vitruvius by Fra Giocondo, Venice, 1511)

9. In theatres, likewise, there are the bronze vessels (in Greek ἠχεῖα) which are placed in niches under the seats in accordance with the musical intervals on mathematical principles. These vessels are arranged with a view to musical concords or harmony, and apportioned in the compass of the fourth, the fifth, and the octave, and so on up to the double octave, in such a way that when the voice of an actor falls in unison with any of them its power is increased, and it reaches the ears of the audience with

greater clearness and sweetness. Water organs, too, and the other instruments which resemble them cannot be made by one who is without the principles of music.

10. The architect should also have a knowledge of the study of medicine on account of the questions of climates (in Greek κλίματα), air, the healthiness and unhealthiness of sites, and the use of different waters. For without these considerations, the healthiness of a dwelling cannot be assured. And as for principles of law, he should know those which are necessary in the case of buildings having party walls, with regard to water dripping from the eaves, and also the laws about drains, windows, and water supply. And other things of this sort should be known to architects, so that, before they begin upon buildings, they may be careful not to leave disputed points for the householders to settle after the works are finished, and so that in drawing up contracts the interests of both employer and contractor may be wisely safe-guarded. For if a contract is skilfully drawn, each may obtain a release from the other without disadvantage. From astronomy we find the east, west, south, and north, as well as the theory of the heavens, the equinox, solstice, and courses of the stars. If one has no knowledge of these matters, he will not be able to have any comprehension of the theory of sundials.

11. Consequently, since this study is so vast in extent, embellished and enriched as it is with many different kinds of learning, I think that men have no right to profess themselves architects hastily, without having climbed from boyhood the steps of these studies and thus, nursed by the knowledge of many arts and sciences, having reached the heights of the holy ground of architecture.

12. But perhaps to the inexperienced it will seem a marvel that human nature can comprehend such a great number of studies and keep them in the memory. Still, the observation that all studies have a common bond of union and intercourse with one another, will lead to the belief that this can easily be realized. For a liberal education forms, as it were, a single body made up of

these members. Those, therefore, who from tender years receive instruction in the various forms of learning, recognize the same stamp on all the arts, and an intercourse between all studies, and so they more readily comprehend them all. This is what led one of the ancient architects, Pytheos, the celebrated builder of the temple of Minerva at Priene, to say in his Commentaries that an architect ought to be able to accomplish much more in all the arts and sciences than the men who, by their own particular kinds of work and the practice of it, have brought each a single subject to the highest perfection. But this is in point of fact not realized.

13. For an architect ought not to be and cannot be such a philologian as was Aristarchus, although not illiterate; nor a musician like Aristoxenus, though not absolutely ignorant of music; nor a painter like Apelles, though not unskilful in drawing; nor a sculptor such as was Myron or Polyclitus, though not unacquainted with the plastic art; nor again a physician like Hippocrates, though not ignorant of medicine; nor in the other sciences need he excel in each, though he should not be unskilful in them. For, in the midst of all this great variety of subjects, an individual cannot attain to perfection in each, because it is scarcely in his power to take in and comprehend the general theories of them.

14. Still, it is not architects alone that cannot in all matters reach perfection, but even men who individually practise specialties in the arts do not all attain to the highest point of merit. Therefore, if among artists working each in a single field not all, but only a few in an entire generation acquire fame, and that with difficulty, how can an architect, who has to be skilful in many arts, accomplish not merely the feat — in itself a great marvel — of being deficient in none of them, but also that of surpassing all those artists who have devoted themselves with unremitting industry to single fields?

15. It appears, then, that Pytheos made a mistake by not observing that the arts are each composed of two things, the actual work and the theory of it. One of these, the doing of the work, is

proper to men trained in the individual subject, while the other, the theory, is common to all scholars: for example, to physicians and musicians the rhythmical beat of the pulse and its metrical movement. But if there is a wound to be healed or a sick man to be saved from danger, the musician will not call, for the business will be appropriate to the physician. So in the case of a musical instrument, not the physician but the musician will be the man to tune it so that the ears may find their due pleasure in its strains.

16. Astronomers likewise have a common ground for discussion with musicians in the harmony of the stars and musical concords in tetrads and triads of the fourth and the fifth, and with geometricians in the subject of vision (in Greek λόγος ὀπτικός); and in all other sciences many points, perhaps all, are common so far as the discussion of them is concerned. But the actual undertaking of works which are brought to perfection by the hand and its manipulation is the function of those who have been specially trained to deal with a single art. It appears, therefore, that he has done enough and to spare who in each subject possesses a fairly good knowledge of those parts, with their principles, which are indispensable for architecture, so that if he is required to pass judgement and to express approval in the case of those things or arts, he may not be found wanting. As for men upon whom nature has bestowed so much ingenuity, acuteness, and memory that they are able to have a thorough knowledge of geometry, astronomy, music, and the other arts, they go beyond the functions of architects and become pure mathematicians. Hence they can readily take up positions against those arts because many are the artistic weapons with which they are armed. Such men, however, are rarely found, but there have been such at times; for example, Aristarchus of Samos, Philolaus and Archytas of Tarentum, Apollonius of Perga, Eratosthenes of Cyrene, and among Syracusans Archimedes and Scopinas, who through mathematics and natural philosophy discovered, expounded, and left to posterity many things in connexion with mechanics and with sundials.

17. Since, therefore, the possession of such talents due to natural capacity is not vouchsafed at random to entire nations, but only to a few great men; since, moreover, the function of the architect requires a training in all the departments of learning; and finally, since reason, on account of the wide extent of the subject, concedes that he may possess not the highest but not even necessarily a moderate knowledge of the subjects of study, I request, Caesar, both of you and of those who may read the said books, that if anything is set forth with too little regard for grammatical rule, it may be pardoned. For it is not as a very great philosopher, nor as an eloquent rhetorician, nor as a grammarian trained in the highest principles of his art, that I have striven to write this work, but as an architect who has had only a dip into those studies. Still, as regards the efficacy of the art and the theories of it, I promise and expect that in these volumes I shall undoubtedly show myself of very considerable importance not only to builders but also to all scholars.

CHAPTER II

THE FUNDAMENTAL PRINCIPLES OF ARCHITECTURE

1. ARCHITECTURE depends on Order (in Greek τάξις), Arrangement (in Greek διάθεσις), Eurythmy, Symmetry, Propriety, and Economy (in Greek οἰκονομία).

2. Order gives due measure to the members of a work considered separately, and symmetrical agreement to the proportions of the whole. It is an adjustment according to quantity (in Greek ποσότης). By this I mean the selection of modules from the members of the work itself and, starting from these individual parts of members, constructing the whole work to correspond. Arrangement includes the putting of things in their proper places and the elegance of effect which is due to adjustments appropriate to the character of the work. Its forms of expression (in Greek ἰδέαι) are these: groundplan, elevation, and perspec-

tive. A groundplan is made by the proper successive use of compasses and rule, through which we get outlines for the plane surfaces of buildings. An elevation is a picture of the front of a building, set upright and properly drawn in the proportions of the contemplated work. Perspective is the method of sketching a front with the sides withdrawing into the background, the lines all meeting in the centre of a circle. All three come of reflexion and invention. Reflexion is careful and laborious thought, and watchful attention directed to the agreeable effect of one's plan. Invention, on the other hand, is the solving of intricate problems and the discovery of new principles by means of brilliancy and versatility. These are the departments belonging under Arrangement.

3. Eurythmy is beauty and fitness in the adjustments of the members. This is found when the members of a work are of a height suited to their breadth, of a breadth suited to their length, and, in a word, when they all correspond symmetrically.

4. Symmetry is a proper agreement between the members of the work itself, and relation between the different parts and the whole general scheme, in accordance with a certain part selected as standard. Thus in the human body there is a kind of symmetrical harmony between forearm, foot, palm, finger, and other small parts; and so it is with perfect buildings. In the case of temples, symmetry may be calculated from the thickness of a column, from a triglyph, or even from a module; in the ballista, from the hole or from what the Greeks call the περίτρητος; in a ship, from the space between the tholepins (διάπηγμα); and in other things, from various members.

5. Propriety is that perfection of style which comes when a work is authoritatively constructed on approved principles. It arises from prescription (Greek θεματισμῷ), from usage, or from nature. From prescription, in the case of hypaethral edifices, open to the sky, in honour of Jupiter Lightning, the Heaven, the Sun, or the Moon: for these are gods whose semblances and manifestations we behold before our very eyes in the sky when it

is cloudless and bright. The temples of Minerva, Mars, and Hercules, will be Doric, since the virile strength of these gods makes daintiness entirely inappropriate to their houses. In temples to Venus, Flora, Proserpine, Spring-Water, and the Nymphs, the Corinthian order will be found to have peculiar significance, because these are delicate divinities and so its rather slender outlines, its flowers, leaves, and ornamental volutes will lend propriety where it is due. The construction of temples of the Ionic order to Juno, Diana, Father Bacchus, and the other gods of that kind, will be in keeping with the middle position which they hold; for the building of such will be an appropriate combination of the severity of the Doric and the delicacy of the Corinthian.

6. Propriety arises from usage when buildings having magnificent interiors are provided with elegant entrance-courts to correspond; for there will be no propriety in the spectacle of an elegant interior approached by a low, mean entrance. Or, if dentils be carved in the cornice of the Doric entablature or triglyphs represented in the Ionic entablature over the cushion-shaped capitals of the columns, the effect will be spoilt by the transfer of the peculiarities of the one order of building to the other, the usage in each class having been fixed long ago.

7. Finally, propriety will be due to natural causes if, for example, in the case of all sacred precincts we select very healthy neighbourhoods with suitable springs of water in the places where the fanes are to be built, particularly in the case of those to Aesculapius and to Health, gods by whose healing powers great numbers of the sick are apparently cured. For when their diseased bodies are transferred from an unhealthy to a healthy spot, and treated with waters from health-giving springs, they will the more speedily grow well. The result will be that the divinity will stand in higher esteem and find his dignity increased, all owing to the nature of his site. There will also be natural propriety in using an eastern light for bedrooms and libraries, a western light in winter for baths and winter apartments, and a northern light for picture galleries and other places in which a steady light is

needed; for that quarter of the sky grows neither light nor dark with the course of the sun, but remains steady and unshifting all day long.

8. Economy denotes the proper management of materials and of site, as well as a thrifty balancing of cost and common sense in the construction of works. This will be observed if, in the first place, the architect does not demand things which cannot be found or made ready without great expense. For example: it is not everywhere that there is plenty of pitsand, rubble, fir, clear fir, and marble, since they are produced in different places and to assemble them is difficult and costly. Where there is no pitsand, we must use the kinds washed up by rivers or by the sea; the lack of fir and clear fir may be evaded by using cypress, poplar, elm, or pine; and other problems we must solve in similar ways.

9. A second stage in Economy is reached when we have to plan the different kinds of dwellings suitable for ordinary householders, for great wealth, or for the high position of the statesman. A house in town obviously calls for one form of construction; that into which stream the products of country estates requires another; this will not be the same in the case of money-lenders and still different for the opulent and luxurious; for the powers under whose deliberations the commonwealth is guided dwellings are to be provided according to their special needs: and, in a word, the proper form of economy must be observed in building houses for each and every class.

CHAPTER III

THE DEPARTMENTS OF ARCHITECTURE

1. THERE are three departments of architecture: the art of building, the making of time-pieces, and the construction of machinery. Building is, in its turn, divided into two parts, of which the first is the construction of fortified towns and of works for general use in public places, and the second is the putting up of structures for private individuals. There are three classes of pub-

lic buildings: the first for defensive, the second for religious, and the third for utilitarian purposes. Under defence comes the planning of walls, towers, and gates, permanent devices for resistance against hostile attacks; under religion, the erection of fanes and temples to the immortal gods; under utility, the provision of meeting places for public use, such as harbours, markets, colonnades, baths, theatres, promenades, and all other similar arrangements in public places.

2. All these must be built with due reference to durability, convenience, and beauty. Durability will be assured when foundations are carried down to the solid ground and materials wisely and liberally selected; convenience, when the arrangement of the apartments is faultless and presents no hindrance to use, and when each class of building is assigned to its suitable and appropriate exposure; and beauty, when the appearance of the work is pleasing and in good taste, and when its members are in due proportion according to correct principles of symmetry.

CHAPTER IV

THE SITE OF A CITY

1. For fortified towns the following general principles are to be observed. First comes the choice of a very healthy site. Such a site will be high, neither misty nor frosty, and in a climate neither hot nor cold, but temperate; further, without marshes in the neighbourhood. For when the morning breezes blow toward the town at sunrise, if they bring with them mists from marshes and, mingled with the mist, the poisonous breath of the creatures of the marshes to be wafted into the bodies of the inhabitants, they will make the site unhealthy. Again, if the town is on the coast with a southern or western exposure, it will not be healthy, because in summer the southern sky grows hot at sunrise and is fiery at noon, while a western exposure grows warm after sunrise, is hot at noon, and at evening all aglow.

2. These variations in heat and the subsequent cooling off are harmful to the people living on such sites. The same conclusion may be reached in the case of inanimate things. For instance, nobody draws the light for covered wine rooms from the south or west, but rather from the north, since that quarter is never subject to change but is always constant and unshifting. So it is with granaries: grain exposed to the sun's course soon loses its good quality, and provisions and fruit, unless stored in a place unexposed to the sun's course, do not keep long.

3. For heat is a universal solvent, melting out of things their power of resistance, and sucking away and removing their natural strength with its fiery exhalations so that they grow soft, and hence weak, under its glow. We see this in the case of iron which, however hard it may naturally be, yet when heated thoroughly in a furnace fire can be easily worked into any kind of shape, and still, if cooled while it is soft and white hot, it hardens again with a mere dip into cold water and takes on its former quality.

4. We may also recognize the truth of this from the fact that in summer the heat makes everybody weak, not only in unhealthy but even in healthy places, and that in winter even the most unhealthy districts are much healthier because they are given a solidity by the cooling off. Similarly, persons removed from cold countries to hot cannot endure it but waste away; whereas those who pass from hot places to the cold regions of the north, not only do not suffer in health from the change of residence but even gain by it.

5. It appears, then, that in founding towns we must beware of districts from which hot winds can spread abroad over the inhabitants. For while all bodies are composed of the four elements (in Greek στοιχεῖα), that is, of heat, moisture, the earthy, and air, yet there are mixtures according to natural temperament which make up the natures of all the different animals of the world, each after its kind.

6. Therefore, if one of these elements, heat, becomes predominant in any body whatsoever, it destroys and dissolves all the

others with its violence. This defect may be due to violent heat from certain quarters of the sky, pouring into the open pores in too great proportion to admit of a mixture suited to the natural temperament of the body in question. Again, if too much moisture enters the channels of a body, and thus introduces disproportion, the other elements, adulterated by the liquid, are impaired, and the virtues of the mixture dissolved. This defect, in turn, may arise from the cooling properties of moist winds and breezes blowing upon the body. In the same way, increase or diminution of the proportion of air or of the earthy which is natural to the body may enfeeble the other elements; the predominance of the earthy being due to overmuch food, that of air to a heavy atmosphere.

7. If one wishes a more accurate understanding of all this, he need only consider and observe the natures of birds, fishes, and land animals, and he will thus come to reflect upon distinctions of temperament. One form of mixture is proper to birds, another to fishes, and a far different form to land animals. Winged creatures have less of the earthy, less moisture, heat in moderation, air in large amount. Being made up, therefore, of the lighter elements, they can more readily soar away into the air. Fish, with their aquatic nature, being moderately supplied with heat and made up in great part of air and the earthy, with as little of moisture as possible, can more easily exist in moisture for the very reason that they have less of it than of the other elements in their bodies; and so, when they are drawn to land, they leave life and water at the same moment. Similarly, the land animals, being moderately supplied with the elements of air and heat, and having less of the earthy and a great deal of moisture, cannot long continue alive in the water, because their portion of moisture is already abundant.

8. Therefore, if all this is as we have explained, our reason showing us that the bodies of animals are made up of the elements, and these bodies, as we believe, giving way and breaking up as a result of excess or deficiency in this or that element, we cannot but believe that we must take great care to select a very

temperate climate for the site of our city, since healthfulness is, as we have said, the first requisite.

9. I cannot too strongly insist upon the need of a return to the method of old times. Our ancestors, when about to build a town or an army post, sacrificed some of the cattle that were wont to feed on the site proposed and examined their livers. If the livers of the first victims were dark-coloured or abnormal, they sacrificed others, to see whether the fault was due to disease or their food. They never began to build defensive works in a place until after they had made many such trials and satisfied themselves that good water and food had made the liver sound and firm. If they continued to find it abnormal, they argued from this that the food and water supply found in such a place would be just as unhealthy for man, and so they moved away and changed to another neighbourhood, healthfulness being their chief object.

10. That pasturage and food may indicate the healthful qualities of a site is a fact which can be observed and investigated in the case of certain pastures in Crete, on each side of the river Pothereus, which separates the two Cretan states of Gnosus and Gortyna. There are cattle at pasture on the right and left banks of that river, but while the cattle that feed near Gnosus have the usual spleen, those on the other side near Gortyna have no perceptible spleen. On investigating the subject, physicians discovered on this side a kind of herb which the cattle chew and thus make their spleen small. The herb is therefore gathered and used as a medicine for the cure of splenetic people. The Cretans call it ἄσπληνον. From food and water, then, we may learn whether sites are naturally unhealthy or healthy.

11. If the walled town is built among the marshes themselves, provided they are by the sea, with a northern or north-eastern exposure, and are above the level of the seashore, the site will be reasonable enough. For ditches can be dug to let out the water to the shore, and also in times of storms the sea swells and comes backing up into the marshes, where its bitter blend prevents the reproductions of the usual marsh creatures, while any that swim

down from the higher levels to the shore are killed at once by the saltness to which they are unused. An instance of this may be found in the Gallic marshes surrounding Altino, Ravenna, Aquileia, and other towns in places of the kind, close by marshes. They are marvellously healthy, for the reasons which I have given.

12. But marshes that are stagnant and have no outlets either by rivers or ditches, like the Pomptine marshes, merely putrefy as they stand, emitting heavy, unhealthy vapours. A case of a town built in such a spot was Old Salpia in Apulia, founded by Diomede on his way back from Troy, or, according to some writers, by Elpias of Rhodes. Year after year there was sickness, until finally the suffering inhabitants came with a public petition to Marcus Hostilius and got him to agree to seek and find them a proper place to which to remove their city. Without delay he made the most skilful investigations, and at once purchased an estate near the sea in a healthy place, and asked the Senate and Roman people for permission to remove the town. He constructed the walls and laid out the house lots, granting one to each citizen for a mere trifle. This done, he cut an opening from a lake into the sea, and thus made of the lake a harbour for the town. The result is that now the people of Salpia live on a healthy site and at a distance of only four miles from the old town.

CHAPTER V

THE CITY WALLS

1. AFTER insuring on these principles the healthfulness of the future city, and selecting a neighbourhood that can supply plenty of food stuffs to maintain the community, with good roads or else convenient rivers or seaports affording easy means of transport to the city, the next thing to do is to lay the foundations for the towers and walls. Dig down to solid bottom, if it can be found, and lay them therein, going as deep as the magnitude of the proposed work seems to require. They should be much thicker than

the part of the walls that will appear above ground, and their structure should be as solid as it can possibly be laid.

2. The towers must be projected beyond the line of wall, so that an enemy wishing to approach the wall to carry it by assault may be exposed to the fire of missiles on his open flank from the towers on his right and left. Special pains should be taken that there be no easy avenue by which to storm the wall. The roads should be encompassed at steep points, and planned so as to approach the gates, not in a straight line, but from the right to the left; for as a result of this, the right hand side of the assailants, unprotected by their shields, will be next the wall. Towns should be laid out not as an exact square nor with salient angles, but in circular form, to give a view of the enemy from many points. Defence is difficult where there are salient angles, because the angle protects the enemy rather than the inhabitants.

3. The thickness of the wall should, in my opinion, be such that armed men meeting on top of it may pass one another without interference. In the thickness there should be set a very close succession of ties made of charred olive wood, binding the two faces of the wall together like pins, to give it lasting endurance. For that is a material which neither decay, nor the weather, nor time can harm, but even though buried in the earth or set in the water it keeps sound and useful forever. And so not only city walls but substructures in general and all walls that require a thickness like that of a city wall, will be long in falling to decay if tied in this manner.

4. The towers should be set at intervals of not more than a bowshot apart, so that in case of an assault upon any one of them, the enemy may be repulsed with scorpiones and other means of hurling missiles from the towers to the right and left. Opposite the inner side of every tower the wall should be interrupted for a space the width of the tower, and have only a wooden flooring across, leading to the interior of the tower but not firmly nailed. This is to be cut away by the defenders in case the enemy gets possession of any portion of the wall; and if the work is quickly

done, the enemy will not be able to make his way to the other towers and the rest of the wall unless he is ready to face a fall.

5. The towers themselves must be either round or polygonal. Square towers are sooner shattered by military engines, for the

CONSTRUCTION OF CITY WALLS
(From the edition of Vitruvius by Fra Giocondo, Venice, 1511)

battering rams pound their angles to pieces; but in the case of round towers they can do no harm, being engaged, as it were, in driving wedges to their centre. The system of fortification by wall and towers may be made safest by the addition of earthen ramparts, for neither rams, nor mining, nor other engineering devices can do them any harm.

6. The rampart form of defence, however, is not required in all places, but only where outside the wall there is high ground from

which an assault on the fortifications may be made over a level space lying between. In places of this kind we must first make very wide, deep ditches; next sink foundations for a wall in the bed of the ditch and build them thick enough to support an earthwork with ease.

7. Then within this substructure lay a second foundation, far enough inside the first to leave ample room for cohorts in line of battle to take position on the broad top of the rampart for its defence. Having laid these two foundations at this distance from one another, build cross walls between them, uniting the outer and inner foundation, in a comb-like arrangement, set like the teeth of a saw. With this form of construction, the enormous burden of earth will be distributed into small bodies, and will not lie with all its weight in one crushing mass so as to thrust out the substructures.

8. With regard to the material of which the actual wall should be constructed or finished, there can be no definite prescription, because we cannot obtain in all places the supplies that we desire. Dimension stone, flint, rubble, burnt or unburnt brick, — use them as you find them. For it is not every neighbourhood or particular locality that can have a wall built of burnt brick like that at Babylon, where there was plenty of asphalt to take the place of lime and sand, and yet possibly each may be provided with materials of equal usefulness so that out of them a faultless wall may be built to last forever.

CHAPTER VI

THE DIRECTIONS OF THE STREETS; WITH REMARKS ON THE WINDS

1. THE town being fortified, the next step is the apportionment of house lots within the wall and the laying out of streets and alleys with regard to climatic conditions. They will be properly laid out if foresight is employed to exclude the winds from the alleys. Cold winds are disagreeable, hot winds enervating, moist

winds unhealthy. We must, therefore, avoid mistakes in this matter and beware of the common experience of many communities. For example, Mytilene in the island of Lesbos is a town built with magnificence and good taste, but its position shows a lack of foresight. In that community when the wind is south, the people fall ill; when it is northwest, it sets them coughing; with a north wind they do indeed recover but cannot stand about in the alleys and streets, owing to the severe cold.

2. Wind is a flowing wave of air, moving hither and thither indefinitely. It is produced when heat meets moisture, the rush of heat generating a mighty current of air. That this is the fact we may learn from bronze eolipiles, and thus by means of a scientific invention discover a divine truth lurking in the laws of the heavens. Eolipiles are hollow bronze balls, with a very small opening through which water is poured into them. Set before a fire, not a breath issues from them before they get warm; but as soon as they begin to boil, out comes a strong blast due to the fire. Thus from this slight and very short experiment we may understand and judge of the mighty and wonderful laws of the heavens and the nature of winds.

3. By shutting out the winds from our dwellings, therefore, we shall not only make the place healthful for people who are well, but also in the case of diseases due perhaps to unfavourable situations elsewhere, the patients, who in other healthy places might be cured by a different form of treatment, will here be more quickly cured by the mildness that comes from the shutting out of the winds. The diseases which are hard to cure in neighbourhoods such as those to which I have referred above are catarrh, hoarseness, coughs, pleurisy, consumption, spitting of blood, and all others that are cured not by lowering the system but by building it up. They are hard to cure, first, because they are originally due to chills; secondly, because the patient's system being already exhausted by disease, the air there, which is in constant agitation owing to winds and therefore deteriorated, takes all the sap of life out of their diseased bodies and leaves them more

meagre every day. On the other hand, a mild, thick air, without draughts and not constantly blowing back and forth, builds up their frames by its unwavering steadiness, and so strengthens and restores people who are afflicted with these diseases.

4. Some have held that there are only four winds: Solanus from due east; Auster from the south; Favonius from due west; Septentrio from the north. But more careful investigators tell us that there are eight. Chief among such was Andronicus of Cyrrhus who in proof built the marble octagonal tower in Athens. On the several sides of the octagon he executed reliefs representing the several winds, each facing the point from which it blows; and on top of the tower he set a conical shaped piece of marble and on this a bronze Triton with a rod outstretched in its right hand. It was so contrived as to go round with the wind, always stopping to face the breeze and holding its rod as a pointer directly over the representation of the wind that was blowing.

5. Thus Eurus is placed to the southeast between Solanus and Auster: Africus to the southwest between Auster and Favonius; Caurus, or, as many call it, Corus, between Favonius and Septentrio; and Aquilo between Septentrio and Solanus. Such, then, appears to have been his device, including the numbers and names of the wind and indicating the directions from which particular winds blow. These facts being thus determined, to find the directions and quarters of the winds your method of procedure should be as follows.

6. In the middle of the city place a marble amussium, laying it true by the level, or else let the spot be made so true by means of rule and level that no amussium is necessary. In the very centre of that spot set up a bronze gnomon or "shadow tracker" (in Greek σκιαθήρας). At about the fifth hour in the morning, take the end of the shadow cast by this gnomon, and mark it with a point. Then, opening your compasses to this point which marks the length of the gnomon's shadow, describe a circle from the centre. In the afternoon watch the shadow of your gnomon as it lengthens, and when it once more touches the circumference of this

THE TOWER OF THE WINDS AT ATHENS

circle and the shadow in the afternoon is equal in length to that of the morning, mark it with a point.

7. From these two points describe with your compasses intersecting arcs, and through their intersection and the centre let a line be drawn to the circumference of the circle to give us the quarters of south and north. Then, using a sixteenth part of the entire circumference of the circle as a diameter, describe a circle with its centre on the line to the south, at the point where it crosses the circumference, and put points to the right and left on the circumference on the south side, repeating the process on the north side. From the four points thus obtained draw lines intersecting the centre from one side of the circumference to the other. Thus we shall have an eighth part of the circumference set out for Auster and another for Septentrio. The rest of the entire circumference is then to be divided into three equal parts on each side, and thus we have designed a figure equally apportioned among the eight winds. Then let the directions of your streets and alleys be laid down on the lines of division between the quarters of two winds.

8. On this principle of arrangement the disagreeable force of the winds will be shut out from dwellings and lines of houses. For if the streets run full in the face of the winds, their constant blasts rushing in from the open country, and then confined by narrow alleys, will sweep through them with great violence. The lines of houses must therefore be directed away from the quarters from which the winds blow, so that as they come in they may strike against the angles of the blocks and their force thus be broken and dispersed.

9. Those who know names for very many winds will perhaps be surprised at our setting forth that there are only eight. Remembering, however, that Eratosthenes of Cyrene, employing mathematical theories and geometrical methods, discovered from the course of the sun, the shadows cast by an equinoctial gnomon, and the inclination of the heaven that the circumference of the earth is two hundred and fifty-two thousand stadia, that is, thirty-

one million five hundred thousand paces, and observing that an eighth part of this, occupied by a wind, is three million nine hundred and thirty-seven thousand five hundred paces, they should not be surprised to find that a single wind, ranging over so wide a field, is subject to shifts this way and that, leading to a variety of breezes.

10. So we often have Leuconotus and Altanus blowing respectively to the right and left of Auster; Libonotus and Subvesperus to the right and left of Africus; Argestes, and at certain periods the Etesiae, on either side of Favonius; Circias and Corus on the sides of Caurus; Thracias and Gallicus on either side of Septentrio; Supernas and Caecias to the right and left of Aquilo; Carbas, and at a certain period the Ornithiae, on either side of Solanus; while Eurocircias and Volturnus blow on the flanks of Eurus which is between them. There are also many other names for winds derived from localities or from the squalls which sweep from rivers or down mountains.

11. Then, too, there are the breezes of early morning; for the sun on emerging from beneath the earth strikes humid air as he returns, and as he goes climbing up the sky he spreads it out before him, extracting breezes from the vapour that was there before the dawn. Those that still blow on after sunrise are classed with Eurus, and hence appears to come the Greek name εὖρος as the child of the breezes, and the word for "to-morrow," αὔριον, named from the early morning breezes. Some people do indeed say that Eratosthenes could not have inferred the true measure of the earth. Whether true or untrue, it cannot affect the truth of what I have written on the fixing of the quarters from which the different winds blow.

12. If he was wrong, the only result will be that the individual winds may blow, not with the scope expected from his measurement, but with powers either more or less widely extended. For the readier understanding of these topics, since I have treated them with brevity, it has seemed best to me to give two figures, or, as the Greeks say, σχήματα, at the end of this book: one de-

Chap. VII]   DIRECTIONS OF THE STREETS   29

signed to show the precise quarters from which the winds arise; the other, how by turning the directions of the rows of houses and the streets away from their full force, we may avoid unhealthy blasts. Let A be the centre of a plane surface, and B the point to

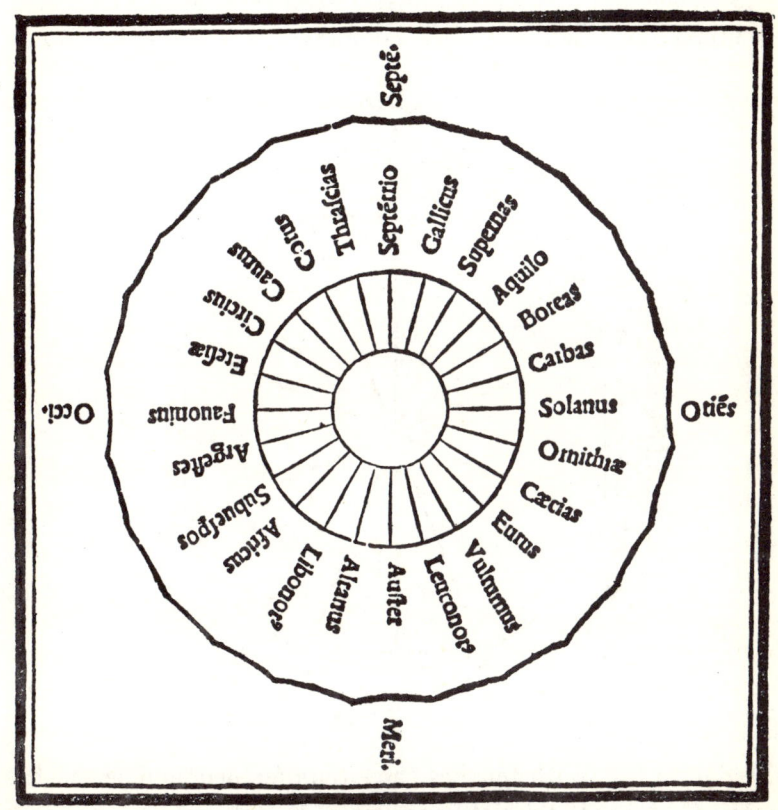

DIAGRAM OF THE WINDS
(From the edition of Vitruvius by Fra Giocondo, Venice, 1511)

which the shadow of the gnomon reaches in the morning. Taking A as the centre, open the compasses to the point B, which marks the shadow, and describe a circle. Put the gnomon back where it was before and wait for the shadow to lessen and grow again until in the afternoon it is equal to its length in the morning, touching the circumference at the point C. Then from the points B and C describe with the compasses two arcs intersecting at D. Next draw a line from the point of intersection D through the centre of the circle to the circumference and call it E F. This line will show where the south and north lie.

13. Then find with the compasses a sixteenth part of the entire circumference; then centre the compasses on the point E where

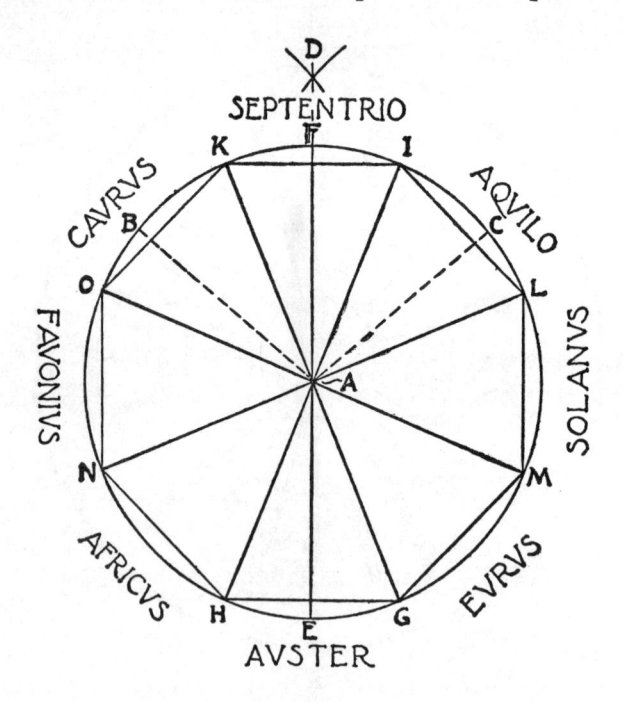

the line to the south touches the circumference, and set off the points G and H to the right and left of E. Likewise on the north side, centre the compasses on the circumference at the point F on the line to the north, and set off the points I and K to the right and left; then draw lines through the centre from G to K and from H to I. Thus the space from G to H will belong to Auster and the south, and the space from I to K will be that of Septentrio. The rest of the circumference is to be divided equally into three parts on the right and three on the left, those to the east at the points L and M, those to the west at the points N and O.

Finally, intersecting lines are to be drawn from M to O and from L to N. Thus we shall have the circumference divided into eight equal spaces for the winds. The figure being finished, we shall have at the eight different divisions, beginning at the south, the letter G between Eurus and Auster, H between Auster and Africus, N between Africus and Favonius, O between Favonius and Caurus, K between Caurus and Septentrio, I between Septentrio and Aquilo, L between Aquilo and Solanus, and M between Solanus and Eurus. This done, apply a gnomon to these eight divisions and thus fix the directions of the different alleys.

CHAPTER VII

THE SITES FOR PUBLIC BUILDINGS

1. HAVING laid out the alleys and determined the streets, we have next to treat of the choice of building sites for temples, the forum, and all other public places, with a view to general convenience and utility. If the city is on the sea, we should choose ground close to the harbour as the place where the forum is to be built; but if inland, in the middle of the town. For the temples, the sites for those of the gods under whose particular protection the state is thought to rest and for Jupiter, Juno, and Minerva, should be on the very highest point commanding a view of the greater part of the city. Mercury should be in the forum, or, like Isis and Serapis, in the emporium: Apollo and Father Bacchus near the theatre: Hercules at the circus in communities which have no gymnasia nor amphitheatres; Mars outside the city but at the training ground, and so Venus, but at the harbour. It is moreover shown by the Etruscan diviners in treatises on their science that the fanes of Venus, Vulcan, and Mars should be situated outside the walls, in order that the young men and married women may not become habituated in the city to the temptations incident to the worship of Venus, and that buildings may be free from the terror of fires through the religious rites and sacrifices which

call the power of Vulcan beyond the walls. As for Mars, when that divinity is enshrined outside the walls, the citizens will never take up arms against each other, and he will defend the city from its enemies and save it from danger in war.

2. Ceres also should be outside the city in a place to which people need never go except for the purpose of sacrifice. That place should be under the protection of religion, purity, and good morals. Proper sites should be set apart for the precincts of the other gods according to the nature of the sacrifices offered to them.

The principle governing the actual construction of temples and their symmetry I shall explain in my third and fourth books. In the second I have thought it best to give an account of the materials used in buildings with their good qualities and advantages, and then in the succeeding books to describe and explain the proportions of buildings, their arrangements, and the different forms of symmetry.

BOOK II

BOOK II

INTRODUCTION

1. DINOCRATES, an architect who was full of confidence in his own ideas and skill, set out from Macedonia, in the reign of Alexander, to go to the army, being eager to win the approbation of the king. He took with him from his country letters from relatives and friends to the principal military men and officers of the court, in order to gain access to them more readily. Being politely received by them, he asked to be presented to Alexander as soon as possible. They promised, but were rather slow, waiting for a suitable opportunity. So Dinocrates, thinking that they were playing with him, had recourse to his own efforts. He was of very lofty stature and pleasing countenance, finely formed, and extremely dignified. Trusting, therefore, to these natural gifts, he undressed himself in his inn, anointed his body with oil, set a chaplet of poplar leaves on his head, draped his left shoulder with a lion's skin, and holding a club in his right hand stalked forth to a place in front of the tribunal where the king was administering justice.

2. His strange appearance made the people turn round, and this led Alexander to look at him. In astonishment he gave orders to make way for him to draw near, and asked who he was. "Dinocrates," quoth he, "a Macedonian architect, who brings thee ideas and designs worthy of thy renown. I have made a design for the shaping of Mount Athos into the statue of a man, in whose left hand I have represented a very spacious fortified city, and in his right a bowl to receive the water of all the streams which are in that mountain, so that it may pour from the bowl into the sea."

3. Alexander, delighted with the idea of his design, immediately inquired whether there were any fields in the neighbour-

hood that could maintain the city in corn. On finding that this was impossible without transport from beyond the sea, "Dinocrates," quoth he, "I appreciate your design as excellent in composition, and I am delighted with it, but I apprehend that anybody who should found a city in that spot would be censured for bad judgement. For as a newborn babe cannot be nourished without the nurse's milk, nor conducted to the approaches that lead to growth in life, so a city cannot thrive without fields and the fruits thereof pouring into its walls, nor have a large population without plenty of food, nor maintain its population without a supply of it. Therefore, while thinking that your design is commendable, I consider the site as not commendable; but I would have you stay with me, because I mean to make use of your services."

4. From that time, Dinocrates did not leave the king, but followed him into Egypt. There Alexander, observing a harbour rendered safe by nature, an excellent centre for trade, cornfields throughout all Egypt, and the great usefulness of the mighty river Nile, ordered him to build the city of Alexandria, named after the king. This was how Dinocrates, recommended only by his good looks and dignified carriage, came to be so famous. But as for me, Emperor, nature has not given me stature, age has marred my face, and my strength is impaired by ill health. Therefore, since these advantages fail me, I shall win your approval, as I hope, by the help of my knowledge and my writings.

5. In my first book, I have said what I had to say about the functions of architecture and the scope of the art, as well as about fortified towns and the apportionment of building sites within the fortifications. Although it would next be in order to explain the proper proportions and symmetry of temples and public buildings, as well as of private houses, I thought best to postpone this until after I had treated the practical merits of the materials out of which, when they are brought together, buildings are constructed with due regard to the proper kind of material for each part, and until I had shown of what natural elements those materials are composed. But before beginning to explain their

INTRODUCTION

natural properties, I will prefix the motives which originally gave rise to buildings and the development of inventions in this field, following in the steps of early nature and of those writers who have devoted treatises to the origins of civilization and the investigation of inventions. My exposition will, therefore, follow the instruction which I have received from them.

CHAPTER I

THE ORIGIN OF THE DWELLING HOUSE

1. THE men of old were born like the wild beasts, in woods, caves, and groves, and lived on savage fare. As time went on, the thickly crowded trees in a certain place, tossed by storms and winds, and rubbing their branches against one another, caught fire, and so the inhabitants of the place were put to flight, being terrified by the furious flame. After it subsided, they drew near, and observing that they were very comfortable standing before the warm fire, they put on logs and, while thus keeping it alive, brought up other people to it, showing them by signs how much comfort they got from it. In that gathering of men, at a time when utterance of sound was purely individual, from daily habits they fixed upon articulate words just as these had happened to come; then, from indicating by name things in common use, the result was that in this chance way they began to talk, and thus originated conversation with one another.

2. Therefore it was the discovery of fire that originally gave rise to the coming together of men, to the deliberative assembly, and to social intercourse. And so, as they kept coming together in greater numbers into one place, finding themselves naturally gifted beyond the other animals in not being obliged to walk with faces to the ground, but upright and gazing upon the splendour of the starry firmament, and also in being able to do with ease whatever they chose with their hands and fingers, they began in that first assembly to construct shelters. Some made them of green boughs, others dug caves on mountain sides, and some, in imitation of the nests of swallows and the way they built, made places of refuge out of mud and twigs. Next, by observing the shelters of others and adding new details to their own incep-

tions, they constructed better and better kinds of huts as time went on.

3. And since they were of an imitative and teachable nature, they would daily point out to each other the results of their building, boasting of the novelties in it; and thus, with their natural gifts sharpened by emulation, their standards improved daily. At first they set up forked stakes connected by twigs and covered these walls with mud. Others made walls of lumps of dried mud, covering them with reeds and leaves to keep out the rain and the heat. Finding that such roofs could not stand the rain during the storms of winter, they built them with peaks daubed with mud, the roofs sloping and projecting so as to carry off the rain water.

4. That houses originated as I have written above, we can see for ourselves from the buildings that are to this day constructed of like materials by foreign tribes: for instance, in Gaul, Spain, Portugal, and Aquitaine, roofed with oak shingles or thatched. Among the Colchians in Pontus, where there are forests in plenty, they lay down entire trees flat on the ground to the right and the left, leaving between them a space to suit the length of the trees, and then place above these another pair of trees, resting on the ends of the former and at right angles with them. These four trees enclose the space for the dwelling. Then upon these they place sticks of timber, one after the other on the four sides, crossing each other at the angles, and so, proceeding with their walls of trees laid perpendicularly above the lowest, they build up high towers. The interstices, which are left on account of the thickness of the building material, are stopped up with chips and mud. As for the roofs, by cutting away the ends of the crossbeams and making them converge gradually as they lay them across, they bring them up to the top from the four sides in the shape of a pyramid. They cover it with leaves and mud, and thus construct the roofs of their towers in a rude form of the "tortoise" style.

5. On the other hand, the Phrygians, who live in an open coun-

try, have no forests and consequently lack timber. They therefore select a natural hillock, run a trench through the middle of it, dig passages, and extend the interior space as widely as the site admits. Over it they build a pyramidal roof of logs fastened together, and this they cover with reeds and brushwood, heaping up very high mounds of earth above their dwellings. Thus their fashion in houses makes their winters very warm and their summers very cool. Some construct hovels with roofs of rushes from the swamps. Among other nations, also, in some places there are huts of the same or a similar method of construction. Likewise at Marseilles we can see roofs without tiles, made of earth mixed with straw. In Athens on the Areopagus there is to this day a relic of antiquity with a mud roof. The hut of Romulus on the Capitol is a significant reminder of the fashions of old times, and likewise the thatched roofs of temples on the Citadel.

6. From such specimens we can draw our inferences with regard to the devices used in the buildings of antiquity, and conclude that they were similar.

Furthermore, as men made progress by becoming daily more expert in building, and as their ingenuity was increased by their dexterity so that from habit they attained to considerable skill, their intelligence was enlarged by their industry until the more proficient adopted the trade of carpenters. From these early beginnings, and from the fact that nature had not only endowed the human race with senses like the rest of the animals, but had also equipped their minds with the powers of thought and understanding, thus putting all other animals under their sway, they next gradually advanced from the construction of buildings to the other arts and sciences, and so passed from a rude and barbarous mode of life to civilization and refinement.

7. Then, taking courage and looking forward from the standpoint of higher ideas born of the multiplication of the arts, they gave up huts and began to build houses with foundations, having

brick or stone walls, and roofs of timber and tiles; next, observation and application led them from fluctuating and indefinite conceptions to definite rules of symmetry. Perceiving that nature had been lavish in the bestowal of timber and bountiful in stores of building material, they treated this like careful nurses, and thus developing the refinements of life, embellished them with luxuries. Therefore I shall now treat, to the best of my ability, of the things which are suitable to be used in buildings, showing their qualities and their excellencies.

8. Some persons, however, may find fault with the position of this book, thinking that it should have been placed first. I will therefore explain the matter, lest it be thought that I have made a mistake. Being engaged in writing a complete treatise on architecture, I resolved to set forth in the first book the branches of learning and studies of which it consists, to define its departments, and to show of what it is composed. Hence I have there declared what the qualities of an architect should be. In the first book, therefore, I have spoken of the function of the art, but in this I shall discuss the use of the building materials which nature provides. For this book does not show of what architecture is composed, but treats of the origin of the building art, how it was fostered, and how it made progress, step by step, until it reached its present perfection.

9. This book is, therefore, in its proper order and place.

I will now return to my subject, and with regard to the materials suited to the construction of buildings will consider their natural formation and in what proportions their elementary constituents were combined, making it all clear and not obscure to my readers. For there is no kind of material, no body, and no thing that can be produced or conceived of, which is not made up of elementary particles; and nature does not admit of a truthful exploration in accordance with the doctrines of the physicists without an accurate demonstration of the primary causes of things, showing how and why they are as they are.

CHAPTER II

ON THE PRIMORDIAL SUBSTANCE ACCORDING TO THE PHYSICISTS

1. First of all Thales thought that water was the primordial substance of all things. Heraclitus of Ephesus, surnamed by the Greeks σκοτεινός on account of the obscurity of his writings, thought that it was fire. Democritus and his follower Epicurus thought that it was the atoms, termed by our writers "bodies that cannot be cut up," or, by some, "indivisibles." The school of the Pythagoreans added air and the earthy to the water and fire. Hence, although Democritus did not in a strict sense name them, but spoke only of indivisible bodies, yet he seems to have meant these same elements, because when taken by themselves they cannot be harmed, nor are they susceptible of dissolution, nor can they be cut up into parts, but throughout time eternal they forever retain an infinite solidity.

2. All things therefore appear to be made up and produced by the coming together of these elements, so that they have been distributed by nature among an infinite number of kinds of things. Hence I believed it right to treat of the diversity and practical peculiarities of these things as well as of the qualities which they exhibit in buildings, so that persons who are intending to build may understand them and so make no mistake, but may gather materials which are suitable to use in their buildings.

CHAPTER III

BRICK

1. Beginning with bricks, I shall state of what kind of clay they ought to be made. They should not be made of sandy or pebbly clay, or of fine gravel, because when made of these kinds they are in the first place heavy; and, secondly, when washed by

the rain as they stand in walls, they go to pieces and break up, and the straw in them does not hold together on account of the roughness of the material. They should rather be made of white and chalky or of red clay, or even of a coarse grained gravelly clay. These materials are smooth and therefore durable; they are not heavy to work with, and are readily laid.

2. Bricks should be made in Spring or Autumn, so that they may dry uniformly. Those made in Summer are defective, because the fierce heat of the sun bakes their surface and makes the brick seem dry while inside it is not dry. And so the shrinking, which follows as they dry, causes cracks in the parts which were dried before, and these cracks make the bricks weak. Bricks will be most serviceable if made two years before using; for they cannot dry thoroughly in less time. When fresh undried bricks are used in a wall, the stucco covering stiffens and hardens into a permanent mass, but the bricks settle and cannot keep the same height as the stucco; the motion caused by their shrinking prevents them from adhering to it, and they are separated from their union with it. Hence the stucco, no longer joined to the core of the wall, cannot stand by itself because it is so thin; it breaks off, and the walls themselves may perhaps be ruined by their settling. This is so true that at Utica in constructing walls they use brick only if it is dry and made five years previously, and approved as such by the authority of a magistrate.

3. There are three kinds of bricks. First, the kind called in Greek Lydian, being that which our people use, a foot and a half long and one foot wide. The other two kinds are used by the Greeks in their buildings. Of these, one is called πεντάδωρον, the other τετράδωρον. Δῶρον is the Greek for "palm," for in Greek δῶρον means the giving of gifts, and the gift is always presented in the palm of the hand. A brick five palms square is called "pentadoron"; one four palms square "tetradoron." Public buildings are constructed of πεντάδωρα, private of τετράδωρα.

4. With these bricks there are also half-bricks. When these are used in a wall, a course of bricks is laid on one face and a course

of half-bricks on the other, and they are bedded to the line on each face. The walls are bonded by alternate courses of the two different kinds, and as the bricks are always laid so as to break joints, this lends strength and a not unattractive appearance to both sides of such walls.

VITRUVIUS' BRICK-BOND ACCORDING TO REBER

In the states of Maxilua and Callet, in Further Spain, as well as in Pitane in Asia Minor, there are bricks which, when finished and dried, will float on being thrown into water. The reason why they can float seems to be that the clay of which they are made is like pumice-stone. So it is light, and also it does not, after being hardened by exposure to the air, take up or absorb liquid. So these bricks, being of this light and porous quality, and admitting no moisture into their texture, must by the laws of nature float in water, like pumice, no matter what their weight may be. They have therefore great advantages; for they are not heavy to use in building and, once made, they are not spoiled by bad weather.

CHAPTER IV

SAND

1. IN walls of masonry the first question must be with regard to the sand, in order that it may be fit to mix into mortar and have no dirt in it. The kinds of pitsand are these: black, gray, red, and carbuncular. Of these the best will be found to be that which crackles when rubbed in the hand, while that which has much dirt in it will not be sharp enough. Again: throw some sand upon a white garment and then shake it out; if the garment is not soiled and no dirt adheres to it, the sand is suitable.

2. But if there are no sandpits from which it can be dug, then we must sift it out from river beds or from gravel or even from the sea beach. This kind, however, has these defects when used in

masonry: it dries slowly; the wall cannot be built up without interruption but from time to time there must be pauses in the work; and such a wall cannot carry vaultings. Furthermore, when sea-sand is used in walls and these are coated with stucco, a salty efflorescence is given out which spoils the surface.

3. But pitsand used in masonry dries quickly, the stucco coating is permanent, and the walls can support vaultings. I am speaking of sand fresh from the sandpits. For if it lies unused too long after being taken out, it is disintegrated by exposure to sun, moon, or hoar frost, and becomes earthy. So when mixed in masonry, it has no binding power on the rubble, which consequently settles and down comes the load which the walls can no longer support. Fresh pitsand, however, in spite of all its excellence in concrete structures, is not equally useful in stucco, the richness of which, when the lime and straw are mixed with such sand, will cause it to crack as it dries on account of the great strength of the mixture. But river sand, though useless in "signinum" on account of its thinness, becomes perfectly solid in stucco when thoroughly worked by means of polishing instruments.

CHAPTER V

LIME

1. SAND and its sources having been thus treated, next with regard to lime we must be careful that it is burned from a stone which, whether soft or hard, is in any case white. Lime made of close-grained stone of the harder sort will be good in structural parts; lime of porous stone, in stucco. After slaking it, mix your mortar, if using pitsand, in the proportions of three parts of sand to one of lime; if using river or sea-sand, mix two parts of sand with one of lime. These will be the right proportions for the composition of the mixture. Further, in using river or sea-sand, the addition of a third part composed of burnt brick, pounded up and sifted, will make your mortar of a better composition to use.

2. The reason why lime makes a solid structure on being combined with water and sand seems to be this: that rocks, like all other bodies, are composed of the four elements. Those which contain a larger proportion of air, are soft; of water, are tough from the moisture; of earth, hard; and of fire, more brittle. Therefore, if limestone, without being burned, is merely pounded up small and then mixed with sand and so put into the work, the mass does not solidify nor can it hold together. But if the stone is first thrown into the kiln, it loses its former property of solidity by exposure to the great heat of the fire, and so with its strength burnt out and exhausted it is left with its pores open and empty. Hence, the moisture and air in the body of the stone being burned out and set free, and only a residuum of heat being left lying in it, if the stone is then immersed in water, the moisture, before the water can feel the influence of the fire, makes its way into the open pores; then the stone begins to get hot, and finally, after it cools off, the heat is rejected from the body of the lime.

3. Consequently, limestone when taken out of the kiln cannot be as heavy as when it was thrown in, but on being weighed, though its bulk remains the same as before, it is found to have lost about a third of its weight owing to the boiling out of the water. Therefore, its pores being thus opened and its texture rendered loose, it readily mixes with sand, and hence the two materials cohere as they dry, unite with the rubble, and make a solid structure.

CHAPTER VI

POZZOLANA

1. THERE is also a kind of powder which from natural causes produces astonishing results. It is found in the neighbourhood of Baiae and in the country belonging to the towns round about Mt. Vesuvius. This substance, when mixed with lime and rub-

ble, not only lends strength to buildings of other kinds, but even when piers of it are constructed in the sea, they set hard under water. The reason for this seems to be that the soil on the slopes of the mountains in these neighbourhoods is hot and full of hot springs. This would not be so unless the mountains had beneath them huge fires of burning sulphur or alum or asphalt. So the fire and the heat of the flames, coming up hot from far within through the fissures, make the soil there light, and the tufa found there is spongy and free from moisture. Hence, when the three substances, all formed on a similar principle by the force of fire, are mixed together, the water suddenly taken in makes them cohere, and the moisture quickly hardens them so that they set into a mass which neither the waves nor the force of the water can dissolve.

2. That there is burning heat in these regions may be proved by the further fact that in the mountains near Baiae, which belongs to the Cumaeans, there are places excavated to serve as sweating-baths, where the intense heat that comes from far below bores its way through the earth, owing to the force of the fire, and passing up appears in these regions, thus making remarkably good sweating-baths. Likewise also it is related that in ancient times the tides of heat, swelling and overflowing from under Mt. Vesuvius, vomited forth fire from the mountain upon the neighbouring country. Hence, what is called "sponge-stone" or "Pompeian pumice" appears to have been reduced by burning from another kind of stone to the condition of the kind which we see.

3. The kind of sponge-stone taken from this region is not produced everywhere else, but only about Aetna and among the hills of Mysia which the Greeks call the "Burnt District," and in other places of the same peculiar nature. Seeing that in such places there are found hot springs and warm vapour in excavations on the mountains, and that the ancients tell us that there were once fires spreading over the fields in those very regions, it seems to be certain that moisture has been extracted from the

tufa and earth, by the force of fire, just as it is from limestone in kilns.

4. Therefore, when different and unlike things have been subjected to the action of fire and thus reduced to the same condition, if after this, while in a warm, dry state, they are suddenly saturated with water, there is an effervescence of the heat latent in the bodies of them all, and this makes them firmly unite and quickly assume the property of one solid mass.

There will still be the question why Tuscany, although it abounds in hot springs, does not furnish a powder out of which, on the same principle, a wall can be made which will set fast under water. I have therefore thought best to explain how this seems to be, before the question should be raised.

5. The same kinds of soil are not found in all places and countries alike, nor is stone found everywhere. Some soils are earthy; others gravelly, and again pebbly; in other places the material is sandy; in a word, the properties of the soil are as different and unlike as are the various countries. In particular, it may be observed that sandpits are hardly ever lacking in any place within the districts of Italy and Tuscany which are bounded by the Apennines; whereas across the Apennines toward the Adriatic none are found, and in Achaea and Asia Minor or, in short, across the sea, the very term is unknown. Hence it is not in all the places where boiling springs of hot water abound, that there is the same combination of favourable circumstances which has been described above. For things are produced in accordance with the will of nature; not to suit man's pleasure, but as it were by a chance distribution.

6. Therefore, where the mountains are not earthy but consist of soft stone, the force of the fire, passing through the fissures in the stone, sets it afire. The soft and delicate part is burned out, while the hard part is left. Consequently, while in Campania the burning of the earth makes ashes, in Tuscany the combustion of the stone makes carbuncular sand. Both are excellent in walls, but one is better to use for buildings on land, the other for piers

TRAVERTINE QUARRIES ON THE ROMAN CAMPAGNA

1. 2. Ancient quarries. 3. A similar modern quarry.

The top of the rock shows the original ground level. The present ground level shows the depth to which the rock has been removed.

under salt water. The Tuscan stone is softer in quality than tufa but harder than earth, and being thoroughly kindled by the violent heat from below, the result is the production in some places of the kind of sand called carbuncular.

CHAPTER VII

STONE

1. I HAVE now spoken of lime and sand, with their varieties and points of excellence. Next comes the consideration of stone-quarries from which dimension stone and supplies of rubble to be used in building are taken and brought together. The stone in quarries is found to be of different and unlike qualities. In some it is soft: for example, in the environs of the city at the quarries of Grotta Rossa, Palla, Fidenae, and of the Alban hills; in others, it is medium, as at Tivoli, at Amiternum, or Mt. Soracte, and in quarries of this sort; in still others it is hard, as in lava quarries. There are also numerous other kinds: for instance, in Campania, red and black tufas; in Umbria, Picenum, and Venetia, white tufa which can be cut with a toothed saw, like wood.

2. All these soft kinds have the advantage that they can be easily worked as soon as they have been taken from the quarries. Under cover they play their part well; but in open and exposed situations the frost and rime make them crumble, and they go to pieces. On the seacoast, too, the salt eats away and dissolves them, nor can they stand great heat either. But travertine and all stone of that class can stand injury whether from a heavy load laid upon it or from the weather; exposure to fire, however, it cannot bear, but splits and cracks to pieces at once. This is because in its natural composition there is but little moisture and not much of the earthy, but a great deal of air and of fire. Therefore, it is not only without the earthy and watery elements, but when fire, expelling the air from it by the operation and force of heat, penetrates into its inmost parts and occupies the empty spaces of the

fissures, there comes a great glow and the stone is made to burn as fiercely as do the particles of fire itself.

3. There are also several quarries called Anician in the territory of Tarquinii, the stone being of the colour of peperino. The principal workshops lie round the lake of Bolsena and in the prefecture of Statonia. This stone has innumerable good qualities. Neither the season of frost nor exposure to fire can harm it, but it remains solid and lasts to a great age, because there is only a little air and fire in its natural composition, a moderate amount of moisture, and a great deal of the earthy. Hence its structure is of close texture and solid, and so it cannot be injured by the weather or by the force of fire.

4. This may best be seen from monuments in the neighbourhood of the town of Ferento which are made of stone from these quarries. Among them are large statues exceedingly well made, images of smaller size, and flowers and acanthus leaves gracefully carved. Old as these are, they look as fresh as if they were only just finished. Bronze workers, also, make moulds for the casting of bronze out of stone from these quarries, and find it very useful in bronze-founding. If the quarries were only near Rome, all our buildings might well be constructed from the products of these workshops.

5. But since, on account of the proximity of the stone-quarries of Grotta Rossa, Palla, and the others that are nearest to the city, necessity drives us to make use of their products, we must proceed as follows, if we wish our work to be finished without flaws. Let the stone be taken from the quarry two years before building is to begin, and not in winter but in summer. Then let it lie exposed in an open place. Such stone as has been damaged by the two years of exposure should be used in the foundations. The rest, which remains unhurt, has passed the test of nature and will endure in those parts of the building which are above ground. This precaution should be observed, not only with dimension stone, but also with the rubble which is to be used in walls.

Photo. Moscioni
EXAMPLE OF OPUS INCERTUM, THE CIRCULAR TEMPLE AT TIVOLI

CHAPTER VIII

METHODS OF BUILDING WALLS

1. THERE are two styles of walls: "opus reticulatum," now used by everybody, and the ancient style called "opus incertum." Of these, the reticulatum looks better, but its construction makes it likely to crack, because its beds and builds spread out in every direction. On the other hand, in the opus incertum, the rubble, lying in courses and imbricated, makes a wall which, though not beautiful, is stronger than the reticulatum.

2. Both kinds should be constructed of the smallest stones, so that the walls, being thoroughly puddled with the mortar, which is made of lime and sand, may hold together longer. Since the stones used are soft and porous, they are apt to suck the moisture out of the mortar and so to dry it up. But when there is abundance of lime and sand, the wall, containing more moisture, will not soon lose its strength, for they will hold it together. But as soon as the moisture is sucked out of the mortar by the porous rubble, and the lime and sand separate and disunite, the rubble can no longer adhere to them and the wall will in time become a ruin.

3. This we may learn from several monuments in the environs of the city, which are built of marble or dimension stone, but on the inside packed with masonry between the outer walls. In the course of time, the mortar has lost its strength, which has been sucked out of it by the porousness of the rubble; and so the monuments are tumbling down and going to pieces, with their joints loosened by the settling of the material that bound them together.

4. He who wishes to avoid such a disaster should leave a cavity behind the facings, and on the inside build walls two feet thick, made of red dimension stone or burnt brick or lava in courses, and then bind them to the fronts by means of iron clamps and lead. For thus his work, being no mere heap of material but regularly laid in courses, will be strong enough to last forever

without a flaw, because the beds and builds, all settling equally and bonded at the joints, will not let the work bulge out, nor allow the fall of the face walls which have been tightly fastened together.

5. Consequently, the method of construction employed by the Greeks is not to be despised. They do not use a structure of soft rubble polished on the outside, but whenever they forsake dimension stone, they lay courses of lava or of some hard stone, and, as though building with brick, they bind the upright joints by interchanging the direction of the stones as they lie in the courses. Thus they attain to a perfection that will endure to eternity. These structures are of two kinds. One of them is called "isodomum," the other "pseudisodomum."

6. A wall is called isodomum when all the courses are of equal height; pseudisodomum, when the rows of courses do not match but run unequally. Both kinds are strong: first, because the rubble itself is of close texture and solid, unable to suck the moisture out of the mortar, but keeping it in its moist condition for a very long period; secondly, because the beds of the stones, being laid smooth and level to begin with, keep the mortar from falling, and, as they are bonded throughout the entire thickness of the wall, they hold together for a very long period.

7. Another method is that which they call ἔμπλεκτον, used also among us in the country. In this the facings are finished, but the other stones left in their natural state and then laid with alternate bonding stones. But our workmen, in their hurry to finish, devote themselves only to the facings of the walls, setting them upright but filling the space between with a lot of broken stones and mortar thrown in anyhow. This makes three different sections in the same structure; two consisting of facing and one of filling between them. The Greeks, however, do not build so; but laying their stones level and building every other stone lengthwise into the thickness, they do not fill the space between, but construct the thickness of their walls in one solid and unbroken mass from the facings to the interior. Further, at intervals they

OPUS RETICULATUM FROM THE THERMAE OF HADRIAN'S VILLA AT TIVOLI

Photo. Moscioni

OPUS RETICULATUM FROM THE DOORWAY OF THE STOA POECILE. VILLA OF HADRIAN AT TIVOLI

Photo. Moscioni

lay single stones which run through the entire thickness of the wall. These stones, which show at each end, are called διάτονοι, and by their bonding powers they add very greatly to the solidity of the walls.

8. One who in accordance with these notes will take pains in selecting his method of construction, may count upon having something that will last. No walls made of rubble and finished with delicate beauty — no such walls can escape ruin as time goes on. Hence, when arbitrators are chosen to set a valuation on party walls, they do not value them at what they cost to build, but look up the written contract in each case and then, after deducting from the cost one eightieth for each year that the wall has been standing, decide that the remainder is the sum to be paid. They thus in effect pronounce that such walls cannot last more than eighty years.

9. In the case of brick walls, however, no deduction is made provided that they are still standing plumb, but they are always valued at what they cost to build. Hence in some states we may see public buildings and private houses, as well as those of kings, built of brick: in Athens, for example, the part of the wall which faces Mt. Hymettus and Pentelicus; at Patras, the cellae of the temple of Jupiter and Hercules, which are brick, although on the outside the entablature and columns of the temple are of stone; in Italy, at Arezzo, an ancient wall excellently built; at Tralles, the house built for the kings of the dynasty of Attalus, which is now always granted to the man who holds the state priesthood. In Sparta, paintings have been taken out of certain walls by cutting through the bricks, then have been placed in wooden frames, and so brought to the Comitium to adorn the aedileship of Varro and Murena.

10. Then there is the house of Croesus which the people of Sardis have set apart as a place of repose for their fellow-citizens in the retirement of age, — a "Gerousia" for the guild of the elder men. At Halicarnassus, the house of that most potent king Mausolus, though decorated throughout with Proconnesian mar-

ble, has walls built of brick which are to this day of extraordinary strength, and are covered with stucco so highly polished that they seem to be as glistening as glass. That king did not use brick from poverty; for he was choke-full of revenues, being ruler of all Caria.

11. As for his skill and ingenuity as a builder, they may be seen from what follows. He was born at Melassa, but recognizing the natural advantages of Halicarnassus as a fortress, and seeing that it was suitable as a trading centre and that it had a good harbour, he fixed his residence there. The place had a curvature like that of the seats in a theatre. On the lowest tier, along the harbour, was built the forum. About half-way up the curving slope, at the point where the curved cross-aisle is in a theatre, a broad wide street was laid out, in the middle of which was built the Mausoleum, a work so remarkable that it is classed among the Seven Wonders of the World. At the top of the hill, in the centre, is the fane of Mars, containing a colossal acrolithic statue by the famous hand of Leochares. That is, some think that this statue is by Leochares, others by Timotheus. At the extreme right of the summit is the fane of Venus and Mercury, close to the spring of Salmacis.

12. There is a mistaken idea that this spring infects those who drink of it with an unnatural lewdness. It will not be out of place to explain how this idea came to spread throughout the world from a mistake in the telling of the tale. It cannot be that the water makes men effeminate and unchaste, as it is said to do; for the spring is of remarkable clearness and excellent in flavour. The fact is that when Melas and Arevanias came there from Argos and Troezen and founded a colony together, they drove out the Carians and Lelegans who were barbarians. These took refuge in the mountains, and, uniting there, used to make raids, plundering the Greeks and laying their country waste in a cruel manner. Later, one of the colonists, to make money, set up a well-stocked shop, near the spring because the water was so good, and the way in which he carried it on attracted the barbarians. So

THE MAUSOLEUM AT HALICARNASSUS AS RESTORED BY FRIEDRICH ADLER

they began to come down, one at a time, and to meet with society, and thus they were brought back of their own accord, giving up their rough and savage ways for the delights of Greek customs. Hence this water acquired its peculiar reputation, not because it really induced unchastity, but because those barbarians were softened by the charm of civilization.

13. But since I have been tempted into giving a description of this fortified place, it remains to finish my account of it. Corresponding to the fane of Venus and the spring described above, which are on the right, we have on the extreme left the royal palace which king Mausolus built there in accordance with a plan all his own. To the right it commands a view of the forum, the harbour, and the entire line of fortifications, while just below it, to the left, there is a concealed harbour, hidden under the walls in such a way that nobody could see or know what was going on in it. Only the king himself could, in case of need, give orders from his own palace to the oarsmen and soldiers, without the knowledge of anybody else.

14. After the death of Mausolus, his wife Artemisia became queen, and the Rhodians, regarding it as an outrage that a woman should be ruler of the states of all Caria, fitted out a fleet and sallied forth to seize upon the kingdom. When news of this reached Artemisia, she gave orders that her fleet should be hidden away in that harbour with oarsmen and marines mustered and concealed, but that the rest of the citizens should take their places on the city wall. After the Rhodians had landed at the larger harbour with their well-equipped fleet, she ordered the people on the wall to cheer them and to promise that they would deliver up the town. Then, when they had passed inside the wall, leaving their fleet empty, Artemisia suddenly made a canal which led to the sea, brought her fleet thus out of the smaller harbour, and so sailed into the larger. Disembarking her soldiers, she towed the empty fleet of the Rhodians out to sea. So the Rhodians were surrounded without means of retreat, and were slain in the very forum.

15. So Artemisia embarked her own soldiers and oarsmen in the ships of the Rhodians and set forth for Rhodes. The Rhodians, beholding their own ships approaching wreathed with laurel, supposed that their fellow-citizens were returning victorious, and admitted the enemy. Then Artemisia, after taking Rhodes and killing its leading men, put up in the city of Rhodes a trophy of her victory, including two bronze statues, one representing the state of the Rhodians, the other herself. Herself she fashioned in the act of branding the state of the Rhodians. In later times the Rhodians, labouring under the religious scruple which makes it a sin to remove trophies once they are dedicated, constructed a building to surround the place, and thus by the erection of the "Grecian Station" covered it so that nobody could see it, and ordered that the building be called "ἄβατον."

16. Since such very powerful kings have not disdained walls built of brick, although with their revenues and from booty they might often have had them not only of masonry or dimension stone but even of marble, I think that one ought not to reject buildings made of brick-work, provided that they are properly "topped." But I shall explain why this kind of structure should not be used by the Roman people within the city, not omitting the reasons and the grounds for them.

17. The laws of the state forbid that walls abutting on public property should be more than a foot and a half thick. The other walls are built of the same thickness in order to save space. Now brick walls, unless two or three bricks thick, cannot support more than one story; certainly not if they are only a foot and a half in thickness. But with the present importance of the city and the unlimited numbers of its population, it is necessary to increase the number of dwelling-places indefinitely. Consequently, as the ground floors could not admit of so great a number living in the city, the nature of the case has made it necessary to find relief by making the buildings high. In these tall piles reared with piers of stone, walls of burnt brick, and partitions of rubble work, and provided with floor after floor, the upper stories can be par-

titioned off into rooms to very great advantage. The accommodations within the city walls being thus multiplied as a result of the many floors high in the air, the Roman people easily find excellent places in which to live.

18. It has now been explained how limitations of building space necessarily forbid the employment of brick walls within the city. When it becomes necessary to use them outside the city, they should be constructed as follows in order to be perfect and durable. On the top of the wall lay a structure of burnt brick, about a foot and a half in height, under the tiles and projecting like a coping. Thus the defects usual in these walls can be avoided. For when the tiles on the roof are broken or thrown down by the wind so that rain-water can leak through, this burnt brick coating will prevent the crude brick from being damaged, and the cornice-like projection will throw off the drops beyond the vertical face, and thus the walls, though of crude brick structure, will be preserved intact.

19. With regard to burnt brick, nobody can tell offhand whether it is of the best or unfit to use in a wall, because its strength can be tested only after it has been used on a roof and exposed to bad weather and time — then, if it is good it is accepted. If not made of good clay or if not baked sufficiently, it shows itself defective there when exposed to frosts and rime. Brick that will not stand exposure on roofs can never be strong enough to carry its load in a wall. Hence the strongest burnt brick walls are those which are constructed out of old roofing tiles.

20. As for "wattle and daub" I could wish that it had never been invented. The more it saves in time and gains in space, the greater and the more general is the disaster that it may cause; for it is made to catch fire, like torches. It seems better, therefore, to spend on walls of burnt brick, and be at expense, than to save with "wattle and daub," and be in danger. And, in the stucco covering, too, it makes cracks from the inside by the arrangement of its studs and girts. For these swell with moisture as they are daubed, and then contract as they dry, and, by their shrinking, cause the

solid stucco to split. But since some are obliged to use it either to save time or money, or for partitions on an unsupported span, the proper method of construction is as follows. Give it a high foundation so that it may nowhere come in contact with the broken stone-work composing the floor; for if it is sunk in this, it rots in course of time, then settles and sags forward, and so breaks through the surface of the stucco covering.

I have now explained to the best of my ability the subject of walls, and the preparation of the different kinds of material employed, with their advantages and disadvantages. Next, following the guidance of Nature, I shall treat of the frame-work and the kinds of wood used in it, showing how they may be procured of a sort that will not give way as time goes on.

CHAPTER IX

TIMBER

1. TIMBER should be felled between early Autumn and the time when Favonius begins to blow. For in Spring all trees become pregnant, and they are all employing their natural vigour in the production of leaves and of the fruits that return every year. The requirements of that season render them empty and swollen, and so they are weak and feeble because of their looseness of texture. This is also the case with women who have conceived. Their bodies are not considered perfectly healthy until the child is born; hence, pregnant slaves, when offered for sale, are not warranted sound, because the fetus as it grows within the body takes to itself as nourishment all the best qualities of the mother's food, and so the stronger it becomes as the full time for birth approaches, the less compact it allows that body to be from which it is produced. After the birth of the child, what was heretofore taken to promote the growth of another creature is now set free by the delivery of the newborn, and the channels being now empty and open, the body will take it in by lapping up its juices, and thus

becomes compact and returns to the natural strength which it had before.

2. On the same principle, with the ripening of the fruits in Autumn the leaves begin to wither and the trees, taking up their sap from the earth through the roots, recover themselves and are restored to their former solid texture. But the strong air of winter compresses and solidifies them during the time above mentioned. Consequently, if the timber is felled on the principle and at the time above mentioned, it will be felled at the proper season.

3. In felling a tree we should cut into the trunk of it to the very heart, and then leave it standing so that the sap may drain out drop by drop throughout the whole of it. In this way the useless liquid which is within will run out through the sapwood instead of having to die in a mass of decay, thus spoiling the quality of the timber. Then and not till then, the tree being drained dry and the sap no longer dripping, let it be felled and it will be in the highest state of usefulness.

4. That this is so may be seen in the case of fruit trees. When these are tapped at the base and pruned, each at the proper time, they pour out from the heart through the tapholes all the superfluous and corrupting fluid which they contain, and thus the draining process makes them durable. But when the juices of trees have no means of escape, they clot and rot in them, making the trees hollow and good for nothing. Therefore, if the draining process does not exhaust them while they are still alive, there is no doubt that, if the same principle is followed in felling them for timber, they will last a long time and be very useful in buildings.

5. Trees vary and are unlike one another in their qualities. Thus it is with the oak, elm, poplar, cypress, fir, and the others which are most suitable to use in buildings. The oak, for instance, has not the efficacy of the fir, nor the cypress that of the elm. Nor in the case of other trees, is it natural that they should be alike; but the individual kinds are effective in building, some in one way, some in another, owing to the different properties of their elements.

6. To begin with fir: it contains a great deal of air and fire with very little moisture and the earthy, so that, as its natural properties are of the lighter class, it is not heavy. Hence, its consistence being naturally stiff, it does not easily bend under the load, and keeps its straightness when used in the framework. But it contains so much heat that it generates and encourages decay, which spoils it; and it also kindles fire quickly because of the air in its body, which is so open that it takes in fire and so gives out a great flame.

7. The part which is nearest to the earth before the tree is cut down takes up moisture through the roots from the immediate neighbourhood and hence is without knots and is "clear." But the upper part, on account of the great heat in it, throws up branches into the air through the knots; and this, when it is cut off about twenty feet from the ground and then hewn, is called "knotwood" because of its hardness and knottiness. The lowest part, after the tree is cut down and the sapwood of the same thrown away, is split up into four pieces and prepared for joiner's work, and so is called "clearstock."

8. Oak, on the other hand, having enough and to spare of the earthy among its elements, and containing but little moisture, air, and fire, lasts for an unlimited period when buried in underground structures. It follows that when exposed to moisture, as its texture is not loose and porous, it cannot take in liquid on account of its compactness, but, withdrawing from the moisture, it resists it and warps, thus making cracks in the structures in which it is used.

9. The winter oak, being composed of a moderate amount of all the elements, is very useful in buildings, but when in a moist place, it takes in water to its centre through its pores, its air and fire being expelled by the influence of the moisture, and so it rots. The Turkey oak and the beech, both containing a mixture of moisture, fire, and the earthy, with a great deal of air, through this loose texture take in moisture to their centre and soon decay. White and black poplar, as well as willow, linden, and the agnus

castus, containing an abundance of fire and air, a moderate amount of moisture, and only a small amount of the earthy, are composed of a mixture which is proportionately rather light, and so they are of great service from their stiffness. Although on account of the mixture of the earthy in them they are not hard, yet their loose texture makes them gleaming white, and they are a convenient material to use in carving.

10. The alder, which is produced close by river banks, and which seems to be altogether useless as building material, has really excellent qualities. It is composed of a very large proportion of air and fire, not much of the earthy, and only a little moisture. Hence, in swampy places, alder piles driven close together beneath the foundations of buildings take in the water which their own consistence lacks and remain imperishable forever, supporting structures of enormous weight and keeping them from decay. Thus a material which cannot last even a little while above ground, endures for a long time when covered with moisture.

11. One can see this at its best in Ravenna; for there all the buildings, both public and private, have piles of this sort beneath their foundations. The elm and the ash contain a very great amount of moisture, a minimum of air and fire, and a moderate mixture of the earthy in their composition. When put in shape for use in buildings they are tough and, having no stiffness on account of the weight of moisture in them, soon bend. But when they become dry with age, or are allowed to lose their sap and die standing in the open, they get harder, and from their toughness supply a strong material for dowels to be used in joints and other articulations.

12. The hornbeam, which has a very small amount of fire and of the earthy in its composition, but a very great proportion of air and moisture, is not a wood that breaks easily, and is very convenient to handle. Hence, the Greeks call it "zygia," because they make of it yokes for their draught-animals, and their word for yoke is ζυγά. Cypress and pine are also just as admirable; for although they contain an abundance of moisture mixed with

an equivalent composed of all the other elements, and so are apt to warp when used in buildings on account of this superfluity of moisture, yet they can be kept to a great age without rotting, because the liquid contained within their substances has a bitter taste which by its pungency prevents the entrance of decay or of those little creatures which are destructive. Hence, buildings made of these kinds of wood last for an unending period of time.

13. The cedar and the juniper tree have the same uses and good qualities, but, while the cypress and pine yield resin, from the cedar is produced an oil called cedar-oil. Books as well as other things smeared with this are not hurt by worms or decay. The foliage of this tree is like that of the cypress but the grain of the wood is straight. The statue of Diana in the temple at Ephesus is made of it, and so are the coffered ceilings both there and in all other famous fanes, because that wood is everlasting. The tree grows chiefly in Crete, Africa, and in some districts of Syria.

14. The larch, known only to the people of the towns on the banks of the river Po and the shores of the Adriatic, is not only preserved from decay and the worm by the great bitterness of its sap, but also it cannot be kindled with fire nor ignite of itself, unless like stone in a limekiln it is burned with other wood. And even then it does not take fire nor produce burning coals, but after a long time it slowly consumes away. This is because there is a very small proportion of the elements of fire and air in its composition, which is a dense and solid mass of moisture and the earthy, so that it has no open pores through which fire can find its way; but it repels the force of fire and does not let itself be harmed by it quickly. Further, its weight will not let it float in water, so that when transported it is loaded on shipboard or on rafts made of fir.

15. It is worth while to know how this wood was discovered. The divine Caesar, being with his army in the neighbourhood of the Alps, and having ordered the towns to furnish supplies, the inhabitants of a fortified stronghold there, called Larignum, trusting in the natural strength of their defences, refused to obey his command. So the general ordered his forces to the assault.

In front of the gate of this stronghold there was a tower, made of beams of this wood laid in alternating directions at right angles to each other, like a funeral pyre, and built high, so that they could drive off an attacking party by throwing stakes and stones from the top. When it was observed that they had no other missiles than stakes, and that these could not be hurled very far from the wall on account of the weight, orders were given to approach and to throw bundles of brushwood and lighted torches at this outwork. These the soldiers soon got together.

16. The flames soon kindled the brushwood which lay about that wooden structure and, rising towards heaven, made everybody think that the whole pile had fallen. But when the fire had burned itself out and subsided, and the tower appeared to view entirely uninjured, Caesar in amazement gave orders that they should be surrounded with a palisade, built beyond the range of missiles. So the townspeople were frightened into surrendering, and were then asked where that wood came from which was not harmed by fire. They pointed to trees of the kind under discussion, of which there are very great numbers in that vicinity. And so, as that stronghold was called Larignum, the wood was called larch. It is transported by way of the Po to Ravenna, and is to be had in Fano, Pesaro, Ancona, and the other towns in that neighbourhood. If there were only a ready method of carrying this material to Rome, it would be of the greatest use in buildings; if not for general purposes, yet at least if the boards used in the eaves running round blocks of houses were made of it, the buildings would be free from the danger of fire spreading across to them, because such boards can neither take fire from flames or from burning coals, nor ignite spontaneously.

17. The leaves of these trees are like those of the pine; timber from them comes in long lengths, is as easily wrought in joiner's work as is the clearwood of fir, and contains a liquid resin, of the colour of Attic honey, which is good for consumptives.

With regard to the different kinds of timber, I have now explained of what natural properties they appear to be composed, and how they were produced. It remains to consider the question why the highland fir, as it is called in Rome, is inferior, while the lowland fir is extremely useful in buildings so far as durability is concerned; and further to explain how it is that their bad or good qualities seem to be due to the peculiarities of their neighbourhood, so that this subject may be clearer to those who examine it.

CHAPTER X

HIGHLAND AND LOWLAND FIR

1. The first spurs of the Apennines arise from the Tuscan sea between the Alps and the most distant borders of Tuscany. The mountain range itself bends round and, almost touching the shores of the Adriatic in the middle of the curve, completes its circuit by extending to the strait on the other shore. Hence, this side of the curve, sloping towards the districts of Tuscany and Campania, lies basking in the sun, being constantly exposed to the full force of its rays all day. But the further side, sloping towards the Upper Sea and having a northern exposure, is constantly shrouded in shadowy darkness. Hence the trees which grow on that side, being nourished by the moisture, not only themselves attain to a very large size, but their fibre too, filled full of moisture, is swollen and distended with abundance of liquid. When they lose their vitality after being felled and hewn, the fibre retains its stiffness, and the trees as they dry become hollow and frail on account of their porosity, and hence cannot last when used in buildings.

2. But trees which grow in places facing the course of the sun are not of porous fibre but are solid, being drained by the dryness; for the sun absorbs moisture and draws it out of trees as well as out of the earth. The trees in sunny neighbourhoods, therefore, being solidified by the compact texture of their fibre, and not being porous from moisture, are very useful, so far as durability goes, when they are hewn into timber. Hence the lowland firs,

being conveyed from sunny places, are better than those highland firs, which are brought here from shady places.

3. To the best of my mature consideration, I have now treated the materials which are necessary in the construction of buildings, the proportionate amount of the elements which are seen to be contained in their natural composition, and the points of excellence and defects of each kind, so that they may be not unknown to those who are engaged in building. Thus those who can follow the directions contained in this treatise will be better informed in advance, and able to select, among the different kinds, those which will be of use in their works. Therefore, since the preliminaries have been explained, the buildings themselves will be treated in the remaining books; and first, as due order requires, I shall in the next book write of the temples of the immortal gods and their symmetrical proportions.

BOOK III

BOOK III

INTRODUCTION

1. Apollo at Delphi, through the oracular utterance of his priestess, pronounced Socrates the wisest of men. Of him it is related that he said with sagacity and great learning that the human breast should have been furnished with open windows, so that men might not keep their feelings concealed, but have them open to the view. Oh that nature, following his idea, had constructed them thus unfolded and obvious to the view! For if it had been so, not merely the virtues and vices of the mind would be easily visible, but also its knowledge of branches of study, displayed to the contemplation of the eyes, would not need testing by untrustworthy powers of judgement, but a singular and lasting influence would thus be lent to the learned and wise. However, since they are not so constructed, but are as nature willed them to be, it is impossible for men, while natural abilities are concealed in the breast, to form a judgement on the quality of the knowledge of the arts which is thus deeply hidden. And if artists themselves testify to their own skill, they can never, unless they are wealthy or famous from the age of their studios, or unless they are also possessed of the public favour and of eloquence, have an influence commensurate with their devotion to their pursuits, so that people may believe them to have the knowledge which they profess to have.

2. In particular we can learn this from the case of the sculptors and painters of antiquity. Those among them who were marked by high station or favourably recommended have come down to posterity with a name that will last forever; for instance, Myron, Polycletus, Phidias, Lysippus, and the others who have attained to fame by their art. For they acquired it by the execution of works for great states or for kings or for citizens of rank. But

those who, being men of no less enthusiasm, natural ability, and dexterity than those famous artists, and who executed no less perfectly finished works for citizens of low station, are unremembered, not because they lacked diligence or dexterity in their art, but because fortune failed them; for instance, Teleas of Athens, Chion of Corinth, Myager the Phocaean, Pharax of Ephesus, Boedas of Byzantium, and many others. Then there were painters like Aristomenes of Thasos, Polycles and Andron of Ephesus, Theo of Magnesia, and others who were not deficient in diligence or enthusiasm for their art or in dexterity, but whose narrow means or ill-luck, or the higher position of their rivals in the struggle for honour, stood in the way of their attaining distinction.

3. Of course, we need not be surprised if artistic excellence goes unrecognized on account of being unknown; but there should be the greatest indignation when, as often, good judges are flattered by the charm of social entertainments into an approbation which is a mere pretence. Now if, as Socrates wished, our feelings, opinions, and knowledge gained by study had been manifest and clear to see, popularity and adulation would have no influence, but men who had reached the height of knowledge by means of correct and definite courses of study, would be given commissions without any effort on their part. However, since such things are not plain and apparent to the view, as we think they should have been, and since I observe that the uneducated rather than the educated are in higher favour, thinking it beneath me to engage with the uneducated in the struggle for honour, I prefer to show the excellence of our department of knowledge by the publication of this treatise.

4. In my first book, Emperor, I described to you the art, with its points of excellence, the different kinds of training with which the architect ought to be equipped, adding the reasons why he ought to be skilful in them, and I divided up the subject of architecture as a whole among its departments, duly defining the limits of each. Next, as was preëminent and necessary, I explained on scientific principles the method of selecting healthy sites for

fortified towns, pointed out by geometrical figures the different winds and the quarters from which they blow, and showed the proper way to lay out the lines of streets and rows of houses within the walls. Here I fixed the end of my first book. In the second, on building materials, I treated their various advantages in structures, and the natural properties of which they are composed. In this third book I shall speak of the temples of the immortal gods, describing and explaining them in the proper manner.

CHAPTER I

ON SYMMETRY: IN TEMPLES AND IN THE HUMAN BODY

1. The design of a temple depends on symmetry, the principles of which must be most carefully observed by the architect. They are due to proportion, in Greek ἀναλογία. Proportion is a correspondence among the measures of the members of an entire work, and of the whole to a certain part selected as standard. From this result the principles of symmetry. Without symmetry and proportion there can be no principles in the design of any temple; that is, if there is no precise relation between its members, as in the case of those of a well shaped man.

2. For the human body is so designed by nature that the face, from the chin to the top of the forehead and the lowest roots of the hair, is a tenth part of the whole height; the open hand from the wrist to the tip of the middle finger is just the same; the head from the chin to the crown is an eighth, and with the neck and shoulder from the top of the breast to the lowest roots of the hair is a sixth; from the middle of the breast to the summit of the crown is a fourth. If we take the height of the face itself, the distance from the bottom of the chin to the under side of the nostrils is one third of it; the nose from the under side of the nostrils to a line between the eyebrows is the same; from there to the lowest roots of the hair is also a third, comprising the forehead. The length of the foot is one sixth of the height of the body; of the forearm, one fourth; and the breadth of the breast is also one fourth. The other members, too, have their own symmetrical proportions, and it was by employing them that the famous painters and sculptors of antiquity attained to great and endless renown.

3. Similarly, in the members of a temple there ought to be the greatest harmony in the symmetrical relations of the different

parts to the general magnitude of the whole. Then again, in the human body the central point is naturally the navel. For if a man be placed flat on his back, with his hands and feet extended, and a pair of compasses centred at his navel, the fingers and toes of his two hands and feet will touch the circumference of a circle described therefrom. And just as the human body yields a circular outline, so too a square figure may be found from it. For if we measure the distance from the soles of the feet to the top of the head, and then apply that measure to the outstretched arms, the breadth will be found to be the same as the height, as in the case of plane surfaces which are perfectly square.

4. Therefore, since nature has designed the human body so that its members are duly proportioned to the frame as a whole, it appears that the ancients had good reason for their rule, that in perfect buildings the different members must be in exact symmetrical relations to the whole general scheme. Hence, while transmitting to us the proper arrangements for buildings of all kinds, they were particularly careful to do so in the case of temples of the gods, buildings in which merits and faults usually last forever.

5. Further, it was from the members of the body that they derived the fundamental ideas of the measures which are obviously necessary in all works, as the finger, palm, foot, and cubit. These they apportioned so as to form the "perfect number," called in Greek τέλειον, and as the perfect number the ancients fixed upon ten. For it is from the number of the fingers of the hand that the palm is found, and the foot from the palm. Again, while ten is naturally perfect, as being made up by the fingers of the two palms, Plato also held that this number was perfect because ten is composed of the individual units, called by the Greeks μονάδες. But as soon as eleven or twelve is reached, the numbers, being excessive, cannot be perfect until they come to ten for the second time; for the component parts of that number are the individual units.

6. The mathematicians, however, maintaining a different view,

have said that the perfect number is six, because this number is composed of integral parts which are suited numerically to their method of reckoning: thus, one is one sixth; two is one third; three is one half; four is two thirds, or δίμοιρος as they call it; five is five sixths, called πεντάμοιρος; and six is the perfect number. As the number goes on growing larger, the addition of a unit above six is the ἔφεκτος; eight, formed by the addition of a third part of six, is the integer and a third, called ἐπίτριτος; the addition of one half makes nine, the integer and a half, termed ἡμιόλιος; the addition of two thirds, making the number ten, is the integer and two thirds, which they call ἐπιδίμοιρος; in the number eleven, where five are added, we have the five sixths, called ἐπίπεμπτος; finally, twelve, being composed of the two simple integers, is called διπλάσιος.

7. And further, as the foot is one sixth of a man's height, the height of the body as expressed in number of feet being limited to six, they held that this was the perfect number, and observed that the cubit consisted of six palms or of twenty-four fingers. This principle seems to have been followed by the states of Greece. As the cubit consisted of six palms, they made the drachma, which they used as their unit, consist in the same way of six bronze coins, like our *asses*, which they call obols; and, to correspond to the fingers, divided the drachma into twenty-four quarter-obols, which some call dichalca others trichalca.

8. But our countrymen at first fixed upon the ancient number and made ten bronze pieces go to the denarius, and this is the origin of the name which is applied to the denarius to this day. And the fourth part of it, consisting of two asses and half of a third, they called "sesterce." But later, observing that six and ten were both of them perfect numbers, they combined the two, and thus made the most perfect number, sixteen. They found their authority for this in the foot. For if we take two palms from the cubit, there remains the foot of four palms; but the palm contains four fingers. Hence the foot contains sixteen fingers, and the denarius the same number of bronze *asses*.

9. Therefore, if it is agreed that number was found out from the human fingers, and that there is a symmetrical correspondence between the members separately and the entire form of the body, in accordance with a certain part selected as standard, we can have nothing but respect for those who, in constructing temples of the immortal gods, have so arranged the members of the works that both the separate parts and the whole design may harmonize in their proportions and symmetry.

CHAPTER II

CLASSIFICATION OF TEMPLES

1. THERE are certain elementary forms on which the general aspect of a temple depends. First there is the temple in antis, or ναὸς ἐν παραστάσιν as it is called in Greek; then the prostyle, amphiprostyle, peripteral, pseudodipteral, dipteral, and hypaethral. These different forms may be described as follows.

2. It will be a temple in antis when it has antae carried out in front of the walls which enclose the cella, and in the middle, between the antae, two columns, and over them the pediment constructed in the symmetrical proportions to be described later in this work. An example will be found at the Three Fortunes, in that one of the three which is nearest the Colline gate.

3. The prostyle is in all respects like the temple in antis, except that at the corners, opposite the antae, it has two columns, and that it has architraves not only in front, as in the case of the temple in antis, but also one to the right and one to the left in the wings. An example of this is the temple of Jove and Faunus in the Island of the Tiber.

4. The amphiprostyle is in all other respects like the prostyle, but has besides, in the rear, the same arrangement of columns and pediment.

5. A temple will be peripteral that has six columns in front and six in the rear, with eleven on each side including the corner col-

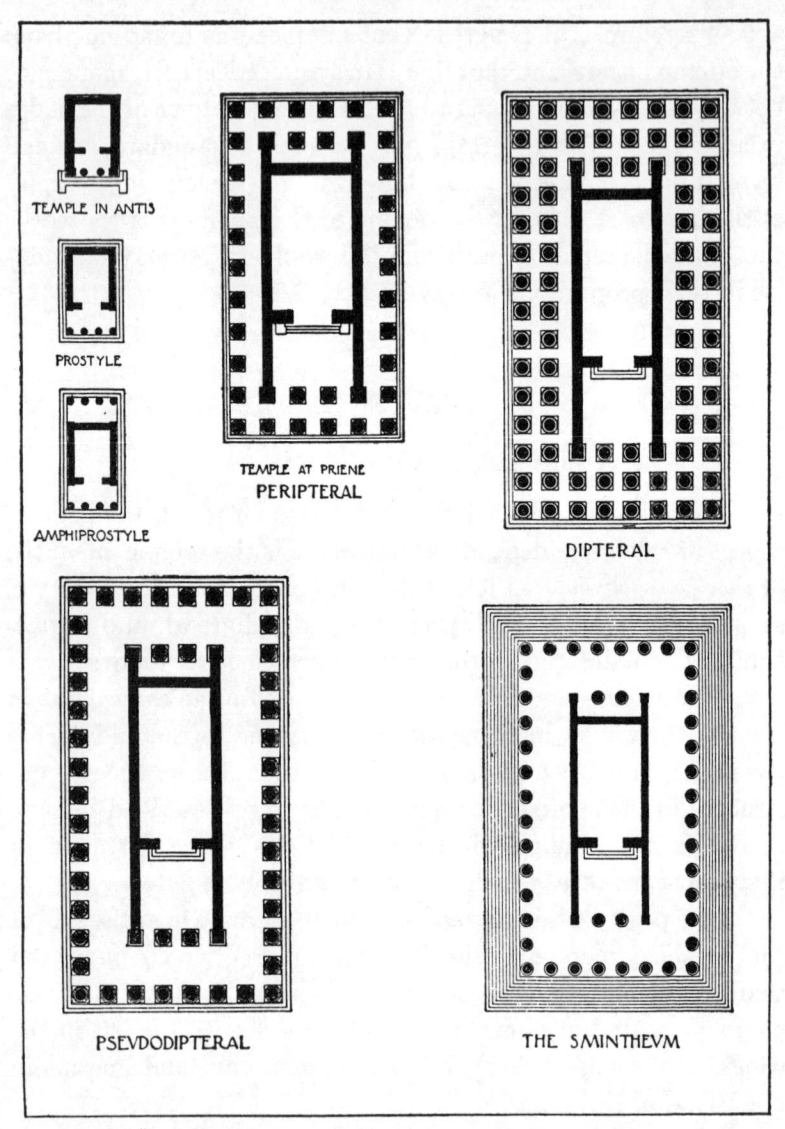

THE CLASSIFICATION OF TEMPLES ACCORDING TO THE ARRANGEMENTS
OF THE COLONNADES

umns. Let the columns be so placed as to leave a space, the width
of an intercolumniation, all round between the walls and the rows
of columns on the outside, thus forming a walk round the cella of

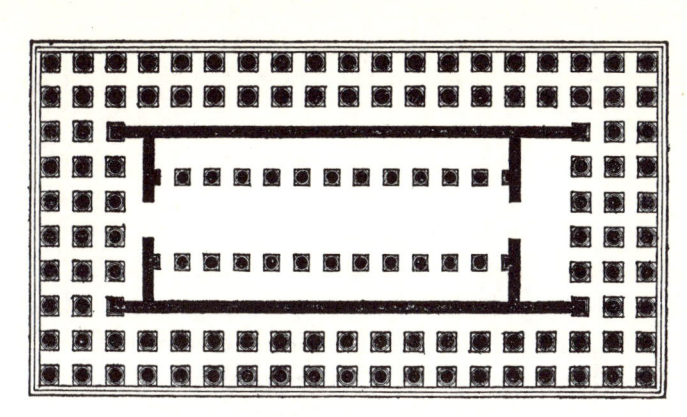

THE HYPAETHRAL TEMPLE

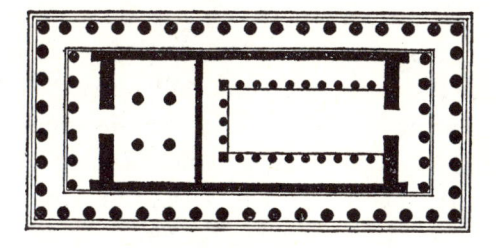

THE PARTHENON

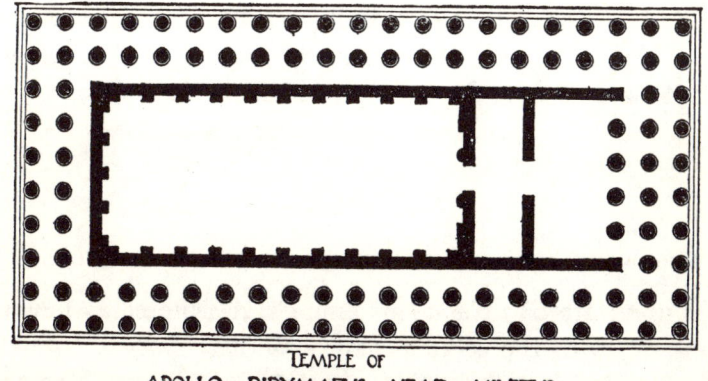

TEMPLE OF
APOLLO DIDYMAEUS NEAR MILETUS
SCALE OF FEET

THE HYPAETHRAL TEMPLE OF VITRUVIUS COMPARED WITH THE PARTHENON
AND THE TEMPLE OF APOLLO NEAR MILETUS

the temple, as in the cases of the temple of Jupiter Stator by Hermodorus in the Portico of Metellus, and the Marian temple of Honour and Valour constructed by Mucius, which has no portico in the rear.

6. The pseudodipteral is so constructed that in front and in the rear there are in each case eight columns, with fifteen on each side, including the corner columns. The walls of the cella in front and in the rear should be directly over against the four middle columns. Thus there will be a space, the width of two intercolumniations plus the thickness of the lower diameter of a column, all round between the walls and the rows of columns on the outside. There is no example of this in Rome, but at Magnesia there is the temple of Diana by Hermogenes, and that of Apollo at Alabanda by Mnesthes.

7. The dipteral also is octastyle in both front and rear porticoes, but it has two rows of columns all round the temple, like the temple of Quirinus, which is Doric, and the temple of Diana at Ephesus, planned by Chersiphron, which is Ionic.

8. The hypaethral is decastyle in both front and rear porticoes. In everything else it is the same as the dipteral, but inside it has two tiers of columns set out from the wall all round, like the colonnade of a peristyle. The central part is open to the sky, without a roof. Folding doors lead to it at each end, in the porticoes in front and in the rear. There is no example of this sort in Rome, but in Athens there is the octastyle in the precinct of the Olympian.

CHAPTER III

THE PROPORTIONS OF INTERCOLUMNIATIONS AND OF COLUMNS

1. There are five classes of temples, designated as follows: pycnostyle, with the columns close together; systyle, with the intercolumniations a little wider; diastyle, more open still; araeostyle, farther apart than they ought to be; eustyle, with the intervals apportioned just right.

CHAP. III] PROPORTIONS 79

2. The pycnostyle is a temple in an intercolumniation of which the thickness of a column and a half can be inserted: for example, the temple of the Divine Caesar, that of Venus in Caesar's forum, and others constructed like them. The systyle is a temple in which

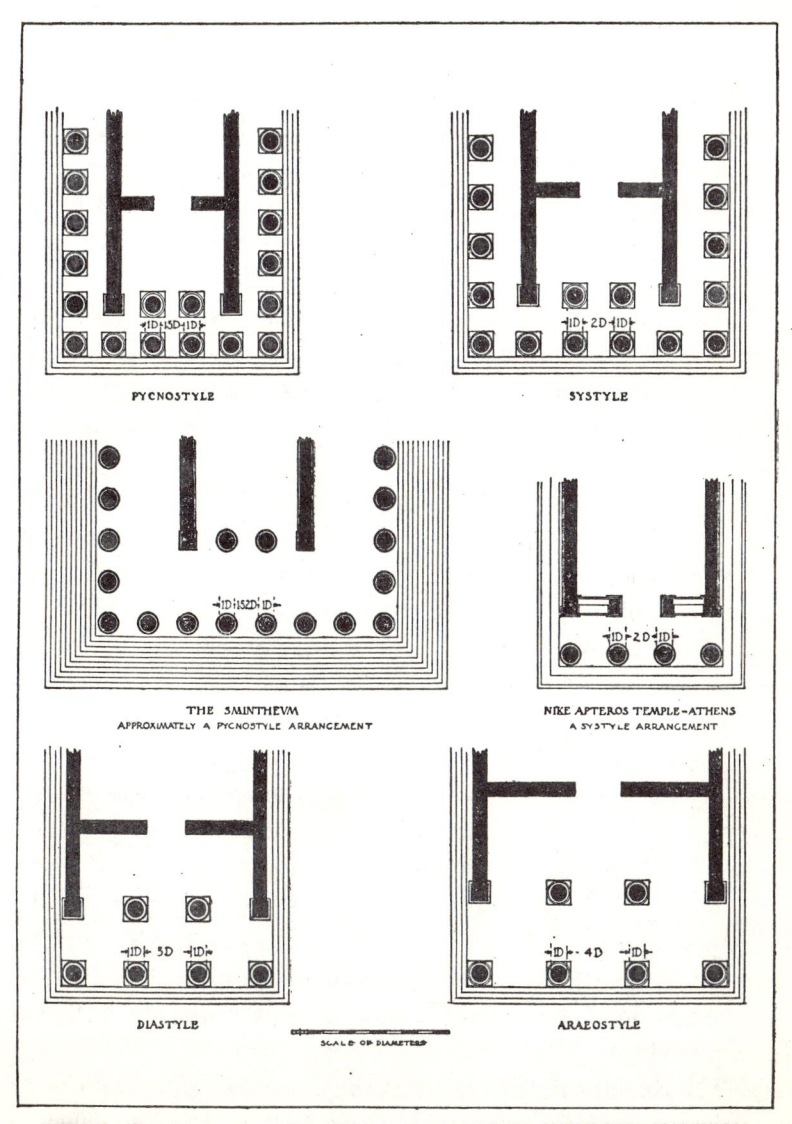

PYCNOSTYLE

SYSTYLE

THE SMINTHEVM
APPROXIMATELY A PYCNOSTYLE ARRANGEMENT

NIKE APTEROS TEMPLE – ATHENS
A SYSTYLE ARRANGEMENT

DIASTYLE

SCALE OF DIAMETERS

ARAEOSTYLE

THE CLASSIFICATION OF TEMPLES ACCORDING TO INTERCOLUMNIATION the thickness of two columns can be placed in an intercolumniation, and in which the plinths of the bases are equivalent to the distance between two plinths: for example, the temple of Equestrian Fortune near the stone theatre, and the others which are constructed on the same principles.

3. These two kinds have practical disadvantages. When the matrons mount the steps for public prayer or thanksgiving, they cannot pass through the intercolumniations with their arms about one another, but must form single file; then again, the effect of the folding doors is thrust out of sight by the crowding of the columns, and likewise the statues are thrown into shadow; the narrow space interferes also with walks round the temple.

4. The construction will be diastyle when we can insert the thickness of three columns in an intercolumniation, as in the case of the temple of Apollo and Diana. This arrangement involves the danger that the architraves may break on account of the great width of the intervals.

5. In araeostyles we cannot employ stone or marble for the architraves, but must have a series of wooden beams laid upon the columns. And moreover, in appearance these temples are clumsy-roofed, low, broad, and their pediments are adorned in the Tuscan fashion with statues of terra-cotta or gilt bronze: for example, near the Circus Maximus, the temple of Ceres and Pompey's temple of Hercules; also the temple on the Capitol.

6. An account must now be given of the eustyle, which is the most approved class, and is arranged on principles developed with a view to convenience, beauty, and strength. The intervals should be made as wide as the thickness of two columns and a quarter, but the middle intercolumniations, one in front and the other in the rear, should be of the thickness of three columns. Thus built, the effect of the design will be beautiful, there will be no obstruction at the entrance, and the walk round the cella will be dignified.

7. The rule of this arrangement may be set forth as follows. If a tetrastyle is to be built, let the width of the front which shall

THE EUSTYLE TEMPLE
ACCORDING TO VITRVVIVS

THE TEMPLE AT TEOS
IN ASIA MINOR

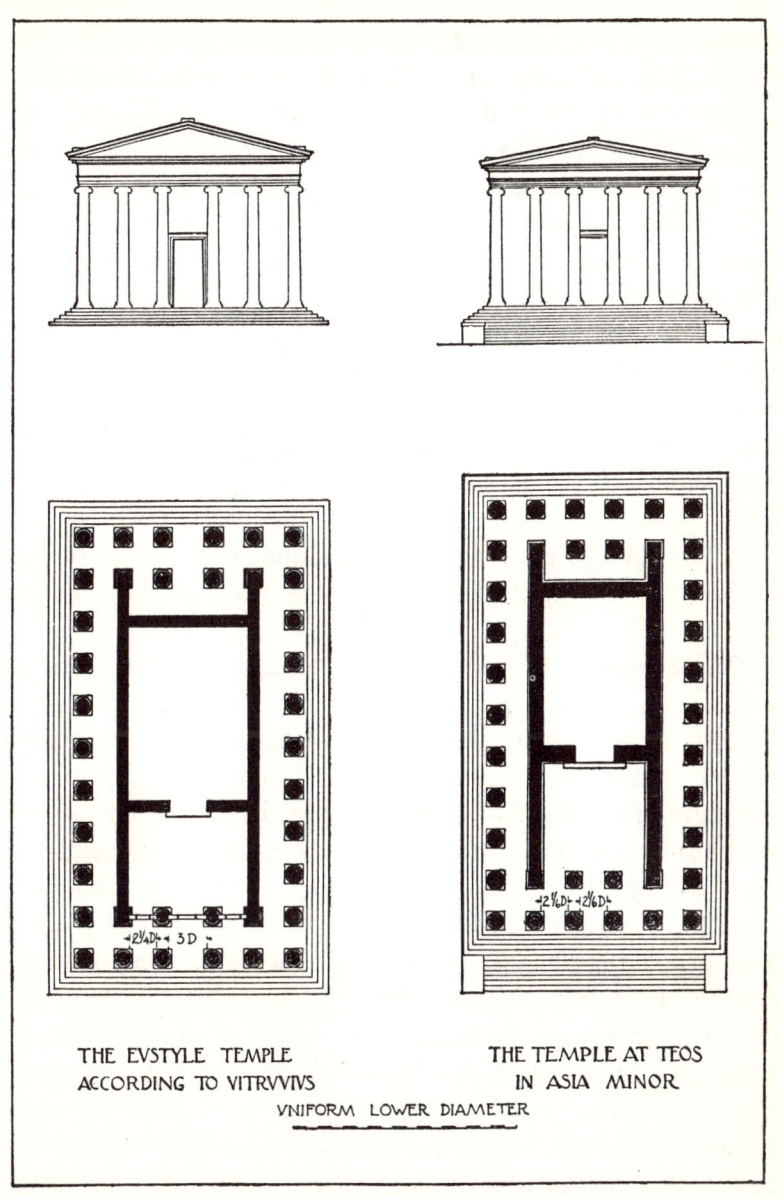

VNIFORM LOWER DIAMETER

THE EUSTYLE TEMPLE OF VITRUVIUS COMPARED WITH THE TEMPLE OF TEOS

have already been determined for the temple, be divided into eleven parts and a half, not including the substructures and the projections of the bases; if it is to be of six columns, into eighteen parts. If an octastyle is to be constructed, let the front be divided into twenty-four parts and a half. Then, whether the temple is to be tetrastyle, hexastyle, or octastyle, let one of these parts be taken, and it will be the module. The thickness of the columns will be equal to one module. Each of the intercolumniations, except those in the middle, will measure two modules and a quarter. The middle intercolumniations in front and in the rear will each measure three modules. The columns themselves will be nine modules and a half in height. As a result of this division, the intercolumniations and the heights of the columns will be in due proportion.

8. We have no example of this in Rome, but at Teos in Asia Minor there is one which is hexastyle, dedicated to Father Bacchus.

These rules for symmetry were established by Hermogenes, who was also the first to devise the principle of the pseudodipteral octastyle. He did so by dispensing with the inner rows of thirty-eight columns which belonged to the symmetry of the dipteral temple, and in this way he made a saving in expense and labour. He thus provided a much wider space for the walk round the cella between it and the columns, and without detracting at all from the general effect, or making one feel the loss of what had been really superfluous, he preserved the dignity of the whole work by his new treatment of it.

9. For the idea of the pteroma and the arrangement of the columns round a temple were devised in order that the intercolumniations might give the imposing effect of high relief; and also, in case a multitude of people should be caught in a heavy shower and detained, that they might have in the temple and round the cella a wide free space in which to wait. These ideas are developed, as I have described, in the pseudodipteral arrangement of a temple. It appears, therefore, that Hermogenes pro-

CHAP. III] PROPORTIONS 83

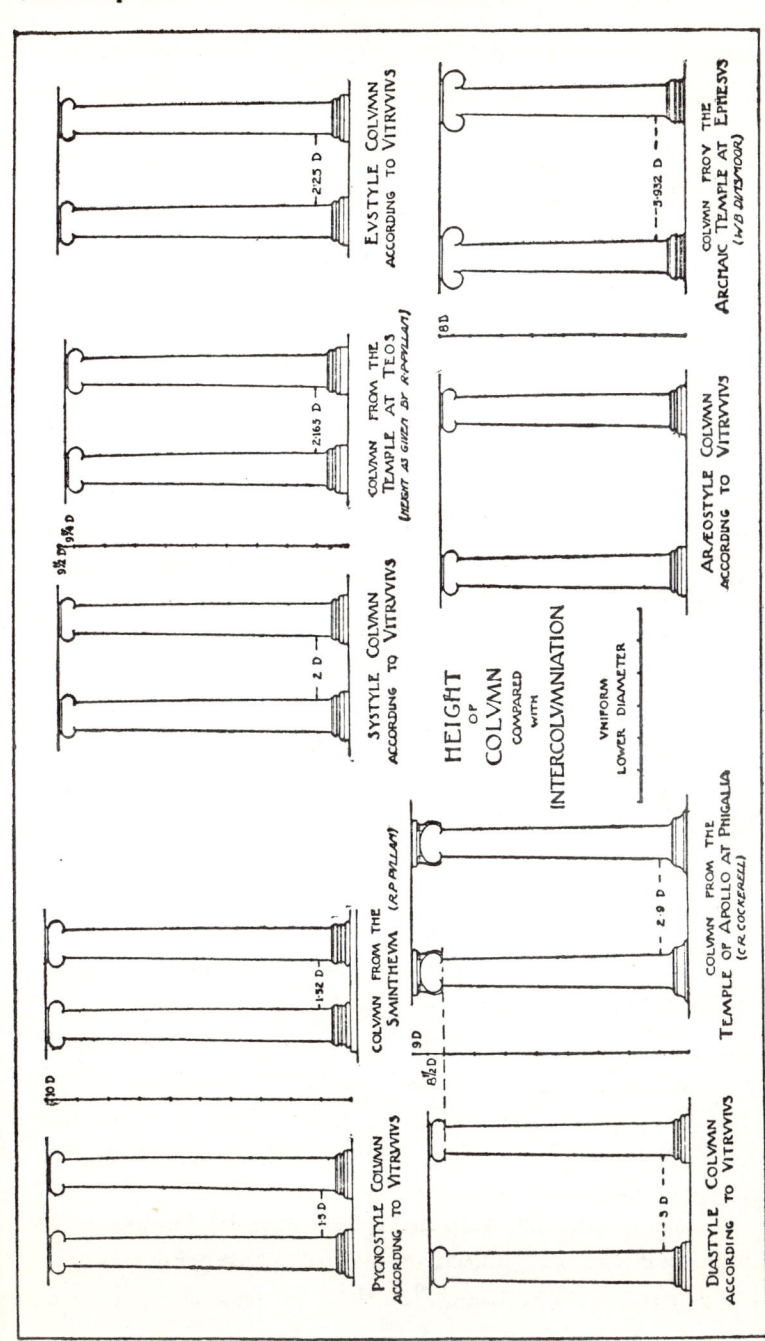

VITRUVIUS' RULES FOR THE DIAMETER AND HEIGHT OF COLUMNS IN THE DIFFERENT CLASSES OF TEMPLE COMPARED WITH ACTUAL EXAMPLES

duced results which exhibit much acute ingenuity, and that he left sources from which those who came after him could derive instructive principles.

10. In araeostyle temples, the columns should be constructed so that their thickness is one eighth part of their height. In the diastyle, the height of a column should be measured off into eight and a half parts, and the thickness of the column fixed at one of these parts. In the systyle, let the height be divided into nine and a half parts, and one of these given to the thickness of the column. In the pycnostyle, the height should be divided into ten parts, and one of these used for the thickness of the column. In the eustyle temple, let the height of a column be divided, as in the systyle, into nine and a half parts, and let one part be taken for the thickness at the bottom of the shaft. With these dimensions we shall be taking into account the proportions of the intercolumniations.

11. For the thickness of the shafts must be enlarged in proportion to the increase of the distance between the columns. In the araeostyle, for instance, if only a ninth or tenth part is given to the thickness, the column will look thin and mean, because the width of the intercolumniations is such that the air seems to eat away and diminish the thickness of such shafts. On the other hand, in pycnostyles, if an eighth part is given to the thickness, it will make the shaft look swollen and ungraceful, because the intercolumniations are so close to each other and so narrow. We must therefore follow the rules of symmetry required by each kind of building. Then, too, the columns at the corners should be made thicker than the others by a fiftieth of their own diameter, because they are sharply outlined by the unobstructed air round them, and seem to the beholder more slender than they are. Hence, we must counteract the ocular deception by an adjustment of proportions.

12. Moreover, the diminution in the top of a column at the necking seems to be regulated on the following principles: if a column is fifteen feet or under, let the thickness at the bottom

CHAP. III]   PROPORTIONS   85

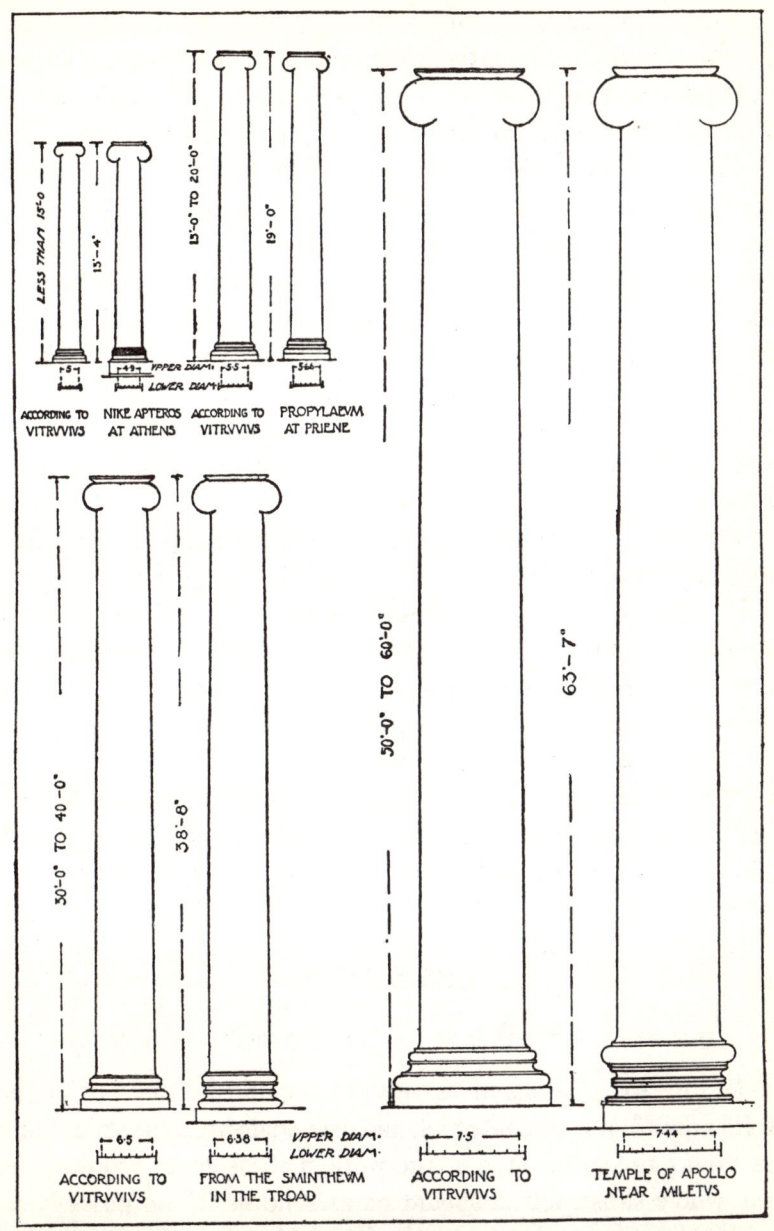

THE DIMINUTION OF COLUMNS IN RELATION TO THEIR DIMENSIONS OF HEIGHT

be divided into six parts, and let five of those parts form the thickness at the top. If it is from fifteen feet to twenty feet, let the bottom of the shaft be divided into six and a half parts, and let five and a half of those parts be the upper thickness of the column. In a column of from twenty feet to thirty feet, let the bottom of the shaft be divided into seven parts, and let the diminished top measure six of these. A column of from thirty to forty feet should be divided at the bottom into seven and a half parts, and, on the principle of diminution, have six and a half of these at the top. Columns of from forty feet to fifty should be divided into eight parts, and diminish to seven of these at the top of the shaft under the capital. In the case of higher columns, let the diminution be determined proportionally, on the same principles.

13. These proportionate enlargements are made in the thickness of columns on account of the different heights to which the eye has to climb. For the eye is always in search of beauty, and if we do not gratify its desire for pleasure by a proportionate enlargement in these measures, and thus make compensation for ocular deception, a clumsy and awkward appearance will be presented to the beholder. With regard to the enlargement made at the middle of columns, which among the Greeks is called ἔντασις, at the end of the book a figure and calculation will be subjoined, showing how an agreeable and appropriate effect may be produced by it.

CHAPTER IV

THE FOUNDATIONS AND SUBSTRUCTURES OF TEMPLES

1. THE foundations of these works should be dug out of the solid ground, if it can be found, and carried down into solid ground as far as the magnitude of the work shall seem to require, and the whole substructure should be as solid as it can possibly be laid. Above ground, let walls be laid under the columns, thicker by one half than the columns are to be, so that the lower may be

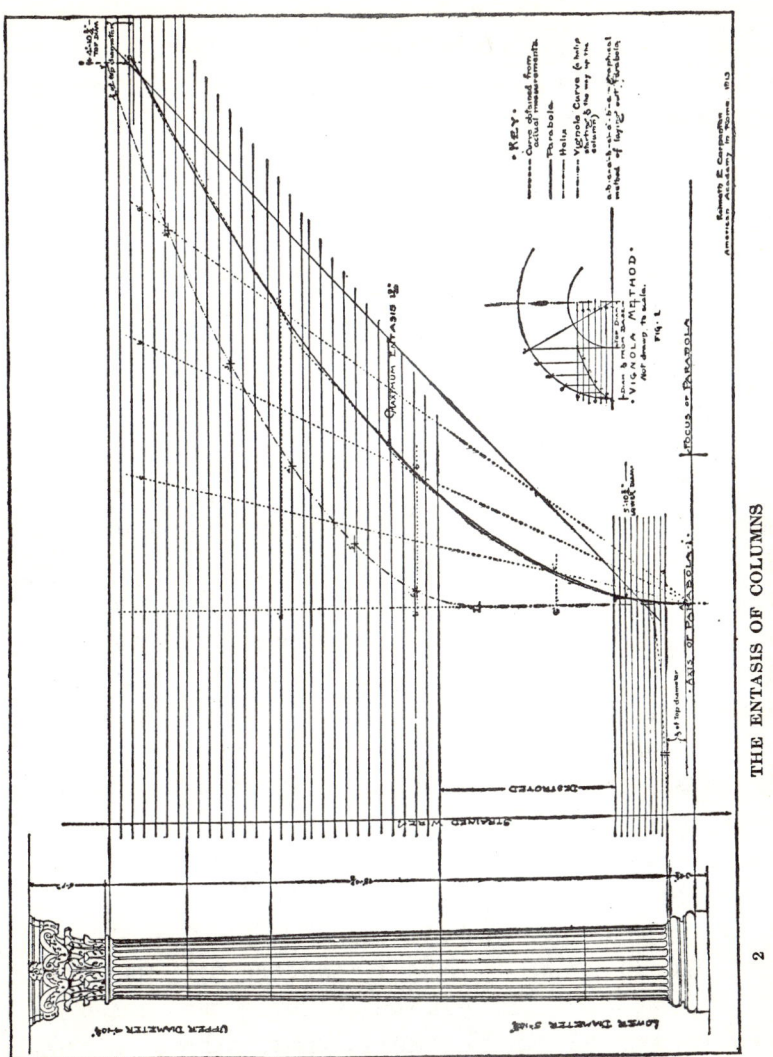

CHAP. IV] FOUNDATIONS AND SUBSTRUCTURES 87

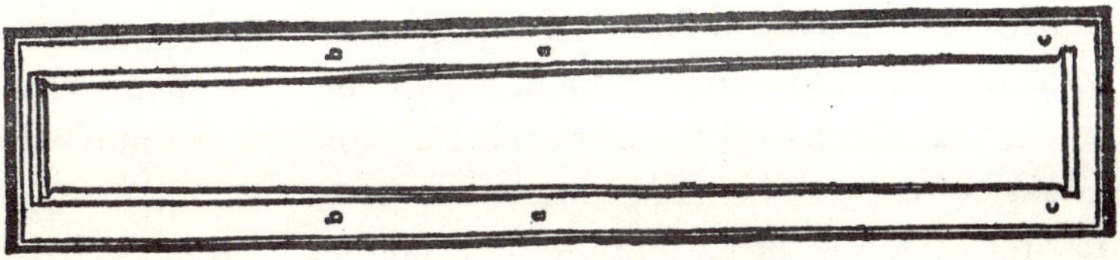

THE ENTASIS OF COLUMNS
1. The entasis as given by Fra Giocondo in the edition of 1511.
2. The entasis from the temple of Mars Ultor in Rome compared with Vignola's rule for entasis.

stronger than the higher. Hence they are called "stereobates"; for they take the load. And the projections of the bases should not extend beyond this solid foundation. The wall-thickness is similarly to be preserved above ground likewise, and the intervals between these walls should be vaulted over, or filled with earth rammed down hard, to keep the walls well apart.

2. If, however, solid ground cannot be found, but the place proves to be nothing but a heap of loose earth to the very bottom, or a marsh, then it must be dug up and cleared out and set with piles made of charred alder or olive wood or oak, and these must be driven down by machinery, very closely together like bridge-piles, and the intervals between them filled in with charcoal, and finally the foundations are to be laid on them in the most solid form of construction. The foundations having been brought up to the level, the stylobates are next to be put in place.

3. The columns are then to be distributed over the stylobates in the manner above described: close together in the pycnostyle; in the systyle, diastyle, or eustyle, as they are described and arranged above. In araeostyle temples one is free to arrange them as far apart as one likes. Still, in peripterals, the columns should be so placed that there are twice as many intercolumniations on the sides as there are in front; for thus the length of the work will be twice its breadth. Those who make the number of columns double, seem to be in error, because then the length seems to be one intercolumniation longer than it ought to be.

4. The steps in front must be arranged so that there shall always be an odd number of them; for thus the right foot, with which one mounts the first step, will also be the first to reach the level of the temple itself. The rise of such steps should, I think, be limited to not more than ten nor less than nine inches; for then the ascent will not be difficult. The treads of the steps ought to be made not less than a foot and a half, and not more than two feet deep. If there are to be steps running all round the temple, they should be built of the same size.

5. But if a podium is to be built on three sides round the

CHAP. IV] **FOUNDATIONS AND SUBSTRUCTURES** 89

temple, it should be so constructed that its plinths, bases, dies, coronae, and cymatiumare appropriate to the actual stylobate which is to be under the bases of the columns.

FRA GIOCONDO'S IDEA OF THE "SCAMILLI IMPARES"
(From his edition of Vitruvius, Venice, 1511)

The level of the stylobate must be increased along the middle by the scamilli impares; for if it is laid perfectly level, it will look to the eye as though it were hollowed a little. At the end of the book a figure will be found, with a description showing how the scamilli may be made to suit this purpose.

CHAPTER V

PROPORTIONS OF THE BASE, CAPITALS, AND ENTABLATURE IN THE IONIC ORDER

1. This finished, let the bases of the columns be set in place, and constructed in such proportions that their height, including the plinth, may be half the thickness of a column, and their projection (called in Greek ἐκφορά) the same.[1] Thus in both length and breadth it will be one and one half thicknesses of a column.

2. If the base is to be in the Attic style, let its height be so divided that the upper part shall be one third part of the thickness of the column, and the rest left for the plinth. Then, excluding the plinth, let the rest be divided into four parts, and of these let one fourth constitute the upper torus, and let the other three be divided equally, one part composing the lower torus, and the other, with its fillets, the scotia, which the Greeks call τροχίλος.

3. But if Ionic bases are to be built, their proportions shall be so determined that the base may be each way equal in breadth to the thickness of a column plus three eighths of the thickness; its height that of the Attic base, and so too its plinth; excluding the plinth, let the rest, which will be a third part of the thickness of a column, be divided into seven parts. Three of these parts constitute the torus at the top, and the other four are to be divided equally, one part constituting the upper trochilus with its astragals and overhang, the other left for the lower trochilus. But the lower will seem to be larger, because it will project to the edge of the plinth. The astragals must be one eighth of the trochilus. The projection of the base will be three sixteenths of the thickness of a column.

4. The bases being thus finished and put in place, the columns are to be put in place: the middle columns of the front and rear porticoes perpendicular to their own centre; the corner columns, and those which are to extend in a line from them along the sides

---

[1] Reading *aeque tantam* as in new *Rose*. Codd. *sextantem;* Schn. *quadrantem.*

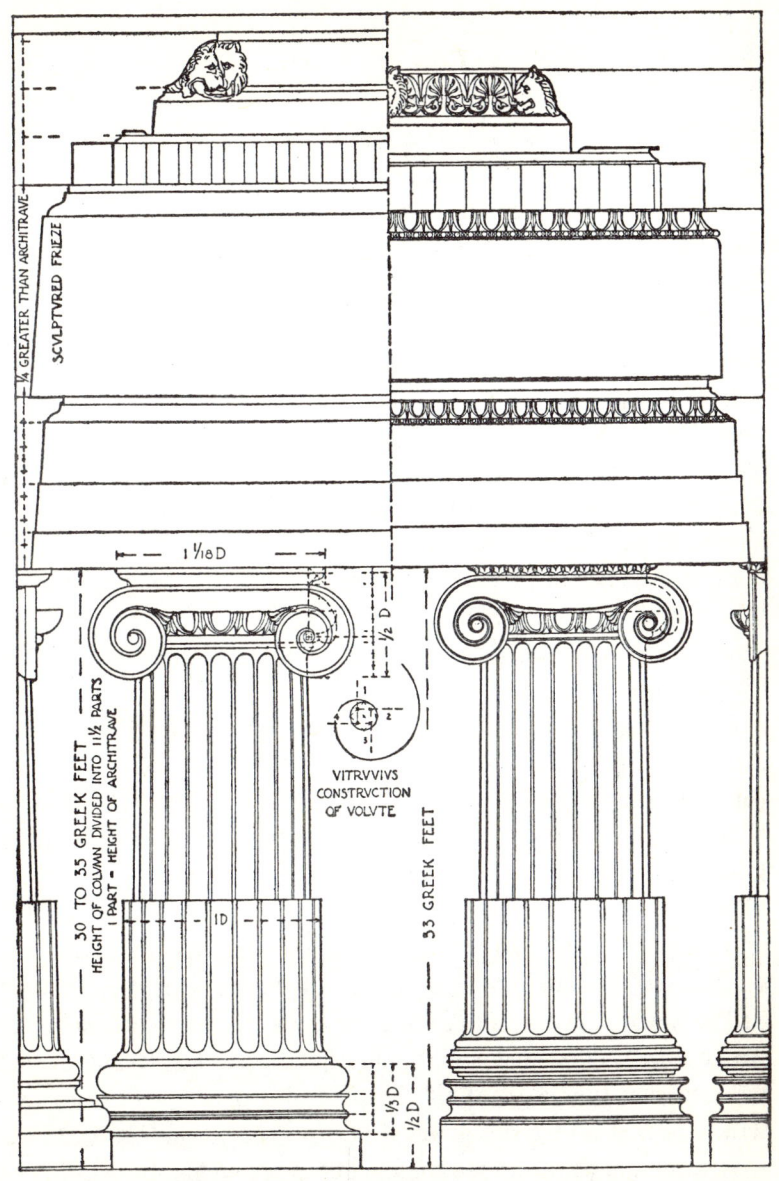

THE IONIC ORDER ACCORDING TO VITRUVIUS COMPARED WITH THE
ORDER OF THE MAUSOLEUM AT HALICARNASSUS

The difference between the Roman and the Greek relation of the baluster-side of the capital to the echinus is to be noted.

of the temple to the right and left, are to be set so that their inner sides, which face toward the cella wall, are perpendicular, but their outer sides in the manner which I have described in speaking of their diminution. Thus, in the design of the temple the lines will be adjusted with due regard to the diminution.

5. The shafts of the columns having been erected, the rule for the capitals will be as follows. If they are to be cushion-shaped, they should be so proportioned that the abacus is in length and breadth equivalent to the thickness of the shaft at its bottom plus one eighteenth thereof, and the height of the capital, including the volutes, one half of that amount. The faces of the volutes must recede from the edge of the abacus inwards by one and a half eighteenths of that same amount. Then, the height of the capital is to be divided into nine and a half parts, and down along the abacus on the four sides of the volutes, down along the fillet at the edge of the abacus, lines called "catheti" are to be let fall. Then, of the nine and a half parts let one and a half be reserved for the height of the abacus, and let the other eight be used for the volutes.

6. Then let another line be drawn, beginning at a point situated at a distance of one and a half parts toward the inside from the line previously let fall down along the edge of the abacus. Next, let these lines be divided in such a way as to leave four and a half parts under the abacus; then, at the point which forms the division between the four and a half parts and the remaining three and a half, fix the centre of the eye, and from that centre describe a circle with a diameter equal to one of the eight parts. This will be the size of the eye, and in it draw a diameter on the line of the "cathetus." Then, in describing the quadrants, let the size of each be successively less, by half the diameter of the eye, than that which begins under the abacus, and proceed from the eye until that same quadrant under the abacus is reached.

7. The height of the capital is to be such that, of the nine and a half parts, three parts are below the level of the astragal at the top of the shaft, and the rest, omitting the abacus and the chan-

nel, belongs to its echinus. The projection of the echinus beyond the fillet of the abacus should be equal to the size of the eye. The projection of the bands of the cushions should be thus obtained: place one leg of a pair of compasses in the centre of the capital and open out the other to the edge of the echinus; bring this leg round and it will touch the outer edge of the bands. The axes of the volutes should not be thicker than the size of the eye, and the volutes themselves should be channelled out to a depth which is one twelfth of their height. These will be the symmetrical proportions for capitals of columns twenty-five feet high and less. For higher columns the other proportions will be the same, but the length and breadth of the abacus will be the thickness of the lower diameter of a column plus one ninth part thereof; thus, just as the higher the column the less the diminution, so the projection of its capital is proportionately increased and its breadth [1] is correspondingly enlarged.

8. With regard to the method of describing volutes, at the end of the book a figure will be subjoined and a calculation showing how they may be described so that their spirals may be true to the compass.

The capitals having been finished and set up in due proportion to the columns (not exactly level on the columns, however, but with the same measured adjustment, so that in the upper members there may be an increase corresponding to that which was made in the stylobates), the rule for the architraves is to be as follows. If the columns are at least twelve feet and not more than fifteen feet high, let the height of the architrave be equal to half the thickness of a column at the bottom. If they are from fifteen feet to twenty, let the height of a column be measured off into thirteen parts, and let one of these be the height of the architrave. If they are from twenty to twenty-five feet, let this height be divided into twelve and one half parts, and let one of them form the height of the architrave. If they are from twenty-five feet to thirty, let it be divided into twelve parts, and let one of

[1] Codd. *altitudo*.

them form the height. If they are higher, the heights of the architraves are to be worked out proportionately in the same manner from the height of the columns.

9. For the higher that the eye has to climb, the less easily can it make its way through the thicker and thicker mass of air. So it fails when the height is great, its strength is sucked out of it, and it conveys to the mind only a confused estimate of the dimensions. Hence there must always be a corresponding increase in the symmetrical proportions of the members, so that whether the buildings are on unusually lofty sites or are themselves somewhat colossal, the size of the parts may seem in due proportion. The depth of the architrave on its under side just above the capital, is to be equivalent to the thickness of the top of the column just under the capital, and on its uppermost side equivalent to the foot of the shaft.

10. The cymatium of the architrave should be one seventh of the height of the whole architrave, and its projection the same. Omitting the cymatium, the rest of the architrave is to be divided into twelve parts, and three of these will form the lowest fascia, four, the next, and five, the highest fascia. The frieze, above the architrave, is one fourth less high than the architrave, but if there are to be reliefs upon it, it is one fourth higher than the architrave, so that the sculptures may be more imposing. Its cymatium is one seventh of the whole height of the frieze, and the projection of the cymatium is the same as its height.

11. Over the frieze comes the line of dentils, made of the same height as the middle fascia of the architrave and with a projection equal to their height. The intersection (or in Greek $\mu\epsilon\tau\acute{o}\pi\eta$) is apportioned so that the face of each dentil is half as wide as its height and the cavity of each intersection two thirds of this face in width. The cymatium here is one sixth of the whole height of this part. The corona with its cymatium, but not including the sima, has the height of the middle fascia of the architrave, and the total projection of the corona and dentils should be equal to the height from the frieze to the cymatium at the top of the corona.

PROPORTIONS

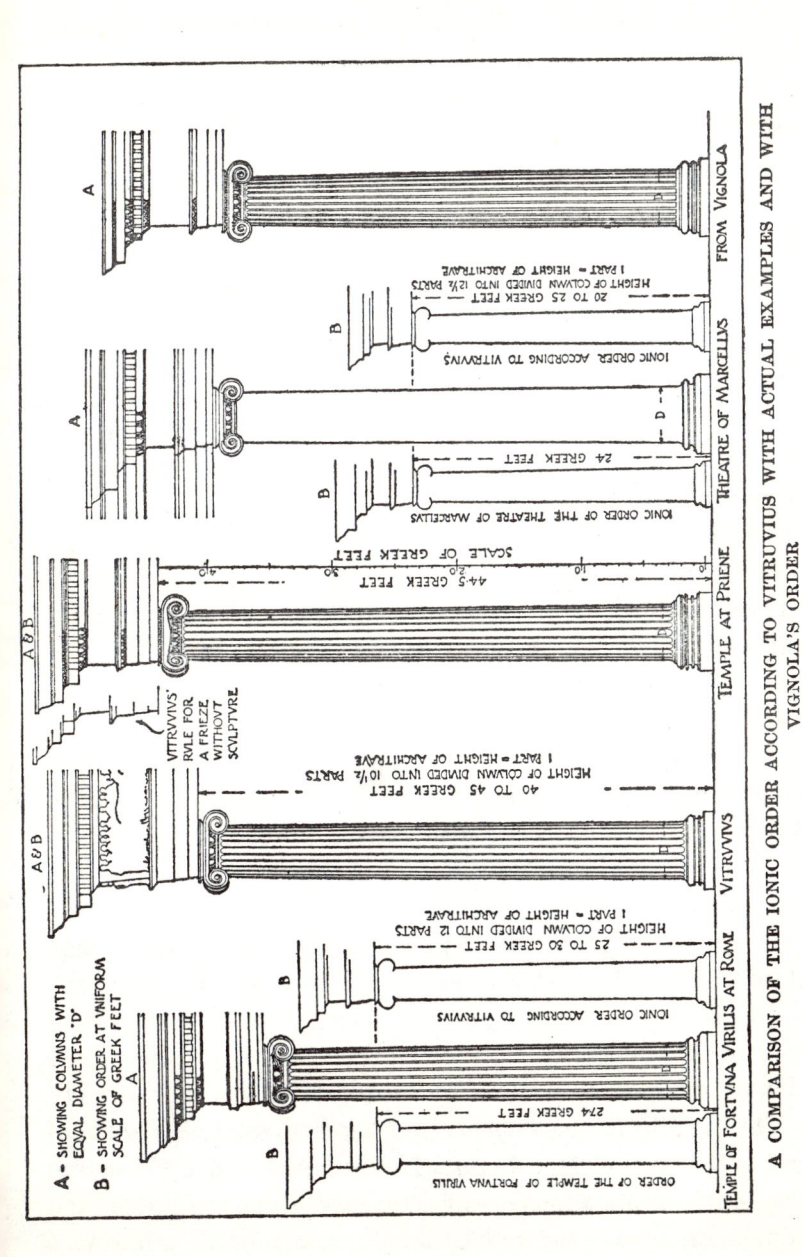

A COMPARISON OF THE IONIC ORDER ACCORDING TO VITRUVIUS WITH ACTUAL EXAMPLES AND WITH VIGNOLA'S ORDER

A: Showing the orders reduced to equal lower diameters.   B: Showing the orders to a uniform scale.

And as a general rule, all projecting parts have greater beauty when their projection is equal to their height.

12. The height of the tympanum, which is in the pediment, is to be obtained thus: let the front of the corona, from the two ends of its cymatium, be measured off into nine parts, and let one of these parts be set up in the middle at the peak of the tympanum, taking care that it is perpendicular to the entablature and the neckings of the columns. The coronae over the tympanum are to be made of equal size with the coronae under it, not including the simae. Above the coronae are the simae (in Greek ἐπαιετίδες), which should be made one eighth higher than the height of the coronae. The acroteria at the corners have the height of the centre of the tympanum, and those in the middle are one eighth part higher than those at the corners.

13. All the members which are to be above the capitals of the columns, that is, architraves, friezes, coronae, tympana, gables, and acroteria, should be inclined to the front a twelfth part of their own height, for the reason that when we stand in front of them, if two lines are drawn from the eye, one reaching to the bottom of the building and the other to the top, that which reaches to the top will be the longer. Hence, as the line of sight to the upper part is the longer, it makes that part look as if it were leaning back. But when the members are inclined to the front, as described above, they will seem to the beholder to be plumb and perpendicular.

14. Each column should have twenty-four flutes, channelled out in such a way that if a carpenter's square be placed in the hollow of a flute and turned, the arm will touch the corners of the fillets on the right and left, and the tip of the square may keep touching some point in the concave surface as it moves through it. The breadth of the flutes is to be equivalent to the enlargement in the middle of a column, which will be found in the figure.

15. In the simae which are over the coronae on the sides of the temple, lion's heads are to be carved and arranged at intervals thus: First one head is marked out directly over the axis of each

column, and then the others are arranged at equal distances apart, and so that there shall be one at the middle of every rooftiling. Those that are over the columns should have holes bored through them to the gutter which receives the rain-water from the tiles, but those between them should be solid. Thus the mass of water that falls by way of the tiles into the gutter will not be thrown down along the intercolumniations nor drench people who are passing through them, while the lion's heads that are over the columns will appear to be vomiting as they discharge streams of water from their mouths.

In this book I have written as clearly as I could on the arrangements of Ionic temples. In the next I shall explain the proportions of Doric and Corinthian temples.

BOOK IV

BOOK IV

INTRODUCTION

1. I HAVE observed, Emperor, that many in their treatises and volumes of commentaries on architecture have not presented the subject with well-ordered completeness, but have merely made a beginning and left, as it were, only desultory fragments. I have therefore thought that it would be a worthy and very useful thing to reduce the whole of this great art to a complete and orderly form of presentation, and then in different books to lay down and explain the required characteristics of different departments. Hence, Caesar, in my first book I have set forth to you the function of the architect and the things in which he ought to be trained. In the second I have discussed the supplies of material of which buildings are constructed. In the third, which deals with the arrangements of temples and their variety of form, I showed the nature and number of their classes, with the adjustments proper to each form according to the usage of the Ionic order, one of the three which exhibit the greatest delicacy of proportion in their symmetrical measurements. In the present book I shall speak of the established rules for the Doric and Corinthian orders, and shall explain their differences and peculiarities.

CHAPTER I

THE ORIGINS OF THE THREE ORDERS, AND THE PROPORTIONS OF THE CORINTHIAN CAPITAL

1. CORINTHIAN columns are, excepting in their capitals, of the same proportions in all respects as Ionic; but the height of their capitals gives them proportionately a taller and more slender effect. This is because the height of the Ionic capital is only one third of the thickness of the column, while that of the Corinthian is the entire thickness of the shaft. Hence, as two thirds are added in Corinthian capitals, their tallness gives a more slender appearance to the columns themselves.

2. The other members which are placed above the columns, are, for Corinthian columns, composed either of the Doric proportions or according to the Ionic usages; for the Corinthian order never had any scheme peculiar to itself for its cornices or other ornaments, but may have mutules in the coronae and guttae on the architraves according to the triglyph system of the Doric style, or, according to Ionic practices, it may be arranged with a frieze adorned with sculptures and accompanied with dentils and coronae.

3. Thus a third architectural order, distinguished by its capital, was produced out of the two other orders. To the forms of their columns are due the names of the three orders, Doric, Ionic, and Corinthian, of which the Doric was the first to arise, and in early times. For Dorus, the son of Hellen and the nymph Phthia, was king of Achaea and all the Peloponnesus, and he built a fane, which chanced to be of this order, in the precinct of Juno at Argolis, a very ancient city, and subsequently others of the same order in the other cities of Achaea, although the rules of symmetry were not yet in existence.

4. Later, the Athenians, in obedience to oracles of the Delphic Apollo, and with the general agreement of all Hellas, despatched

thirteen colonies at one time to Asia Minor, appointing leaders for each colony and giving the command-in-chief to Ion, son of Xuthus and Creusa (whom further Apollo at Delphi in the oracles had acknowledged as his son). Ion conducted those colonies to Asia Minor, took possession of the land of Caria, and there founded the grand cities of Ephesus, Miletus, Myus (long ago engulfed by the water, and its sacred rites and suffrage handed over by the Ionians to the Milesians), Priene, Samos, Teos, Colophon, Chius, Erythrae, Phocaea, Clazomenae, Lebedos, and Melite. This Melite, on account of the arrogance of its citizens, was destroyed by the other cities in a war declared by general agreement, and in its place, through the kindness of King Attalus and Arsinoe, the city of the Smyrnaeans was admitted among the Ionians.

5. Now these cities, after driving out the Carians and Lelegans, called that part of the world Ionia from their leader Ion, and there they set off precincts for the immortal gods and began to build fanes: first of all, a temple to Panionion Apollo such as they had seen in Achaea, calling it Doric because they had first seen that kind of temple built in the states of the Dorians.

6. Wishing to set up columns in that temple, but not having rules for their symmetry, and being in search of some way by which they could render them fit to bear a load and also of a satisfactory beauty of appearance, they measured the imprint of a man's foot and compared this with his height. On finding that, in a man, the foot was one sixth of the height, they applied the same principle to the column, and reared the shaft, including the capital, to a height six times its thickness at its base. Thus the Doric column, as used in buildings, began to exhibit the proportions, strength, and beauty of the body of a man.

7. Just so afterwards, when they desired to construct a temple to Diana in a new style of beauty, they translated these footprints into terms characteristic of the slenderness of women, and thus first made a column the thickness of which was only one eighth of its height, so that it might have a taller look. At the

foot they substituted the base in place of a shoe; in the capital they placed the volutes, hanging down at the right and left like curly ringlets, and ornamented its front with cymatia and with festoons of fruit arranged in place of hair, while they brought the flutes down the whole shaft, falling like the folds in the robes worn by matrons. Thus in the invention of the two different kinds of columns, they borrowed manly beauty, naked and unadorned, for the one, and for the other the delicacy, adornment, and proportions characteristic of women.

8. It is true that posterity, having made progress in refinement and delicacy of feeling, and finding pleasure in more slender proportions, has established seven diameters of the thickness as the height of the Doric column, and nine as that of the Ionic. The Ionians, however, originated the order which is therefore named Ionic.

The third order, called Corinthian, is an imitation of the slenderness of a maiden; for the outlines and limbs of maidens, being more slender on account of their tender years, admit of prettier effects in the way of adornment.

9. It is related that the original discovery of this form of capital was as follows. A freeborn maiden of Corinth, just of marriageable age, was attacked by an illness and passed away. After her burial, her nurse, collecting a few little things which used to give the girl pleasure while she was alive, put them in a basket, carried it to the tomb, and laid it on top thereof, covering it with a roof-tile so that the things might last longer in the open air. This basket happened to be placed just above the root of an acanthus. The acanthus root, pressed down meanwhile though it was by the weight, when springtime came round put forth leaves and stalks in the middle, and the stalks, growing up along the sides of the basket, and pressed out by the corners of the tile through the compulsion of its weight, were forced to bend into volutes at the outer edges.

10. Just then Callimachus, whom the Athenians called κατατηξίτεχνος for the refinement and delicacy of his artistic work,

THE BASILICA AT POMPEII

Photo. Sommer

CHAP. I]   ORIGINS OF THE THREE ORDERS   105

1
AFTER VITRVVIVS

2
FROM THE TEMPLE OF VESTA AT TIVOLI

3
FROM THE TEMPLE OF MINERVA AT ASSISI

4
FROM THE TEMPLE OF CASTOR & POLLVX, CORI

5
FROM THE TEMPLE OF VESTA AT ROME.

6
THE CORINTHIAN CAPITAL FROM CORI

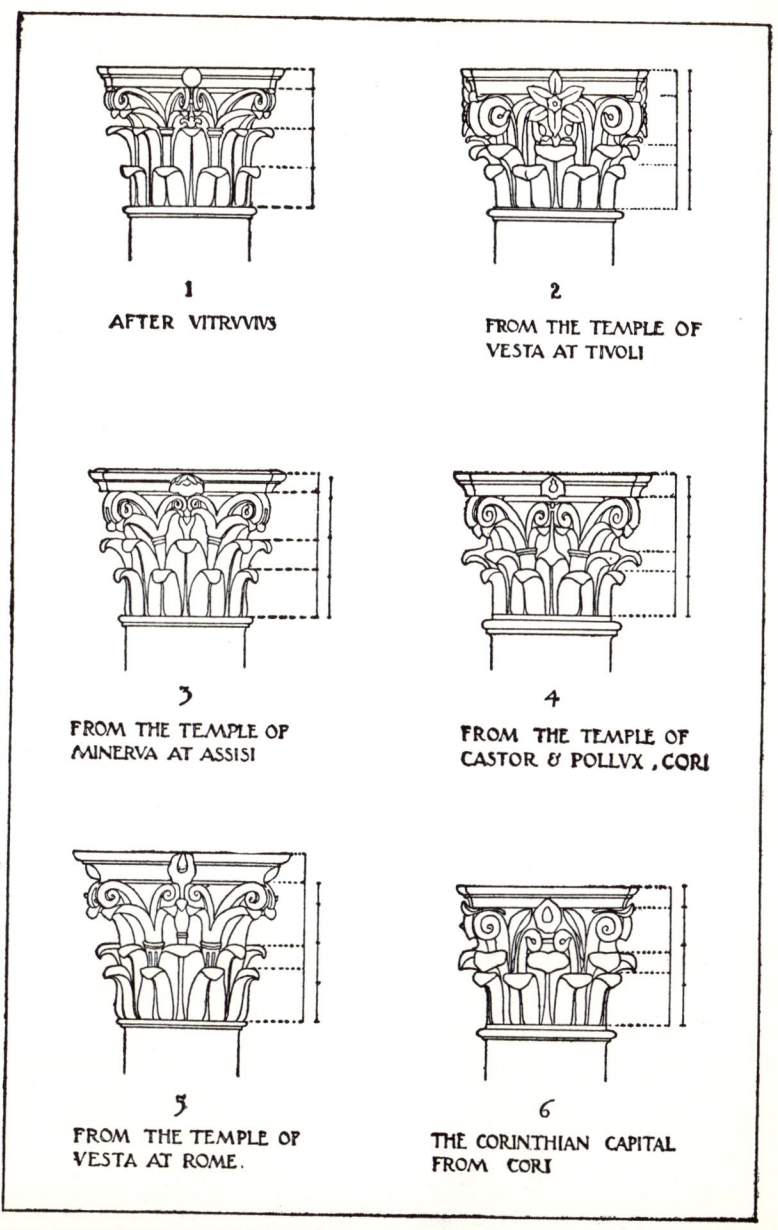

THE CORINTHIAN CAPITAL OF VITRUVIUS COMPARED WITH THE MONUMENTS

passed by this tomb and observed the basket with the tender young leaves growing round it. Delighted with the novel style and form, he built some columns after that pattern for the Corinthians, determined their symmetrical proportions, and established from that time forth the rules to be followed in finished works of the Corinthian order.

11. The proportions of this capital should be fixed as follows. Let the height of the capital, including its abacus, be equivalent to the thickness of the base of a column. Let the breadth of the abacus be proportioned so that diagonals drawn from one corner of it to the other shall be twice the height of the capitals, which will give the proper breadth to each face of the abacus. The faces should curve inwards, by one ninth of the breadth of the face, from the outside edge of the corners of the abacus. At the bottom the capital should be of the thickness of the top of the column omitting the congé and astragal. The height of the abacus is one seventh of the height of the capital.

12. Omitting the height of the abacus, let the rest be divided into three parts, of which one should be given to the lowest leaf. Let the second leaf occupy the middle part of the height. Of the same height should be the stalks, out of which grow leaves projected so as to support the volutes which proceed from the stalks, and run out to the utmost corners of the abacus; the smaller spirals between them should be carved just under the flower which is on the abacus. The flowers on the four sides are to be made as large as the height of the abacus. On these principles of proportion, Corinthian capitals will be finished as they ought to be.

There are other kinds of capitals set upon these same columns and called by various names, but they have no peculiarities of proportion of which we can speak, nor can we recognize from them another order of columns. Even their very names are, as we can see, derived with some changes from the Corinthian, the cushion-shaped, and the Doric, whose symmetrical proportions have been thus transferred to delicate sculptures of novel form.

CHAPTER II

THE ORNAMENTS OF THE ORDERS

1. Since the origin and invention of the orders of columns have been described above, I think it not out of place to speak in the same way about their ornaments, showing how these arose and from what original elements they were devised. The upper parts of all buildings contain timber work to which various terms are applied. And not only in its terminology but actually in its uses it exhibits variety. The main beams are those which are laid upon columns, pilasters, and antae; tie-beams and rafters are found in the framing. Under the roof, if the span is pretty large, are the crossbeams and struts; if it is of moderate extent, only the ridgepole, with the principal rafters extending to the outer edge of the eaves. Over the principal rafters are the purlines, and then above these and under the roof-tiles come the common rafters, extending so far that the walls are covered by their projection.

2. Thus each and every detail has a place, origin, and order of its own. In accordance with these details, and starting from carpenter's work, artists in building temples of stone and marble imitated those arrangements in their sculptures, believing that they must follow those inventions. So it was that some ancient carpenters, engaged in building somewhere or other, after laying the tie-beams so that they projected from the inside to the outside of the walls, closed up the space between the beams, and above them ornamented the coronae and gables with carpentry work of beauty greater than usual; then they cut off the projecting ends of the beams, bringing them into line and flush with the face of the walls; next, as this had an ugly look to them, they fastened boards, shaped as triglyphs are now made, on the ends of the beams, where they had been cut off in front, and painted them with blue wax so that the cutting off of the ends of the beams, being concealed, would not offend the eye. Hence it was in imitation of the arrangement of the tie-beams that men

began to employ, in Doric buildings, the device of triglyphs and the metopes between the beams.

3. Later, others in other buildings allowed the projecting principal rafters to run out till they were flush with the triglyphs, and then formed their projections into simae. From that practice, like the triglyphs from the arrangement of the tie-beams, the system of mutules under the coronae was devised from the projections of the principal rafters. Hence generally, in buildings of stone and marble, the mutules are carved with a downward slant, in imitation of the principal rafters. For these necessarily have a slanting and projecting position to let the water drip down. The scheme of triglyphs and mutules in Doric buildings was, therefore, the imitative device that I have described.

4. It cannot be that the triglyphs represent windows, as some have erroneously said, since the triglyphs are placed at the corners and over the middle of columns — places where, from the nature of the case, there can be no windows at all. For buildings are wholly disconnected at the corners if openings for windows are left at those points. Again, if we are to suppose that there were open windows where the triglyphs now stand, it will follow, on the same principle, that the dentils of the Ionic order have likewise taken the places of windows. For the term "metope" is used of the intervals between dentils as well as of those between triglyphs. The Greeks call the seats of tie-beams and rafters ὀπαί, while our people call these cavities columbaria (dovecotes). Hence, the space between the tie-beams, being the space between two "opae," was named by them μετόπη.

5. The system of triglyphs and mutules was invented for the Doric order, and similarly the scheme of dentils belongs to the Ionic, in which there are proper grounds for its use in buildings. Just as mutules represent the projection of the principal rafters, so dentils in the Ionic are an imitation of the projections of the common rafters. And so in Greek works nobody ever put dentils under mutules, as it is impossible that common rafters should be underneath principal rafters. Therefore, if that which

in the original must be placed above the principal rafters, is put in the copy below them, the result will be a work constructed on false principles. Neither did the ancients approve of or employ mutules or dentils in pediments, but only plain coronae, for the reason that neither principal nor common rafters tail into the fronts of pediments, nor can they overhang them, but they are laid with a slope towards the eaves. Hence the ancients held that what could not happen in the original would have no valid reason for existence in the copy.

6. For in all their works they proceeded on definite principles of fitness and in ways derived from the truth of Nature. Thus they reached perfection, approving only those things which, if challenged, can be explained on grounds of the truth. Hence, from the sources which have been described they established and left us the rules of symmetry and proportion for each order. Following in their steps, I have spoken above on the Ionic and Corinthian styles, and I shall now briefly explain the theory of the Doric and its general appearance.

CHAPTER III

PROPORTIONS OF DORIC TEMPLES

1. SOME of the ancient architects said that the Doric order ought not to be used for temples, because faults and incongruities were caused by the laws of its symmetry. Arcesius and Pytheos said so, as well as Hermogenes. He, for instance, after getting together a supply of marble for the construction of a Doric temple, changed his mind and built an Ionic temple to Father Bacchus with the same materials. This is not because it is unlovely in appearance or origin or dignity of form, but because the arrangement of the triglyphs and metopes (lacunaria) is an embarrassment and inconvenience to the work.

2. For the triglyphs ought to be placed so as to correspond to the centres of the columns, and the metopes between the triglyphs

ought to be as broad as they are high. But in violation of this rule, at the corner columns triglyphs are placed at the outside edges and not corresponding to the centre of the columns. Hence the metopes next to the corner columns do not come out perfectly square, but are too broad by half the width of a triglyph. Those who would make the metopes all alike, make the outermost intercolumniations narrower by half the width of a triglyph. But the result is faulty, whether it is attained by broader metopes or narrower intercolumniations. For this reason, the ancients appear to have avoided the scheme of the Doric order in their temples.

3. However, since our plan calls for it, we set it forth as we have received it from our teachers, so that if anybody cares to set to work with attention to these laws, he may find the proportions stated by which he can construct correct and faultless examples of temples in the Doric fashion.

Let the front of a Doric temple, at the place where the columns are put up, be divided, if it is to be tetrastyle, into twenty-seven parts; if hexastyle, into forty-two. One of these parts will be the module (in Greek ἐμβάτης); and this module once fixed, all the parts of the work are adjusted by means of calculations based upon it.

4. The thickness of the columns will be two modules, and their height, including the capitals, fourteen. The height of a capital will be one module, and its breadth two and one sixth modules. Let the height of the capital be divided into three parts, of which one will form the abacus with its cymatium, the second the echinus with its annulets, and the third the necking. The diminution of the column should be the same as described for Ionic columns in the third book. The height of the architrave, including taenia and guttae, is one module, and of the taenia, one seventh of a module. The guttae, extending as wide as the triglyphs and beneath the taenia, should hang down for one sixth of a module, including their regula. The depth of the architrave on its under side should answer to the necking at the top of the column. Above

CHAP. III] PROPORTIONS OF DORIC TEMPLES

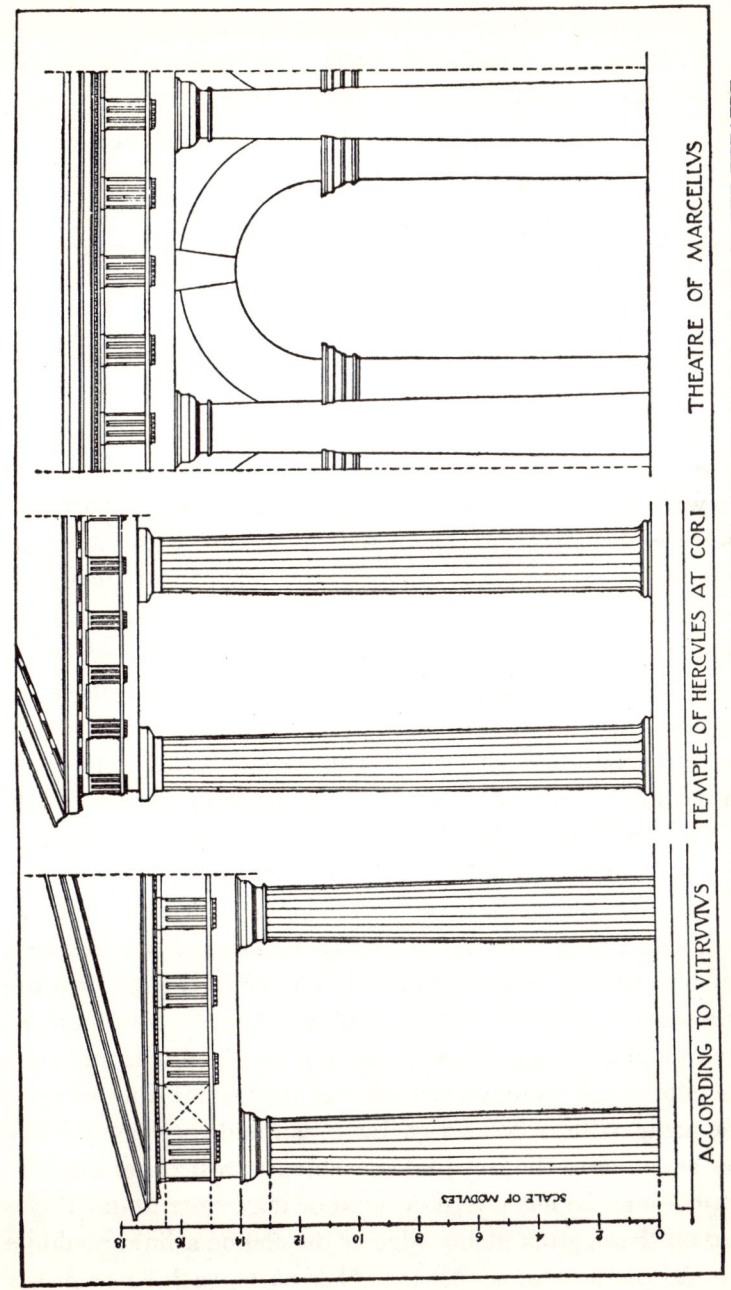

VITRUVIUS' DORIC ORDER COMPARED WITH THE TEMPLE AT CORI AND THE DORIC ORDER OF THE THEATRE OF MARCELLUS

the architrave, the triglyphs and metopes are to be placed: the triglyphs one and one half modules high, and one module wide in front. They are to be arranged so that one is placed to correspond to the centre of each corner and intermediate column, and two over each intercolumniation except the middle intercolumniations of the front and rear porticoes, which have three each. The intervals in the middle being thus extended, a free passage will be afforded to those who would approach the statues of the gods.

5. The width of the triglyph should be divided into six parts, and five of these marked off in the middle by means of the rule, and two half parts at the right and left. Let one part, that in the centre, form a "femur" (in Greek $\mu\eta\rho\acute{o}s$). On each side of it are the channels, to be cut in to fit the tip of a carpenter's square, and in succession the other femora, one at the right and the other at the left of a channel. To the outsides are relegated the semichannels. The triglyphs having been thus arranged, let the metopes between the triglyphs be as high as they are wide, while at the outer corners there should be semimetopes inserted, with the width of half a module.

In these ways all defects will be corrected, whether in metopes or intercolumniations or lacunaria, as all the arrangements have been made with uniformity.

6. The capitals of each triglyph are to measure one sixth of a module. Over the capitals of the triglyphs the corona is to be placed, with a projection of two thirds of a module, and having a Doric cymatium at the bottom and another at the top. So the corona with its cymatia is half a module in height. Set off on the under side of the corona, vertically over the triglyphs and over the middle of the metopes, are the viae in straight lines and the guttae arranged in rows, six guttae broad and three deep. The spaces left (due to the fact that the metopes are broader than the triglyphs) may be left unornamented or may have thunderbolts carved on them. Just at the edge of the corona a line should be cut in, called the scotia. All the other parts, such as tympana

and the simae of the corona, are to be constructed as described above in the case of the Ionic order.

7. Such will be the scheme established for diastyle buildings. But if the building is to be systyle and monotriglyphic, let the front of the temple, if tetrastyle, be divided into nineteen and a half parts; if hexastyle, into twenty-nine and a half parts. One of these parts will form the module in accordance with which the adjustments are to be made as above described.

8. Thus, over each portion of the architrave two metopes and two triglyphs[1] will be placed; and, in addition, at the corners half a triglyph and besides a space large enough for a half triglyph. At the centre, vertically under the gable, there should be room for three triglyphs and three metopes, in order that the centre intercolumniation, by its greater width, may give ample room for people to enter the temple, and may lend an imposing effect to the view of the statues of the gods.

9. The columns should be fluted with twenty flutes. If these are to be left plane, only the twenty angles need be marked off. But if they are to be channelled out, the contour of the channelling may be determined thus: draw a square with sides equal in length to the breadth of the fluting, and centre a pair of compasses in the middle of this square. Then describe a circle with a circumference touching the angles of the square, and let the channellings have the contour of the segment formed by the circumference and the side of the square. The fluting of the Doric column will thus be finished in the style appropriate to it.

10. With regard to the enlargement to be made in the column at its middle, let the description given for Ionic columns in the third book be applied here also in the case of Doric.

Since the external appearance of the Corinthian, Doric, and Ionic proportions has now been described, it is necessary next to explain the arrangements of the cella and the pronaos.

[1] That is: two metopes with a triglyph between them, and half of the triglyph on either side.

CHAPTER IV

THE CELLA AND PRONAOS

1. THE length of a temple is adjusted so that its width may be half its length, and the actual cella one fourth greater in length than in width, including the wall in which the folding doors are placed. Let the remaining three parts, constituting the pronaos, extend to the antae terminating the walls, which antae ought to be of the same thickness as the columns. If the temple is to be more than twenty feet in width, let two columns be placed between the two antae, to separate the pteroma from the pronaos. The three intercolumniations between the antae and the columns should be closed by low walls made of marble or of joiner's work, with doors in them to afford passages into the pronaos.

2. If the width is to be more than forty feet, let columns be placed inside and opposite to the columns between the antae. They should have the same height as the columns in front of them, but their thickness should be proportionately reduced: thus, if the columns in front are in thickness one eighth of their height, these should be one tenth; if the former are one ninth or one tenth, these should be reduced in the same proportion. For their reduction will not be discernible, as the air has not free play about them. Still, in case they look too slender, when the outer columns have twenty or twenty-four flutes, these may have twenty-eight or thirty-two. Thus the additional number of flutes will make up proportionately for the loss in the body of the shaft, preventing it from being seen, and so in a different way the columns will be made to look equally thick.

3. The reason for this result is that the eye, touching thus upon a greater number of points, set closer together, has a larger compass to cover with its range of vision. For if two columns, equally thick but one unfluted and the other fluted, are measured by drawing lines round them, one line touching the body of the columns in the hollows of the channels and on the edges of the flutes,

CHAP. IV] THE CELLA AND PRONAOS 115

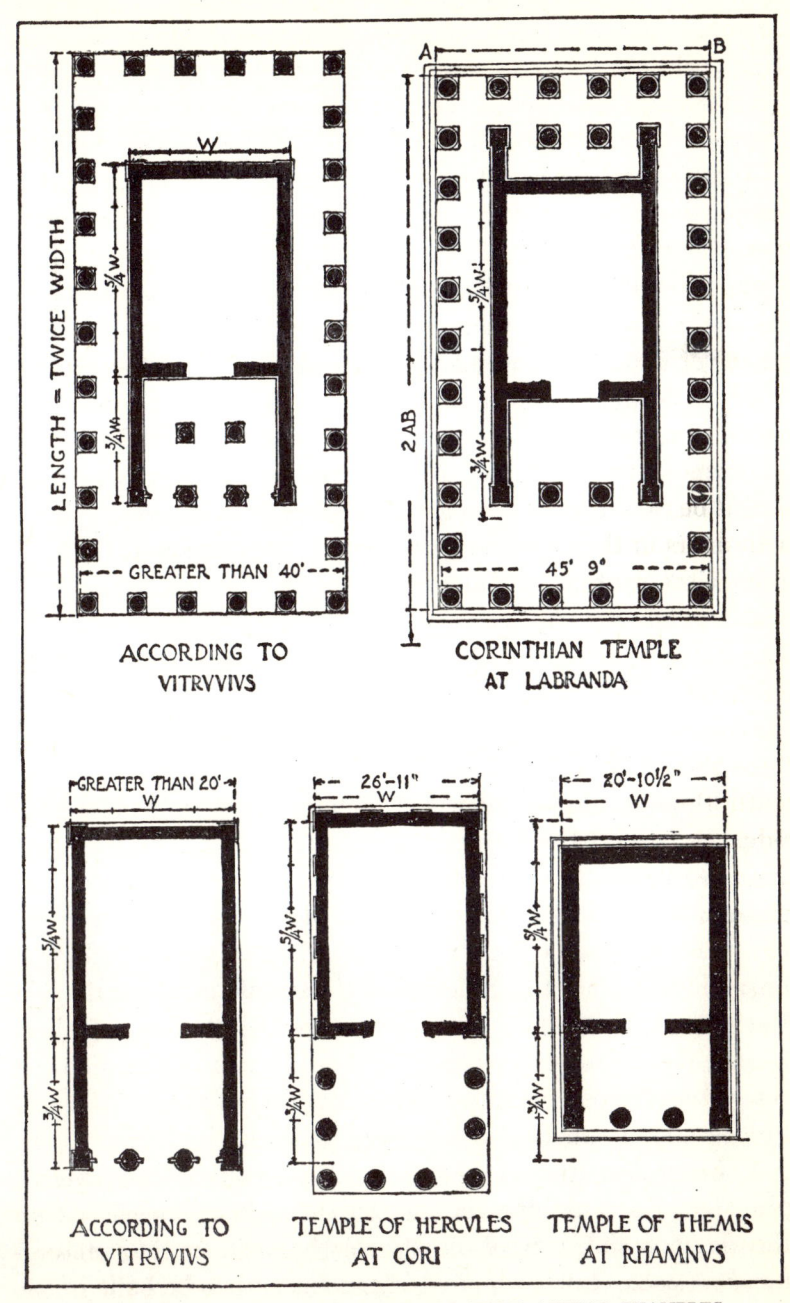

VITRUVIUS' TEMPLE PLAN COMPARED WITH ACTUAL EXAMPLES

these surrounding lines, even though the columns are equally thick, will not be equal to each other, because it takes a line of greater length to compass the channels and the flutes. This being granted, it is not improper, in narrow quarters or where the space is enclosed, to use in a building columns of somewhat slender proportions, since we can help out by a duly proportionate number of flutings.

4. The walls of the cella itself should be thick in proportion to its size, provided that their antae are kept of the same thickness as the columns. If the walls are to be of masonry, let the rubble used be as small as possible; but if they are to be of dimension stone or marble, the material ought to be of a very moderate and uniform size; for the laying of the stones so as to break joints will make the whole work stronger, and their bevelled edges, standing up about the builds and beds, will give it an agreeable look, somewhat like that of a picture.

CHAPTER V

HOW THE TEMPLE SHOULD FACE

1. THE quarter toward which temples of the immortal gods ought to face is to be determined on the principle that, if there is no reason to hinder and the choice is free, the temple and the statue placed in the cella should face the western quarter of the sky. This will enable those who approach the altar with offerings or sacrifices to face the direction of the sunrise in facing the statue in the temple, and thus those who are undertaking vows look toward the quarter from which the sun comes forth, and likewise the statues themselves appear to be coming forth out of the east to look upon them as they pray and sacrifice.

2. But if the nature of the site is such as to forbid this, then the principle of determining the quarter should be changed, so that the widest possible view of the city may be had from the sanctuaries of the gods. Furthermore, temples that are to be built beside

rivers, as in Egypt on both sides of the Nile, ought, as it seems, to face the river banks. Similarly, houses of the gods on the sides of public roads should be arranged so that the passers-by can have a view of them and pay their devotions face to face.

CHAPTER VI

THE DOORWAYS OF TEMPLES

1. For the doorways of temples and their casings the rules are as follows, first determining of what style they are to be. The styles of portals are Doric, Ionic, and Attic.

In the Doric, the symmetrical proportions are distinguished by the following rules. Let the top of the corona, which is laid above the casing, be on a level with the tops of the capitals of the columns in the pronaos. The aperture of the doorway should be determined by dividing the height of the temple, from floor to coffered ceiling, into three and one half parts and letting two and one half [1] thereof constitute the height of the aperture of the folding doors. Let this in turn be divided into twelve parts, and let five and a half of these form the width of the bottom of the aperture. At the top, this width should be diminished, if the aperture is sixteen feet in height, by one third the width of the door-jamb; if the aperture is from sixteen to twenty-five feet, let the upper part of it be diminished by one quarter of the jamb; if from twenty-five to thirty feet, let the top be diminished by one eighth of the jamb. Other and higher apertures should, as it seems, have their sides perpendicular.

2. Further, the jambs themselves should be diminished at the top by one fourteenth of their width. The height of the lintel should be equivalent to the width of the jambs at the top. Its cymatium ought to be one sixth of the jamb, with a projection equivalent to its height. The style of carving of the cymatium with its astragal should be the Lesbian. Above the cymatium of

[1] Codd. *duae*.

the lintel, place the frieze of the doorway, of the same height as the lintel, and having a Doric cymatium and Lesbian astragal carved upon it. Let the corona and its cymatium at the top of all be carved without ornamentation, and have a projection equal to its height. To the right and left of the lintel, which rests upon the jambs, there are to be projections fashioned like projecting bases and jointed to a nicety with the cymatium itself.

3. If the doorways are to be of the Ionic style, the height of the aperture should be reached in the same manner as in the Doric. Let its width be determined by dividing the height into two and one half parts and letting one of them form the width at the bottom. The diminutions should be the same as for Doric. The width of the faces of the jambs should be one fourteenth of the height of the aperture, and the cymatium one sixth of the width. Let the rest, excluding the cymatium, be divided into twelve parts. Let three of these compose the first fascia with its astragal, four the second, and five the third, the fasciae with their astragals running side by side all round.

4. The cornices of Ionic doorways should be constructed in the same manner as those of Doric, in due proportions. The consoles, otherwise called brackets, carved at the right and left, should hang down to the level of the bottom of the lintel, exclusive of the leaf. Their width on the face should be two thirds of the width of the jamb, but at the bottom one fourth slenderer than above.

Doors should be constructed with the hinge-stiles one twelfth of the width of the whole aperture. The panels between two stiles should each occupy three of the twelve parts.

5. The rails will be apportioned thus: divide the height into five parts, of which assign two to the upper portion and three to the lower; above the centre place the middle rails; insert the others at the top and at the bottom. Let the height of a rail be one third of the breadth of a panel, and its cymatium one sixth of the rail. The width of the meeting-stiles should be one half the rail, and the cover-joint two thirds of the rail. The stiles toward

CHAP. VI] THE DOORWAYS OF TEMPLES

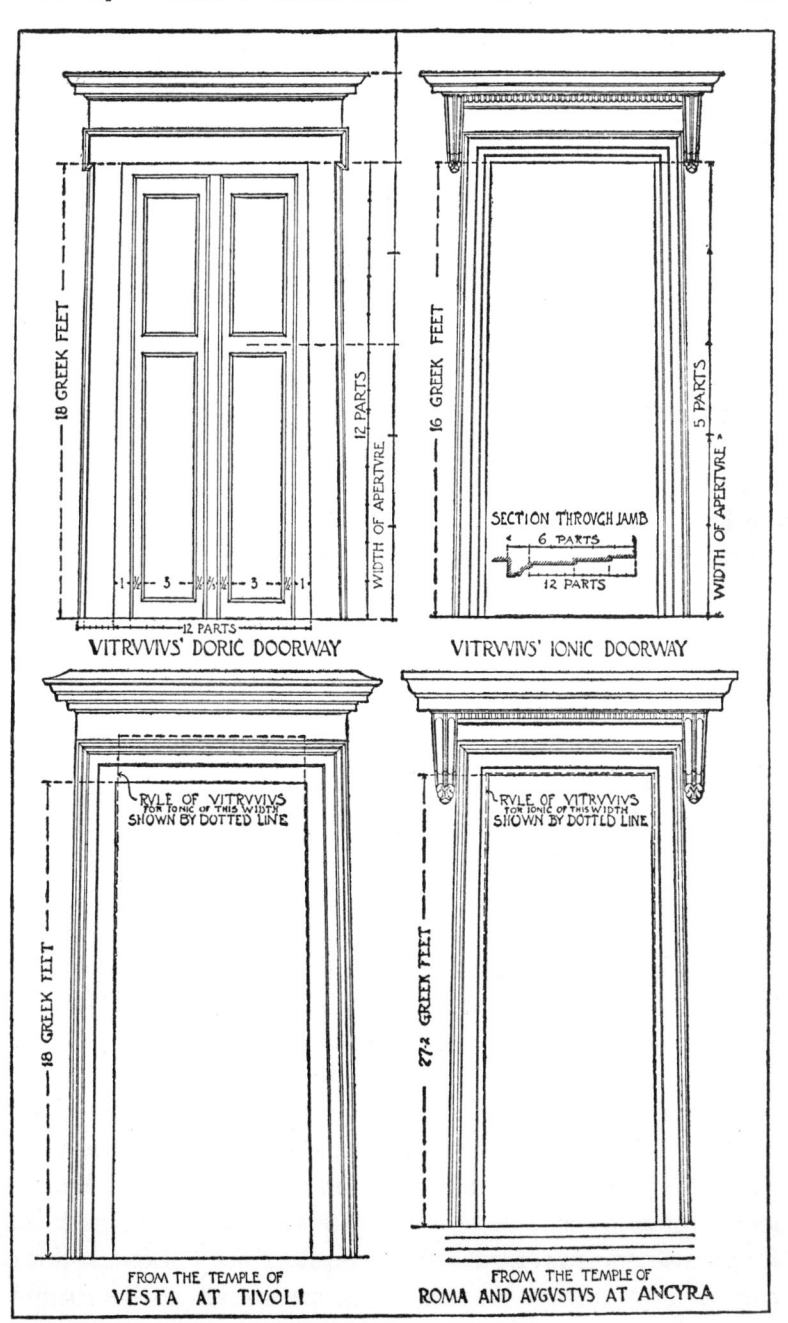

VITRVVIVS' DORIC DOORWAY

VITRVVIVS' IONIC DOORWAY

FROM THE TEMPLE OF
VESTA AT TIVOLI

FROM THE TEMPLE OF
ROMA AND AVGVSTVS AT ANCYRA

VITRUVIUS' RULE FOR DOORWAYS COMPARED WITH TWO EXAMPLES

the side of the jambs should be one half the rail. If the doors have folds in them, the height will remain as before, but the width should be double that of a single door; if the door is to have four folds, its height should be increased.

6. Attic doorways are built with the same proportions as Doric. Besides, there are fasciae running all round under the cymatia on the jambs, and apportioned so as to be equal to three sevenths of a jamb, excluding the cymatium. The doors are without latticework, are not double but have folds in them, and open outward.

The laws which should govern the design of temples built in the Doric, Ionic, and Corinthian styles, have now, so far as I could arrive at them, been set forth according to what may be called the accepted methods. I shall next speak of the arrangements in the Tuscan style, showing how they should be treated.

CHAPTER VII

TUSCAN TEMPLES

1. THE place where the temple is to be built having been divided on its length into six parts, deduct one and let the rest be given to its width. Then let the length be divided into two equal parts, of which let the inner be reserved as space for the cellae, and the part next the front left for the arrangement of the columns.

2. Next let the width be divided into ten parts. Of these, let three on the right and three on the left be given to the smaller cellae, or to the alae if there are to be alae, and the other four devoted to the middle of the temple. Let the space in front of the cellae, in the pronaos, be marked out for columns thus: the corner columns should be placed opposite the antae on the line of the outside walls; the two middle columns, set out on the line of the walls which are between the antae and the middle of the temple; and through the middle, between the antae and the front columns, a second row, arranged on the same lines. Let the thickness of the columns at the bottom be one seventh of their height,

TUSCAN TEMPLES

THE TUSCAN TEMPLE ACCORDING TO VITRUVIUS

TUSCAN TEMPLE AT MARZABOTTO

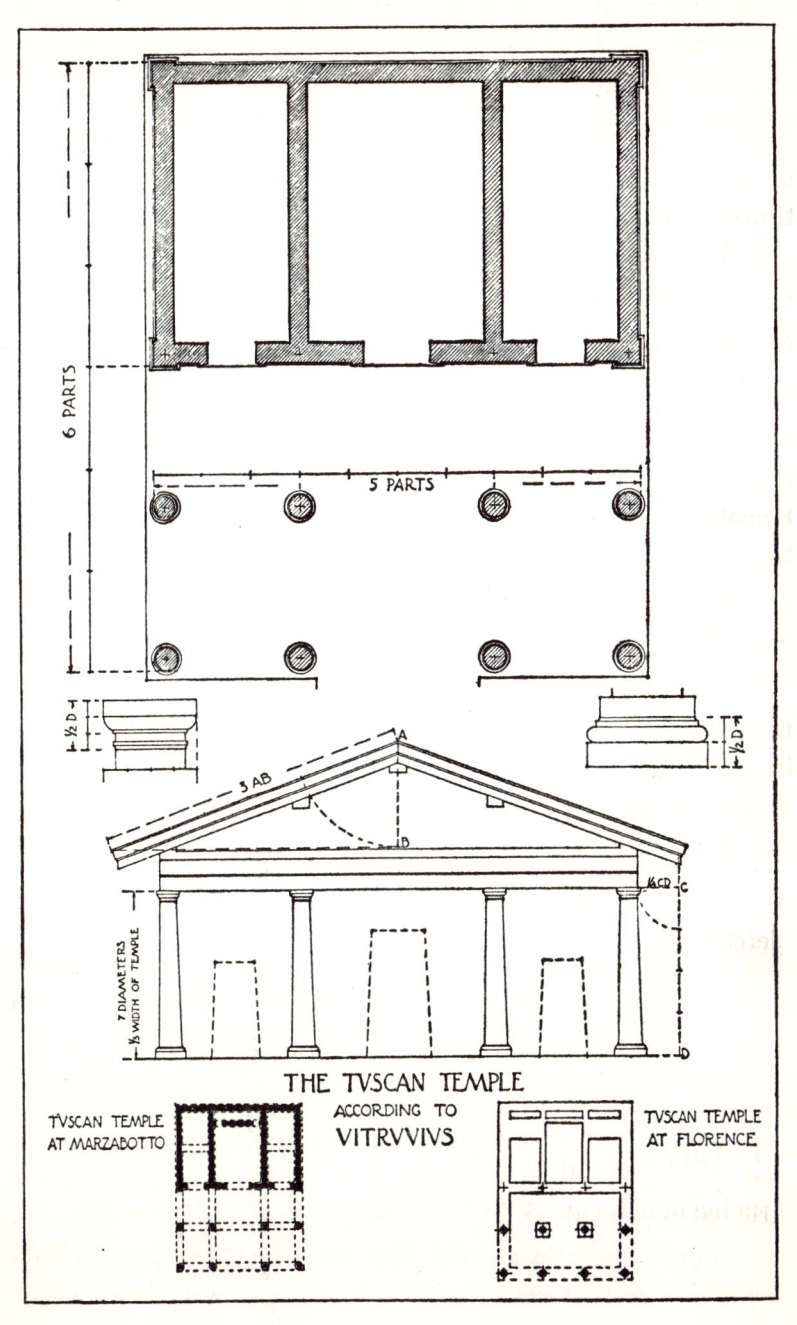

TUSCAN TEMPLE AT FLORENCE

their height one third of the width of the temple, and the diminution of a column at the top, one fourth of its thickness at the bottom.

3. The height of their bases should be one half of that thickness. The plinth of their bases should be circular, and in height one half the height of the bases, the torus above it and congé being of the same height as the plinth. The height of the capital is one half the thickness of a column. The abacus has a width equivalent to the thickness of the bottom of a column. Let the height of the capital be divided into three parts, and give one to the plinth (that is, the abacus), the second to the echinus, and the third to the necking with its congé.

4. Upon the columns lay the main beams, fastened together, to a height commensurate with the requirements of the size of the building. These beams fastened together should be laid so as to be equivalent in thickness to the necking at the top of a column, and should be fastened together by means of dowels and dove-tailed tenons in such a way that there shall be a space two fingers broad between them at the fastening. For if they touch one another, and so do not leave airholes and admit draughts of air to blow between them, they get heated and soon begin to rot.

5. Above the beams and walls let the mutules project to a distance equal to one quarter of the height of a column; along the front of them nail casings; above, build the tympanum of the pediment either in masonry or in wood. The pediment with its ridgepole, principal rafters, and purlines are to be built in such a way that the eaves shall be equivalent to one third of the completed roof.

CHAPTER VIII

CIRCULAR TEMPLES AND OTHER VARIETIES

1. THERE are also circular temples, some of which are constructed in monopteral form, surrounded by columns but without

THE CIRCULAR TEMPLE AT TIVOLI

THE MAISON CARRÉE AT NÎMES, A PSEUDO-PERIPTERAL TEMPLE

CIRCULAR TEMPLES

a cella, while others are termed peripteral. Those that are without a cella have a raised platform and a flight of steps leading to it, one third of the diameter of the temple. The columns upon the stylobates are constructed of a height equivalent to the diameter taken between the outer edges of the stylobate walls, and of a

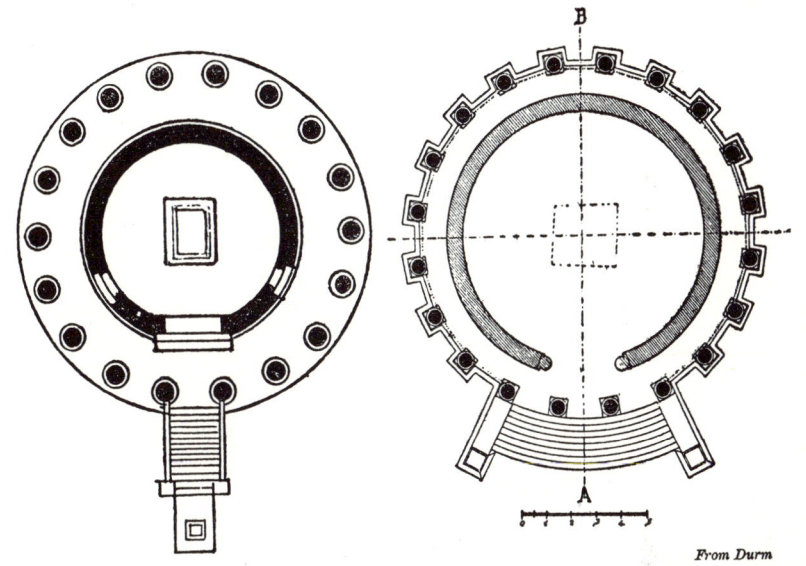

TEMPLE AT TIVOLI PLAN OF THE TEMPLE OF VESTA AT ROME

From Durm

thickness equivalent to one tenth of their height including the capitals and bases. The architrave has the height of one half of the thickness of a column. The frieze and the other parts placed above it are such as I have described in the third [1] book, on the subject of symmetrical proportions.

2. But if such a temple is to be constructed in peripteral form, let two steps and then the stylobate be constructed below. Next, let the cella wall be set up, recessed within the stylobate about one fifth of the breadth thereof, and let a place for folding doors be left in the middle to afford entrance. This cella, excluding its walls and the passage round the outside, should have a diameter equivalent to the height of a column above the stylobate. Let

[1] Codd. *quarto.*

the columns round the cella be arranged in the symmetrical proportions just given.

3. The proportions of the roof in the centre should be such that the height of the rotunda, excluding the finial, is equivalent to one half the diameter of the whole work. The finial, excluding

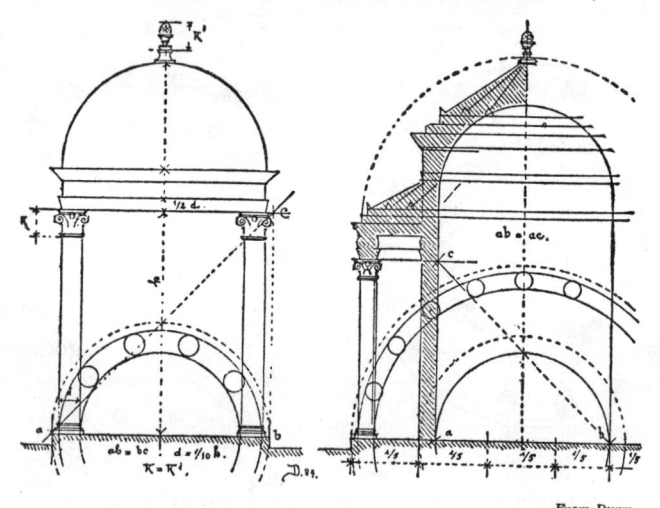

THE CIRCULAR TEMPLE ACCORDING TO VITRUVIUS

its pyramidal base, should have the dimensions of the capital of a column. All the rest must be built in the symmetrical proportions described above.

4. There are also other kinds of temples, constructed in the same symmetrical proportions and yet with a different kind of plan: for example, the temple of Castor in the district of the Circus Flaminius, that of Vejovis between the two groves, and still more ingeniously the temple of Diana in her sacred grove, with columns added on the right and left at the flanks of the pronaos. Temples of this kind, like that of Castor in the Circus, were first built in Athens on the Acropolis, and in Attica at Sunium to Pallas Minerva. The proportions of them are not different, but the same as usual. For the length of their cellae is twice the width, as in other temples; but all that we regularly find in the fronts of others is in these transferred to the sides.

5. Some take the arrangement of columns belonging to the Tuscan order and apply it to buildings in the Corinthian and Ionic styles, and where there are projecting antae in the pronaos, set up two columns in a line with each of the cella walls, thus making a combination of the principles of Tuscan and Greek buildings.

6. Others actually remove the temple walls, transferring them to the intercolumniations, and thus, by dispensing with the space needed for a pteroma, greatly increase the extent of the cella. So, while leaving all the rest in the same symmetrical proportions, they appear to have produced a new kind of plan with the new name "pseudoperipteral." These kinds, however, vary according to the requirements of the sacrifices. For we must not build temples according to the same rules to all gods alike, since the performance of the sacred rites varies with the various gods.

7. I have now set forth, as they have come down to me, all the principles governing the building of temples, have marked out under separate heads their arrangements and proportions, and have set forth, so far as I could express them in writing, the differences in their plans and the distinctions which make them unlike one another. Next, with regard to the altars of the immortal gods, I shall state how they may be constructed so as to conform to the rules governing sacrifices.

CHAPTER IX

ALTARS

ALTARS should face the east, and should always be placed on a lower level than are the statues in the temples, so that those who are praying and sacrificing may look upwards towards the divinity. They are of different heights, being each regulated so as to be appropriate to its own god. Their heights are to be adjusted thus: for Jupiter and all the celestials, let them be constructed as high as possible; for Vesta and Mother Earth, let them be built low. In accordance with these rules will altars be adjusted when one is preparing his plans.

Having described the arrangements of temples in this book, in the following we shall give an exposition of the construction of public buildings.

BOOK V

BOOK V

INTRODUCTION

1. Those who have filled books of unusually large size, Emperor, in setting forth their intellectual ideas and doctrines, have thus made a very great and remarkable addition to the authority of their writings. I could wish that circumstances made this as permissible in the case of our subject, so that the authority of the present treatise might be increased by amplifications; but this is not so easy as it may be thought. Writing on architecture is not like history or poetry. History is captivating to the reader from its very nature; for it holds out the hope of various novelties. Poetry, with its measures and metrical feet, its refinement in the arrangement of words, and the delivery in verse of the sentiments expressed by the several characters to one another, delights the feelings of the reader, and leads him smoothly on to the very end of the work.

2. But this cannot be the case with architectural treatises, because those terms which originate in the peculiar needs of the art, give rise to obscurity of ideas from the unusual nature of the language. Hence, while the things themselves are not well known, and their names not in common use, if besides this the principles are described in a very diffuse fashion without any attempt at conciseness and explanation in a few pellucid sentences, such fullness and amplitude of treatment will be only a hindrance, and will give the reader nothing but indefinite notions. Therefore, when I mention obscure terms, and the symmetrical proportions of members of buildings, I shall give brief explanations, so that they may be committed to memory; for thus expressed, the mind will be enabled to understand them the more easily.

3. Furthermore, since I have observed that our citizens are distracted with public affairs and private business, I have thought

it best to write briefly, so that my readers, whose intervals of leisure are small, may be able to comprehend in a short time.

Then again, Pythagoras and those who came after him in his school thought it proper to employ the principles of the cube in composing books on their doctrines, and, having determined that the cube consisted of 216 [1] lines, held that there should be no more than three cubes in any one treatise.

4. A cube is a body with sides all of equal breadth and their surfaces perfectly square. When thrown down, it stands firm and steady so long as it is untouched, no matter on which of its sides it has fallen, like the dice which players throw on the board. The Pythagoreans appear to have drawn their analogy from the cube, because the number of lines mentioned will be fixed firmly and steadily in the memory when they have once settled down, like a cube, upon a man's understanding. The Greek comic poets, also, divided their plays into parts by introducing a choral song, and by this partition on the principle of the cubes, they relieve the actor's speeches by such intermissions.

5. Since these rules, founded on the analogy of nature, were followed by our predecessors, and since I observe that I have to write on unusual subjects which many persons will find obscure, I have thought it best to write in short books, so that they may the more readily strike the understanding of the reader: for they will thus be easy to comprehend. I have also arranged them so that those in search of knowledge on a subject may not have to gather it from different places, but may find it in one complete treatment, with the various classes set forth each in a book by itself. Hence, Caesar, in the third and fourth books I gave the rules for temples; in this book I shall treat of the laying out of public places. I shall speak first of the proper arrangement of the forum, for in it the course of both public and private affairs is directed by the magistrates.

---

[1] Codd. *CC.* & *L.*

CHAPTER I

THE FORUM AND BASILICA

1. THE Greeks lay out their forums in the form of a square surrounded by very spacious double colonnades, adorn them with columns set rather closely together, and with entablatures of stone or marble, and construct walks above in the upper story. But in the cities of Italy the same method cannot be followed, for the reason that it is a custom handed down from our ancestors that gladiatorial shows should be given in the forum.

2. Therefore let the intercolumniations round the show place be pretty wide; round about in the colonnades put the bankers' offices; and have balconies on the upper floor properly arranged so as to be convenient, and to bring in some public revenue.

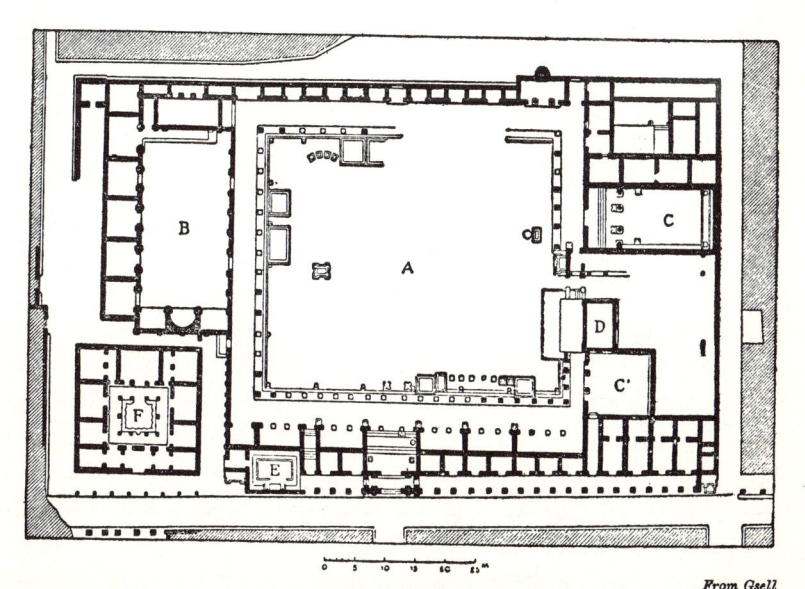

FORUM AT TIMGAD

From Gsell

A, Forum.   B, Basilica.   C, Curia.   C', Official Building.   D, Small Temple.
E, Latrina.   F, Atrium.

The size of a forum should be proportionate to the number of inhabitants, so that it may not be too small a space to be useful, nor look like a desert waste for lack of population. To determine its breadth, divide its length into three parts and assign two of them to the breadth. Its shape will then be oblong, and its ground plan conveniently suited to the conditions of shows.

3. The columns of the upper tier should be one fourth smaller than those of the lower, because, for the purpose of bearing the load, what is below ought to be stronger than what is above, and also, because we ought to imitate nature as seen in the case of things growing; for example, in round smooth-stemmed trees, like the fir, cypress, and pine, every one of which is rather thick just above the roots and then, as it goes on increasing in height, tapers off naturally and symmetrically in growing up to the top. Hence, if nature requires this in things growing, it is the right arrangement that what is above should be less in height and thickness than what is below.

4. Basilicas should be constructed on a site adjoining the forum and in the warmest possible quarter, so that in winter business men may gather in them without being troubled by the weather. In breadth they should be not less than one third nor more than one half of their length, unless the site is naturally such as to prevent this and to oblige an alteration in these proportions. If the length of the site is greater than necessary, Chalcidian porches may be constructed at the ends, as in the Julia Aquiliana.

5. It is thought that the columns of basilicas ought to be as high as the side-aisles are broad; an aisle should be limited to one third of the breadth which the open space in the middle is to have. Let the columns of the upper tier be smaller than those of the lower, as written above. The screen, to be placed between the upper and the lower tiers of columns, ought to be, it is thought, one fourth lower than the columns of the upper tier, so that people walking in the upper story of the basilica may not be seen by the business men. The architraves, friezes, and cornices should

FORUM AT POMPEII

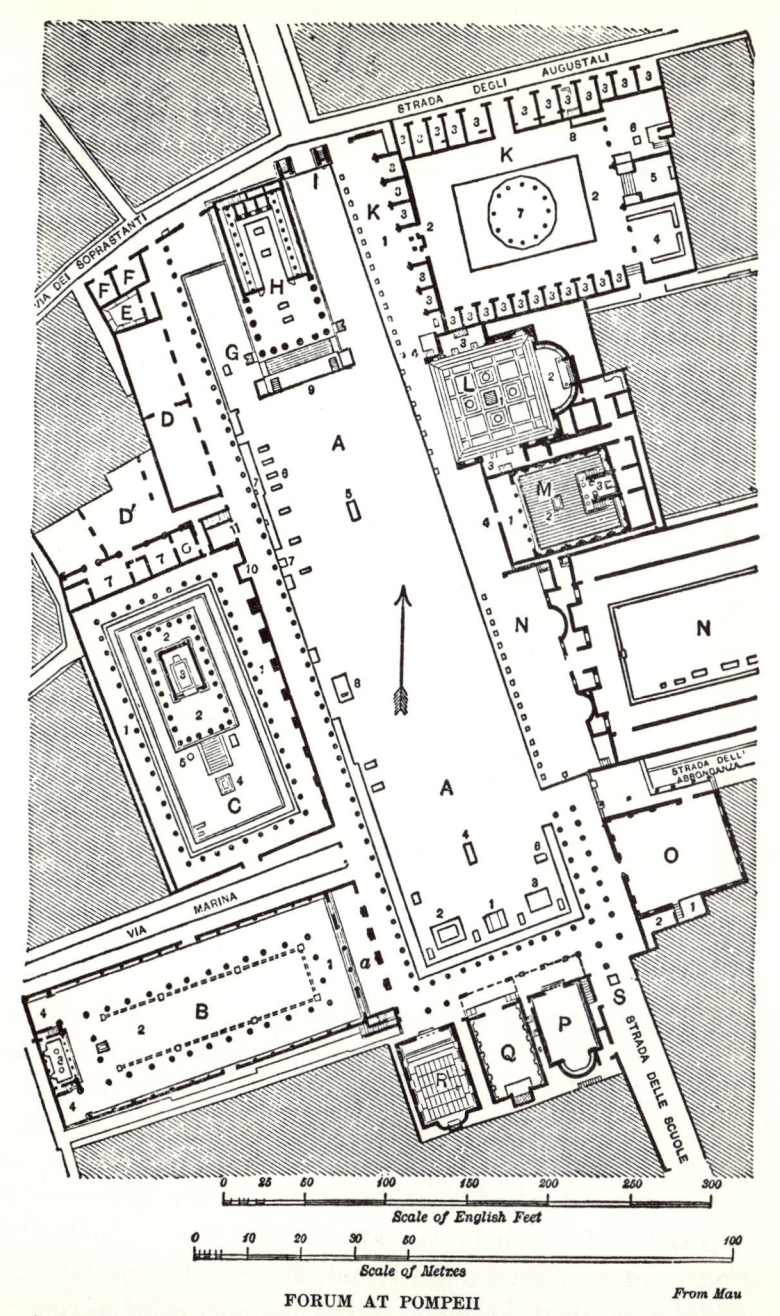

From Mau

A, Forum. B, Basilica. C, Temple of Apollo. D, D', Market Buildings. E, Latrina. F, City Treasury. G, Memorial Arch. H, Temple of Jupiter. I, Arch of Tiberius. K, Macellum (provision market). L, Sanctuary of the City Lares. M, Temple of Vespasian. N, Building of Eumachia. O, Comitium. P, Office of the Duumvirs. Q, The City Council. R, Office of the Aediles.

be adjusted to the proportions of the columns, as we have stated in the third book.

6. But basilicas of the greatest dignity and beauty may also be constructed in the style of that one which I erected, and the building of which I superintended at Fano. Its proportions and symmetrical relations were established as follows. In the middle, the main roof between the columns is 120 feet long and sixty feet wide. Its aisle round the space beneath the main roof and between the walls and the columns is twenty feet broad. The columns, of unbroken height, measuring with their capitals fifty feet, and being each five feet thick, have behind them pilasters, twenty feet high, two and one half feet broad, and one and one half feet thick, which support the beams on which is carried the upper flooring of the aisles. Above them are other pilasters, eighteen feet high, two feet broad, and a foot thick, which carry the beams supporting the principal raftering and the roof of the aisles, which is brought down lower than the main roof.

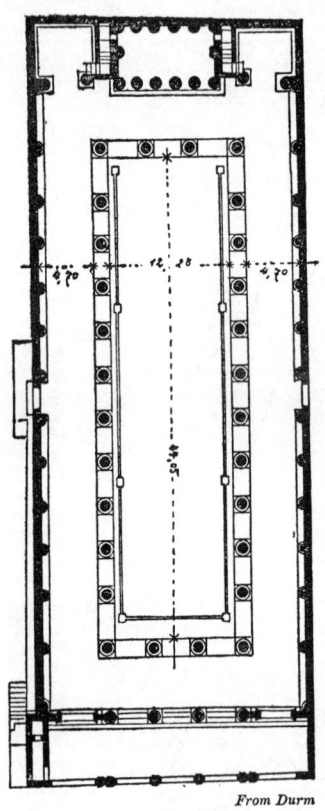

From Durm

PLAN OF THE BASILICA AT POMPEII

7. The spaces remaining between the beams supported by the pilasters and the columns, are left for windows between the intercolumniations. The columns are: on the breadth of the main roof at each end, four, including the corner columns at right and left; on the long side which is next to the forum, eight, including the same corner columns; on the other side, six, including the corner columns. This is because the

THE TRIBVNAL
AFTER REBER

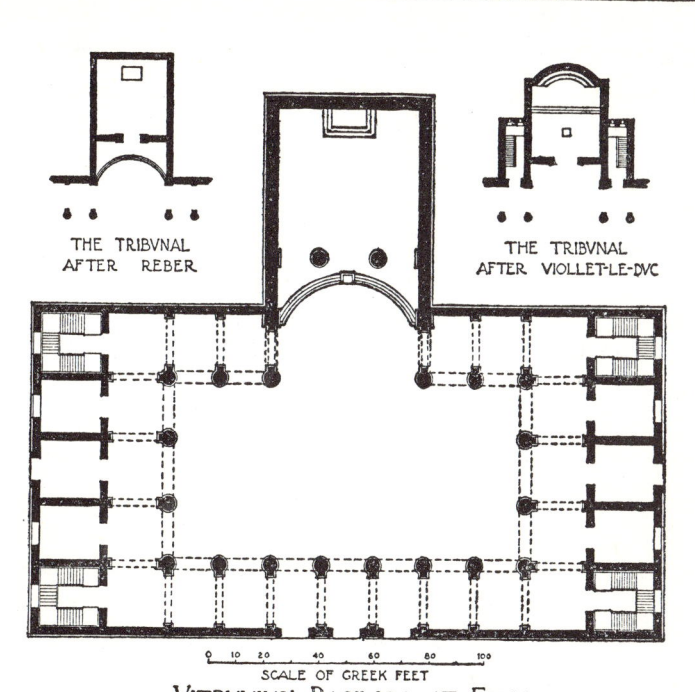

THE TRIBVNAL
AFTER VIOLLET-LE-DVC

SCALE OF GREEK FEET
VITRVVIVS' BASILICA AT FANO

two middle columns on that side are omitted, in order not to obstruct the view of the pronaos of the temple of Augustus (which is built at the middle of the side wall of the basilica, facing the middle of the forum and the temple of Jupiter) and also the tribunal which is in the former temple, shaped as a hemicycle whose curvature is less than a semicircle.

8. The open side of this hemicycle is forty-six feet along the front, and its curvature inwards is fifteen feet, so that those who are standing before the magistrates may not be in the way of the business men in the basilica. Round about, above the columns, are placed the architraves, consisting of three two-foot timbers fastened together. These return from the columns which stand third on the inner side to the antae which project from the pronaos, and which touch the edges of the hemicycle at right and left.

9. Above the architraves and regularly dispersed on supports directly over the capitals, piers are placed, three feet high and four feet broad each way. Above them is placed the projecting cornice round about, made of two two-foot timbers. The tie-beams and struts, being placed above them, and directly over the shafts of the columns and the antae and walls of the pronaos, hold up one gable roof along the entire basilica, and another from the middle of it, over the pronaos of the temple.

10. Thus the gable tops run in two directions, like the letter T, and give a beautiful effect to the outside and inside of the main roof. Further, by the omission of an ornamental entablature and of a line of screens and a second tier of columns, troublesome labour is saved and the total cost greatly diminished. On the other hand, the carrying of the columns themselves in unbroken height directly up to the beams that support the main roof, seems to add an air of sumptuousness and dignity to the work.

CHAPTER II

THE TREASURY, PRISON, AND SENATE HOUSE

1. THE treasury, prison, and senate house ought to adjoin the forum, but in such a way that their dimensions may be proportionate to those of the forum. Particularly, the senate house should be constructed with special regard to the importance of the town or city. If the building is square, let its height be fixed at one and one half times its breadth; but if it is to be oblong, add together its length and breadth and, having got the total, let half of it be devoted to the height up to the coffered ceiling.

2. Further, the inside walls should be girdled, at a point halfway up their height, with coronae made of woodwork or of stucco. Without these, the voice of men engaged in discussion there will be carried up to the height above, and so be unintelligible to their listeners. But when the walls are girdled with coronae, the voice from below, being detained before rising and becoming lost in the air, will be intelligible to the ear.

CHAPTER III

THE THEATRE: ITS SITE, FOUNDATIONS, AND ACOUSTICS

1. AFTER the forum has been arranged, next, for the purpose of seeing plays or festivals of the immortal gods, a site as healthy as possible should be selected for the theatre, in accordance with what has been written in the first book, on the principles of healthfulness in the sites of cities. For when plays are given, the spectators, with their wives and children, sit through them spellbound, and their bodies, motionless from enjoyment, have the pores open, into which blowing winds find their way. If these winds come from marshy districts or from other unwholesome quarters, they will introduce noxious exhalations into the system. Hence, such faults will be avoided if the site of the theatre is somewhat carefully selected.

2. We must also beware that it has not a southern exposure. When the sun shines full upon the rounded part of it, the air, being shut up in the curved enclosure and unable to circulate, stays there and becomes heated; and getting glowing hot it burns up, dries out, and impairs the fluids of the human body. For these reasons, sites which are unwholesome in such respects are to be avoided, and healthy sites selected.

3. The foundation walls will be an easier matter if they are on a hillside; but if they have to be laid on a plain or in a marshy place, solidity must be assured and substructures built in accordance with what has been written in the third book, on the foundations of temples. Above the foundation walls, the ascending rows of seats, from the substructures up, should be built of stone and marble materials.

4. The curved cross-aisles should be constructed in proportionate relation, it is thought, to the height of the theatre, but not higher than the footway of the passage is broad. If they are loftier, they will throw back the voice and drive it away from the upper portion, thus preventing the case-endings of words from reaching with distinct meaning the ears of those who are in the uppermost seats above the cross-aisles. In short, it should be so contrived that a line drawn from the lowest to the highest seat will touch the top edges and angles of all the seats. Thus the voice will meet with no obstruction.

5. The different entrances ought to be numerous and spacious, the upper not connected with the lower, but built in a continuous straight line from all parts of the house, without turnings, so that the people may not be crowded together when let out from shows, but may have separate exits from all parts without obstructions.

Particular pains must also be taken that the site be not a "deaf" one, but one through which the voice can range with the greatest clearness. This can be brought about if a site is selected where there is no obstruction due to echo.

6. Voice is a flowing breath of air, perceptible to the hearing by contact. It moves in an endless number of circular rounds,

like the innumerably increasing circular waves which appear when a stone is thrown into smooth water, and which keep on spreading indefinitely from the centre unless interrupted by narrow limits, or by some obstruction which prevents such waves from reaching their end in due formation. When they are interrupted by obstructions, the first waves, flowing back, break up the formation of those which follow.

7. In the same manner the voice executes its movements in concentric circles; but while in the case of water the circles move horizontally on a plane surface, the voice not only proceeds horizontally, but also ascends vertically by regular stages. Therefore, as in the case of the waves formed in the water, so it is in the case of the voice: the first wave, when there is no obstruction to interrupt it, does not break up the second or the following waves, but they all reach the ears of the lowest and highest spectators without an echo.

8. Hence the ancient architects, following in the footsteps of nature, perfected the ascending rows of seats in theatres from their investigations of the ascending voice, and, by means of the canonical theory of the mathematicians and that of the musicians, endeavoured to make every voice uttered on the stage come with greater clearness and sweetness to the ears of the audience. For just as musical instruments are brought to perfection of clearness in the sound of their strings by means of bronze plates or horn ἠχεῖα, so the ancients devised methods of increasing the power of the voice in theatres through the application of harmonics.

CHAPTER IV

HARMONICS

1. HARMONICS is an obscure and difficult branch of musical science, especially for those who do not know Greek. If we desire to treat of it, we must use Greek words, because some of them have no Latin equivalents. Hence, I will explain it as clearly as

I can from the writings of Aristoxenus, append his scheme, and define the boundaries of the notes, so that with somewhat careful attention anybody may be able to understand it pretty easily.

2. The voice, in its changes of position when shifting pitch, becomes sometimes high, sometimes low, and its movements are of two kinds, in one of which its progress is continuous, in the other by intervals. The continuous voice does not become stationary at the "boundaries" or at any definite place, and so the extremities of its progress are not apparent, but the fact that there are differences of pitch is apparent, as in our ordinary speech in *sol, lux, flos, vox;* for in these cases we cannot tell at what pitch the voice begins, nor at what pitch it leaves off, but the fact that it becomes low from high and high from low is apparent to the ear. In its progress by intervals the opposite is the case. For here, when the pitch shifts, the voice, by change of position, stations itself on one pitch, then on another, and, as it frequently repeats this alternating process, it appears to the senses to become stationary, as happens in singing when we produce a variation of the mode by changing the pitch of the voice. And so, since it moves by intervals, the points at which it begins and where it leaves off are obviously apparent in the boundaries of the notes, but the intermediate points escape notice and are obscure, owing to the intervals.

3. There are three classes of modes: first, that which the Greeks term the enharmonic; second, the chromatic; third, the diatonic. The enharmonic mode is an artistic conception, and therefore execution in it has a specially severe dignity and distinction. The chromatic, with its delicate subtlety and with the "crowding" of its notes, gives a sweeter kind of pleasure. In the diatonic, the distance between the intervals is easier to understand, because it is natural. These three classes differ in their arrangement of the tetrachord. In the enharmonic, the tetrachord consists of two tones and two "dieses." A diesis is a quarter tone; hence in a semitone there are included two dieses. In the chromatic there are two semitones arranged in succession, and the

Chap. IV] **HARMONICS** 141

third interval is a tone and a half. In the diatonic, there are two consecutive tones, and the third interval of a semitone completes the tetrachord. Hence, in the three classes, the tetrachords are equally composed of two tones and a semitone, but when they are regarded separately according to the terms of each class, they differ in the arrangement of their intervals.

4. Now then, these intervals of tones and semitones of the tetrachord are a division introduced by nature in the case of the voice, and she has defined their limits by measures according to the magnitude of the intervals, and determined their characteristics in certain different ways. These natural laws are followed by the skilled workmen who fashion musical instruments, in bringing them to the perfection of their proper concords.

5. In each class there are eighteen notes, termed in Greek φθόγγοι, of which eight in all the three classes are constant and fixed, while the other ten, not being tuned to the same pitch, are variable. The fixed notes are those which, being placed between the moveable, make up the unity of the tetrachord, and remain unaltered in their boundaries according to the different classes. Their names are proslambanomenos, hypate hypaton, hypate meson, mese, nete synhemmenon, paramese, nete diezeugmenon, nete hyperbolaeon. The moveable notes are those which, being arranged in the tetrachord between the immoveable, change from place to place according to the different classes. They are called

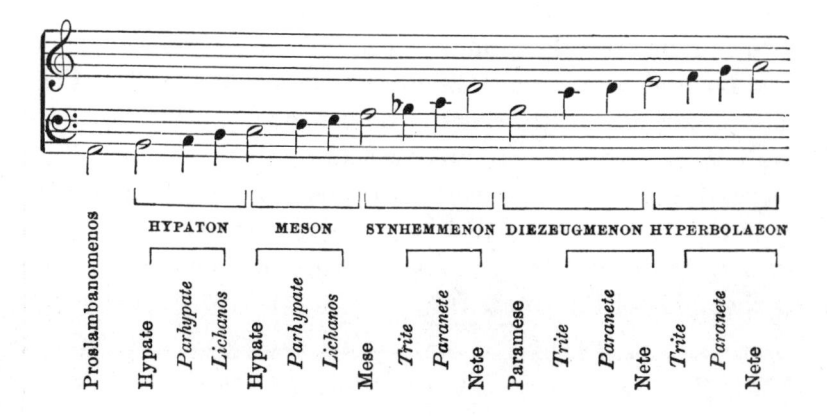

parhypate hypaton, lichanos hypaton, parhypate meson, lichanos meson, trite synhemmenon, paranete synhemmenon, trite diezeugmenon, paranete diezeugmenon, trite hyperbolaeon, paranete hyperbolaeon.

6. These notes, from being moveable, take on different qualities; for they may stand at different intervals and increasing distances. Thus, parhypate, which in the enharmonic is at the interval of half a semitone from hypate, has a semitone interval when transferred to the chromatic. What is called lichanos in the enharmonic is at the interval of a semitone from hypate; but when shifted to the chromatic, it goes two semitones away; and in the diatonic it is at an interval of three semitones from hypate. Hence the ten notes produce three different kinds of modes on account of their changes of position in the classes.

7. There are five tetrachords: first, the lowest, termed in Greek ὕπατον; second, the middle, called μέσον; third, the conjunct, termed συνημμένον; fourth, the disjunct, named διεζευγμένον; the fifth, which is the highest, is termed in Greek ὑπερβόλαιον. The concords, termed in Greek συμφωνίαι, of which human modulation will naturally admit, are six in number: the fourth, the fifth, the octave, the octave and fourth, the octave and fifth, and the double octave.

8. Their names are therefore due to numerical value; for when the voice becomes stationary on some one note, and then, shifting its pitch, changes its position and passes to the limit of the fourth note from that one, we use the term "fourth"; when it passes to the fifth, the term is "fifth." [1]

9. For there can be no consonancies either in the case of the notes of stringed instruments or of the singing voice, between two intervals or between three or six or seven; but, as written above, it is only the harmonies of the fourth, the fifth, and so on up to the double octave, that have boundaries naturally corresponding to those of the voice: and these concords are produced by the union of the notes.

---

[1] The remainder of this section is omitted from the translation as being an obvious interpolation.

CHAPTER V

SOUNDING VESSELS IN THE THEATRE

1. In accordance with the foregoing investigations on mathematical principles, let bronze vessels be made, proportionate to the size of the theatre, and let them be so fashioned that, when touched, they may produce with one another the notes of the fourth, the fifth, and so on up to the double octave. Then, having constructed niches in between the seats of the theatre, let the vessels be arranged in them, in accordance with musical laws, in such a way that they nowhere touch the wall, but have a clear space all round them and room over their tops. They should be set upside down, and be supported on the side facing the stage by wedges not less than half a foot high. Opposite each niche, apertures should be left in the surface of the seat next below, two feet long and half a foot deep.

2. The arrangement of these vessels, with reference to the situations in which they should be placed, may be described as follows. If the theatre be of no great size, mark out a horizontal range halfway up, and in it construct thirteen arched niches with twelve equal spaces between them, so that of the above mentioned "echea" those which give the note nete hyperbolaeon may be placed first on each side, in the niches which are at the extreme ends; next to the ends and a fourth below in pitch, the note nete diezeugmenon; third, paramese, a fourth below; fourth, nete synhemmenon; fifth, mese, a fourth below; sixth, hypate meson, a fourth below; and in the middle and another fourth below, one vessel giving the note hypate hypaton.

3. On this principle of arrangement, the voice, uttered from the stage as from a centre, and spreading and striking against the cavities of the different vessels, as it comes in contact with them, will be increased in clearness of sound, and will wake an harmonious note in unison with itself.

But if the theatre be rather large, let its height be divided into four parts, so that three horizontal ranges of niches may be marked out and constructed: one for the enharmonic, another for the chromatic, and the third for the diatonic system. Beginning with the bottom range, let the arrangement be as described above in the case of a smaller theatre, but on the enharmonic system.

4. In the middle range, place first at the extreme ends the vessels which give the note of the chromatic hyperbolaeon; next

[musical notation: §§ 2, 3]

[musical notation: § 4]

[musical notation: § 5]

to them, those which give the chromatic diezeugmenon, a fourth below; third, the chromatic synhemmenon; fourth, the chromatic meson, a fourth below; fifth, the chromatic hypaton, a fourth below; sixth, the paramese, for this is both the concord of the fifth to the chromatic hyperbolaeon, and the concord[1] of the chromatic synhemmenon.

5. No vessel is to be placed in the middle, for the reason that there is no other note in the chromatic system that forms a natural concord of sound.

In the highest division and range of niches, place at the extreme ends vessels fashioned so as to give the note of the diatonic hyperbolaeon; next, the diatonic diezeugmenon, a fourth below; third, the diatonic synhemmenon; fourth, the diatonic meson, a fourth below; fifth, the diatonic hypaton, a fourth below; sixth, the

---

[1] Codd. *diatessaron*, which is impossible, paramese being the concord of the fourth to the chromatic meson, and identical with the chromatic synhemmenon.

proslambanomenos, a fourth below; in the middle, the note mese, for this is both the octave to proslambanomenos, and the concord of the fifth to the diatonic hypaton.

6. Whoever wishes to carry out these principles with ease, has only to consult the scheme at the end of this book, drawn up in accordance with the laws of music. It was left by Aristoxenus, who with great ability and labour classified and arranged in it the different modes. In accordance with it, and by giving heed to these theories, one can easily bring a theatre to perfection, from the point of view of the nature of the voice, so as to give pleasure to the audience.

7. Somebody will perhaps say that many theatres are built every year in Rome, and that in them no attention at all is paid to these principles; but he will be in error, from the fact that all our public theatres made of wood contain a great deal of boarding, which must be resonant. This may be observed from the behaviour of those who sing to the lyre, who, when they wish to sing in a higher key, turn towards the folding doors on the stage, and thus by their aid are reinforced with a sound in harmony with the voice. But when theatres are built of solid materials like masonry, stone, or marble, which cannot be resonant, then the principles of the "echea" must be applied.

8. If, however, it is asked in what theatre these vessels have been employed, we cannot point to any in Rome itself, but only to those in the districts of Italy and in a good many Greek states. We have also the evidence of Lucius Mummius, who, after destroying the theatre in Corinth, brought its bronze vessels to Rome, and made a dedicatory offering at the temple of Luna with the money obtained from the sale of them. Besides, many skilful architects, in constructing theatres in small towns, have, for lack of means, taken large jars made of clay, but similarly resonant, and have produced very advantageous results by arranging them on the principles described.

CHAPTER VI

PLAN OF THE THEATRE

1. THE plan of the theatre itself is to be constructed as follows. Having fixed upon the principal centre, draw a line of circumference equivalent to what is to be the perimeter at the bottom, and in it inscribe four equilateral triangles, at equal distances apart and touching the boundary line of the circle, as the astrologers do in a figure of the twelve signs of the zodiac, when they are making computations from the musical harmony of the stars. Taking that one of these triangles whose side is nearest to the scaena, let the front of the scaena be determined by the line where that side cuts off a segment of the circle (A–B), and draw, through the centre, a parallel line (C–D) set off from that position, to separate the platform of the stage from the space of the orchestra.

2. The platform has to be made deeper than that of the Greeks, because all our artists perform on the stage, while the orchestra contains the places reserved for the seats of senators. The height of this platform must be not more than five feet, in order that those who sit in the orchestra may be able to see the performances of all the actors. The sections (cunei) for spectators in the theatre should be so divided, that the angles of the triangles which run about the circumference of the circle may give the direction for the flights of steps between the sections, as far as up to the first curved cross-aisle. Above this, the upper sections are to be laid out, midway between (the lower sections), with alternating passage-ways.

3. The angles at the bottom, which give the directions for the flights of steps, will be seven in number (C, E, F, G, H, I, D); the other five angles will determine the arrangement of the scene: thus, the angle in the middle ought to have the "royal door" (K) opposite to it; the angles to the right and left (L, M) will designate the position of the doors for guest chambers; and the two

CHAP. VI] PLAN OF THE THEATRE 147

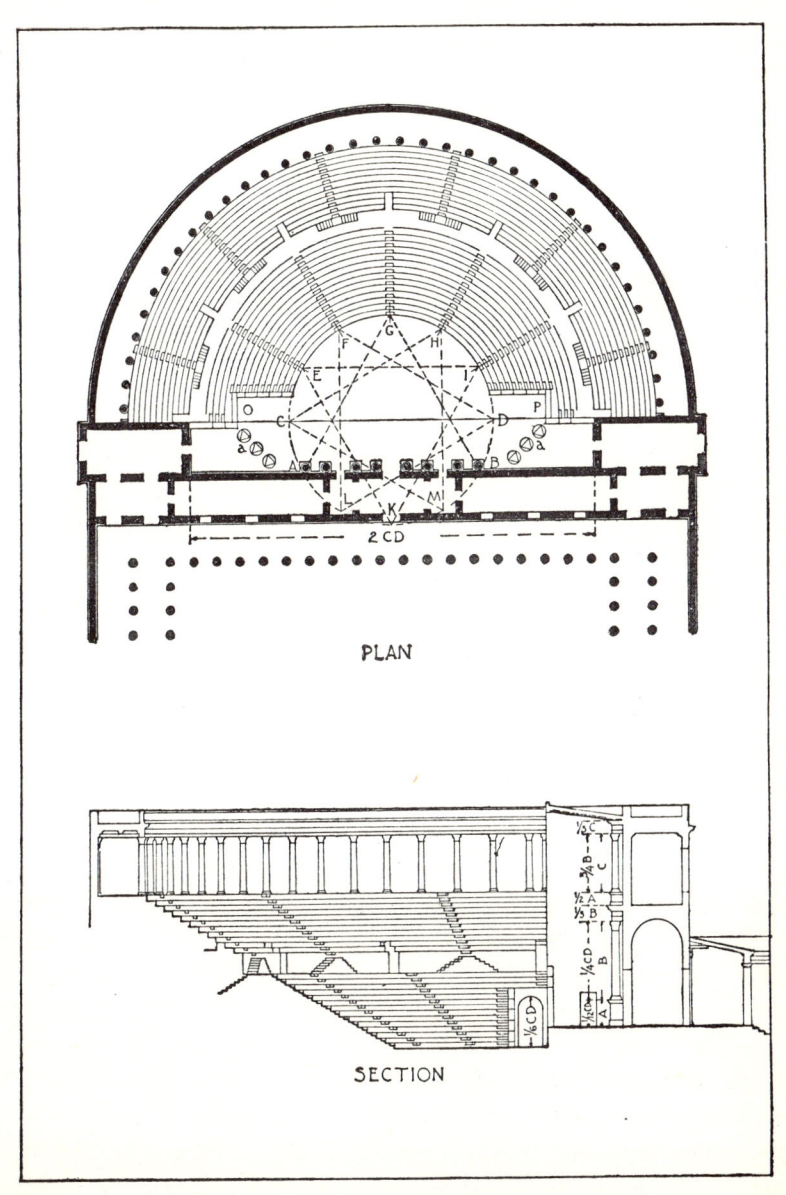

PLAN

SECTION

THE ROMAN THEATRE ACCORDING TO VITRUVIUS

outermost angles (A, B) will point to the passages in the wings. The steps for the spectators' places, where the seats are arranged, should be not less than a foot and a palm in height, nor more than a foot and six fingers; their depth should be fixed at not more than two and a half feet, nor less than two feet.

4. The roof of the colonnade to be built at the top of the rows of seats, should lie level with the top of the "scaena," for the reason that the voice will then rise with equal power until it reaches the highest rows of seats and the roof. If the roof is not so high, in proportion as it is lower, it will check the voice at the point which the sound first reaches.

5. Take one sixth of the diameter of the orchestra between the lowest steps, and let the lower seats at the ends on both sides be cut away to a height of that dimension so as to leave entrances (O, P). At the point where this cutting away occurs, fix the soffits of the passages. Thus their vaulting will be sufficiently high.

6. The length of the "scaena" ought to be double the diameter of the orchestra. The height of the podium, starting from the level of the stage, is, including the corona and cymatium, one twelfth of the diameter of the orchestra. Above the podium, the columns, including their capitals and bases, should have a height of one quarter of the same diameter, and the architraves and ornaments of the columns should be one fifth of their height. The parapet above, including its cyma and corona, is one half the height of the parapet below. Let the columns above this parapet be one fourth less in height than the columns below, and the architraves and ornaments of these columns one fifth of their height. If the "scaena" is to have three stories, let the uppermost parapet be half the height of the intermediate one, the columns at the top one fourth less high than the intermediate, and the architraves and coronae of these columns one fifth of their height as before.

7. It is not possible, however, that in all theatres these rules of symmetry should answer all conditions and purposes, but the

CHAP. VI]   PLAN OF THE THEATRE   149

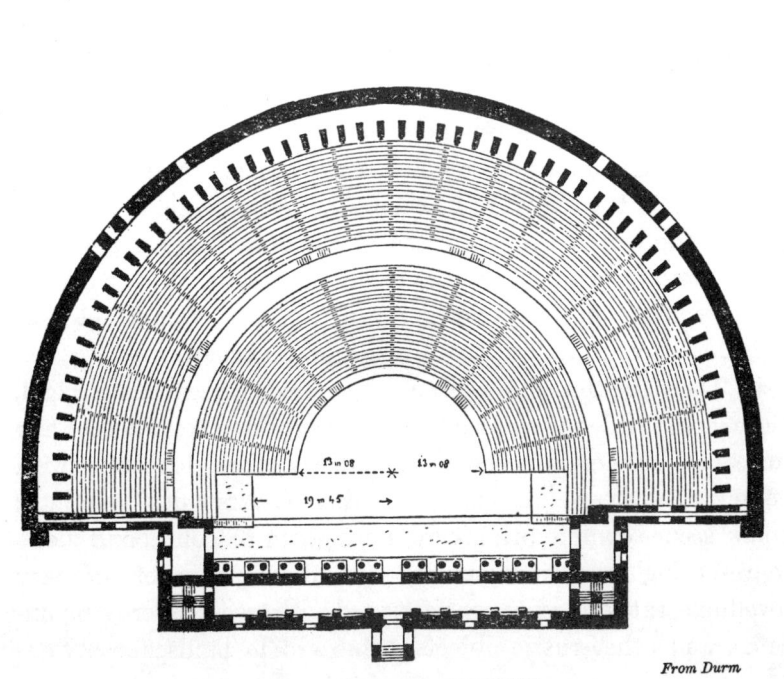

THE THEATRE AT ASPENDUS

From Durm

architect ought to consider to what extent he must follow the principle of symmetry, and to what extent it may be modified to suit the nature of the site or the size of the work. There are, of course, some things which, for utility's sake, must be made of the same size in a small theatre, and a large one: such as the steps, curved cross-aisles, their parapets, the passages, stairways, stages, tribunals, and any other things which occur that make it necessary to give up symmetry so as not to interfere with utility. Again, if in the course of the work any of the material fall short, such as marble, timber, or anything else that is provided, it will not be amiss to make a slight reduction or addition, provided that it is done without going too far, but with intelligence. This will be possible, if the architect is a man of practical experience and, besides, not destitute of cleverness and skill.

8. The "scaena" itself displays the following scheme. In the centre are double doors decorated like those of a royal palace. At the right and left are the doors of the guest chambers. Beyond are spaces provided for decoration — places that the Greeks call περίακτοι, because in these places are triangular pieces of machinery (Δ, Δ) which revolve, each having three decorated faces. When the play is to be changed, or when gods enter to the accompaniment of sudden claps of thunder, these may be revolved and present a face differently decorated. Beyond these places are the projecting wings which afford entrances to the stage, one from the forum, the other from abroad.

9. There are three kinds of scenes, one called the tragic, second, the comic, third, the satyric. Their decorations are different and unlike each other in scheme. Tragic scenes are delineated with columns, pediments, statues, and other objects suited to kings; comic scenes exhibit private dwellings, with balconies and views representing rows of windows, after the manner of ordinary dwellings; satyric scenes are decorated with trees, caverns, mountains, and other rustic objects delineated in landscape style.

CHAPTER VII

GREEK THEATRES

1. In the theatres of the Greeks, these same rules of construction are not to be followed in all respects. First, in the circle at the bottom where the Roman has four triangles, the Greek has three squares with their angles touching the line of circumference. The square whose side is nearest to the "scaena," and cuts off a segment of the circle, determines by this line the limits of the "proscaenium" (A, B). Parallel to this line and tangent to the outer circumference of the segment, a line is drawn which fixes the front of the "scaena" (C–D). Through the centre of the orchestra and parallel to the direction of the "proscaenium," a line is laid off, and centres are marked where it cuts the circumference to the right and left (E, F) at the ends of the half-circle. Then, with the compasses fixed at the right, an arc is described from the horizontal distance at the left to the left hand side of the "proscaenium" (F, G); again with the centre at the left end, an arc is described from the horizontal distance at the right to the right hand side of the "proscaenium" (E, H).

2. As a result of this plan with three centres, the Greeks have a roomier orchestra, and a "scaena" set further back, as well as a stage of less depth. They call this the λογεῖον, for the reason that there the tragic and comic actors perform on the stage, while other artists give their performances in the entire orchestra; hence, from this fact they are given in Greek the distinct names "Scenic" and "Thymelic." The height of this "logeum" ought to be not less than ten feet nor more than twelve. Let the ascending flights of steps between the wedges of seats, as far up as the first curved cross-aisle, be laid out on lines directly opposite to the angles of the squares. Above the cross-aisle, let other flights be laid out in the middle between the first; and at the top, as often as there is a new cross-aisle, the number of flights of steps is always increased to the same extent.

THEATRE AT EPIDAVRVS

THE GREEK THEATRE
ACCORDING TO VITRVVIVS

THEATRE AT OROPVS

RVLE OF VITRVVIVS
AS EXECVTED
(from Durm)

RVLE OF VITRVVIVS
AS EXECVTED
(from Durm)

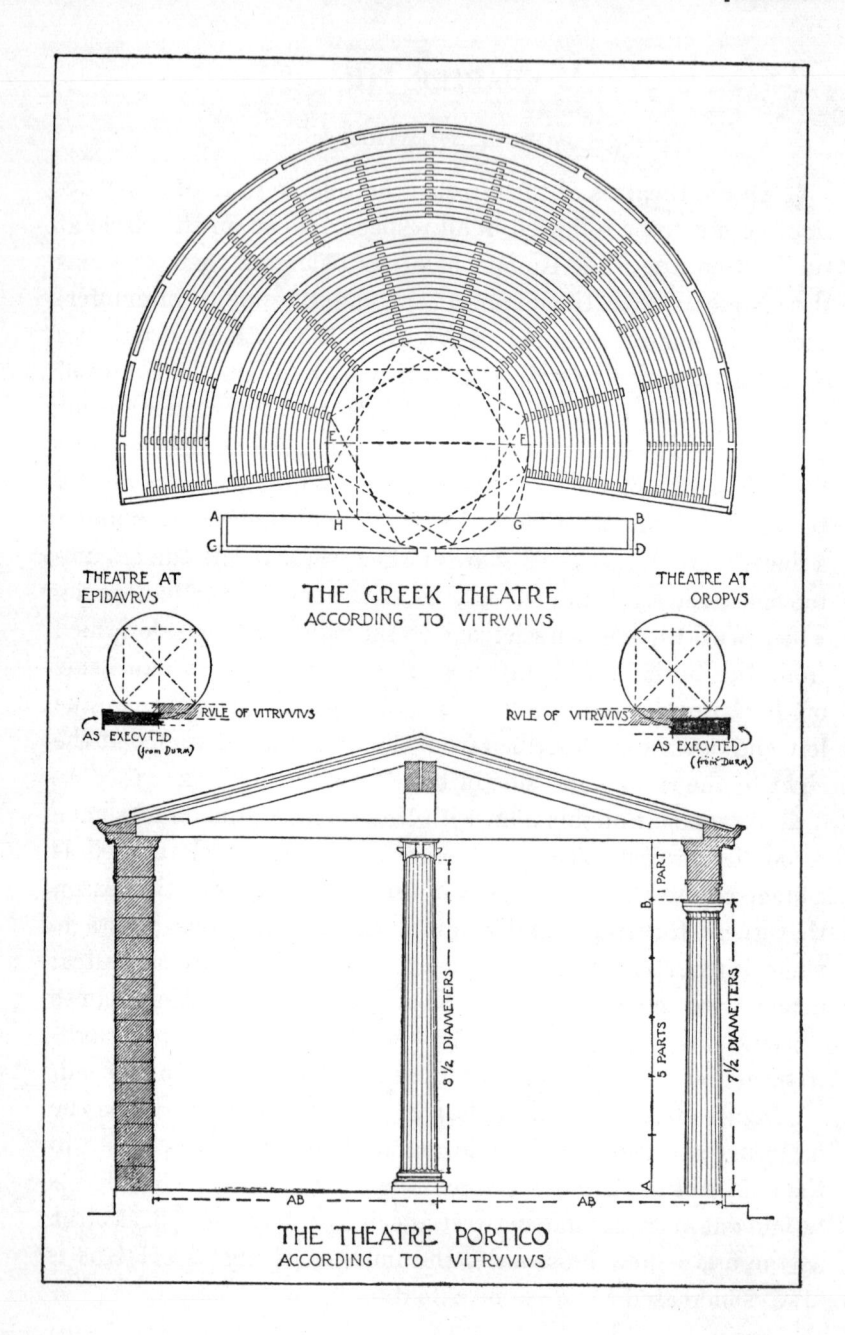

THE THEATRE PORTICO
ACCORDING TO VITRVVIVS

CHAPTER VIII

ACOUSTICS OF THE SITE OF A THEATRE

1. ALL this having been settled with the greatest pains and skill, we must see to it, with still greater care, that a site has been selected where the voice has a gentle fall, and is not driven back with a recoil so as to convey an indistinct meaning to the ear. There are some places which from their very nature interfere with the course of the voice, as for instance the dissonant, which are termed in Greek κατηχοῦντες; the circumsonant, which with them are named περιηχοῦντες; again the resonant, which are termed ἀντηχοῦντες; and the consonant, which they call συνηχοῦντες. The dissonant are those places in which the first sound uttered that is carried up high, strikes against solid bodies above, and, being driven back, checks as it sinks to the bottom the rise of the succeeding sound.

2. The circumsonant are those in which the voice spreads all round, and then is forced into the middle, where it dissolves, the case-endings are not heard, and it dies away there in sounds of indistinct meaning. The resonant are those in which it comes into contact with some solid substance and recoils, thus producing an echo, and making the terminations of cases sound double. The consonant are those in which it is supported from below, increases as it goes up, and reaches the ears in words which are distinct and clear in tone. Hence, if there has been careful attention in the selection of the site, the effect of the voice will, through this precaution, be perfectly suited to the purposes of a theatre.

The drawings of the plans may be distinguished from each other by this difference, that theatres designed from squares are meant to be used by Greeks, while Roman theatres are designed from equilateral triangles. Whoever is willing to follow these directions will be able to construct perfectly correct theatres.

CHAPTER IX

COLONNADES AND WALKS

1. COLONNADES must be constructed behind the scaena, so that when sudden showers interrupt plays, the people may have somewhere to retire from the theatre, and so that there may be room for the preparation of all the outfit of the stage. Such places, for instance, are the colonnades of Pompey, and also, in Athens, the colonnades of Eumenes and the fane of Father Bacchus; also, as you leave the theatre, the music hall which Themistocles surrounded with stone columns, and roofed with the yards and masts of ships captured from the Persians. It was burned during the war with Mithridates, and afterwards restored by King Ariobarzanes. At Smyrna there is the Stratoniceum, at Tralles, a colonnade on each side of the scaena above the race course, and in other cities which have had careful architects there are colonnades and walks about the theatres.

2. The approved way of building them requires that they should be double, and have Doric columns on the outside, with the architraves and their ornaments finished according to the law of modular proportion. The approved depth for them requires that the depth, from the lower part of the outermost columns to the columns in the middle, and from the middle columns to the wall enclosing the walk under the colonnade, should be equal to the height of the outer columns. Let the middle columns be one fifth higher than the outer columns, and designed in the Ionic or Corinthian style.

3. The columns will not be subject to the same rules of symmetry and proportion which I prescribed in the case of sanctuaries; for the dignity which ought to be their quality in temples of the gods is one thing, but their elegance in colonnades and other public works is quite another. Hence, if the columns are to be of the Doric order, let their height, including the capital, be measured off into fifteen parts. Of these parts, let one be fixed

upon to form the module, and in accordance with this module the whole work is to be developed. Let the thickness of the columns at the bottom be two modules; an intercolumniation, five and a half modules; the height of a column, excluding the capital, fourteen modules; the capital, one module in height and two and one sixth modules in breadth. Let the modular proportions of the rest of the work be carried out as written in the fourth book in the case of temples.

4. But if the columns are to be Ionic, let the shaft, excluding base and capital, be divided into eight and one half parts, and let one of these be assigned to the thickness of a column. Let the base, including the plinth, be fixed at half the thickness, and let the proportions of the capital be as shown in the third book. If the column is to be Corinthian, let its shaft and base be proportioned as in the Ionic, but its capital, as has been written in the fourth book. In the stylobates, let the increase made there by means of the "scamilli impares" be taken from the description written above in the third book. Let the architraves, coronae, and all the rest be developed, in proportion to the columns, from what has been written in the foregoing books.

5. The space in the middle, between the colonnades and open to the sky, ought to be embellished with green things; for walking in the open air is very healthy, particularly for the eyes, since the refined and rarefied air that comes from green things, finding its way in because of the physical exercise, gives a clean-cut image, and, by clearing away the gross humours from the eyes, leaves the sight keen and the image distinct. Besides, as the body gets warm with exercise in walking, this air, by sucking out the humours from the frame, diminishes their superabundance, and disperses and thus reduces that superfluity which is more than the body can bear.

6. That this is so may be seen from the fact that misty vapours never arise from springs of water which are under cover, nor even from watery marshes which are underground; but in uncovered places which are open to the sky, when the rising

sun begins to act upon the world with its heat, it brings out the vapour from damp and watery spots, and rolls it in masses upwards. Therefore, if it appears that in places open to the sky the more noxious humours are sucked out of the body by the air, as they obviously are from the earth in the form of mists, I think there is no doubt that cities should be provided with the roomiest and most ornamented walks, laid out under the free and open sky.

7. That they may be always dry and not muddy, the following is to be done. Let them be dug down and cleared out to the lowest possible depth. At the right and left construct covered drains, and in their walls, which are directed towards the walks, lay earthen pipes with their lower ends inclined into the drains. Having finished these, fill up the place with charcoal, and then strew sand over the walks and level them off. Hence, on account of the porous nature of the charcoal and the insertion of the pipes into the drains, quantities of water will be conducted away, and the walks will thus be rendered perfectly dry and without moisture.

8. Furthermore, our ancestors in establishing these works provided cities with storehouses for an indispensable material. The fact is that in sieges everything else is easier to procure than is wood. Salt can easily be brought in beforehand; corn can be got together quickly by the State or by individuals, and if it gives out, the defence may be maintained on cabbage, meat, or beans; water can be had by digging wells, or when there are sudden falls of rain, by collecting it from the tiles. But a stock of wood, which is absolutely necessary for cooking food, is a difficult and troublesome thing to provide; for it is slow to gather and a good deal is consumed.

9. On such occasions, therefore, these walks are thrown open, and a definite allowance granted to each inhabitant according to tribes. Thus these uncovered walks insure two excellent things: first, health in time of peace; secondly, safety in time of war. Hence, walks that are developed on these principles, and built

Photo Brooklyn Institute
THE TEPIDARIUM OF THE STABIAN BATHS AT POMPEII

Photo Brooklyn Institute
APODYTERIUM FOR WOMEN IN THE STABIAN BATHS AT POMPEII

not only behind the "scaena" of theatres, but also at the temples of all the gods, will be capable of being of great use to cities.

As it appears that we have given an adequate account of them, next will follow descriptions of the arrangements of baths.

CHAPTER X

BATHS

1. In the first place, the warmest possible situation must be selected; that is, one which faces away from the north and northeast. The rooms for the hot and tepid baths should be lighted from the southwest, or, if the nature of the situation prevents this, at all events from the south, because the set time for bathing is principally from midday to evening. We must also see to it that the hot bath rooms in the women's and men's departments adjoin each other, and are situated in the same quarter; for thus it will be possible that the same furnace should serve both of them and their fittings. Three bronze cauldrons are to be set over the furnace, one for hot, another for tepid, and the third for cold water, placed in such positions that the amount of water which flows out of the hot water cauldron may be replaced from that for tepid water, and in the same way the cauldron for tepid water may be supplied from that for cold. The arrangement must allow the semi-cylinders for the bath basins to be heated from the same furnace.

2. The hanging floors of the hot bath rooms are to be constructed as follows. First the surface of the ground should be laid with tiles a foot and a half square, sloping towards the furnace in such a way that, if a ball is thrown in, it cannot stop inside but must return of itself to the furnace room; thus the heat of the fire will more readily spread under the hanging flooring. Upon them, pillars made of eight-inch bricks are built, and set at such a distance apart that two-foot tiles may be used to cover them. These pillars should be two feet in height, laid with clay mixed with hair, and covered on top with the two-foot tiles which support the floor.

3. The vaulted ceilings will be more serviceable if built of masonry; but if they are of framework, they should have tile work on the under side, to be constructed as follows. Let iron bars or arcs be made, and hang them to the framework by means of iron hooks set as close together as possible; and let these bars or arcs be placed at such distances apart that each pair of them may support and carry an unflanged tile. Thus the entire vaulting will be

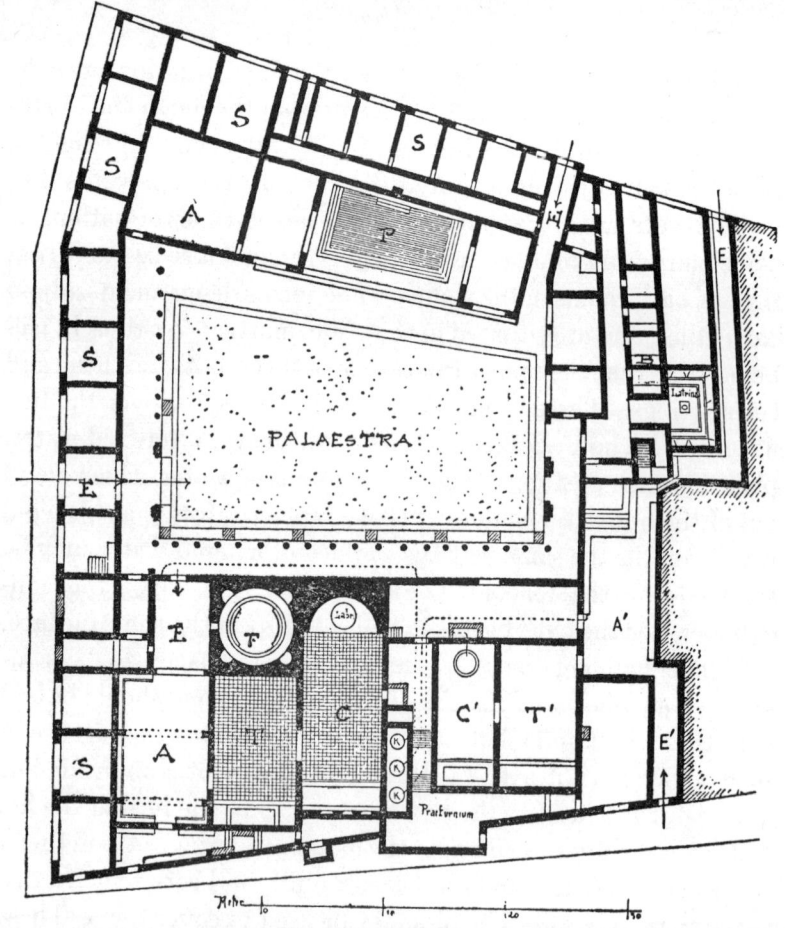

THE STABIAN BATHS AT POMPEII

S,S. Shops. B. Private Baths. A–T. Men's Bath. A'–T'. Women's Baths. E,E'. Entrances. A,A'. Apodyteria. F. Frigidarium. T,T'. Tepidarium. C,C'. Caldarium. K,K,K. Kettles in furnace room. P. Piscina.

completely supported on iron. These vaults should have the joints on their upper side daubed with clay mixed with hair, and their under side, facing the floor, should first be plastered with pounded tile mixed with lime, and then covered with polished stucco in relief or smooth. Vaults in hot bath rooms will be more serviceable if they are doubled; for then the moisture from the heat will not be able to spoil the timber in the framework, but will merely circulate between the two vaults.

4. The size of the baths must depend upon the number of the population. The rooms should be thus proportioned: let their breadth be one third of their length, excluding the niches for the washbowl and the bath basin. The washbowl ought without fail to be placed under a window, so that the shadows of those who stand round it may not obstruct the light. Niches for washbowls must be made so roomy that when the first comers have taken their places, the others who are waiting round may have proper standing room. The bath basin should be not less than six feet broad from the wall to the edge, the lower step and the "cushion" taking up two feet of this space.

5. The Laconicum and other sweating baths must adjoin the tepid room, and their height to the bottom of the curved dome should be equal to their width. Let an aperture be left in the middle of the dome with a bronze disc hanging from it by chains. By raising and lowering it, the temperature of the sweating bath can be regulated. The chamber itself ought, as it seems, to be circular, so that the force of the fire and heat may spread evenly from the centre all round the circumference.

CHAPTER XI

THE PALAESTRA

1. NEXT, although the building of palaestrae is not usual in Italy, I think it best to set forth the traditional way, and to show how they are constructed among the Greeks. The square or ob-

long peristyle in a palaestra should be so formed that the circuit of it makes a walk of two stadia, a distance which the Greeks call the δίαυλος. Let three of its colonnades be single, but let the fourth, which is on the south side, be double, so that when there is bad weather accompanied by wind, the drops of rain may not be able to reach the interior.

2. In the three colonnades construct roomy recesses (A) with seats in them, where philosophers, rhetoricians, and others who delight in learning may sit and converse. In the double colonnade let the rooms be arranged thus: the young men's hall (B) in the middle; this is a very spacious recess (exedra) with seats in it, and it should be one third longer than it is broad. At the right, the bag room (C); then next, the dust room (D); beyond the dust room, at the corner of the colonnade, the cold washing room (E), which the Greeks call λουτρόν. At the left of the young men's hall is the anointing room (F); then, next to the anointing room, the cold bath room (G), and beyond that a passage into the furnace room (H) at the corner of the colonnade. Next, but inside and on a line with the cold bath room, put the vaulted sweating bath (I), its length twice its breadth, and having at the ends on one side a Laconicum (K), proportioned in the same manner as above described, and opposite the Laconicum the warm washing room (L). Inside a palaestra, the peristyle ought to be laid out as described above.

3. But on the outside, let three colonnades be arranged, one as you leave the peristyle and two at the right and left, with running-tracks in them. That one of them which faces the north should be a double colonnade of very ample breadth, while the other should be single, and so constructed that on the sides next the walls and the side along the columns it may have edges, serving as paths, of not less than ten feet, with the space between them sunken, so that steps are necessary in going down from the edges a foot and a half to the plane, which plane should be not less than twelve feet wide. Thus people walking round on the edges will not be interfered with by the anointed who are exercising.

4. This kind of colonnade is called among the Greeks ξυστός, because athletes during the winter season exercise in covered running tracks. Next to this "xystus" and to the double colon-

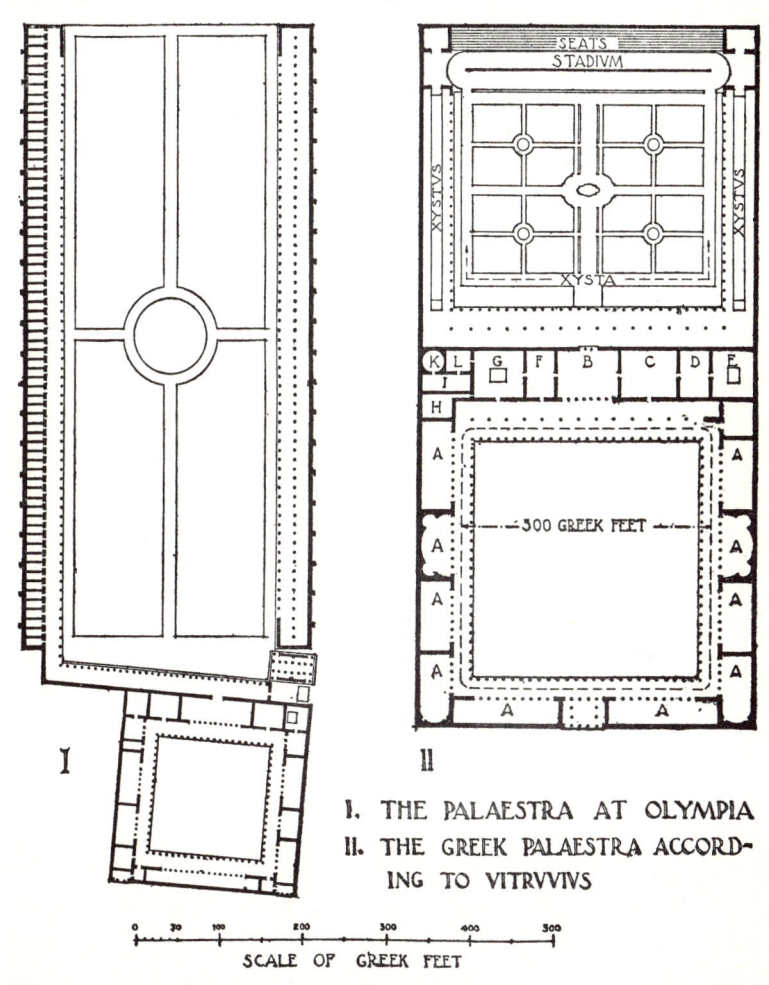

I. THE PALAESTRA AT OLYMPIA
II. THE GREEK PALAESTRA ACCORDING TO VITRVVIVS

SCALE OF GREEK FEET

nade should be laid out the uncovered walks which the Greeks term παραδρομίδες and our people "xysta," into which, in fair weather during the winter, the athletes come out from the "xystus" for exercise. The "xysta" ought to be so constructed that there may be plantations between the two colonnades, or groves of plane trees, with walks laid out in them among the trees and resting places there, made of "opus signinum." Behind the "xystus" a stadium, so designed that great numbers of people may have plenty of room to look on at the contests between the athletes.

I have now described all that seemed necessary for the proper arrangement of things within the city walls.

CHAPTER XII

HARBOURS, BREAKWATERS, AND SHIPYARDS

1. THE subject of the usefulness of harbours is one which I must not omit, but must explain by what means ships are sheltered in them from storms. If their situation has natural advantages, with projecting capes or promontories which curve or return inwards by their natural conformation, such harbours are obviously of the greatest service. Round them, of course, colonnades or shipyards must be built, or passages from the colonnades to the business quarters, and towers must be set up on both sides, from which chains can be drawn across by machinery.

2. But if we have a situation without natural advantages, and unfit to shelter ships from storms, it is obvious that we must proceed as follows. If there is no river in the neighbourhood, but if there can be a roadstead on one side, then, let the advances be made from the other side by means of walls or embankments, and let the enclosing harbour be thus formed. Walls which are to be under water should be constructed as follows. Take the powder which comes from the country extending from Cumae to the promontory of Minerva, and mix it in the mortar trough in the proportion of two to one.

3. Then, in the place previously determined, a cofferdam, with its sides formed of oaken stakes with ties between them, is to be driven down into the water and firmly propped there; then, the lower surface inside, under the water, must be levelled off and

dredged, working from beams laid across; and finally, concrete from the mortar trough — the stuff having been mixed as prescribed above — must be heaped up until the empty space which was within the cofferdam is filled up by the wall. This, however, is possessed as a gift of nature by such places as have been described above.

But if by reason of currents or the assaults of the open sea the props cannot hold the cofferdam together, then, let a platform of the greatest possible strength be constructed, beginning on the ground itself or on a substructure; and let the platform be constructed with a level surface for less than half its extent, while the rest, which is close to the beach, slopes down and out.

4. Then, on the water's edge and at the sides of the platform, let marginal walls be constructed, about one and one half feet thick and brought up to a level with the surface above mentioned; next, let the sloping part be filled in with sand and levelled off with the marginal wall and the surface of the platform. Then, upon this level surface construct a block as large as is required, and when it is finished, leave it for not less than two months to dry. Then, cut away the marginal wall which supports the sand. Thus, the sand will be undermined by the waves, and this will cause the block to fall into the sea. By this method, repeated as often as necessary, an advance into the water can be made.

5. But in places where this powder is not found, the following method must be employed. A cofferdam with double sides, composed of charred stakes fastened together with ties, should be constructed in the appointed place, and clay in wicker baskets made of swamp rushes should be packed in among the props. After this has been well packed down and filled in as closely as possible, set up your water-screws, wheels, and drums, and let the space now bounded by the enclosure be emptied and dried. Then, dig out the bottom within the enclosure. If it proves to be of earth, it must be cleared out and dried till you come to solid bottom and for a space wider than the wall which is to be built upon it,

and then filled in with masonry consisting of rubble, lime, and sand.

6. But if the place proves to be soft, the bottom must be staked with piles made of charred alder or olive wood, and then filled in with charcoal as has been prescribed in the case of the foundations of theatres and the city wall. Finally, build the wall of dimension stone, with the bond stones as long as possible, so that particularly the stones in the middle may be held together by the joints. Then, fill the inside of the wall with broken stone or masonry. It will thus be possible for even a tower to be built upon it.

7. When all this is finished, the general rule for shipyards will be to build them facing the north. Southern exposures from their heat produce rot, the wood worm, shipworms, and all sorts of other destructive creatures, and strengthen and keep them alive. And these buildings must by no means be constructed of wood, for fear of fire. As for their size, no definite limit need be set, but they must be built to suit the largest type of ship, so that if even larger ships are hauled up, they may find plenty of room there.

I have described in this book the construction and completion of all that I could remember as necessary for general use in the public places of cities. In the following book I shall consider private houses, their conveniences, and symmetrical proportions.

# BOOK VI

BOOK VI

INTRODUCTION

1. It is related of the Socratic philosopher Aristippus that, being shipwrecked and cast ashore on the coast of the Rhodians, he observed geometrical figures drawn thereon, and cried out to his companions: "Let us be of good cheer, for I see the traces of man." With that he made for the city of Rhodes, and went straight to the gymnasium. There he fell to discussing philosophical subjects, and presents were bestowed upon him, so that he could not only fit himself out, but could also provide those who accompanied him with clothing and all other necessaries of life. When his companions wished to return to their country, and asked him what message he wished them to carry home, he bade them say this: that children ought to be provided with property and resources of a kind that could swim with them even out of a shipwreck.

2. These are indeed the true supports of life, and neither Fortune's adverse gale, nor political revolution, nor ravages of war can do them any harm. Developing the same idea, Theophrastus, urging men to acquire learning rather than to put their trust in money, states the case thus: "The man of learning is the only person in the world who is neither a stranger when in a foreign land, nor friendless when he has lost his intimates and relatives; on the contrary, he is a citizen of every country, and can fearlessly look down upon the troublesome accidents of fortune. But he who thinks himself entrenched in defences not of learning but of luck, moves in slippery paths, struggling through life unsteadily and insecurely."

3. And Epicurus, in much the same way, says that the wise owe little to fortune; all that is greatest and essential is under the direction of the thinking power of the mind and the understanding. Many other philosophers have said the same thing. Likewise the

poets who wrote the ancient comedies in Greek have expressed the same sentiments in their verses on the stage: for example, Eucrates, Chionides, Aristophanes, and with them Alexis in particular, who says that the Athenians ought to be praised for the reason that, while the laws of all Greeks require the maintenance of parents by their children, the laws of the Athenians require this only in the case of those who have educated their children in the arts. All the gifts which fortune bestows she can easily take away; but education, when combined with intelligence, never fails, but abides steadily on to the very end of life.

4. Hence, I am very much obliged and infinitely grateful to my parents for their approval of this Athenian law, and for having taken care that I should be taught an art, and that of a sort which cannot be brought to perfection without learning and a liberal education in all branches of instruction. Thanks, therefore, to the attention of my parents and the instruction given by my teachers, I obtained a wide range of knowledge, and by the pleasure which I take in literary and artistic subjects, and in the writing of treatises, I have acquired intellectual possessions whose chief fruits are these thoughts: that superfluity is useless, and that not to feel the want of anything is true riches. There may be some people, however, who deem all this of no consequence, and think that the wise are those who have plenty of money. Hence it is that very many, in pursuit of that end, take upon themselves impudent assurance, and attain notoriety and wealth at the same time.

5. But for my part, Caesar, I have never been eager to make money by my art, but have gone on the principle that slender means and a good reputation are preferable to wealth and disrepute. For this reason, only a little celebrity has followed; but still, my hope is that, with the publication of these books, I shall become known even to posterity. And it is not to be wondered at that I am so generally unknown. Other architects go about and ask for opportunities to practise their profession; but I have been taught by my instructors that it is the proper thing to undertake a charge only after being asked, and not to ask for it; since a gentleman will

blush with shame at petitioning for a thing that arouses suspicion. It is in fact those who can grant favours that are courted, not those who receive them. What are we to think must be the suspicions of a man who is asked to allow his private means to be expended in order to please a petitioner? Must he not believe that the thing is to be done for the profit and advantage of that individual?

6. Hence it was that the ancients used to entrust their work in the first place to architects of good family, and next inquired whether they had been properly educated, believing that one ought to trust in the honour of a gentleman rather than in the assurance of impudence. And the architects themselves would teach none but their own sons or kinsmen, and trained them to be good men, who could be trusted without hesitation in matters of such importance.

But when I see that this grand art is boldly professed by the uneducated and the unskilful, and by men who, far from being acquainted with architecture, have no knowledge even of the carpenter's trade, I can find nothing but praise for those householders who, in the confidence of learning, are emboldened to build for themselves. Their judgment is that, if they must trust to inexperienced persons, it is more becoming to them to use up a good round sum at their own pleasure than at that of a stranger.

7. Nobody, therefore, attempts to practise any other art in his own home — as, for instance, the shoemaker's, or the fuller's, or any other of the easier kinds — but only architecture, and this is because the professionals do not possess the genuine art but term themselves architects falsely. For these reasons I have thought proper to compose most carefully a complete treatise on architecture and its principles, believing that it will be no unacceptable gift to all the world. In the fifth book I have said what I had to say about the convenient arrangement of public works; in this I shall set forth the theoretical principles and the symmetrical proportions of private houses.

CHAPTER I

ON CLIMATE AS DETERMINING THE STYLE OF THE HOUSE

1. IF our designs for private houses are to be correct, we must at the outset take note of the countries and climates in which they are built. One style of house seems appropriate to build in Egypt, another in Spain, a different kind in Pontus, one still different in Rome, and so on with lands and countries of other characteristics. This is because one part of the earth is directly under the sun's course, another is far away from it, while another lies midway between these two. Hence, as the position of the heaven with regard to a given tract on the earth leads naturally to different characteristics, owing to the inclination of the circle of the zodiac and the course of the sun, it is obvious that designs for houses ought similarly to conform to the nature of the country and to diversities of climate.

2. In the north, houses should be entirely roofed over and sheltered as much as possible, not in the open, though having a warm exposure. But on the other hand, where the force of the sun is great in the southern countries that suffer from heat, houses must be built more in the open and with a northern or northeastern exposure. Thus we may amend by art what nature, if left to herself, would mar. In other situations, also, we must make modifications to correspond to the position of the heaven and its effects on climate.

3. These effects are noticeable and discernible not only in things in nature, but they also are observable in the limbs and bodies of entire races. In places on which the sun throws out its heat in moderation, it keeps human bodies in their proper condition, and where its path is very close at hand, it parches them up, and burns out and takes away the proportion of moisture which they ought to possess. But, on the other hand, in the cold re-

gions that are far away from the south, the moisture is not drawn out by hot weather, but the atmosphere is full of dampness which diffuses moisture into the system, and makes the frame larger and the pitch of the voice deeper. This is also the reason why the races that are bred in the north are of vast height, and have fair complexions, straight red hair, grey eyes, and a great deal of blood, owing to the abundance of moisture and the coolness of the atmosphere.

4. On the contrary, those that are nearest to the southern half of the axis, and that lie directly under the sun's course, are of lower stature, with a swarthy complexion, hair curling, black eyes, strong legs, and but little blood on account of the force of the sun. Hence, too, this poverty of blood makes them over-timid to stand up against the sword, but great heat and fevers they can endure without timidity, because their frames are bred up in the raging heat. Hence, men that are born in the north are rendered over-timid and weak by fever, but their wealth of blood enables them to stand up against the sword without timidity.

5. The pitch of the voice is likewise different and varying in quality with different nations, for the following reasons. The terminating points east and west on the level of the earth, where the upper and lower parts of the heaven are divided, seem to lie in a naturally balanced circle which mathematicians call the Horizon. Keeping this idea definitely in mind, if we imagine a line drawn from the northern side of the circumference (N) to the side which lies above the southern half of the axis (S), and from here another line obliquely up to the pivot at the summit, beyond the stars composing the Great Bear (the pole star P), we shall doubtless see that we have in the heaven a triangular figure like that of the musical instrument which the Greeks call the "sambuca."

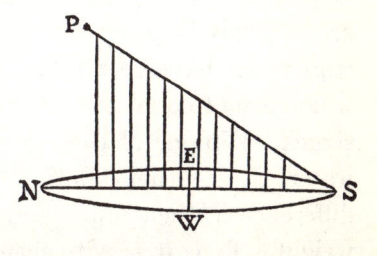

6. And so, under the space which is nearest to the pivot at the bottom, off the southern portions of the line of the axis, are found nations that on account of the slight altitude of the heaven above them, have shrill and very high-pitched voices, like the string nearest to the angle in the musical instrument. Next in order come other nations as far as the middle of Greece, with lower elevations of the voice; and from this middle point they go on in regular order up to the extreme north, where, under high altitudes, the vocal utterance of the inhabitants is, under natural laws, produced in heavier tones. Thus it is obvious that the system of the universe as a whole is, on account of the inclination of the heaven, composed in a most perfect harmony through the temporary power of the sun.

7. The nations, therefore, that lie midway between the pivots at the southern and the northern extremities of the axis, converse in a voice of middle pitch, like the notes in the middle of a musical scale; but, as we proceed towards the north, the distances to the heaven become greater, and so the nations there, whose vocal utterance is reduced by the moisture to the "hypatès" and to "proslambanomenon," are naturally obliged to speak in heavier tones. In the same way, as we proceed from the middle point to the south, the voices of the nations there correspond in extreme height of pitch and in shrillness to the "paranetès" and "netès."

8. That it is a fact that things are made heavier from being in places naturally moist, and higher pitched from places that are hot, may be proved from the following experiment. Take two cups which have been baked in the same oven for an equal time, which are of equal weight, and which give the same note when struck. Dip one of them into water and, after taking it out of water, strike them both. This done, there will be a great difference in their notes, and the cups can no longer be equal in weight. Thus it is with men: though born in the same general form and under the same all-embracing heaven, yet in some of them, on account of the heat in their country, the voice strikes

the air on a high note, while in others, on account of abundance of moisture, the quality of tones produced is very heavy.

9. Further, it is owing to the rarity of the atmosphere that southern nations, with their keen intelligence due to the heat, are very free and swift in the devising of schemes, while northern nations, being enveloped in a dense atmosphere, and chilled by moisture from the obstructing air, have but a sluggish intelligence. That this is so, we may see from the case of snakes. Their movements are most active in hot weather, when they have got rid of the chill due to moisture, whereas at the winter solstice, and in winter weather, they are chilled by the change of temperature, and rendered torpid and motionless. It is therefore no wonder that man's intelligence is made keener by warm air and duller by cold.

10. But although southern nations have the keenest wits, and are infinitely clever in forming schemes, yet the moment it comes to displaying valour, they succumb because all manliness of spirit is sucked out of them by the sun. On the other hand, men born in cold countries are indeed readier to meet the shock of arms with great courage and without timidity, but their wits are so slow that they will rush to the charge inconsiderately and inexpertly, thus defeating their own devices. Such being nature's arrangement of the universe, and all these nations being allotted temperaments which are lacking in due moderation, the truly perfect territory, situated under the middle of the heaven, and having on each side the entire extent of the world and its countries, is that which is occupied by the Roman people.

11. In fact, the races of Italy are the most perfectly constituted in both respects — in bodily form and in mental activity to correspond to their valour. Exactly as the planet Jupiter is itself temperate, its course lying midway between Mars, which is very hot, and Saturn, which is very cold, so Italy, lying between the north and the south, is a combination of what is found on each side, and her preëminence is well regulated and indisputable. And so by her wisdom she breaks the courageous onsets of the

barbarians, and by her strength of hand thwarts the devices of the southerners. Hence, it was the divine intelligence that set the city of the Roman people in a peerless and temperate country, in order that it might acquire the right to command the whole world.

12. Now if it is a fact that countries differ from one another, and are of various classes according to climate, so that the very nations born therein naturally differ in mental and physical conformation and qualities, we cannot hesitate to make our houses suitable in plan to the peculiarities of nations and races, since we have the expert guidance of nature herself ready to our hand.

I have now set forth the peculiar characteristics of localities, so far as I could note them, in the most summary way, and have stated how we ought to make our houses conform to the physical qualities of nations, with due regard to the course of the sun and to climate. Next I shall treat the symmetrical proportions of the different styles of houses, both as wholes and in their separate parts.

CHAPTER II

SYMMETRY, AND MODIFICATIONS IN IT TO SUIT THE SITE

1. THERE is nothing to which an architect should devote more thought than to the exact proportions of his building with reference to a certain part selected as the standard. After the standard of symmetry has been determined, and the proportionate dimensions adjusted by calculations, it is next the part of wisdom to consider the nature of the site, or questions of use or beauty, and modify the plan by diminutions or additions in such a manner that these diminutions or additions in the symmetrical relations may be seen to be made on correct principles, and without detracting at all from the effect.

2. The look of a building when seen close at hand is one thing, on a height it is another, not the same in an enclosed place, still

different in the open, and in all these cases it takes much judgment to decide what is to be done. The fact is that the eye does not always give a true impression, but very often leads the mind to form a false judgment. In painted scenery, for example, columns may appear to jut out, mutules to project, and statues to be standing in the foreground, although the picture is of course perfectly flat. Similarly with ships, the oars when under the water are straight, though to the eye they appear to be broken. To the point where they touch the surface of the sea they look straight, as indeed they are, but when dipped under the water they emit from their bodies undulating images which come swimming up through the naturally transparent medium to the surface of the water, and, being there thrown into commotion, make the oars look broken.

3. Now whether this appearance is due to the impact of the images, or to the effusion of the rays from the eye, as the physicists hold, in either case it is obvious that the vision may lead us to false impressions.

4. Since, therefore, the reality may have a false appearance, and since things are sometimes represented by the eyes as other than they are, I think it certain that diminutions or additions should be made to suit the nature or needs of the site, but in such fashion that the buildings lose nothing thereby. These results, however, are also attainable by flashes of genius, and not only by mere science.

5. Hence, the first thing to settle is the standard of symmetry, from which we need not hesitate to vary. Then, lay out the ground lines of the length and breadth of the work proposed, and when once we have determined its size, let the construction follow this with due regard to beauty of proportion, so that the beholder may feel no doubt of the eurythmy of its effect. I must now tell how this may be brought about, and first I will speak of the proper construction of a cavaedium.

CHAPTER III

PROPORTIONS OF THE PRINCIPAL ROOMS

1. There are five different styles of cavaedium, termed according to their construction as follows: Tuscan, Corinthian, tetrastyle, displuviate, and testudinate.

In the Tuscan, the girders that cross the breadth of the atrium have crossbeams on them, and valleys sloping in and running from the angles of the walls to the angles formed by the beams, and the rainwater falls down along the rafters to the roof-opening (compluvium) in the middle.

In the Corinthian, the girders and roof-opening are constructed on these same principles, but the girders run in from the side walls, and are supported all round on columns.

In the tetrastyle, the girders are supported at the angles by columns, an arrangement which relieves and strengthens the girders; for thus they have themselves no great span to support, and they are not loaded down by the crossbeams.

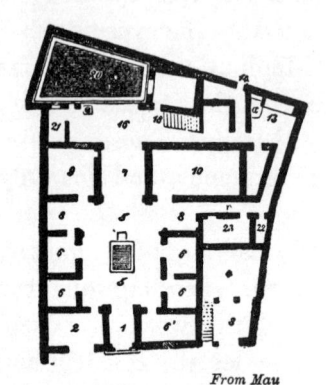

From Mau
THE HOUSE OF THE SURGEON, POMPEII
Illustrating the Tuscan Atrium

1. Fauces
2, 3. Shops
4. Storage
5. Atrium
6. Chambers
7. Tablinum
8. Alae
9, 10. Dining Rooms
13. Kitchen, *a*, hearth
14. Rear Entrance
16. Portico
18. Stairs to rooms over the rear of the house
20. Garden

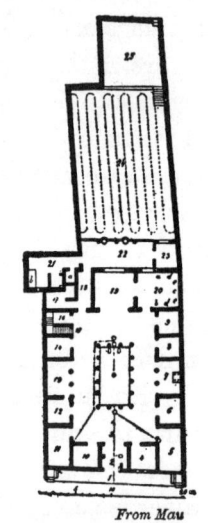

From Mau
HOUSE OF EPIDIUS RUFUS AT POMPEII
Illustrating Corinthian Atrium

2. In the displuviate, there are beams which slope outwards, supporting the roof and throwing the rainwater off. This style is suitable chiefly in winter residences, for its roof-opening, being high up, is not an obstruction to the light of the dining rooms. It is, however, very troublesome to keep in repair, because the pipes, which are intended to hold the water that comes dripping down the walls all round, cannot take it quickly enough as it runs down from the channels, but get too full and run over, thus spoiling the woodwork and the walls of houses of this style.

The testudinate is employed where the span is not great, and where large rooms are provided in upper stories.

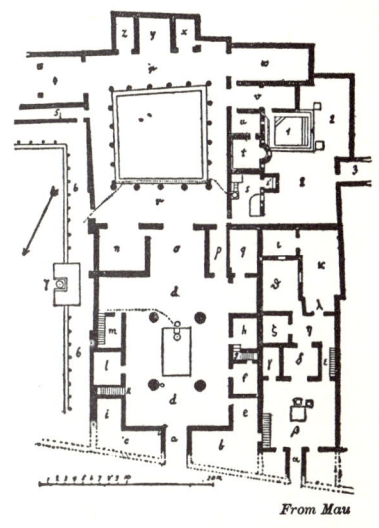

From Mau

HOUSE OF THE SILVER WEDDING AT POMPEII

Illustrating the Tetrastyle Atrium

a. fauces
d. tetrastyle atrium
n. dining room
o. tablinum
p. audron
r. peristyle
w. summer dining room

3. In width and length, atriums are designed according to three classes. The first is laid out by dividing the length into five parts and giving three parts to the width; the second, by dividing it into three parts and assigning two parts to the width; the third, by using the width to describe a square figure with equal sides, drawing a diagonal line in this square, and giving the atrium the length of this diagonal line.

4. Their height up to the girders should be one fourth less than their width, the rest being the proportion assigned to the ceiling and the roof above the girders.

The alae, to the right and left, should have a width equal to one third of the length of the atrium, when that is from thirty to forty feet long. From forty to fifty feet, divide the length by three and one half, and give the alae the result. When it is from fifty to sixty feet in length, devote one fourth of the length to the alae. From sixty to eighty feet, divide the length by four and one half and let the result be the width of the alae. From eighty feet to one hundred feet, the length divided into five parts will produce the right width for the alae. Their lintel beams should be placed high enough to make the height of the alae equal to their width.

5. The tablinum should be given two thirds of the width of the atrium when the latter is twenty feet wide. If it is from thirty to forty feet, let half the width of the atrium be devoted to the tablinum. When it is from forty to sixty feet, divide the width into five parts and let two of these be set apart for the tablinum. In the case of smaller atriums, the symmetrical proportions cannot be the same as in larger. For if, in the case of the smaller, we employ the proportion that belong to the larger, both tablina and alae must be unserviceable, while if, in the case of the larger, we employ the proportions of the smaller, the rooms mentioned will be huge monstrosities. Hence, I have thought it best to describe exactly their respective proportionate sizes, with a view both to convenience and to beauty.

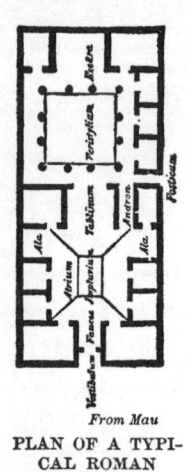

6. The height of the tablinum at the lintel should be one eighth more than its width. Its ceiling should exceed this height by one third of the width. The fauces in the case of smaller atriums should be two thirds, and in the case of larger one half the width of the tablinum. Let the busts of ancestors with their ornaments be set up at a height corresponding to the width of the alae. The proportionate width and height of doors may be settled, if they are Doric, in the Doric manner, and if Ionic, in the Ionic manner, according to the rules of symmetry which have been given about portals in the fourth book. In the roof-opening let

From Mau
PLAN OF A TYPI-
CAL ROMAN
HOUSE

THE PERISTYLE OF THE HOUSE OF THE VETTII AT POMPEII

an aperture be left with a breadth of not less than one fourth nor more than one third the width of the atrium, and with a length proportionate to that of the atrium.

7. Peristyles, lying athwart, should be one third longer than they are deep, and their columns as high as the colonnades are wide. Intercolumniations of peristyles should be not less than three nor more than four times the thickness of the columns. If the columns of the peristyle are to be made in the Doric style, take the modules which I have given in the fourth book, on the Doric order, and arrange the columns with reference to these modules and to the scheme of the triglyphs.

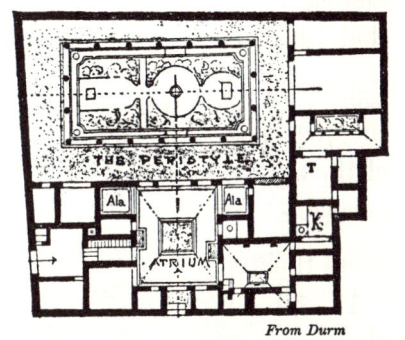

PLAN OF THE HOUSE OF THE VETTII, POMPEII
From Durm

8. Dining rooms ought to be twice as long as they are wide. The height of all oblong rooms should be calculated by adding together their measured length and width, taking one half of this total, and using the result for the height. But in the case of exedrae or square oeci, let the height be brought up to one and one half times the width. Picture galleries, like exedrae, should be constructed of generous dimensions. Corinthian and tetrastyle oeci, as well as those termed Egyptian, should have the same symmetrical proportions in width and length as the dining rooms described above, but, since they have columns in them, their dimensions should be ampler.

9. The following will be the distinction between Corinthian and Egyptian oeci: the Corinthian have single tiers of columns, set either on a podium or on the ground, with architraves over them and coronae either of woodwork or of stucco, and carved vaulted ceilings above the coronae. In the Egyptian there are architraves over the columns, and joists laid thereon from the architraves to the surrounding walls, with a floor in the upper

story to allow of walking round under the open sky. Then, above the architrave and perpendicularly over the lower tier of columns, columns one fourth smaller should be imposed. Above their architraves and ornaments are decorated ceilings, and the upper columns have windows set in between them. Thus the Egyptian are not like Corinthian dining rooms, but obviously resemble basilicas.

10. There are also, though not customary in Italy, the oeci which the Greeks call Cyzicene. These are built with a northern exposure and generally command a view of gardens, and have folding doors in the middle. They are also so long and so wide that two sets of dining couches, facing each other, with room to pass round them, can be placed therein. On the right and left they have windows which open like folding doors, so that views of the garden may be had from the dining couches through the opened windows. The height of such rooms is one and one half times their width.

11. All the above-mentioned symmetrical relations should be observed, in these kinds of buildings, that can be observed without embarrassment caused by the situation. The windows will be an easy matter to arrange if they are not darkened by high walls; but in cases of confined space, or when there are other unavoidable obstructions, it will be permissible to make diminutions or additions in the symmetrical relations, — with ingenuity and acuteness, however, so that the result may be not unlike the beauty which is due to true symmetry.

CHAPTER IV

THE PROPER EXPOSURES OF THE DIFFERENT ROOMS

1. WE shall next explain how the special purposes of different rooms require different exposures, suited to convenience and to the quarters of the sky. Winter dining rooms and bathrooms should have a southwestern exposure, for the reason that they

need the evening light, and also because the setting sun, facing them in all its splendour but with abated heat, lends a gentler warmth to that quarter in the evening. Bedrooms and libraries ought to have an eastern exposure, because their purposes require the morning light, and also because books in such libraries will not decay. In libraries with southern exposures the books are ruined by worms and dampness, because damp winds come up, which breed and nourish the worms, and destroy the books with mould, by spreading their damp breath over them.

2. Dining rooms for Spring and Autumn to the east; for when the windows face that quarter, the sun, as he goes on his career from over against them to the west, leaves such rooms at the proper temperature at the time when it is customary to use them. Summer dining rooms to the north, because that quarter is not, like the others, burning with heat during the solstice, for the reason that it is unexposed to the sun's course, and hence it always keeps cool, and makes the use of the rooms both healthy and agreeable. Similarly with picture galleries, embroiderers' work rooms, and painters' studios, in order that the fixed light may permit the colours used in their work to last with qualities unchanged.

CHAPTER V

HOW THE ROOMS SHOULD BE SUITED TO THE STATION OF THE OWNER

1. AFTER settling the positions of the rooms with regard to the quarters of the sky, we must next consider the principles on which should be constructed those apartments in private houses which are meant for the householders themselves, and those which are to be shared in common with outsiders. The private rooms are those into which nobody has the right to enter without an invitation, such as bedrooms, dining rooms, bathrooms, and all others used for the like purposes. The common are those which any of the people have a perfect right to enter, even without an invita-

tion: that is, entrance courts, cavaedia, peristyles, and all intended for the like purpose. Hence, men of everyday fortune do not need entrance courts, tablina, or atriums built in grand style, because such men are more apt to discharge their social obligations by going round to others than to have others come to them.

2. Those who do business in country produce must have stalls and shops in their entrance courts, with crypts, granaries, storerooms, and so forth in their houses, constructed more for the purpose of keeping the produce in good condition than for ornamental beauty.

For capitalists and farmers of the revenue, somewhat comfortable and showy apartments must be constructed, secure against robbery; for advocates and public speakers, handsomer and more roomy, to accommodate meetings; for men of rank who, from holding offices and magistracies, have social obligations to their fellow-citizens, lofty entrance courts in regal style, and most spacious atriums and peristyles, with plantations and walks of some extent in them, appropriate to their dignity. They need also libraries, picture galleries, and basilicas, finished in a style similar to that of great public buildings, since public councils as well as private law suits and hearings before arbitrators are very often held in the houses of such men.

3. If, therefore, houses are planned on these principles to suit different classes of persons, as prescribed in my first book, under the subject of Propriety, there will be no room for criticism; for they will be arranged with convenience and perfection to suit every purpose. The rules on these points will hold not only for houses in town, but also for those in the country, except that in town atriums are usually next to the front door, while in country seats peristyles come first, and then atriums surrounded by paved colonnades opening upon palaestrae and walks.

I have now set forth the rules for houses in town so far as I could describe them in a summary way. Next I shall state how farmhouses may be arranged with a view to convenience in use, and shall give the rules for their construction.

CHAPTER VI

THE FARMHOUSE

1. In the first place, inspect the country from the point of view of health, in accordance with what is written in my first book, on the building of cities, and let your farmhouses be situated accordingly. Their dimensions should depend upon the size of the farm and the amount of produce. Their courtyards and the dimensions thereof should be determined by the number of cattle and the number of yokes of oxen that will need to be kept therein. Let the kitchen be placed on the warmest side of the courtyard, with the stalls for the oxen adjoining, and their cribs facing the kitchen fire and the eastern quarter of the sky, for the reason that oxen facing the light and the fire do not get rough-coated. Even peasants wholly without knowledge of the quarters of the sky believe that oxen ought to face only in the direction of the sunrise.

2. Their stalls ought to be not less than ten nor more than fifteen feet wide, and long enough to allow not less than seven feet for each yoke. Bathrooms, also, should adjoin the kitchen; for in this situation it will not take long to get ready a bath in the country.

Let the pressing room, also,

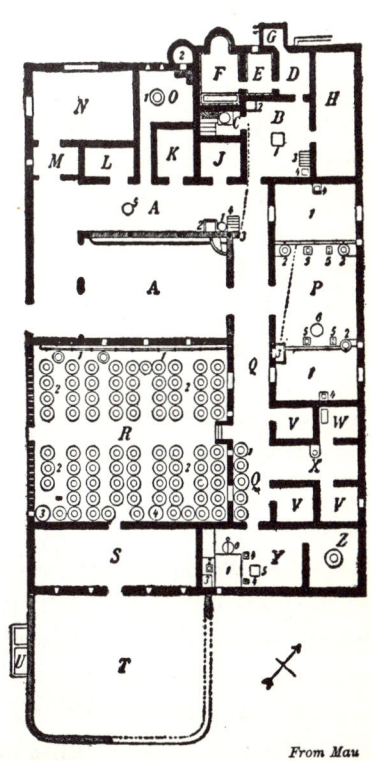

From Mau

THE VILLA RUSTICA AT BOSCOREALE NEAR POMPEII

A. Court. *B.* Kitchen. *C–F.* Baths. *H.* Stable. *J.* Toolroom. *K, L, V, V.* Bedrooms. *N.* Dining Room. *M.* Anteroom. *O.* Bakery. *P.* Room with two winepresses. *Q.* Corridor. *R.* Court for fermentation of wine. *S.* Barn. *T.* Threshing-floor. *Y.* Room with oil press.

be next to the kitchen; for in this situation it will be easy to deal with the fruit of the olive. Adjoining it should be the wine room with its windows lighted from the north. In a room with windows on any other quarter so that the sun can heat it, the heat will get into the wine and make it weak.

3. The oil room must be situated so as to get its light from the south and from warm quarters; for oil ought not to be chilled, but should be kept thin by gentle heat. In dimensions, oil rooms should be built to accommodate the crop and the proper number of jars, each of which, holding about one hundred and twenty gallons, must take up a space four feet in diameter. The pressing room itself, if the pressure is exerted by means of levers and a beam, and not worked by turning screws, should be not less than forty feet long, which will give the lever man a convenient amount of space. It should be not less than sixteen feet wide, which will give the men who are at work plenty of free space to do the turning conveniently. If two presses are required in the place, allow twenty-four feet for the width.

4. Folds for sheep and goats must be made large enough to allow each animal a space of not less than four and a half, nor more than six feet. Rooms for grain should be set in an elevated position and with a northern or north-eastern exposure. Thus the grain will not be able to heat quickly, but, being cooled by the wind, keeps a long time. Other exposures produce the corn weevil and the other little creatures that are wont to spoil the grain. To the stable should be assigned the very warmest place in the farmhouse, provided that it is not exposed to the kitchen fire; for when draught animals are stabled very near a fire, their coats get rough.

5. Furthermore, there are advantages in building cribs apart from the kitchen and in the open, facing the east; for when the oxen are taken over to them on early winter mornings in clear weather, their coats get sleeker as they take their fodder in the sunlight. Barns for grain, hay, and spelt, as well as bakeries, should be built apart from the farmhouse, so that farmhouses

may be better protected against danger from fire. If something more refined is required in farmhouses, they may be constructed on the principles of symmetry which have been given above in the case of town houses, provided that there is nothing in such buildings to interfere with their usefulness on a farm.

6. We must take care that all buildings are well lighted, but this is obviously an easier matter with those which are on country estates, because there can be no neighbour's wall to interfere, whereas in town high party walls or limited space obstruct the light and make them dark. Hence we must apply the following test in this matter. On the side from which the light should be obtained let a line be stretched from the top of the wall that seems to obstruct the light to the point at which it ought to be introduced, and if a considerable space of open sky can be seen when one looks up above that line, there will be no obstruction to the light in that situation.

7. But if there are timbers in the way, or lintels, or upper stories, then, make the opening higher up and introduce the light in this way. And as a general rule, we must arrange so as to leave places for windows on all sides on which a clear view of the sky can be had, for this will make our buildings light. Not only in dining rooms and other rooms for general use are windows very necessary, but also in passages, level or inclined, and on stairs; for people carrying burdens too often meet and run against each other in such places.

I have now set forth the plans used for buildings in our native country so that they may be clear to builders. Next, I shall describe summarily how houses are planned in the Greek fashion, so that these also may be understood.

CHAPTER VII

THE GREEK HOUSE

1. THE Greeks, having no use for atriums, do not build them, but make passage-ways for people entering from the front door,

not very wide, with stables on one side and doorkeepers' rooms on the other, and shut off by doors at the inner end. This place between the two doors is termed in Greek θυρωρεῖον. From it one enters the peristyle. This peristyle has colonnades on three sides, and on the side facing the south it has two antae, a considerable distance apart, carrying an architrave, with a recess for a distance one third less than the space between the antae. This space is called by some writers "prostas," by others "pastas."

2. Hereabouts, towards the inner side, are the large rooms in which mistresses of houses sit with their wool-spinners. To the right and left of the prostas there are chambers, one of which is called the "thalamos," the other the "amphithalamos." All round the colonnades are dining rooms for everyday use, chambers, and rooms for the slaves. This part of the house is termed "gynaeconitis."

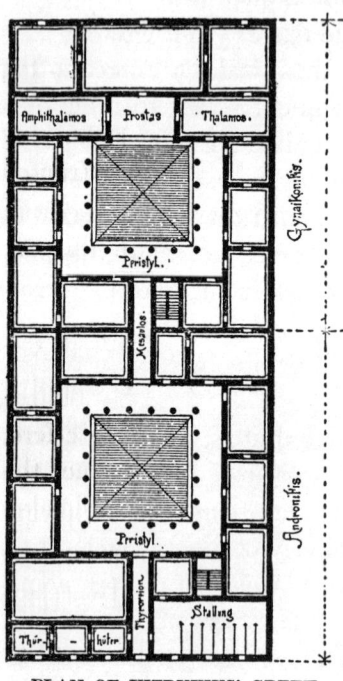

PLAN OF VITRUVIUS' GREEK HOUSE ACCORDING TO BECKER

3. In connexion with these there are ampler sets of apartments with more sumptuous peristyles, surrounded by four colonnades of equal height, or else the one which faces the south has higher columns than the others. A peristyle that has one such higher colonnade is called a Rhodian peristyle. Such apartments have fine entrance courts with imposing front doors of their own; the colonnades of the peristyles are decorated with polished stucco in relief and plain, and with coffered ceilings of woodwork; off the colonnades that face the north they have Cyzicene dining rooms and picture galleries; to the east, libraries; exedrae to the

west; and to the south, large square rooms of such generous dimensions that four sets of dining couches can easily be arranged in them, with plenty of room for serving and for the amusements.

4. Men's dinner parties are held in these large rooms; for it was not the practice, according to Greek custom, for the mistress of the house to be present. On the contrary, such peristyles are called the men's apartments, since in them the men can stay without interruption from the women. Furthermore, small sets of apartments are built to the right and left, with front doors of their own and suitable dining rooms and chambers, so that guests from abroad need not be shown into the peristyles, but rather into such guests' apartments. For when the Greeks became more luxurious, and their circumstances more opulent, they began to provide dining rooms, chambers, and store-rooms of provisions for their guests from abroad, and on the first day they would invite them to dinner, sending them on the next chickens, eggs, vegetables, fruits, and other country produce. This is why artists called pictures representing the things which were sent to guests "xenia." Thus, too, the heads of families, while being entertained abroad, had the feeling that they were not away from home, since they enjoyed privacy and freedom in such guests' apartments.

5. Between the two peristyles and the guests' apartments are the passage-ways called "mesauloe," because they are situated midway between two courts; but our people called them "andrones."

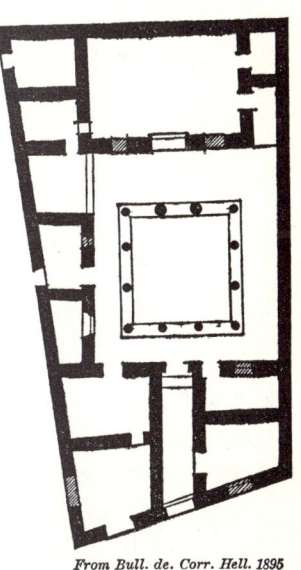

From Bull. de. Corr. Hell. 1895
GREEK HOUSE AT DELOS

This, however, is a very strange fact, for the term does not fit either the Greek or the Latin use of it. The Greeks call the large rooms in which men's dinner parties are usually held ἀνδρῶνες, because women do not go there. There are other similar instances as in the case of "xystus," "prothyrum," "telamones," and some others of the sort. As a Greek term, ξυστός means a colonnade of large dimensions in which athletes exercise in the winter time. But our people apply the term "xysta" to uncovered walks,

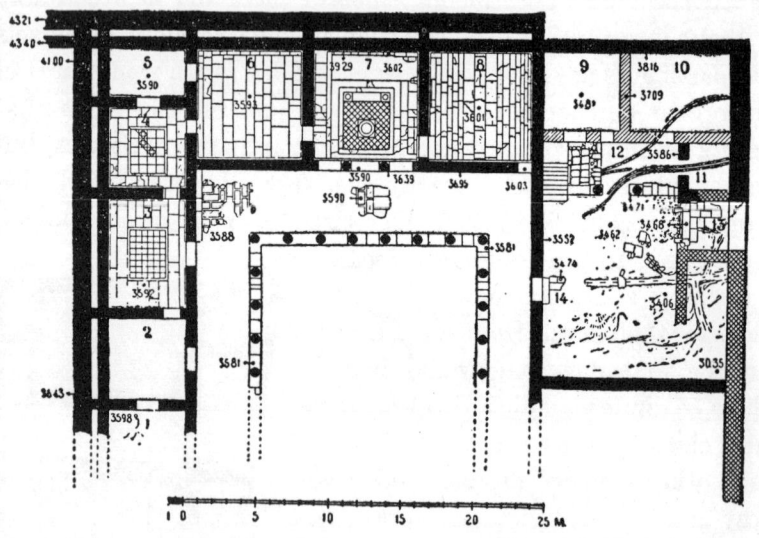

From Mitt. d. Deutsch. Arch. Inst.
GREEK HOUSE DISCOVERED AT PERGAMUM IN 1903
13. Prothyron.   7. Tablinum.

which the Greeks call παραδρομίδες. Again, πρόθυρα means in Greek the entrance courts before the front doors; we, however, use the term "prothyra" in the sense of the Greek διάθυρα.

6. Again, figures in the form of men supporting mutules or coronae, we term "telamones" — the reasons why or wherefore they are so called are not found in any story — but the Greeks name them ἄτλαντες. For Atlas is described in story as holding up the firmament because, through his vigorous intelligence and ingenuity, he was the first to cause men to be taught about the courses of the sun and moon, and the laws governing the revolutions of all the constellations. Consequently, in recognition of

this benefaction, painters and sculptors represent him as holding up the firmament, and the Atlantides, his daughters, whom we call "Vergiliae" and the Greeks Πλειάδες, are consecrated in the firmament among the constellations.

7. All this, however, I have not set forth for the purpose of changing the usual terminology or language, but I have thought that it should be explained so that it may be known to scholars.

I have now explained the usual ways of planning houses both in the Italian fashion and according to the practices of the Greeks, and have described, with regard to their symmetry, the proportions of the different classes. Having, therefore, already written of their beauty and propriety, I shall next explain, with reference to durability, how they may be built to last to a great age without defects.

CHAPTER VIII

ON FOUNDATIONS AND SUBSTRUCTURES

1. Houses which are set level with the ground will no doubt last to a great age, if their foundations are laid in the manner which we have explained in the earlier books, with regard to city walls and theatres. But if underground rooms and vaults are intended, their foundations ought to be thicker than the walls which are to be constructed in the upper part of the house, and the walls, piers, and columns of the latter should be set perpendicularly over the middle of the foundation walls below, so that they may have solid bearing; for if the load of the walls or columns rests on the middle of spans, they can have no permanent durability.

2. It will also do no harm to insert posts between lintels and sills where there are piers or antae; for where the lintels and beams have received the load of the walls, they may sag in the middle, and gradually undermine and destroy the walls. But

when there are posts set up underneath and wedged in there, they prevent the beams from settling and injuring such walls.

3. We must also manage to discharge the load of the walls by means of archings composed of voussoirs with joints radiating to the centre. For when arches with voussoirs are sprung from the ends of beams, or from the bearings of lintels, in the first place they will discharge the load and the wood will not sag; secondly, if in course of time the wood becomes at all defective, it can easily be replaced without the construction of shoring.

4. Likewise in houses where piers are used in the construction, when there are arches composed of voussoirs with joints radiating to the centre, the outermost piers at these points must be made broader than the others, so that they may have the strength to resist when the wedges, under the pressure of the load of the walls, begin to press along their joints towards the centre, and thus to thrust out the abutments. Hence, if the piers at the ends are of large dimensions, they will hold the voussoirs together, and make such works durable.

5. Having taken heed in these matters to see that proper attention is paid to them, we must also be equally careful that all walls are perfectly vertical, and that they do not lean forward anywhere. Particular pains, too, must be taken with substructures, for here an endless amount of harm is usually done by the earth used as filling. This cannot always remain of the same weight that it usually has in summer, but in winter time it increases in weight and bulk by taking up a great deal of rain water, and then it bursts its enclosing walls and thrusts them out.

6. The following means must be taken to provide against such a defect. First, let the walls be given a thickness proportionate to the amount of filling; secondly, build counterforts or buttresses at the same time as the wall, on the outer side, at distances from each other equivalent to what is to be the height of the substructure and with the thickness of the substructure. At the bottom let them run out to a distance corresponding to the thickness that has been determined for the substructure, and then gradu-

CHAP. VIII] FOUNDATIONS 191

ally diminish in extent so that at the surface their projection is equal to the thickness of the wall of the building.

7. Furthermore, inside, to meet the mass of earth, there should be saw-shaped constructions attached to the wall, the single

RETAINING WALLS
(From the edition of Vitruvius by Fra Giocondo, Venice 1511)

teeth extending from the wall for a distance equivalent to what is to be the height of the substructure, and the teeth being constructed with the same thickness as the wall. Then at the outermost angles take a distance inwards, from the inside of the angle, equal to the height of the substructure, and mark it off on each side; from these marks build up a diagonal structure and from the middle of it a second, joined on to the angle of the wall. With this arrangement, the teeth and diagonal structures will not allow the filling to thrust with all its force against the wall, but will check and distribute the pressure.

8. I have now shown how buildings can be constructed without defects, and the way to take precautions against the occurrence

of them. As for replacing tiles, roof timbers, and rafters, we need not be so particular about them as about the parts just mentioned, because they can easily be replaced, however defective they may become. Hence, I have shown by what methods the parts which are not considered solid can be rendered durable, and how they are constructed.

9. As for the kind of material to be used, this does not depend upon the architect, for the reason that all kinds of materials are not found in all places alike, as has been shown in the first book. Besides, it depends on the owner whether he desires to build in brick, or rubble work, or dimension stone. Consequently the question of approving any work may be considered under three heads: that is, delicacy of workmanship, sumptuousness, and design. When it appears that a work has been carried out sumptuously, the owner will be the person to be praised for the great outlay which he has authorized; when delicately, the master workman will be approved for his execution; but when proportions and symmetry lend it an imposing effect, then the glory of it will belong to the architect.

10. Such results, however, may very well be brought about when he allows himself to take the advice both of workmen and of laymen. In fact, all kinds of men, and not merely architects, can recognize a good piece of work, but between laymen and the latter there is this difference, that the layman cannot tell what it is to be like without seeing it finished, whereas the architect, as soon as he has formed the conception, and before he begins the work, has a definite idea of the beauty, the convenience, and the propriety that will distinguish it.

I have now described as clearly as I could what I thought necessary for private houses, and how to build them. In the following book I shall treat of the kinds of polished finish employed to make them elegant, and durable without defects to a great age.

BOOK VII

BOOK VII

INTRODUCTION

1. It was a wise and useful provision of the ancients to transmit their thoughts to posterity by recording them in treatises, so that they should not be lost, but, being developed in succeeding generations through publication in books, should gradually attain in later times, to the highest refinement of learning. And so the ancients deserve no ordinary, but unending thanks, because they did not pass on in envious silence, but took care that their ideas of every kind should be transmitted to the future in their writings.

2. If they had not done so, we could not have known what deeds were done in Troy, nor what Thales, Democritus, Anaxagoras, Xenophanes, and the other physicists thought about nature, and what rules Socrates, Plato, Aristotle, Zeno, Epicurus, and other philosophers laid down for the conduct of human life; nor would the deeds and motives of Croesus, Alexander, Darius, and other kings have been known, unless the ancients had compiled treatises, and published them in commentaries to be had in universal remembrance with posterity.

3. So, while they deserve our thanks, those, on the contrary, deserve our reproaches, who steal the writings of such men and publish them as their own; and those also, who depend in their writings, not on their own ideas, but who enviously do wrong to the works of others and boast of it, deserve not merely to be blamed, but to be sentenced to actual punishment for their wicked course of life. With the ancients, however, it is said that such things did not pass without pretty strict chastisement. What the results of their judgments were, it may not be out of place to set forth as they are transmitted to us.

4. The kings of the house of Attalus having established, under the influence of the great charms of literature, an excellent

library at Pergamus to give pleasure to the public, Ptolemy also was aroused with no end of enthusiasm and emulation into exertions to make a similar provision with no less diligence at Alexandria. Having done so with the greatest care, he felt that this was not enough without providing for its increase and development, for which he sowed the seed. He established public contests in honour of the Muses and Apollo, and appointed prizes and honours for victorious authors in general, as is done in the case of athletes.

5. These arrangements having been made, and the contests being at hand, it became necessary to select literary men as judges to decide them. The king soon selected six of the citizens, but could not so easily find a proper person to be the seventh. He therefore turned to those who presided over the library, and asked whether they knew anybody who was suitable for the purpose. Then they told him that there was one Aristophanes who was daily engaged in reading through all the books with the greatest enthusiasm and the greatest care. Hence, when the gathering for the contests took place, and separate seats were set apart for the judges, Aristophanes was summoned with the rest, and sat down in the place assigned to him.

6. A group of poets was first brought in to contend, and, as they recited their compositions, the whole audience by its applause showed the judges what it approved. So, when they were individually asked for their votes, the six agreed, and awarded the first prize to the poet who, as they observed, had most pleased the multitude, and the second to the one who came next. But Aristophanes, on being asked for his vote, urged that the poet who had least pleased the audience should be declared to be the first.

7. As the king and the entire assembly showed great indignation, he arose, and asked and received permission to speak. Silence being obtained, he stated that only one of them — his man — was a poet, and that the rest had recited things not their own; furthermore, that judges ought to give their approval, not to

INTRODUCTION 197

thefts, but to original compositions. The people were amazed, and the king hesitated, but Aristophanes, trusting to his memory, had a vast number of volumes brought out from bookcases which he specified, and, by comparing them with what had been recited, obliged the thieves themselves to make confession. So, the king gave orders that they should be accused of theft, and after condemnation sent them off in disgrace; but he honoured Aristophanes with the most generous gifts, and put him in charge of the library.

8. Some years later, Zoilus, who took the surname of Homeromastix, came from Macedonia to Alexandria and read to the king his writings directed against the Iliad and Odyssey. Ptolemy, seeing the father of poets and captain of all literature abused in his absence, and his works, to which all the world looked up in admiration, disparaged by this person, made no rejoinder, although he thought it an outrage. Zoilus, however, after remaining in the kingdom some time, sank into poverty, and sent a message to the king, requesting that something might be bestowed upon him.

9. But it is said that the king replied, that Homer, though dead a thousand years ago, had all that time been the means of livelihood for many thousands of men; similarly, a person who laid claim to higher genius ought to be able to support not one man only, but many others. And in short, various stories are told about his death, which was like that of one found guilty of parricide. Some writers have said that he was crucified by Philadelphus; others that he was stoned at Chios; others again that he was thrown alive upon a funeral pyre at Smyrna. Whichever of these forms of death befell him, it was a fitting punishment and his just due; for one who accuses men that cannot answer and show, face to face, what was the meaning of their writings, obviously deserves no other treatment.

10. But for my part, Caesar, I am not bringing forward the present treatise after changing the titles of other men's books and inserting my own name, nor has it been my plan to win approbation by finding fault with the ideas of another. On the con-

trary, I express unlimited thanks to all the authors that have in the past, by compiling from antiquity remarkable instances of the skill shown by genius, provided us with abundant materials of different kinds. Drawing from them as it were water from springs, and converting them to our own purposes, we find our powers of writing rendered more fluent and easy, and, relying upon such authorities, we venture to produce new systems of instruction.

11. Hence, as I saw that such beginnings on their part formed an introduction suited to the nature of my own purpose, I set out to draw from them, and to go somewhat further.

In the first place Agatharcus, in Athens, when Aeschylus was bringing out a tragedy, painted a scene, and left a commentary about it. This led Democritus and Anaxagoras to write on the same subject, showing how, given a centre in a definite place, the lines should naturally correspond with due regard to the point of sight and the divergence of the visual rays, so that by this deception a faithful representation of the appearance of buildings might be given in painted scenery, and so that, though all is drawn on a vertical flat façade, some parts may seem to be withdrawing into the background, and others to be standing out in front.

12. Afterwards Silenus published a book on the proportions of Doric structures; Theodorus, on the Doric temple of Juno which is in Samos; Chersiphron and Metagenes, on the Ionic temple at Ephesus which is Diana's; Pytheos, on the Ionic fane of Minerva which is at Priene; Ictinus and Carpion, on the Doric temple of Minerva which is on the acropolis of Athens; Theodorus the Phocian, on the Round Building which is at Delphi; Philo, on the proportions of temples, and on the naval arsenal which was [1] at the port of Peiraeus; Hermogenes, on the Ionic temple of Diana which is at Magnesia, a pseudodipteral, and on that of Father Bacchus at Teos, a monopteral; Arcesius, on the Corinthian proportions, and on the Ionic temple of Aesculapius at Tralles, which it is said that he built with his own hands; on

[1] Codd. *fuerat.*

the Mausoleum, Satyrus and Pytheos who were favoured with the greatest and highest good fortune.

13. For men whose artistic talents are believed to have won them the highest renown for all time, and laurels forever green, devised and executed works of supreme excellence in this building. The decoration and perfection of the different façades were undertaken by different artists in emulation with each other: Leochares, Bryaxis, Scopas, Praxiteles, and, as some think, Timotheus; and the distinguished excellence of their art made that building famous among the seven wonders of the world.

14. Then, too, many less celebrated men have written treatises on the laws of symmetry, such as Nexaris, Theocydes, Demophilus, Pollis, Leonidas, Silanion, Melampus, Sarnacus, and Euphranor; others again on machinery, such as Diades, Archytas, Archimedes, Ctesibius, Nymphodorus, Philo of Byzantium, Diphilus, Democles, Charias, Polyidus, Pyrrus, and Agesistratus. From their commentaries I have gathered what I saw was useful for the present subject, and formed it into one complete treatise, and this principally, because I saw that many books in this field had been published by the Greeks, but very few indeed by our countrymen. Fuficius, in fact, was the first to undertake to publish a book on this subject. Terentius Varro, also, in his work "On the Nine Sciences" has one book on architecture, and Publius Septimius, two.

15. But to this day nobody else seems to have bent his energies to this branch of literature, although there have been, even among our fellow-citizens in old times, great architects who could also have written with elegance. For instance, in Athens, the architects Antistates, Callaeschrus, Antimachides, and Pormus laid the foundations when Peisistratus began the temple of Olympian Jove, but after his death they abandoned the undertaking, on account of political troubles. Hence it was that when, about four hundred years later, King Antiochus promised to pay the expenses of that work, the huge cella, the surrounding columns in dipteral arrangement, and the architraves and other orna-

ments, adjusted according to the laws of symmetry, were nobly constructed with great skill and supreme knowledge by Cossutius, a citizen of Rome. Moreover, this work has a name for its grandeur, not only in general, but also among the select few.

16. There are, in fact, four places possessing temples embellished with workmanship in marble that causes them to be mentioned in a class by themselves with the highest renown. To their great excellence and the wisdom of their conception they owe their place of esteem in the ceremonial worship of the gods. First there is the temple of Diana at Ephesus, in the Ionic style, undertaken by Chersiphron of Gnosus and his son Metagenes, and said to have been finished later by Demetrius, who was himself a slave of Diana, and by Paeonius the Milesian. At Miletus, the temple of Apollo, also Ionic in its proportions, was the undertaking of the same Paeonius and of the Ephesian Daphnis. At Eleusis, the cella of Ceres and Proserpine, of vast size, was completed to the roof by Ictinus in the Doric style, but without exterior columns and with plenty of room for the customary sacrifices.

17. Afterwards, however, when Demetrius of Phalerum was master of Athens, Philo set up columns in front before the temple, and made it prostyle. Thus, by adding an entrance hall, he gave the initiates more room, and imparted the greatest dignity to the building. Finally, in Athens, the temple of the Olympion with its dimensions on a generous scale, and built in the Corinthian style and proportions, is said to have been constructed, as written above, by Cossutius, no commentary by whom has been found. But Cossutius is not the only man by whom we should like to have writings on our subject. Another is Gaius Mucius, who, having great knowledge on which to rely, completed the cella, columns, and entablature of the Marian temple of Honour and Valour, in symmetrical proportions according to the accepted rules of the art. If this building had been of marble, so that besides the refinement of its art it possessed the dignity coming from

magnificence and great outlay, it would be reckoned among the first and greatest of works.

18. Since it appears, then, that our architects in the old days, and a good many even in our own times, have been as great as those of the Greeks, and nevertheless only a few of them have published treatises, I resolved not to be silent, but to treat the different topics methodically in different books. Hence, since I have given an account of private houses in the sixth book, in this, which is the seventh in order, I shall treat of polished finishings and the methods of giving them both beauty and durability.

CHAPTER I

FLOORS

1. FIRST I shall begin with the concrete flooring, which is the most important of the polished finishings, observing that great pains and the utmost precaution must be taken to ensure its durability. If this concrete flooring is to be laid level with the ground, let the soil be tested to see whether it is everywhere solid, and if it is, level it off and upon it lay the broken stone with its bedding. But if the floor is either wholly or partly filling, it should be rammed down hard with great care. In case a wooden framework is used, however, we must see that no wall which does not reach up to the top of the house is constructed under the floor. Any wall which is there should preferably fall short, so as to leave the wooden planking above it an unsupported span. If a wall comes up solid, the unyielding nature of its solid structure must, when the joists begin to dry, or to sag and settle, lead to cracks in the floor on the right and left along the line of wall.

2. We must also be careful that no common oak gets in with the winter oak boards, for as soon as common oak boards get damp, they warp and cause cracks in floors. But if there is no winter oak, and necessity drives, for lack of this it seems advisable to use common oak boards cut pretty thin; for the less thick they are, the more easily they can be held in place by being nailed on. Then, at the ends of every joist, nail on two boards so that they shall not be able to warp and stick up at the edges. As for Turkey oak or beech or ash, none of them can last to a great age.

When the wooden planking is finished, cover it with fern, if there is any, otherwise with straw, to protect the wood from being hurt by the lime.

3. Then, upon this lay the bedding, composed of stones not smaller than can fill the hand. After the bedding is laid, mix the

broken stone in the proportions, if it is new, of three parts to one of lime; if it is old material used again, five parts may answer to two in the mixture. Next, lay the mixture of broken stone, bring on your gangs, and beat it again and again with wooden beetles into a solid mass, and let it be not less than three quarters of a foot in thickness when the beating is finished. On this lay the nucleus, consisting of pounded tile mixed with lime in the proportions of three parts to one, and forming a layer not less than six digits thick. On top of the nucleus, the floor, whether made of cut slips or of cubes, should be well and truly laid by rule and level.

4. After it is laid and set at the proper inclination, let it be rubbed down so that, if it consists of cut slips, the lozenges, or triangles, or squares, or hexagons may not stick up at different levels, but be all jointed together on the same plane with one another; if it is laid in cubes, so that all the edges may be level; for the rubbing down will not be properly finished unless all the edges are on the same level plane. The herring-bone pattern, made of Tibur burnt brick, must also be carefully finished, so as to be without gaps or ridges sticking up, but all flat and rubbed down to rule. When the rubbing down is completely finished by means of the smoothing and polishing processes, sift powdered marble on top, and lay on a coating of lime and sand.

5. In the open air, specially adapted kinds of floors must be made, because their framework, swelling with dampness, or shrinking from dryness, or sagging and settling, injures the floors by these changes; besides, the frost and rime will not let them go unhurt. Hence, if necessity drives, we must proceed as follows in order to make them as free from defects as possible. After finishing the plank flooring, lay a second plank flooring over it at right angles, and nail it down so as to give double protection to the framework. Then, mix with new broken stone one third the quantity of pounded tile, and let lime be added to the mixture in the mortar trough in the proportion of two parts to five.

6. Having made the bedding, lay on this mixture of broken

stone, and let it be not less than a foot thick when the beating is finished. Then, after laying the nucleus, as above described, construct the floor of large cubes cut about two digits each way, and let it have an inclination of two digits for every ten feet. If it is well put together and properly rubbed down, it will be free from all flaws. In order that the mortar in the joints may not suffer from frosts, drench it with oil-dregs every year before winter begins. Thus treated, it will not let the hoarfrost enter it.

7. If, however, it seems needful to use still greater care, lay two-foot tiles, jointed together in a bed of mortar, over the broken stone, with little channels of one finger's breadth cut in the faces of all the joints. Connect these channels and fill them with a mixture of lime and oil; then, rub the joints hard and make them compact. Thus, the lime sticking in the channels will harden and solidify into a mass, and so prevent water or anything else from penetrating through the joints. After this layer is finished, spread the nucleus upon it, and work it down by beating it with rods. Upon this lay the floor, at the inclination above described, either of large cubes or burnt brick in herring-bone pattern, and floors thus constructed will not soon be spoiled.

CHAPTER II

THE SLAKING OF LIME FOR STUCCO

1. LEAVING the subject of floors, we must next treat of stucco work. This will be all right if the best lime, taken in lumps, is slaked a good while before it is to be used, so that if any lump has not been burned long enough in the kiln, it will be forced to throw off its heat during the long course of slaking in the water, and will thus be thoroughly burned to the same consistency. When it is taken not thoroughly slaked but fresh, it has little crude bits concealed in it, and so, when applied, it blisters. When such bits complete their slaking after they are on the building, they break up and spoil the smooth polish of the stucco.

2. But when the proper attention has been paid to the slaking, and greater pains have thus been employed in the preparation for the work, take a hoe, and apply it to the slaked lime in the mortar bed just as you hew wood. If it sticks to the hoe in bits, the lime is not yet tempered; and when the iron is drawn out dry and clean, it will show that the lime is weak and thirsty; but when the lime is rich and properly slaked, it will stick to the tool like glue, proving that it is completely tempered. Then get the scaffolding ready, and proceed to construct the vaultings in the rooms, unless they are to be decorated with flat coffered ceilings.

CHAPTER III

VAULTINGS AND STUCCO WORK

1. WHEN vaulting is required, the procedure should be as follows. Set up horizontal furring strips at intervals of not more than two feet apart, using preferably cypress, as fir is soon spoiled by decay and by age. Arrange these strips so as to form a curve, and make them fast to the joists of the floor above or to the roof, if it is there, by nailing them with many iron nails to ties fixed at intervals. These ties should be made of a kind of wood that neither decay nor time nor dampness can spoil, such as box, juniper, olive, oak, cypress, or any other similar wood except common oak; for this warps, and causes cracks in work in which it is used.

2. Having arranged the furring strips, take cord made of Spanish broom, and tie Greek reeds, previously pounded flat, to them in the required contour. Immediately above the vaulting spread some mortar made of lime and sand, to check any drops that may fall from the joists or from the roof. If a supply of Greek reed is not to be had, gather slender marsh reeds, and make them up with silk cord into bundles all of the same thickness and adjusted to the proper length, provided that the bundles are not more than two feet long between any two knots. Then tie them with cord

to the beams, as above described, and drive wooden pegs into them. Make all the other preparations as above described.

3. Having thus set the vaultings in their places and interwoven them, apply the rendering coat to their lower surface; then lay on the sand mortar, and afterwards polish it off with the powdered marble. After the vaultings have been polished, set the impost mouldings directly beneath them. These obviously ought to be made extremely slender and delicate, for when they are large, their weight carries them down, and they cannot support themselves. Gypsum should by no means be used in their composition, but powdered marble should be laid on uniformly, lest gypsum, by setting too quickly should keep the work from drying uniformly. We must also beware of the ancients' scheme for vaultings; for in their mouldings the soffits overhang very heavily, and are dangerous.

4. Some mouldings are flat, others in relief. In rooms where there has to be a fire or a good many lights, they should be flat, so that they can be wiped off more easily. In summer apartments and in exedrae where there is no smoke nor soot to hurt them, they should be made in relief. It is always the case that stucco, in the pride of its dazzling white, gathers smoke not only from its own house but also from others.

5. Having finished the mouldings, apply a very rough rendering coat to the walls, and afterwards, when the rendering coat gets pretty dry, spread upon it the layers of sand mortar, exactly adjusted in length to rule and line, in height to the plummet, and at the angles to the square. The stucco will thus present a faultless appearance for paintings. When it gets pretty dry, spread on a second coat and then a third. The better the foundation of sand mortar that is laid on, the stronger and more durable in its solidity will be the stucco.

6. When not less than three coats of sand mortar, besides the rendering coat, have been laid on, then, we must make the mixture for the layers of powdered marble, the mortar being so tempered that when mixed it does not stick to the trowel, but

the iron comes out freely and clean from the mortar trough. After this powdered marble has been spread on and gets dry, lay on a medium second coat. When that has been applied and well rubbed down, spread on a finer coat. The walls, being thus rendered solid by three coats of sand mortar and as many of marble, will not possibly be liable to cracks or to any other defect.

7. And further, such walls, owing to the solid foundation given by thorough working with polishing instruments, and the smoothness of it, due to the hard and dazzling white marble, will bring out in brilliant splendour the colours which are laid on at the same time with the polishing.

These colours, when they are carefully laid on stucco still wet, do not fade but are permanent. This is because the lime, having had its moisture burned out in the kiln, becomes porous and loses its strength, and its dryness makes it take up anything that may come in contact with it. On mixing with the seeds or elements that come from other substances, it forms a solid mass with them and, no matter what the constituent parts may then be, it must, obviously, on becoming dry, possess the qualities which are peculiar to its own nature.

8. Hence, stucco that is properly made does not get rough as time goes on, nor lose its colours when it is wiped off, unless they have been laid on with little care and after it is dry. So, when the stucco on walls is made as described above, it will have strength and brilliancy, and an excellence that will last to a great age. But when only one coat of sand mortar and one of fine marble have been spread on, its thin layer is easily cracked from want of strength, and from its lack of thickness it will not take on the brilliance, due to polishing, which it ought to have.

9. Just as a silver mirror that is formed of a thin plate reflects indistinctly and with a feeble light, while one that is substantially made can take on a very high polish, and reflects a brilliant and distinct image when one looks therein, so it is with stucco. When the stuff of which it is formed is thin, it not only cracks but also soon fades; when, however, it has a solid foundation of sand mor-

tar and of marble, thickly and compactly applied, it is not only brilliant after being subjected to repeated polishings, but also reflects from its surface a clear image of the beholder.

10. The Greek stucco-workers not only employ these methods to make their works durable, but also construct a mortar trough, mix the lime and sand in it, bring on a gang of men, and beat the stuff with wooden beetles, and do not use it until it has been thus vigorously worked. Hence, some cut slabs out of old walls and use them as panels, and the stucco of such panels and "reflectors" has projecting bevelled edges all round it.

11. But if stucco has to be made on "wattle and daub," where there must be cracks at the uprights and cross-sticks, because they must take in moisture when they are daubed with the mud, and cause cracks in the stucco when they dry and shrink, the following method will prevent this from happening. After the whole wall has been smeared with the mud, nail rows of reeds to it by means of "fly-nails," then spread on the mud a second time, and, if the first rows have been nailed with the shafts transverse, nail on a second set with the shafts vertical, and then, as above described, spread on the sand mortar, the marble, and the whole mass of stucco. Thus, the double series of reeds with their shafts crossing on the walls will prevent any chipping or cracking from taking place.

CHAPTER IV

ON STUCCO WORK IN DAMP PLACES, AND ON THE DECORATION OF DINING ROOMS

1. HAVING spoken of the method by which stucco work should be done in dry situations, I shall next explain how the polished finish is to be accomplished in places that are damp, in such a way that it can last without defects. First, in apartments which are level with the ground, apply a rendering coat of mortar, mixed with burnt brick instead of sand, to a height of about three feet above the floor, and then lay on the stucco so that those portions

of it may not be injured by the dampness. But if a wall is in a state of dampness all over, construct a second thin wall a little way from it on the inside, at a distance suited to circumstances, and in the space between these two walls run a channel, at a lower level than that of the apartment, with vents to the open air. Similarly, when the wall is brought up to the top, leave airholes there. For if the moisture has no means of getting out by vents at the bottom and at the top, it will not fail to spread all over the new wall. This done, apply a rendering coat of mortar made with burnt brick to this wall, spread on the layer of stucco, and polish it.

2. But if there is not room enough for the construction of a wall, make channels with their vents extending to the open air. Then lay two-foot tiles resting on the margin of the channel on one side, and on the other side construct a foundation of pillars for them, made of eight-inch bricks, on top of each of which the edges of two tiles may be supported, each pillar being not more than a hand's breadth distant from the wall. Then, above, set hooked tiles fastened to the wall from bottom to top, carefully covering the inner sides of them with pitch so that they will reject moisture. Both at the bottom and at the top above the vaulting they should have airholes.

3. Then, whitewash them with lime and water so that they will not reject the rendering coat of burnt brick. For, as they are dry from the loss of water burnt out in the kiln, they can neither take nor hold the rendering coat unless lime has been applied beneath it to stick the two substances together, and make them unite. After spreading the rendering coat upon this, apply layers of burnt brick mortar instead of sand mortar, and finish up all the rest in the manner described above for stucco work.

4. The decorations of the polished surfaces of the walls ought to be treated with due regard to propriety, so as to be adapted to their situations, and not out of keeping with differences in kind. In winter dining rooms, neither paintings on grand subjects nor delicacy of decoration in the cornice work of the vaultings is a

serviceable kind of design, because they are spoiled by the smoke from the fire and the constant soot from the lamps. In these rooms there should be panels above the dadoes, worked in black, and polished, with yellow ochre or vermilion blocks interposed between them. After the vaulting has been treated in the flat style, and polished, the Greek method of making floors for use in winter dining rooms may not be unworthy of one's notice, as being very inexpensive and yet serviceable.

5. An excavation is made below the level of the dining room to a depth of about two feet, and, after the ground has been rammed down, the mass of broken stones or the pounded burnt brick is spread on, at such an inclination that it can find vents in the drain. Next, having filled in with charcoal compactly trodden down, a mortar mixed of gravel, lime, and ashes is spread on to a depth of half a foot. The surface having been made true to rule and level, and smoothed off with whetstone, gives the look of a black pavement. Hence, at their dinner parties, whatever is poured out of the cups, or spirted from the mouth, no sooner falls than it dries up, and the servants who wait there do not catch cold from that kind of floor, although they may go barefoot.

CHAPTER V

THE DECADENCE OF FRESCO PAINTING

1. For the other apartments, that is, those intended to be used in Spring, Autumn, and Summer, as well as for atriums and peristyles, the ancients required realistic pictures of real things. A picture is, in fact, a representation of a thing which really exists or which can exist: for example, a man, a house, a ship, or anything else from whose definite and actual structure copies resembling it can be taken. Consequently the ancients who introduced polished finishings began by representing different kinds of marble slabs in different positions, and then cornices and blocks of yellow ochre arranged in various ways.

FRESCO PAINTING

2. Afterwards they made such progress as to represent the forms of buildings, and of columns, and projecting and overhanging pediments; in their open rooms, such as exedrae, on account of the size, they depicted the façades of scenes in the tragic, comic, or satyric style; and their walks, on account of the great length, they decorated with a variety of landscapes, copying the characteristics of definite spots. In these paintings there are harbours, promontories, seashores, rivers, fountains, straits, fanes, groves, mountains, flocks, shepherds; in some places there are also pictures designed in the grand style, with figures of the gods or detailed mythological episodes, or the battles at Troy, or the wanderings of Ulysses, with landscape backgrounds, and other subjects reproduced on similar principles from real life.

3. But those subjects which were copied from actual realities are scorned in these days of bad taste. We now have fresco paintings of monstrosities, rather than truthful representations of definite things. For instance, reeds are put in the place of columns, fluted appendages with curly leaves and volutes, instead of pediments, candelabra supporting representations of shrines, and on top of their pediments numerous tender stalks and volutes growing up from the roots and having human figures senselessly seated upon them; sometimes stalks having only half-length figures, some with human heads, others with the heads of animals.

4. Such things do not exist and cannot exist and never have existed. Hence, it is the new taste that has caused bad judges of poor art to prevail over true artistic excellence. For how is it possible that a reed should really support a roof, or a candelabrum a pediment with its ornaments, or that such a slender, flexible thing as a stalk should support a figure perched upon it, or that roots and stalks should produce now flowers and now half-length figures? Yet when people see these frauds, they find no fault with them but on the contrary are delighted, and do not care whether any of them can exist or not. Their understanding is darkened by decadent critical principles, so that it is not capable of giving

its approval authoritatively and on the principle of propriety to that which really can exist. The fact is that pictures which are unlike reality ought not to be approved, and even if they are technically fine, this is no reason why they should offhand be judged to be correct, if their subject is lacking in the principles of reality carried out with no violations.

5. For instance, at Tralles, Apaturius of Alabanda designed with skilful hand the scaena of the little theatre which is there called the ἐκκλησιαστήριον, representing columns in it and statues, Centaurs supporting the architraves, rotundas with round roofs on them, pediments with overhanging returns, and cornices ornamented with lions' heads, which are meant for nothing but the rainwater from the roofs, — and then on top of it all he made an episcaenium in which were painted rotundas, porticoes, half-pediments, and all the different kinds of decoration employed in a roof. The effect of high relief in this scaena was very attractive to all who beheld it, and they were ready to give their approval to the work, when Licymnius the mathematician came forward and said that (6.) the Alabandines were considered bright enough in all matters of politics, but that on account of one slight defect, the lack of the sense of propriety, they were believed to be unintelligent. "In their gymnasium the statues are all pleading causes, in their forum, throwing the discus, running, or playing ball. This disregard of propriety in the interchange of statues appropriate to different places has brought the state as a whole into disrepute. Let us then beware lest this scaena of Apaturius make Alabandines or Abderites of us. Which of you can have houses or columns or extensive pediments on top of his tiled roof? Such things are built above the floors, not above the tiled roofs. Therefore, if we give our approval to pictures of things which can have no reason for existence in actual fact, we shall be voluntarily associating ourselves with those communities which are believed to be unintelligent on account of just such defects."

7. Apaturius did not venture to make any answer, but removed

the scaena, altered it so that it conformed to reality, and gave satisfaction with it in its improved state. Would to God that Licymnius could come to life again and reform the present condition of folly and mistaken practices in fresco painting! However, it may not be out of place to explain why this false method prevails over the truth. The fact is that the artistic excellence which the ancients endeavoured to attain by working hard and taking pains, is now attempted by the use of colours and the brave show which they make, and expenditure by the employer prevents people from missing the artistic refinements that once lent authority to works.

8. For example, which of the ancients can be found to have used vermilion otherwise than sparingly, like a drug? But to-day whole walls are commonly covered with it everywhere. Then, too, there is malachite green, purple, and Armenian blue. When these colours are laid on, they present a brilliant appearance to the eye even although they are inartistically applied, and as they are costly, they are made exceptions in contracts, to be furnished by the employer, not by the contractor.

I have now sufficiently explained all that I could suggest for the avoidance of mistakes in stucco work. Next, I shall speak of the components as they occur to me, and first I shall treat of marble, since I spoke of lime at the beginning.

CHAPTER VI

MARBLE FOR USE IN STUCCO

MARBLE is not produced everywhere of the same kind. In some places the lumps are found to contain transparent grains like salt, and this kind when crushed and ground is extremely serviceable in stucco work. In places where this is not found, the broken bits of marble or "chips," as they are called, which marble-workers throw down as they work, may be crushed and ground and used in stucco after being sifted. In still other places

— for example, on the borderland of Magnesia and Ephesus — there are places where it can be dug out all ready to use, without the need of grinding or sifting, but as fine as any that is crushed and sifted by hand.

CHAPTER VII

NATURAL COLOURS

As for colours, some are natural products found in fixed places, and dug up there, while others are artificial compounds of different substances treated and mixed in proper proportions so as to be equally serviceable.

1. We shall first set forth the natural colours that are dug up as such, like yellow ochre, which is termed ὤχρα in Greek. This is found in many places, including Italy, but Attic, which was the best, is not now to be had because in the times when there were slaves in the Athenian silver mines, they would dig galleries underground in order to find the silver. Whenever a vein of ochre was found there, they would follow it up like silver, and so the ancients had a fine supply of it to use in the polished finishings of their stucco work.

2. Red earths are found in abundance in many places, but the best in only a few, for instance at Sinope in Pontus, in Egypt, in the Balearic islands of Spain, as well as in Lemnos, an island the enjoyment of whose revenues the Senate and Roman people granted to the Athenians.

3. Paraetonium white gets its name from the place where it is dug up. The same is the case with Melian white, because there is said to be a mine of it in Melos, one of the islands of the Cyclades.

4. Green chalk is found in numerous places, but the best at Smyrna. The Greeks call it θεοδοτεῖον, because this kind of chalk was first found on the estate of a person named Theodotus.

5. Orpiment, which is termed ἀρσενικόν in Greek, is dug up in Pontus. Sandarach, in many places, but the best is mined in Pontus close by the river Hypanis.

CHAPTER VIII

CINNABAR AND QUICKSILVER

1. I SHALL now proceed to explain the nature of cinnabar. It is said that it was first found in the Cilbian country belonging to Ephesus, and both it and its properties are certainly very strange. First, before getting to the vermilion itself by methods of treatment, they dig out what is called the clod, an ore like iron, but rather of a reddish colour and covered with a red dust. During the digging it sheds, under the blows of the tools, tear after tear of quicksilver, which is at once gathered up by the diggers.

2. When these clods have been collected, they are so full of moisture that they are thrown into an oven in the laboratory to dry, and the fumes that are sent up from them by the heat of the fire settle down on the floor of the oven, and are found to be quicksilver. When the clods are taken out, the drops which remain are so small that they cannot be gathered up, but they are swept into a vessel of water, and there they run together and combine into one. Four pints of it, when measured and weighed, will be found to be one hundred pounds.

3. If the quicksilver is poured into a vessel, and a stone weighing one hundred pounds is laid upon it, the stone swims on the surface, and cannot depress the liquid, nor break through, nor separate it. If we remove the hundred pound weight, and put on a scruple of gold, it will not swim, but will sink to the bottom of its own accord. Hence, it is undeniable that the gravity of a substance depends not on the amount of its weight, but on its nature.

4. Quicksilver is a useful thing for many purposes. For instance, neither silver nor copper can be gilded properly without it. And when gold has been woven into a garment, and the garment becomes worn out with age so that it is no longer respectable to use, the pieces of cloth are put into earthen pots, and burned up over a fire. The ashes are then thrown into water and

quicksilver added thereto. This attracts all the bits of gold, and makes them combine with itself. The water is then poured off, and the rest emptied into a cloth and squeezed in the hands, whereupon the quicksilver, being a liquid, escapes through the loose texture of the cloth, but the gold, which has been brought together by the squeezing, is found inside in a pure state.

CHAPTER IX

CINNABAR (*continued*)

1. I WILL now return to the preparation of vermilion. When the lumps of ore are dry, they are crushed in iron mortars, and repeatedly washed and heated until the impurities are gone, and the colours come. When the cinnabar has given up its quicksilver, and thus lost the natural virtues that it previously had, it becomes soft in quality and its powers are feeble.

2. Hence, though it keeps its colour perfectly when applied in the polished stucco finish of closed apartments, yet in open apartments, such as peristyles or exedrae or other places of the sort, where the bright rays of the sun and moon can penetrate, it is spoiled by contact with them, loses the strength of its colour, and turns black. Among many others, the secretary Faberius, who wished to have his house on the Aventine finished in elegant style, applied vermilion to all the walls of the peristyle; but after thirty days they turned to an ugly and mottled colour. He therefore made a contract to have other colours applied instead of vermilion.

3. But anybody who is more particular, and who wants a polished finish of vermilion that will keep its proper colour, should, after the wall has been polished and is dry, apply with a brush Pontic wax melted over a fire and mixed with a little oil; then after this he should bring the wax to a sweat by warming it and the wall at close quarters with charcoal enclosed in an iron vessel; and finally he should smooth it all off by rubbing it down with

a wax candle and clean linen cloths, just as naked marble statues are treated.

4. This process is termed γάνωσις in Greek. The protecting coat of Pontic wax prevents the light of the moon and the rays of the sun from licking up and drawing the colour out of such polished finishing.

The manufactories which were once at the mines of the Ephesians have now been transferred to Rome, because this kind of ore was later discovered in Spain. The clods are brought from the mines there, and treated in Rome by public contractors. These manufactories are between the temples of Flora and Quirinus.

5. Cinnabar is adulterated by mixing lime with it. Hence, one will have to proceed as follows, if one wishes to prove that it is unadulterated. Take an iron plate, put the cinnabar upon it, and lay it on the fire until the plate gets red hot. When the glowing heat makes the colour change and turn black, remove the plate from the fire, and if the cinnabar when cooled returns to its former colour, it will be proved to be unadulterated; but if it keeps the black colour, it will show that it has been adulterated.

6. I have now said all that I could think of about cinnabar. Malachite green is brought from Macedonia, and is dug up in the neighbourhood of copper mines. The names Armenian blue and India ink show in what places these substances are found.

CHAPTER X

ARTIFICIAL COLOURS. BLACK

1. I SHALL now pass to those substances which by artificial treatment are made to change their composition, and to take on the properties of colours; and first I shall treat of black, the use of which is indispensable in many works, in order that the fixed technical methods for the preparation of that compound may be known.

2. A place is built like a Laconicum, and nicely finished in marble, smoothly polished. In front of it, a small furnace is constructed with vents into the Laconicum, and with a stokehole that can be very carefully closed to prevent the flames from escaping and being wasted. Resin is placed in the furnace. The force of the fire in burning it compels it to give out soot into the Laconicum through the vents, and the soot sticks to the walls and the curved vaulting. It is gathered from them, and some of it is mixed and worked with gum for use as writing ink, while the rest is mixed with size, and used on walls by fresco painters.

3. But if these facilities are not at hand, we must meet the exigency as follows, so that the work may not be hindered by tedious delay. Burn shavings and splinters of pitch pine, and when they turn to charcoal, put them out, and pound them in a mortar with size. This will make a pretty black for fresco painting.

4. Again, if the lees of wine are dried and roasted in an oven, and then ground up with size and applied to a wall, the result will be a colour even more delightful than ordinary black; and the better the wine of which it is made, the better imitation it will give, not only of the colour of ordinary black, but even of that of India ink.

CHAPTER XI

BLUE. BURNT OCHRE

1. METHODS of making blue were first discovered in Alexandria, and afterwards Vestorius set up the making of it at Puzzuoli. The method of obtaining it from the substances of which it has been found to consist, is strange enough. Sand and the flowers of natron are brayed together so finely that the product is like meal, and copper is grated by means of coarse files over the mixture, like sawdust, to form a conglomerate. Then it is made into balls by rolling it in the hands and thus bound together for drying. The dry balls are put in an earthern jar, and the jars in

an oven. As soon as the copper and the sand grow hot and unite under the intensity of the fire, they mutually receive each other's sweat, relinquishing their peculiar qualities, and having lost their properties through the intensity of the fire, they are reduced to a blue colour.

2. Burnt ochre, which is very serviceable in stucco work, is made as follows. A clod of good yellow ochre is heated to a glow on a fire. It is then quenched in vinegar, and the result is a purple colour.

CHAPTER XII

WHITE LEAD, VERDIGRIS, AND ARTIFICIAL SANDARACH

1. It is now in place to describe the preparation of white lead and of verdigris, which with us is called "aeruca." In Rhodes they put shavings in jars, pour vinegar over them, and lay pieces of lead on the shavings; then they cover the jars with lids to prevent evaporation. After a definite time they open them, and find that the pieces of lead have become white lead. In the same way they put in plates of copper and make verdigris, which is called "aeruca."

2. White lead on being heated in an oven changes its colour on the fire, and becomes sandarach. This was discovered as the result of an accidental fire. It is much more serviceable than the natural sandarach dug up in mines.

CHAPTER XIII

PURPLE

1. I shall now begin to speak of purple, which exceeds all the colours that have so far been mentioned both in costliness and in the superiority of its delightful effect. It is obtained from a marine shellfish, from which is made the purple dye, which is as wonderful to the careful observer as anything else in nature;

for it has not the same shade in all the places where it is found, but is naturally qualified by the course of the sun.

2. That which is found in Pontus and Gaul is black, because those countries are nearest to the north. As one passes on from north to west, it is found of a bluish shade. Due east and west, what is found is of a violet shade. That which is obtained in southern countries is naturally red in quality, and therefore this is found in the island of Rhodes and in other such countries that are nearest to the course of the sun.

3. After the shellfish have been gathered, they are broken up with iron tools, the blows of which drive out the purple fluid like a flood of tears, and then it is prepared by braying it in mortars. It is called "ostrum" because it is taken from the shells of marine shellfish. On account of its saltness, it soon dries up unless it has honey poured over it.

CHAPTER XIV

SUBSTITUTES FOR PURPLE, YELLOW OCHRE, MALACHITE GREEN, AND INDIGO

1. PURPLE colours are also manufactured by dyeing chalk with madder root and with hysginum. Other colours are made from flowers. Thus, when fresco painters wish to imitate Attic yellow ochre, they put dried violets into a vessel of water, and heat them over a fire; then, when the mixture is ready, they pour it onto a linen cloth, and squeeze it out with the hands, catching the water which is now coloured by the violets, in a mortar. Into this they pour chalk and bray it, obtaining the colour of Attic yellow ochre.

2. They make a fine purple colour by treating bilberry in the same way and mixing it with milk. Those who cannot use malachite green on account of its dearness, dye blue with the plant called dyer's weed, and thus obtain a most vivid green. This is called dyer's malachite green. Again, for want of indigo, they dye Selinusian or anularian chalk with woad, which the Greeks call ἰσάτις, and make an imitation of indigo.

3. In this book I have written down, so far as I could recall them, the methods and means of attaining durability in polished finishings, how pictures that are appropriate should be made, and also the natural qualities of all the colours. And so, having prescribed in seven books the suitable principles which should govern the construction of all kinds of buildings, I shall treat in the next of water, showing how it may be found in places where it is wanting, by what method it may be conducted, and by what means its wholesomeness and fitness may be tested.

BOOK VIII

BOOK VIII

INTRODUCTION

1. Among the Seven Sages, Thales of Miletus pronounced for water as the primordial element in all things; Heraclitus, for fire; the priests of the Magi, for water and fire; Euripides, a pupil of Anaxagoras, and called by the Athenians "the philosopher of the stage," for air and earth. Earth, he held, was impregnated by the rains of heaven and, thus conceiving, brought forth the young of mankind and of all the living creatures in the world; whatever is sprung from her goes back to her again when the compelling force of time brings about a dissolution; and whatever is born of the air returns in the same way to the regions of the sky; nothing suffers annihilation, but at dissolution there is a change, and things fall back to the essential element in which they were before. But Pythagoras, Empedocles, Epicharmus, and other physicists and philosophers have set forth that the primordial elements are four in number: air, fire, earth, and water; and that it is from their coherence to one another under the moulding power of nature that the qualities of things are produced according to different classes.

2. And, in fact, we see not only that all which comes to birth is produced by them, but also that nothing can be nourished without their influence, nor grow, nor be preserved. The body, for example, can have no life without the flow of the breath to and fro, that is, unless an abundance of air flows in, causing dilations and contractions in regular succession. Without the right proportion of heat, the body will lack vitality, will not be well set up, and will not properly digest strong food. Again, without the fruits of the earth to nourish the bodily frame, it will be enfeebled, and so lose its admixture of the earthy element.

3. Finally, without the influence of moisture, living creatures will be bloodless and, having the liquid element sucked out of

them, will wither away. Accordingly the divine intelligence has not made what is really indispensable for man either hard to get or costly, like pearls, gold, silver, and so forth, the lack of which neither our body nor our nature feels, but has spread abroad, ready to hand through all the world, the things without which the life of mortals cannot be maintained. Thus, to take examples, suppose there is a deficiency of breath in the body, the air, to which is assigned the function of making up the deficiency, performs that service. To supply heat, the mighty sun is ready, and the invention of fire makes life more secure. Then again, the fruits of the earth, satisfying our desires with a more than sufficient store of food stuffs, support and maintain living beings with regular nourishment. Finally, water, not merely supplying drink but filling an infinite number of practical needs, does us services which make us grateful because it is gratis.

4. Hence, too, those who are clothed in priesthoods of the Egyptian orders declare that all things depend upon the power of the liquid element. So, when the waterpot is brought back to precinct and temple with water, in accordance with the holy rite, they throw themselves upon the ground and, raising their hands to heaven, thank the divine benevolence for its invention.

Therefore, since it is held by physicists and philosophers and priests that all things depend upon the power of water, I have thought that, as in the former seven books the rules for buildings have been set forth, in this I ought to write on the methods of finding water, on those special merits which are due to the qualities of localities, on the ways of conducting it, and how it may be tested in advance. For it is the chief requisite for life, for happiness, and for everyday use.

CHAPTER I

HOW TO FIND WATER

1. This will be easier if there are open springs of running water. But if there are no springs which gush forth, we must search for them underground, and conduct them together. The following test should be applied. Before sunrise, lie down flat in the place where the search is to be made, and placing the chin on the earth and supporting it there, take a look out over the country. In this way the sight will not range higher than it ought, the chin being immovable, but will range over a definitely limited height on the same level through the country. Then, dig in places where vapours are seen curling and rising up into the air. This sign cannot show itself in a dry spot.

2. Searchers for water must also study the nature of different localities; for those in which it is found are well defined. In clay the supply is poor, meagre, and at no great depth. It will not have the best taste. In fine gravel the supply is also poor, but it will be found at a greater depth. It will be muddy and not sweet. In black earth some slight drippings and drops are found that gather from the storms of winter and settle down in compact, hard places. They have the best taste. Among pebbles the veins found are moderate, and not to be depended upon. These, too, are extremely sweet. In coarse grained gravel and carbuncular sand the supply is surer and more lasting, and it has a good taste. In red tufa it is copious and good, if it does not run down through the fissures and escape. At the foot of mountains and in lava it is more plentiful and abundant, and here it is also colder and more wholesome. In flat countries the springs are salt, heavy-bodied, tepid, and ill-flavoured, excepting those which run underground from mountains, and burst forth in the middle of a plain, where, if protected by the shade of trees, their taste is equal to that of mountain springs.

3. In the kinds of soil described above, signs will be found growing, such as slender rushes, wild willows, alders, agnus castus trees, reeds, ivy, and other plants of the same sort that cannot spring up of themselves without moisture. But they are also accustomed to grow in depressions which, being lower than the rest of the country, receive water from the rains and the surrounding fields during the winter, and keep it for a comparatively long time on account of their holding power. These must not be trusted, but the search must be made in districts and soils, yet not in depressions, where those signs are found growing not from seed, but springing up naturally of themselves.

4. If the indications mentioned appear in such places, the following test should be applied. Dig out a place not less than three feet square and five feet deep, and put into it about sunset a bronze or leaden bowl or basin, whichever is at hand. Smear the inside with oil, lay it upside down, and cover the top of the excavation with reeds or green boughs, throwing earth upon them. Next day uncover it, and if there are drops and drippings in the vessel, the place will contain water.

5. Again, if a vessel made of unbaked clay be put in the hole, and covered in the same way, it will be wet when uncovered, and already beginning to go to pieces from dampness, if the place contains water. If a fleece of wool is placed in the excavation, and water can be wrung out of it on the following day, it will show that the place has a supply. Further, if a lamp be trimmed, filled with oil, lighted, and put in that place and covered up, and if on the next day it is not burnt out, but still contains some remains of oil and wick, and is itself found to be damp, it will indicate that the place contains water; for all heat attracts moisture. Again, if a fire is made in that place, and if the ground, when thoroughly warmed and burned, sends up a misty vapour from its surface, the place will contain water.

6. After applying these tests and finding the signs described above, a well must next be sunk in the place, and if a spring of water is found, more wells must be dug thereabouts,

and all conducted by means of subterranean channels into one place.

The mountains and districts with a northern exposure are the best spots in which to search, for the reason that springs are sweeter, more wholesome, and more abundant when found there. Such places face away from the sun's course, and the trees are thick in them, and the mountains, being themselves full of woods, cast shadows of their own, preventing the rays of the sun from striking uninterruptedly upon the ground and drying up the moisture.

7. The valleys among the mountains receive the rains most abundantly, and on account of the thick woods the snow is kept in them longer by the shade of the trees and mountains. Afterwards, on melting, it filters through the fissures in the ground, and thus reaches the very foot of the mountains, from which gushing springs come belching out.

But in flat countries, on the contrary, a good supply cannot be had. For however great it is, it cannot be wholesome, because, as there is no shade in the way, the intense force of the sun draws up and carries off the moisture from the flat plains with its heat, and if any water shows itself there, the lightest and purest and the delicately wholesome part of it is summoned away by the air, and dispersed to the skies, while the heaviest and the hard and unpleasant parts are left in springs that are in flat places.

CHAPTER II

RAINWATER

1. RAINWATER has, therefore, more wholesome qualities, because it is drawn from the lightest and most delicately pure parts of all the springs, and then, after being filtered through the agitated air, it is liquefied by storms and so returns to the earth. And rainfall is not abundant in the plains, but rather on the mountains or close to mountains, for the reason that the vapour which

is set in motion at sunrise in the morning, leaves the earth, and drives the air before it through the heaven in whatever direction it inclines; then, when once in motion, it has currents of air rushing after it, on account of the void which it leaves behind.

2. This air, driving the vapour everywhere as it rushes along, produces gales and constantly increasing currents by its mighty blasts. Wherever the winds carry the vapour which rolls in masses from springs, rivers, marshes, and the sea, it is brought together by the heat of the sun, drawn off, and carried upward in the form of clouds; then these clouds are supported by the current of air until they come to mountains, where they are broken up from the shock of the collision and the gales, turn into water on account of their own fulness and weight, and in that form are dispersed upon the earth.

3. That vapour, mists, and humidity come forth from the earth, seems due to the reason that it contains burning heat, mighty currents of air, intense cold, and a great quantity of water. So, as soon as the earth, which has cooled off during the night, is struck by the rays of the rising sun, and the winds begin to blow while it is yet dark, mists begin to rise upward from damp places. That the air when thoroughly heated by the sun can make vapours rise rolling up from the earth, may be seen by means of an example drawn from baths.

4. Of course there can be no springs above the vaultings of hot bathrooms, but the atmosphere in such rooms, becoming well warmed by the hot air from the furnaces, seizes upon the water on the floors, and takes it up to the curved vaultings and holds it up there, for the reason that hot vapour always pushes upwards. At first it does not let the moisture go, for the quantity is small; but as soon as it has collected a considerable amount, it cannot hold it up, on account of the weight, but sprinkles it upon the heads of the bathers. In the same way, when the atmospheric air feels the heat of the sun, it draws the moisture from all about, causes it to rise, and gathers it into clouds. For the earth gives out

moisture under the influence of heat just as a man's heated body emits sweat.

5. The winds are witnesses to this fact. Those that are produced and come from the coolest directions, the north and northeast winds, blow in blasts that are rarefied by the great dryness in the atmosphere, but the south wind and the others that assail us from the direction of the sun's course are very damp, and always bring rain, because they reach us from warm regions after being well heated there, and licking up and carrying off the moisture from the whole country, they pour it out on the regions in the north.

6. That this is the state of the case may be proved by the sources of rivers, the majority and the longest of which, as drawn and described in geographies of the world, are found to rise in the north. First in India, the Ganges and Indus spring from the Caucasus; in Syria, the Tigris and Euphrates; in Pontus in Asia, the Dnieper, Bug, and Don; in Colchis, the Phasis; in Gaul, the Rhone; in Celtica, the Rhine; on this side of the Alps, the Timavo and Po; in Italy, the Tiber; in Maurusia, which we call Mauretania, the Dyris, rising in the Atlas range and running westerly to Lake Heptagonus, where it changes its name and is called Agger; then from Lake Heptabolus it runs at the base of barren mountains, flowing southerly and emptying into the marsh called [1] ... It surrounds Meroë, which is a kingdom in southern Ethiopia, and from the marsh grounds there, winding round by the rivers Astansoba and Astoboa and a great many others, it passes through the mountains to the Cataract, and from there it dashes down, and passes to the north between Elephantis and Syene and the plains of Thebes into Egypt, where it is called the Nile.

7. That the source of the Nile is in Mauretania is known principally from the fact that there are other springs on the other side of the Atlas range flowing into the ocean to the west, and that ichneumons, crocodiles, and other animals and fishes of

---

[1] Here something is lost, as also in chapter III, sections 5 and 6.

like nature are found there, although there are no hippopotamuses.

8. Therefore, since in descriptions of the world it appears that all rivers of any size flow from the north, and since in the plains of Africa, which are exposed to the course of the sun in the south, the moisture is deeply hidden, springs not common, and rivers rare, it follows that the sources of springs which lie to the north or northeast are much better, unless they hit upon a place which is full of sulphur, alum, or asphalt. In this case they are completely changed, and flow in springs which have a bad smell and taste, whether the water is hot or cold.

9. The fact is, heat is not at all a property of water, but when a stream of cold water happens upon a hot place, it boils up, and issues through the fissures and out of the ground in a state of heat. This cannot last very long, but in a short time the water becomes cold. If it were naturally hot, it would not cool off and lose its heat. Its taste, however, and its smell and colour are not restored, because it has become saturated and compounded with these qualities on account of the rarity of its nature.

CHAPTER III

VARIOUS PROPERTIES OF DIFFERENT WATERS

1. THERE are, however, some hot springs that supply water of the best taste, which is so delightful to drink that one does not think with regret of the Fountain of the Muses or the Marcian aqueduct. These hot springs are produced naturally, in the following manner. When fire is kindled down beneath in alum or asphalt or sulphur, it makes the earth immediately over it very hot, and emits a glowing heat to the parts still farther above it, so that if there are any springs of sweet water found in the upper strata, they begin to boil in their fissures when they are met by this heat, and so they run out with their taste unimpaired.

2. And there are some cold springs that have a bad smell and

taste. They rise deep down in the lower strata, cross places which are on fire, and then are cooled by running a long distance through the earth, coming out above ground with their taste, smell, and colour spoiled; as, for instance, the river Albula on the road to Tivoli and the cold springs of Ardea, which have the same smell and are called sulphur springs, and others in similar places. Although they are cold, yet at first sight they seem to be hot for the reason that when they happen upon a burning spot deep down below, the liquid and the fire meet, and with a great noise at the collision they take in strong currents of air, and thus, swollen by a quantity of compressed wind, they come out at the springs in a constant state of ebullition. When such springs are not open but confined by rocks, the force of the air in them drives them up through the narrow fissures to the summits of hills.

3. Consequently those who think that they have excavated sources of springs at the height of such hills find themselves mistaken when they open up their excavations. Suppose a bronze vase filled not to the very lips, but containing two thirds of the quantity of water which forms its capacity, and with a cover placed upon it. When it is subjected to a very hot fire, the water must become thoroughly heated, and from the rarity of its nature it greatly expands by taking in the heat, so that it not only fills the vase but raises its cover by means of the currents of air in it, and swells and runs over. But if you take the cover off, the expanding forces are released into the open air, and the water settles down again to its proper level. So it is with the sources of springs. As long as they are confined in narrow channels, the currents of air in the water rush up in bubbles to the top, but as soon as they are given a wider outlet, they lose their air on account of the rarity peculiar to water, and so settle down and resume their proper level.

4. Every hot spring has healing properties because it has been boiled with foreign substances, and thus acquires a new useful quality. For example, sulphur springs cure pains in the sinews,

by warming up and burning out the corrupt humours of the body by their heat. Aluminous springs, used in the treatment of the limbs when enfeebled by paralysis or the stroke of any such malady, introduce warmth through the open pores, counteracting the chill by the opposite effect of their heat, and thus equably restoring the limbs to their former condition. Asphaltic springs, taken as purges, cure internal maladies.

5. There is also a kind of cold water containing natron, found for instance at Penne in the Vestine country, at Cutiliae, and at other similar places. It is taken as a purge and in passing through the bowels reduces scrofulous tumours. Copious springs are found where there are mines of gold, silver, iron, copper, lead, and the like, but they are very harmful. For they contain, like hot springs, sulphur, alum, asphalt, . . . and when it passes into the body in the form of drink, and spreading through the veins reaches the sinews and joints, it expands and hardens them. Hence the sinews, swelling with this expansion, are contracted in length and so give men the cramp or the gout, for the reason that their veins are saturated with very hard, dense, and cold substances.

6. There is also a sort of water which, since it contains . . . that are not perfectly clear, and it floats like a flower on the surface, in colour like purple glass. This may be seen particularly in Athens, where there are aqueducts from places and springs of that sort leading to the city and the port of Piraeus, from which nobody drinks, for the reason mentioned, but they use them for bathing and so forth, and·drink from wells, thus avoiding their unwholesomeness. At Troezen it cannot be avoided, because no other kind of water at all is found, except what the Cibdeli furnish, and so in that city all or most of the people have diseases of the feet. At the city of Tarsus in Cilicia is a river named Cydnus, in which gouty people soak their legs and find relief from pain.

7. There are also many other kinds of water which have peculiar properties; for example, the river Himera in Sicily, which,

after leaving its source, is divided into two branches. One flows in the direction of Etruria and has an exceedingly sweet taste on account of a sweet juice in the soil through which it runs; the other runs through a country where there are salt pits, and so it has a salt taste. At Paraetonium, and on the road to Ammon, and at Casius in Egypt there are marshy lakes which are so salt that they have a crust of salt on the surface. In many other places there are springs and rivers and lakes which are necessarily rendered salt because they run through salt pits.

8. Others flow through such greasy veins of soil that they are overspread with oil when they burst out as springs: for example, at Soli, a town in Cilicia, the river named Liparis, in which swimmers or bathers get anointed merely by the water. Likewise there is a lake in Ethiopia which anoints people who swim in it, and one in India which emits a great quantity of oil when the sky is clear. At Carthage is a spring that has oil swimming on its surface and smelling like sawdust from citrus wood, with which oil sheep are anointed. In Zacynthus and about Dyrrachium and Apollonia are springs which discharge a great quantity of pitch with their water. In Babylon, a lake of very great extent, called Lake Asphaltitis, has liquid asphalt swimming on its surface, with which asphalt and with burnt brick Semiramis built the wall surrounding Babylon. At Jaffa in Syria and among the Nomads in Arabia, are lakes of enormous size that yield very large masses of asphalt, which are carried off by the inhabitants thereabouts.

9. There is nothing marvellous in this, for quarries of hard asphalt are numerous there. So, when a quantity of water bursts its way through the asphaltic soil, it carries asphalt out with it, and after passing out of the ground, the water is separated and so rejects the asphalt from itself. Again, in Cappadocia on the road from Mazaca to Tyana, there is an extensive lake into which if a part of a reed or of some other thing be plunged, and withdrawn the next day, it will be found that the part thus withdrawn has turned into stone, while the part which remained above water retains its original nature.

10. In the same way, at Hierapolis in Phrygia there is a multitude of boiling hot springs from which water is let into ditches surrounding gardens and vineyards, and this water becomes an incrustation of stone at the end of a year. Hence, every year they construct banks of earth to the right and left, let in the water, and thus out of these incrustations make walls for their fields. This seems due to natural causes, since there is a juice having a coagulating potency like rennet underground in those spots and in that country. When this potency appears above ground mingled with spring water, the mixture cannot but be hardened by the heat of the sun and air, as appears in salt pits.

11. There are also springs which issue exceedingly bitter, owing to a bitter juice in the soil, such as the river Hypanis in Pontus. For about forty miles from its source its taste is very sweet; then it reaches a point about one hundred and sixty miles from its mouth, where it is joined by a very small brook. This runs into it, and at once makes that vast river bitter, for the reason that the water of the brook becomes bitter by flowing through the kind of soil and the veins in which there are sandarach mines.

12. These waters are given their different flavours by the properties of the soil, as is also seen in the case of fruits. If the roots of trees, vines, or other plants did not produce their fruits by drawing juices from soil of different properties, the flowers of all would be of the same kind in all places and districts. But we find in the island of Lesbos the protropum wine, in Maeonia, the catacecaumenites, in Lydia, the Tmolian, in Sicily, the Mamertine, in Campania, the Falernian, between Terracina and Fondi, the Caecuban, and wines of countless varieties and qualities produced in many other places. This could not be the case, were it not that the juice of the soil, introduced with its proper flavours into the roots, feeds the stem, and, mounting along it to the top, imparts a flavour to the fruit which is peculiar to its situation and kind.

PROPERTIES OF WATERS

13. If soils were not different and unlike in their kinds of juices, Syria and Arabia would not be the only places in which the reeds, rushes, and all the plants are aromatic, and in which there are trees bearing frankincense or yielding pepper berries and lumps of myrrh, nor would assafoetida be found only in the stalks growing in Cyrene, but everything would be of the same sort, and produced in the soil of all countries. It is the inclination of the firmament and the force of the sun, as it draws nearer or recedes in its course, that make these diversities such as we find them in different countries and places, through the nature of the soil and its juices. And not only in the case of the things mentioned, but also in that of sheep and cattle. These diversities would not exist if the different properties of soils and their juices were not qualified by the power of the sun.

14. For instance, there are in Boeotia the rivers Cephisus and Melas, in Lucania, the Crathis, in Troy, the Xanthus, and certain springs in the country of the Clazomenians, the Erythraeans, and the Laodiceans. When sheep are ready for breeding at the proper season of the year, they are driven every day during that season to those rivers to drink, and the result is that, however white they may be, they beget in some places whity-brown lambs, in other places gray, and in others black as a raven. Thus, the peculiar character of the liquid, entering their body, produces in each case the quality with which it is imbued. Hence, it is said that the people of Ilium gave the river Xanthus its name because reddish cattle and whity-brown sheep are found in the plains of Troy near that river.

15. Deadly kinds of water are also found, which run through soil containing a noxious juice, and take in its poisonous quality: for instance, there is said to have been a spring at Terracina, called the spring of Neptune, which caused the death of those who thoughtlessly drank from it. In consequence, it is said that the ancients stopped it up. At Chrobs in Thrace there is a lake which causes the death not only of those who drink of it, but also of those who bathe in it. In Thessaly there is a gushing

fount of which sheep never taste, nor does any sort of creature draw near to it, and close by this fount there is a tree with crimson flowers.

16. In Macedonia, at the place where Euripides is buried, two streams approach from the right and left of his tomb, and unite. By one of these, travellers are in the habit of lying down and taking luncheon, because its water is good; but nobody goes near the stream on the other side of the tomb, because its water is said to be death-dealing. In Arcadia there is a tract of land called Nonacris, which has extremely cold water trickling from a rock in the mountains. This water is called "Water of the Styx," and no vessel, whether of silver, bronze, or iron, can stand it without flying to pieces and breaking up. Nothing but a mule's hoof can keep it together and hold it, and tradition says that it was thus conveyed by Antipater through his son Iollas into the province where Alexander was staying, and that the king was killed by him with this water.

17. Among the Alps in the kingdom of Cottius there is a water those who taste of which immediately fall lifeless. In the Faliscan country on the Via Campana in the Campus Cornetus is a grove in which rises a spring, and there the bones of birds and of lizards and other reptiles are seen lying.

Some springs are acid, as at Lyncestus and in Italy in the Velian country, at Teano in Campania, and in many other places. These when used as drinks have the power of breaking up stones in the bladder, which form in the human body.

18. This seems to be due to natural causes, as there is a sharp and acid juice contained in the soil there, which imparts a sharpness to these springs as they issue from it; and so, on entering the body, they disperse all the deposits and concretions, due to the use of other waters, which they find in the body. Why such things are broken up by acid waters we can see from the following experiments. If an egg is left for some time in vinegar, its shell will soften and dissolve. Again, if a piece of lead, which is very flexible and heavy, is put in a vase and vinegar poured over it, and

the vase covered and sealed up, the lead will be dissolved and turn into white lead.

19. On the same principle, copper, which is naturally more solid, will disperse and turn into verdigris if similarly treated. So, also, a pearl. Even rocks of lava, which neither iron nor fire alone can dissolve, split into pieces and dissolve when heated with fire and then sprinkled with vinegar. Hence, since we see these things taking place before our very eyes, we can infer that on the same principle even patients with the stone may, in the nature of things, be cured in like manner by means of acid waters, on account of the sharpness of the potion.

20. Then there are springs in which wine seems to be mingled, like the one in Paphlagonia, the water of which intoxicates those who drink of the spring alone without wine. The Aequians in Italy and the tribe of the Medulli in the Alps have a kind of water which causes swellings in the throats of those who drink it.

21. In Arcadia is the well-known town of Clitor, in whose territory is a cave with running water which makes people who drink of it abstemious. At this spring, there is an epigram in Greek verses inscribed on stone to the effect that the water is unsuitable for bathing, and also injurious to vines, because it was at this spring that Melampus cleansed the daughters of Proetus of their madness by sacrificial rites, and restored those maidens to their former sound state of mind. The inscription runs as written below:

> Swain, if by noontide thirst thou art opprest
>   When with thy flocks to Cleitor's bounds thou'st hied,
> Take from this fount a draught, and grant a rest
>   To all thy goats the water nymphs beside.
> But bathe not in't when full of drunken cheer,
>   Lest the mere vapour may bring thee to bane;
> Shun my vine-hating spring — Melampus here
>   From madness once washed Proetus' daughters sane,
> And all th' offscouring here did hide, when they
> From Argos came to rugged Arcady.

22. In the island of Zea is a spring of which those who thoughtlessly drink lose their understanding, and an epigram is cut there

to the effect that a draught from the spring is delightful, but that he who drinks will become dull as a stone. These are the verses:

> This stone sweet streams of cooling drink doth drip,
> But stone his wits become who doth it sip.

23. At Susa, the capital of the Persian kingdom, there is a little spring, those who drink of which lose their teeth. An epigram is written there, the significance of which is to this effect, that the water is excellent for bathing, but that taken as drink, it knocks out the teeth by the roots. The verses of this epigram are, in Greek, as follows:

> Stranger, you see the waters of a spring
>   In which 't is safe for men their hands to lave;
> But if the weedy basin entering
>   You drink of its unpalatable wave,
> Your grinders tumble out that self-same day
> From jaws that orphaned sockets will display.

24. There are also in some places springs which have the peculiarity of giving fine singing voices to the natives, as at Tarsus in Magnesia and in other countries of that kind. Then there is Zama, an African city, which King Juba fortified by enclosing it with a double wall, and he established his royal residence there. Twenty miles from it is the walled town of Ismuc, the lands belonging to which are marked off by a marvellous kind of boundary. For although Africa was the mother and nurse of wild animals, particularly serpents, yet not one is ever born in the lands of that town, and if ever one is imported and put there, it dies at once; and not only this, but if soil is taken from this spot to another place, the same is true there. It is said that this kind of soil is also found in the Balearic Islands. The above mentioned soil has a still more wonderful property, of which I have learned in the following way.

25. Caius Julius, Masinissa's son, who owned all the lands about that town, served with Caesar the father. He was once my guest. Hence, in our daily intercourse, we naturally talked of

literary subjects. During a conversation between us on the efficacy of water and its qualities, he stated that there were springs in that country of a kind which caused people born there to have fine singing voices, and that consequently they always sent abroad and bought handsome lads and ripe girls, and mated them, so that their progeny might have not only fine voices but also beautiful forms.

26. This great variety in different things is a distribution due to nature, for even the human body, which consists in part of the earthy, contains many kinds of juices, such as blood, milk, sweat, urine, and tears. If all this variation of flavours is found in a small portion of the earthy, we should not be surprised to find in the great earth itself countless varieties of juices, through the veins of which the water runs, and becomes saturated with them before reaching the outlets of springs. In this way, different varieties of springs of peculiar kinds are produced, on account of diversity of situation, characteristics of country, and dissimilar properties of soils.

27. Some of these things I have seen for myself, others I have found written in Greek books, the authorities for these writings being Theophrastus, Timaeus, Posidonius, Hegesias, Herodotus, Aristides, and Metrodorus. These men with much attention and endless pains showed by their writings that the peculiarities of sites, the properties of waters, and the characteristics of countries are conditioned by the inclination of the heaven. Following their investigations, I have set down in this book what I thought sufficient about different kinds of water, to make it easier, by means of these directions, for people to pick out springs from which they can conduct the water in aqueducts for the use of cities and towns.

28. For it is obvious that nothing in the world is so necessary for use as water, seeing that any living creature can, if deprived of grain or fruit or meat or fish, or any one of them, support life by using other foodstuffs; but without water no animal nor any proper food can be produced, kept in good condition, or prepared.

Consequently we must take great care and pains in searching for springs and selecting them, keeping in view the health of mankind.

CHAPTER IV

TESTS OF GOOD WATER

1. SPRINGS should be tested and proved in advance in the following ways. If they run free and open, inspect and observe the physique of the people who dwell in the vicinity before beginning to conduct the water, and if their frames are strong, their complexions fresh, legs sound, and eyes clear, the springs deserve complete approval. If it is a spring just dug out, its water is excellent if it can be sprinkled into a Corinthian vase or into any other sort made of good bronze without leaving a spot on it. Again, if such water is boiled in a bronze cauldron, afterwards left for a time, and then poured off without sand or mud being found at the bottom of the cauldron, that water also will have proved its excellence.

2. And if green vegetables cook quickly when put into a vessel of such water and set over a fire, it will be a proof that the water is good and wholesome. Likewise if the water in the spring is itself limpid and clear, if there is no growth of moss or reeds where it spreads and flows, and if its bed is not polluted by filth of any sort but has a clean appearance, these signs indicate that the water is light and wholesome in the highest degree.

CHAPTER V

LEVELLING AND LEVELLING INSTRUMENTS

1. I SHALL now treat of the ways in which water should be conducted to dwellings and cities. First comes the method of taking the level. Levelling is done either with dioptrae, or with water levels, or with the chorobates, but it is done with greater

accuracy by means of the chorobates, because dioptrae and levels are deceptive. The chorobates is a straightedge about twenty feet long. At the extremities it has legs, made exactly alike and jointed on perpendicularly to the extremities of the straightedge, and also crosspieces, fastened by tenons, connecting the straightedge and the legs. These crosspieces have vertical lines drawn upon them, and there are plumblines hanging from the straightedge over each of the lines. When the straightedge is in position, and the plumblines strike both the lines alike and at the same time, they show that the instrument stands level.

2. But if the wind interposes, and constant motion prevents any definite indication by the lines, then have a groove on the upper side, five feet long, one digit wide, and a digit and a half deep, and pour water into it. If the water comes up uniformly to the rims of the groove, it will be known that the instrument is level. When the level is thus found by means of the chorobates, the amount of fall will also be known.

3. Perhaps some reader of the works of Archimedes will say that there can be no true levelling by means of water, because he holds that water has not a level surface, but is of a spherical form, having its centre at the centre of the earth. Still, whether water is plane or spherical, it necessarily follows that when the straightedge is level, it will support the water evenly at its extremities on the right and left, but that if it slopes down at one end, the water at the higher end will not reach the rim of the groove in the straightedge. For though the water, wherever poured in, must have a swelling and curvature in the centre, yet the extremities on the right and left must be on a level with each other. A picture of the chorobates will be found drawn at the end of the book. If there is to be a considerable fall, the conducting of the water will be comparatively easy. But if the course is broken by depressions, we must have recourse to substructures.

CHAPTER VI

AQUEDUCTS, WELLS, AND CISTERNS

1. THERE are three methods of conducting water, in channels through masonry conduits, or in lead pipes, or in pipes of baked clay. If in conduits, let the masonry be as solid as possible, and let the bed of the channel have a gradient of not less than a quarter of an inch for every hundred feet, and let the masonry structure be arched over, so that the sun may not strike the water at all. When it has reached the city, build a reservoir with a distribution tank in three compartments connected with the reservoir to receive the water, and let the reservoir have three pipes, one for each of the connecting tanks, so that when the water runs over from the tanks at the ends, it may run into the one between them.

2. From this central tank, pipes will be laid to all the basins and fountains; from the second tank, to baths, so that they may yield an annual income to the state; and from the third, to private houses, so that water for public use will not run short; for people will be unable to divert it if they have only their own supplies from headquarters. This is the reason why I have made these divisions, and also in order that individuals who take water into their houses may by their taxes help to maintain the conducting of the water by the contractors.

3. If, however, there are hills between the city and the source of supply, subterranean channels must be dug, and brought to a level at the gradient mentioned above. If the bed is of tufa or other stone, let the channel be cut in it; but if it is of earth or sand, there must be vaulted masonry walls for the channel, and the water should thus be conducted, with shafts built at every two hundred and forty feet.

4. But if the water is to be conducted in lead pipes, first build a reservoir at the source; then, let the pipes have an interior area corresponding to the amount of water, and lay these pipes from

this reservoir to the reservoir which is inside the city walls. The pipes should be cast in lengths of at least ten feet. If they are hundreds, they should weigh 1200 pounds each length; if eighties, 960 pounds; if fifties, 600 pounds; forties, 480 pounds; thirties, 360 pounds; twenties, 240 pounds; fifteens, 180 pounds; tens, 120 pounds; eights, 100 pounds; fives, 60 pounds. The pipes get the names of their sizes from the width of the plates, taken in digits, before they are rolled into tubes. Thus, when a pipe is made from a plate fifty digits in width, it will be called a "fifty," and so on with the rest.

5. The conducting of the water through lead pipes is to be managed as follows. If there is a regular fall from the source to the city, without any intervening hills that are high enough to interrupt it, but with depressions in it, then we must build substructures to bring it up to the level as in the case of channels and conduits. If the distance round such depressions is not great, the water may be carried round circuitously; but if the valleys are extensive, the course will be directed down their slope. On reaching the bottom, a low substructure is built so that the level there may continue as long as possible. This will form the "venter," termed Κοιλία by the Greeks. Then, on reaching the hill on the opposite side, the length of the venter makes the water slow in swelling up to rise to the top of the hill.

6. But if there is no such venter made in the valleys, nor any substructure built on a level, but merely an elbow, the water will break out, and burst the joints of the pipes. And in the venter, water cushions must be constructed to relieve the pressure of the air. Thus, those who have to conduct water through lead pipes will do it most successfully on these principles, because its descents, circuits, venters, and risings can be managed in this way, when the level of the fall from the sources to the city is once obtained.

7. It is also not ineffectual to build reservoirs at intervals of 24,000 feet, so that if a break occurs anywhere, it will not completely ruin the whole work, and the place where it has occurred

can easily be found; but such reservoirs should not be built at a descent, nor in the plane of a venter, nor at risings, nor anywhere in valleys, but only where there is an unbroken level.

8. But if we wish to spend less money, we must proceed as follows. Clay pipes with a skin at least two digits thick should be made, but these pipes should be tongued at one end so that they can fit into and join one another. Their joints must be coated with quicklime mixed with oil, and at the angles of the level of the venter a piece of red tufa stone, with a hole bored through it, must be placed right at the elbow, so that the last length of pipe used in the descent is jointed into the stone, and also the first length of the level of the venter; similarly at the hill on the opposite side the last length of the level of the venter should stick into the hole in the red tufa, and the first of the rise should be similarly jointed into it.

9. The level of the pipes being thus adjusted, they will not be sprung out of place by the force generated at the descent and at the rising. For a strong current of air is generated in an aqueduct which bursts its way even through stones unless the water is let in slowly and sparingly from the source at first, and checked at the elbows or turns by bands, or by the weight of sand ballast. All the other arrangements should be made as in the case of lead pipes. And ashes are to be put in beforehand when the water is let in from the source for the first time, so that if any of the joints have not been sufficiently coated, they may be coated with ashes.

10. Clay pipes for conducting water have the following advantages. In the first place, in construction: — if anything happens to them, anybody can repair the damage. Secondly, water from clay pipes is much more wholesome than that which is conducted through lead pipes, because lead is found to be harmful for the reason that white lead is derived from it, and this is said to be hurtful to the human system. Hence, if what is produced from it is harmful, no doubt the thing itself is not wholesome.

11. This we can exemplify from plumbers, since in them the natural colour of the body is replaced by a deep pallor. For when

lead is smelted in casting, the fumes from it settle upon their members, and day after day burn out and take away all the virtues of the blood from their limbs. <u>Hence, water ought by no means to be conducted in lead pipes, if we want to have it wholesome.</u> That the taste is better when it comes from clay pipes may be proved by everyday life, for though our tables are loaded with silver vessels, yet everybody uses earthenware for the sake of purity of taste.

12. But if there are no springs from which we can construct aqueducts, it is necessary to dig wells. Now in the digging of wells we must not disdain reflection, but must devote much acuteness and skill to the consideration of the natural principles of things, because the earth contains many various substances in itself; for like everything else, it is composed of the four elements. In the first place, it is itself earthy, and of moisture it contains springs of water, also heat, which produces sulphur, alum, and asphalt; and finally, it contains great currents of air, which, coming up in a pregnant state through the porous fissures to the places where wells are being dug, and finding men engaged in digging there, stop up the breath of life in their nostrils by the natural strength of the exhalation. So those who do not quickly escape from the spot, are killed there.

13. To guard against this, we must proceed as follows. Let down a lighted lamp, and if it keeps on burning, a man may make the descent without danger. But if the light is put out by the strength of the exhalation, then dig air shafts beside the well on the right and left. Thus the vapours will be carried off by the air shafts as if through nostrils. When these are finished and we come to the water, then a wall should be built round the well without stopping up the vein.

14. But if the ground is hard, or if the veins lie too deep, the water supply must be obtained from roofs or higher ground, and collected in cisterns of "signinum work." Signinum work is made as follows. In the first place, procure the cleanest and sharpest sand, break up lava into bits of not more than a pound in weight,

and mix the sand in a mortar trough with the strongest lime in the proportion of five parts of sand to two of lime. The trench for the signinum work, down to the level of the proposed depth of the cistern, should be beaten with wooden beetles covered with iron.

15. Then after having beaten the walls, let all the earth between them be cleared out to a level with the very bottom of the walls. Having evened this off, let the ground be beaten to the proper density. If such constructions are in two compartments or in three so as to insure clearing by changing from one to another, they will make the water much more wholesome and sweeter to use. For it will become more limpid, and keep its taste without any smell, if the mud has somewhere to settle; otherwise it will be necessary to clear it by adding salt.

In this book I have put what I could about the merits and varieties of water, its usefulness, and the ways in which it should be conducted and tested; in the next I shall write about the subject of dialling and the principles of timepieces.

BOOK IX

BOOK IX

INTRODUCTION

1. THE ancestors of the Greeks have appointed such great honours for the famous athletes who are victorious at the Olympian, Pythian, Isthmian, and Nemean games, that they are not only greeted with applause as they stand with palm and crown at the meeting itself, but even on returning to their several states in the triumph of victory, they ride into their cities and to their fathers' houses in four-horse chariots, and enjoy fixed revenues for life at the public expense. When I think of this, I am amazed that the same honours and even greater are not bestowed upon those authors whose boundless services are performed for all time and for all nations. This would have been a practice all the more worth establishing, because in the case of athletes it is merely their own bodily frame that is strengthened by their training, whereas in the case of authors it is the mind, and not only their own but also man's in general, by the doctrines laid down in their books for the acquiring of knowledge and the sharpening of the intellect.

2. What does it signify to mankind that Milo of Croton and other victors of his class were invincible? Nothing, save that in their lifetime they were famous among their countrymen. But the doctrines of Pythagoras, Democritus, Plato, and Aristotle, and the daily life of other learned men, spent in constant industry, yield fresh and rich fruit, not only to their own countrymen, but also to all nations. And they who from their tender years are filled with the plenteous learning which this fruit affords, attain to the highest capacity of knowledge, and can introduce into their states civilized ways, impartial justice, and laws, things without which no state can be sound.

3. Since, therefore, these great benefits to individuals and to communities are due to the wisdom of authors, I think that not

only should palms and crowns be bestowed upon them, but that they should even be granted triumphs, and judged worthy of being consecrated in the dwellings of the gods.

Of their many discoveries which have been useful for the development of human life, I will cite a few examples. On reviewing these, people will admit that honours ought of necessity to be bestowed upon them.

4. First of all, among the many very useful theorems of Plato, I will cite one as demonstrated by him. Suppose there is a place or a field in the form of a square and we are required to double it. This has to be effected by means of lines correctly drawn, for it will take a kind of calculation not to be made by means of mere multiplication. The following is the demonstration. A square place ten feet long and ten feet wide gives an area of one hundred feet. Now if it is required to double the square, and to make one of two hundred feet, we must ask how long will be the side of that square so as to get from this the two hundred feet corresponding to the doubling of the area. Nobody can find this by means of arithmetic. For if we take fourteen, multiplication will give one hundred and ninety-six feet; if fifteen, two hundred and twenty-five feet.

5. Therefore, since this is inexplicable by arithmetic, let a diagonal line be drawn from angle to angle of that square of ten feet in length and width, dividing it into two triangles of equal size, each fifty feet in area. Taking this diagonal line as the length, describe another square. Thus we shall have in the larger square four triangles of the same size and the same number of feet as the two of fifty feet each which were formed by the diagonal line in the smaller square. In this way Plato demonstrated the doubling by means of lines, as the figure appended at the bottom of the page will show.

6. Then again, Pythagoras showed that a right angle can be formed without the contrivances of the artisan. Thus, the result which carpenters reach very laboriously, but scarcely to exactness, with their squares, can be demonstrated to perfec-

tion from the reasoning and methods of his teaching. If we take three rules, one three feet, the second four feet, and the third five feet in length, and join these rules together with their tips touching each other so as to make a triangular figure, they will form a right angle. Now if a square be described on the length of each one of these rules, the square on the side of three feet in length will have an area of nine feet; of four feet, sixteen; of five, twenty-five.

7. Thus the area in number of feet made up of the two squares on the sides three and four feet in length is equalled by that of the one square described on the side of five. When Pythagoras discovered this fact, he had no doubt that the Muses had guided him in the discovery, and it is said that he very gratefully offered sacrifice to them.

This theorem affords a useful means of measuring many things, and it is particularly serviceable in the building of staircases in buildings, so that the steps may be at the proper levels.

8. Suppose the height of the story, from the flooring above to the ground below, to be divided into three parts. Five of these will give the right length for the stringers of the stairway. Let four parts, each equal to one of the three composing the height between the upper story and the ground, be set off from the perpendicular, and there fix the lower ends of the stringers. In this manner the steps and the stairway itself will be properly placed. A figure of this also will be found appended below.

9. In the case of Archimedes, although he made many wonderful discoveries of diverse kinds, yet of them all, the following, which I shall relate, seems to have been the result of a boundless ingenuity. Hiero, after gaining the royal power in Syracuse, resolved, as a consequence of his successful exploits, to place in a certain temple a golden crown which he had vowed to the immortal gods. He contracted for its making at a fixed price, and weighed out a precise amount of gold to the contractor. At the appointed time the latter delivered to the king's satisfaction an exquisitely finished piece of handiwork, and it appeared that in

weight the crown corresponded precisely to what the gold had weighed.

10. But afterwards a charge was made that gold had been abstracted and an equivalent weight of silver had been added in the manufacture of the crown. Hiero, thinking it an outrage that he had been tricked, and yet not knowing how to detect the theft, requested Archimedes to consider the matter. The latter, while the case was still on his mind, happened to go to the bath, and on getting into a tub observed that the more his body sank into it the more water ran out over the tub. As this pointed out the way to explain the case in question, without a moment's delay, and transported with joy, he jumped out of the tub and rushed home naked, crying with a loud voice that he had found what he was seeking; for as he ran he shouted repeatedly in Greek, "Εὕρηκα, εὕρηκα."

11. Taking this as the beginning of his discovery, it is said that he made two masses of the same weight as the crown, one of gold and the other of silver. After making them, he filled a large vessel with water to the very brim, and dropped the mass of silver into it. As much water ran out as was equal in bulk to that of the silver sunk in the vessel. Then, taking out the mass, he poured back the lost quantity of water, using a pint measure, until it was level with the brim as it had been before. Thus he found the weight of silver corresponding to a definite quantity of water.

12. After this experiment, he likewise dropped the mass of gold into the full vessel and, on taking it out and measuring as before, found that not so much water was lost, but a smaller quantity: namely, as much less as a mass of gold lacks in bulk compared to a mass of silver of the same weight. Finally, filling the vessel again and dropping the crown itself into the same quantity of water, he found that more water ran over for the crown than for the mass of gold of the same weight. Hence, reasoning from the fact that more water was lost in the case of the crown than in that of the mass, he detected the mixing of silver with the gold, and made the theft of the contractor perfectly clear.

INTRODUCTION

13. Now let us turn our thoughts to the researches of Archytas of Tarentum and Eratosthenes of Cyrene. They made many discoveries from mathematics which are welcome to men, and so, though they deserve our thanks for other discoveries, they are particularly worthy of admiration for their ideas in that field. For example, each in a different way solved the problem enjoined upon Delos by Apollo in an oracle, the doubling of the number of cubic feet in his altars; this done, he said, the inhabitants of the island would be delivered from an offence against religion.

14. Archytas solved it by his figure of the semicylinders; Eratosthenes, by means of the instrument called the mesolabe.

Noting all these things with the great delight which learning gives, we cannot but be stirred by these discoveries when we reflect upon the influence of them one by one. I find also much for admiration in the books of Democritus on nature, and in his commentary entitled Χειρόκμητα, in which he made use of his ring to seal with soft wax the principles which he had himself put to the test.

15. These, then, were men whose researches are an everlasting possession, not only for the improvement of character but also for general utility. The fame of athletes, however, soon declines with their bodily powers. Neither when they are in the flower of their strength, nor afterwards with posterity, can they do for human life what is done by the researches of the learned.

16. But although honours are not bestowed upon authors for excellence of character and teaching, yet as their minds, naturally looking up to the higher regions of the air, are raised to the sky on the steps of history, it must needs be, that not merely their doctrines, but even their appearance, should be known to posterity through time eternal. Hence, men whose souls are aroused by the delights of literature cannot but carry enshrined in their hearts the likeness of the poet Ennius, as they do those of the gods. Those who are devotedly attached to the poems of Accius seem to have before them not merely his vigorous language but even his very figure.

17. So, too, numbers born after our time will feel as if they were discussing nature face to face with Lucretius, or the art of rhetoric with Cicero; many of our posterity will confer with Varro on the Latin language; likewise, there will be numerous scholars who, as they weigh many points with the wise among the Greeks, will feel as if they were carrying on private conversations with them. In a word, the opinions of learned authors, though their bodily forms are absent, gain strength as time goes on, and, when taking part in councils and discussions, have greater weight than those of any living men.

18. Such, Caesar, are the authorities on whom I have depended, and applying their views and opinions I have written the present books, in the first seven treating of buildings and in the eighth of water. In this I shall set forth the rules for dialling, showing how they are found through the shadows cast by the gnomon from the sun's rays in the firmament, and on what principles these shadows lengthen and shorten.

CHAPTER I

THE ZODIAC AND THE PLANETS

1. It is due to the divine intelligence and is a very great wonder to all who reflect upon it, that the shadow of a gnomon at the equinox is of one length in Athens, of another in Alexandria, of another in Rome, and not the same at Piacenza, or at other places in the world. Hence drawings for dials are very different from one another, corresponding to differences of situation. This is because the length of the shadow at the equinox is used in constructing the figure of the analemma, in accordance with which the hours are marked to conform to the situation and the shadow of the gnomon. The analemma is a basis for calculation deduced from the course of the sun, and found by observation of the shadow as it increases until the winter solstice. By means of this, through architectural principles and the employment of the compasses, we find out the operation of the sun in the universe.

2. The word "universe" means the general assemblage of all nature, and it also means the heaven that is made up of the constellations and the courses of the stars. The heaven revolves steadily round earth and sea on the pivots at the ends of its axis. The architect at these points was the power of Nature, and she put the pivots there, to be, as it were, centres, one of them above the earth and sea at the very top of the firmament and even beyond the stars composing the Great Bear, the other on the opposite side under the earth in the regions of the south. Round these pivots (termed in Greek πόλοι) as centres, like those of a turning lathe, she formed the circles in which the heaven passes on its everlasting way. In the midst thereof, the earth and sea naturally occupy the central point.

3. It follows from this natural arrangement that the central point in the north is high above the earth, while on the south, the

region below, it is beneath the earth and consequently hidden by it. Furthermore, across the middle, and obliquely inclined to the south, there is a broad circular belt composed of the twelve signs, whose stars, arranged in twelve equivalent divisions, represent each a shape which nature has depicted. And so with the firmament and the other constellations, they move round the earth and sea in glittering array, completing their orbits according to the spherical shape of the heaven.

4. They are all visible or invisible according to fixed times. While six of the signs are passing along with the heaven above the earth, the other six are moving under the earth and hidden by its shadow. But there are always six of them making their way above the earth; for, corresponding to that part of the last sign which in the course of its revolution has to sink, pass under the earth, and become concealed, an equivalent part of the sign opposite to it is obliged by the law of their common revolution to pass up and, having completed its circuit, to emerge out of the darkness into the light of the open space on the other side. This is because the rising and setting of both are subject to one and the same power and law.

5. While these signs, twelve in number and occupying each one twelfth part of the firmament, steadily revolve from east to west, the moon, Mercury, Venus, the sun, as well as Mars, Jupiter, and Saturn, differing from one another in the magnitude of their orbits as though their courses were at different points in a flight of steps, pass through those signs in just the opposite direction, from west to east in the firmament. The moon makes her circuit of the heaven in twenty-eight days plus about an hour, and with her return to the sign from which she set forth, completes a lunar month.

6. The sun takes a full month to move across the space of one sign, that is, one twelfth of the firmament. Consequently, in twelve months he traverses the spaces of the twelve signs, and, on returning to the sign from which he began, completes the period of a full year. Hence, the circuit made by the moon thir-

teen times in twelve months, is measured by the sun only once in the same number of months. But Mercury and Venus, their paths wreathing around the sun's rays as their centre, retrograde and delay their movements, and so, from the nature of that circuit, sometimes wait at stopping-places within the spaces of the signs.

7. This fact may best be recognized from Venus. When she is following the sun, she makes her appearance in the sky after his setting, and is then called the Evening Star, shining most brilliantly. At other times she precedes him, rising before daybreak, and is named the Morning Star. Thus Mercury and Venus sometimes delay in one sign for a good many days, and at others advance pretty rapidly into another sign. They do not spend the same number of days in every sign, but the longer they have previously delayed, the more rapidly they accomplish their journeys after passing into the next sign, and thus they complete their appointed course. Consequently, in spite of their delay in some of the signs, they nevertheless soon reach the proper place in their orbits after freeing themselves from their enforced delay.

8. Mercury, on his journey through the heavens, passes through the spaces of the signs in three hundred and sixty days, and so arrives at the sign from which he set out on his course at the beginning of his revolution. His average rate of movement is such that he has about thirty days in each sign.

9. Venus, on becoming free from the hindrance of the sun's rays, crosses the space of a sign in thirty days. Though she thus stays less than forty days in particular signs, she makes good the required amount by delaying in one sign when she comes to a pause. Therefore she completes her total revolution in heaven in four hundred and eighty-five days, and once more enters the sign from which she previously began to move.

10. Mars, after traversing the spaces of the constellations for about six hundred and eighty-three days, arrives at the point from which he had before set out at the beginning of his course,

and while he passes through some of the signs more rapidly than others, he makes up the required number of days whenever he comes to a pause. Jupiter, climbing with gentler pace against the revolution of the firmament, travels through each sign in about three hundred and sixty days, and finishes in eleven years and three hundred and thirteen days, returning to the sign in which he had been twelve years before. Saturn, traversing the space of one sign in twenty-nine months plus a few days, is restored after twenty-nine years and about one hundred and sixty days to that in which he had been thirty years before. He is, as it appears, slower, because the nearer he is to the outermost part of the firmament, the greater is the orbit through which he has to pass.

11. The three that complete their circuits above the sun's course do not make progress while they are in the triangle which he has entered, but retrograde and pause until the sun has crossed from that triangle into another sign. Some hold that this takes place because, as they say, when the sun is a great distance off, the paths on which these stars wander are without light on account of that distance, and so the darkness retards and hinders them. But I do not think that this is so. The splendour of the sun is clearly to be seen, and manifest without any kind of obscurity, throughout the whole firmament, so that those very retrograde movements and pauses of the stars are visible even to us.

12. If then, at this great distance, our human vision can discern that sight, why, pray, are we to think that the divine splendour of the stars can be cast into darkness? Rather will the following way of accounting for it prove to be correct. Heat summons and attracts everything towards itself; for instance, we see the fruits of the earth growing up high under the influence of heat, and that spring water is vapourised and drawn up to the clouds at sunrise. On the same principle, the mighty influence of the sun, with his rays diverging in the form of a triangle, attracts the stars which follow him, and, as it were, curbs and restrains those that precede, not allowing them to make progress, but obliging them

to retrograde towards himself until he passes out into the sign that belongs to a different triangle.

13. Perhaps the question will be raised, why the sun by his great heat causes these detentions in the fifth sign from himself rather than in the second or third, which are nearer. I will therefore set forth what seems to be the reason. His rays diverge through the firmament in straight lines as though forming an equilateral triangle, that is, to the fifth sign from the sun, no more, no less. If his rays were diffused in circuits spreading all over the firmament, instead of in straight lines diverging so as to form a triangle, they would burn up all the nearer objects. This is a fact which the Greek poet Euripides seems to have remarked; for he says that places at a greater distance from the sun are in a violent heat, and that those which are nearer he keeps temperate. Thus in the play of Phaethon, the poet writes: καίει τὰ πόρρω, τἄγγυθεν δ' εὔκρατ' ἔχει.

14. If then, fact and reason and the evidence of an ancient poet point to this explanation, I do not see why we should decide otherwise than as I have written above on this subject.

Jupiter, whose orbit is between those of Mars and Saturn, traverses a longer course than Mars, and a shorter than Saturn. Likewise with the rest of these stars: the farther they are from the outermost limits of the heaven, and the nearer their orbits to the earth, the sooner they are seen to finish their courses; for those of them that have a smaller orbit often pass those that are higher, going under them.

15. For example, place seven ants on a wheel such as potters use, having made seven channels on the wheel about the centre, increasing successively in circumference; and suppose those ants obliged to make a circuit in these channels while the wheel is turned in the opposite direction. In spite of having to move in a direction contrary to that of the wheel, the ants must necessarily complete their journeys in the opposite direction, and that ant which is nearest the centre must finish its circuit sooner, while the ant that is going round at the outer edge of the disc of

the wheel must, on account of the size of its circuit, be much slower in completing its course, even though it is moving just as quickly as the other. In the same way, these stars, which struggle on against the course of the firmament, are accomplishing an orbit on paths of their own; but, owing to the revolution of the heaven, they are swept back as it goes round every day.

16. The reason why some of these stars are temperate, others hot, and others cold, appears to be this: that the flame of every kind of fire rises to higher places. Consequently, the burning rays of the sun make the ether above him white hot, in the regions of the course of Mars, and so the heat of the sun makes him hot. Saturn, on the contrary, being nearest to the outermost limit of the firmament and bordering on the quarters of the heaven which are frozen, is excessively cold. Hence, Jupiter, whose course is between the orbits of these two, appears to have a moderate and very temperate influence, intermediate between their cold and heat.

I have now described, as I have received them from my teacher, the belt of the twelve signs and the seven stars that work and move in the opposite direction, with the laws and numerical relations under which they pass from sign to sign, and how they complete their orbits. I shall next speak of the waxing and waning of the moon, according to the accounts of my predecessors.

CHAPTER II

THE PHASES OF THE MOON

1. ACCORDING to the teaching of Berosus, who came from the state, or rather nation, of the Chaldees, and was the pioneer of Chaldean learning in Asia, the moon is a ball, one half luminous and the rest of a blue colour. When, in the course of her orbit, she has passed below the disc of the sun, she is attracted by his rays and great heat, and turns thither her luminous side, on account of the sympathy between light and light. Being thus summoned

by the sun's disc and facing upward, her lower half, as it is not luminous, is invisible on account of its likeness to the air. When she is perpendicular to the sun's rays, all her light is confined to her upper surface, and she is then called the new moon.

2. As she moves on, passing by to the east, the effect of the sun upon her relaxes, and the outer edge of the luminous side sheds its light upon the earth in an exceedingly thin line. This is called the second day of the moon. Day by day she is further relieved and turns, and thus are numbered the third, fourth, and following days. On the seventh day, the sun being in the west and the moon in the middle of the firmament between the east and west, she is half the extent of the firmament distant from the sun, and therefore half of the luminous side is turned toward the earth. But when the sun and moon are separated by the entire extent of the firmament, and the moon is in the east with the sun over against her in the west, she is completely relieved by her still greater distance from his rays, and so, on the fourteenth day, she is at the full, and her entire disc emits its light. On the succeeding days, up to the end of the month, she wanes daily as she turns in her course, being recalled by the sun until she comes under his disc and rays, thus completing the count of the days of the month.

3. But Aristarchus of Samos, a mathematician of great powers, has left a different explanation in his teaching on this subject, as I shall now set forth. It is no secret that the moon has no light of her own, but is, as it were, a mirror, receiving brightness from the influence of the sun. Of all the seven stars, the moon traverses the shortest orbit, and her course is nearest to the earth. Hence in every month, on the day before she gets past the sun, she is under his disc and rays, and is consequently hidden and invisible. When she is thus in conjunction with the sun, she is called the new moon. On the next day, reckoned as her second, she gets past the sun and shows the thin edge of her sphere. Three days away from the sun, she waxes and grows brighter. Removing further every day till she reaches the seventh, when her distance from the sun at his setting is about one half the extent of the

firmament, one half of her is luminous: that is, the half which faces toward the sun is lighted up by him.

4. On the fourteenth day, being diametrically across the whole extent of the firmament from the sun, she is at her full and rises when the sun is setting. For, as she takes her place over against him and distant the whole extent of the firmament, she thus receives the light from the sun throughout her entire orb. On the seventeenth day, at sunrise, she is inclining to the west. On the twenty-second day, after sunrise, the moon is about mid-heaven; hence, the side exposed to the sun is bright and the rest dark. Continuing thus her daily course, she passes under the rays of the sun on about the twenty-eighth day, and so completes the account of the month.

I will next explain how the sun, passing through a different sign each month, causes the days and hours to increase and diminish in length.

CHAPTER III

THE COURSE OF THE SUN THROUGH THE TWELVE SIGNS

1. The sun, after entering the sign Aries and passing through one eighth of it, determines the vernal equinox. On reaching the tail of Taurus and the constellation of the Pleiades, from which the front half of Taurus projects, he advances into a space greater than half the firmament, moving toward the north. From Taurus he enters Gemini at the time of the rising of the Pleiades, and, getting higher above the earth, he increases the length of the days. Next, coming from Gemini into Cancer, which occupies the shortest space in heaven, and after traversing one eighth of it, he determines the summer solstice. Continuing on, he reaches the head and breast of Leo, portions which are reckoned as belonging to Cancer.

2. After leaving the breast of Leo and the boundaries of Cancer, the sun, traversing the rest of Leo, makes the days shorter, diminishing the size of his circuit, and returning to the same

course that he had in Gemini. Next, crossing from Leo into Virgo, and advancing as far as the bosom of her garment, he still further shortens his circuit, making his course equal to what it was in Taurus. Advancing from Virgo by way of the bosom of her garment, which forms the first part of Libra, he determines the autumn equinox at the end of one eighth of Libra. Here his course is equal to what his circuit was in the sign Aries.

3. When the sun has entered Scorpio, at the time of the setting of the Pleiades, he begins to make the days shorter as he advances toward the south. From Scorpio he enters Sagittarius and, on reaching the thighs, his daily course is still further diminished. From the thighs of Sagittarius, which are reckoned as part of Capricornus, he reaches the end of the first eighth of the latter, where his course in heaven is shortest. Consequently, this season, from the shortness of the day, is called bruma or dies brumales. Crossing from Capricornus into Aquarius, he causes the days to increase to the length which they had when he was in Sagittarius. From Aquarius he enters Pisces at the time when Favonius begins to blow, and here his course is the same as in Scorpio. In this way the sun passes round through the signs, lengthening or shortening the days and hours at definite seasons.

I shall next speak of the other constellations formed by arrangements of stars, and lying to the right and left of the belt of the signs, in the southern and northern portions of the firmament.

CHAPTER IV

THE NORTHERN CONSTELLATIONS

1. THE Great Bear, called in Greek ἄρκτος or ἑλίκη, has her Warden behind her. Near him is the Virgin, on whose right shoulder rests a very bright star which we call Harbinger of the Vintage, and the Greeks προτρυγητής. But Spica in that constellation is brighter. Opposite there is another star, coloured, between

the knees of the Bear Warden, dedicated there under the name of Arcturus.

2. Opposite the head of the Bear, at an angle with the feet of the Twins, is the Charioteer, standing on the tip of the horn of the Bull; hence, one and the same star is found in the tip of the left horn of the Bull and in the right foot of the Charioteer. Supported on the hand of the Charioteer are the Kids, with the She-Goat at his left shoulder. Above the Bull and the Ram is Perseus, having at his right . . .[1] with the Pleiades moving beneath, and at his left the head of the Ram. His right hand rests on the likeness of Cassiopea, and with his left he holds the Gorgon's head by its top over the Ram, laying it at the feet of Andromeda.

3. Above Andromeda are the Fishes, one above her belly and the other above the backbone of the Horse. A very bright star terminates both the belly of the Horse and the head of Andromeda. Andromeda's right hand rests above the likeness of Cassiopea, and her left above the Northern Fish. The Waterman's head is above that of the Horse. The Horse's hoofs lie close to the Waterman's knees. Cassiopea is set apart in the midst. High above the He-Goat are the Eagle and the Dolphin, and near them is the Arrow. Farther on is the Bird, whose right wing grazes the head and sceptre of Cepheus, with its left resting over Cassiopea. Under the tail of the Bird lie the feet of the Horse.

4. Above the Archer, Scorpion, and Balance, is the Serpent, reaching to the Crown with the end of its snout. Next, the Serpent-holder grasps the Serpent about the middle in his hands, and with his left foot treads squarely on the foreparts of the Scorpion. A little way from the head of the Serpent-holder is the head of the so-called Kneeler. Their heads are the more readily to be distinguished as the stars which compose them are by no means dim.

[1] From this point to the end of section 3 the text is often hopelessly corrupt. The translation follows, approximately, the manuscript reading, but cannot pretend to be exact.

5. The foot of the Kneeler rests on the temple of that Serpent which is entwined between the She-Bears (called Septentriones). The little Dolphin moves in front of the Horse. Opposite the bill of the Bird is the Lyre. The Crown is arranged between the shoulders of the Warden and the Kneeler. In the northern circle are the two She-Bears with their shoulder-blades confronting and their breasts turned away from one another. The Greeks call the Lesser Bear κυνόσουρα, and the Greater ἑλίκη. Their heads face different ways, and their tails are shaped so that each is in front of the head of the other Bear; for the tails of both stick up over them.

6. The Serpent is said to lie stretched out between their tails, and in it there is a star, called Polus, shining near the head of the Greater Bear. At the nearest point, the Serpent winds its head round, but is also flung in a fold round the head of the Lesser Bear, and stretches out close to her feet. Here it twists back, making another fold, and, lifting itself up, bends its snout and right temple from the head of the Lesser Bear round towards the Greater. Above the tail of the Lesser Bear are the feet of Cepheus, and at this point, at the very top, are stars forming an equilateral triangle. There are a good many stars common to the Lesser Bear and to Cepheus.

I have now mentioned the constellations which are arranged in the heaven to the right of the east, between the belt of the signs and the north. I shall next describe those that Nature has distributed to the left of the east and in the southern regions.

CHAPTER V

THE SOUTHERN CONSTELLATIONS

1. First, under the He-Goat lies the Southern Fish, facing towards the tail of the Whale. The Censer is under the Scorpion's sting. The fore parts of the Centaur are next to the Balance and the Scorpion, and he holds in his hands the figure which astrono-

mers call the Beast. Beneath the Virgin, Lion, and Crab is the twisted girdle formed by the Snake, extending over a whole line of stars, his snout raised near the Crab, supporting the Bowl with the middle of his body near the Lion, and bringing his tail, on which is the Raven, under and near the hand of the Virgin. The region above his shoulders is equally bright.

2. Beneath the Snake's belly, at the tail, lies the Centaur. Near the Bowl and the Lion is the ship named Argo. Her bow is invisible, but her mast and the parts about the helm are in plain sight, the stern of the vessel joining the Dog at the tip of his tail. The Little Dog follows the Twins, and is opposite the Snake's head. The Greater Dog follows the Lesser. Orion lies aslant, under the Bull's hoof; in his left hand grasping his club, and raising the other toward the Twins.

3. At his feet is the Dog, following a little behind the Hare. The Whale lies under the Ram and the Fishes, and from his mane there is a slight sprinkling of stars, called in Greek ἁρπεδόναι, regularly disposed towards each of the Fishes. This ligature by which they hang is carried a great way inwards, but reaches out to the top of the mane of the Whale. The River, formed of stars, flows from a source at the left foot of Orion. But the Water, said to pour from the Waterman, flows between the head of the Southern Fish and the tail of the Whale.

4. These constellations, whose outlines and shapes in the heavens were designed by Nature and the divine intelligence, I have described according to the view of the natural philosopher Democritus, but only those whose risings and settings we can observe and see with our own eyes. Just as the Bears turn round the pivot of the axis without ever setting or sinking under the earth, there are likewise stars that keep turning round the southern pivot, which on account of the inclination of the firmament lies always under the earth, and, being hidden there, they never rise and emerge above the earth. Consequently, the figures which they form are unknown to us on account of the interposition of the earth. The star Canopus proves this. It is unknown to our

vicinity; but we have reports of it from merchants who have been to the most distant part of Egypt, and to regions bordering on the uttermost boundaries of the earth.

CHAPTER VI

ASTROLOGY AND WEATHER PROGNOSTICS

1. I HAVE shown how the firmament, and the twelve signs with the constellations arranged to the north and south of them, fly round the earth, so that the matter may be clearly understood. For it is from this revolution of the firmament, from the course of the sun through the signs in the opposite direction, and from the shadows cast by equinoctial gnomons, that we find the figure of the analemma.

2. As for the branch of astronomy which concerns the influences of the twelve signs, the five stars, the sun, and the moon upon human life, we must leave all this to the calculations of the Chaldeans, to whom belongs the art of casting nativities, which enables them to declare the past and the future by means of calculations based on the stars. These discoveries have been transmitted by the men of genius and great acuteness who sprang directly from the nation of the Chaldeans; first of all, by Berosus, who settled in the island state of Cos, and there opened a school. Afterwards Antipater pursued the subject; then there was Archinapolus, who also left rules for casting nativities, based not on the moment of birth but on that of conception.

3. When we come to natural philosophy, however, Thales of Miletus, Anaxagoras of Clazomenae, Pythagoras of Samos, Xenophanes of Colophon, and Democritus of Abdera have in various ways investigated and left us the laws and the working of the laws by which nature governs it. In the track of their discoveries, Eudoxus, Euctemon, Callippus, Meto, Philippus, Hipparchus, Aratus, and others discovered the risings and settings of the constellations, as well as weather prognostications from astronomy through

the study of the calendars, and this study they set forth and left to posterity. Their learning deserves the admiration of mankind; for they were so solicitous as even to be able to predict, long beforehand, with divining mind, the signs of the weather which was to follow in the future. On this subject, therefore, reference must be made to their labours and investigations.

CHAPTER VII

THE ANALEMMA AND ITS APPLICATIONS

1. In distinction from the subjects first mentioned, we must ourselves explain the principles which govern the shortening and lengthening of the day. When the sun is at the equinoxes, that is, passing through Aries or Libra, he makes the gnomon cast a shadow equal to eight ninths of its own length, in the latitude of Rome. In Athens, the shadow is equal to three fourths of the length of the gnomon; at Rhodes to five sevenths; at Tarentum, to nine elevenths; at Alexandria, to three fifths; and so at other places it is found that the shadows of equinoctial gnomons are naturally different from one another.

2. Hence, wherever a sundial is to be constructed, we must take the equinoctial shadow of the place. If it is found to be, as in Rome, equal to eight ninths of the gnomon, let a line be drawn on a plane surface, and in the middle thereof erect a perpendicular, plumb to the line, which perpendicular is called the gnomon. Then, from the line in the plane, let the line of the gnomon be divided off by the compasses into nine parts, and take the point designating the ninth part as a centre, to be marked by the letter A. Then, opening the compasses from that centre to the line in the plane at the point B, describe a circle. This circle is called the meridian.

3. Then, of the nine parts between the plane and the centre on the gnomon, take eight, and mark them off on the line in the plane to the point C. This will be the equinoctial shadow of the

gnomon. From that point, marked by C, let a line be drawn through the centre at the point A, and this will represent a ray of the sun at the equinox. Then, extending the compasses from the centre to the line in the plane, mark off the equidistant points E on the left and I on the right, on the two sides of the circum-

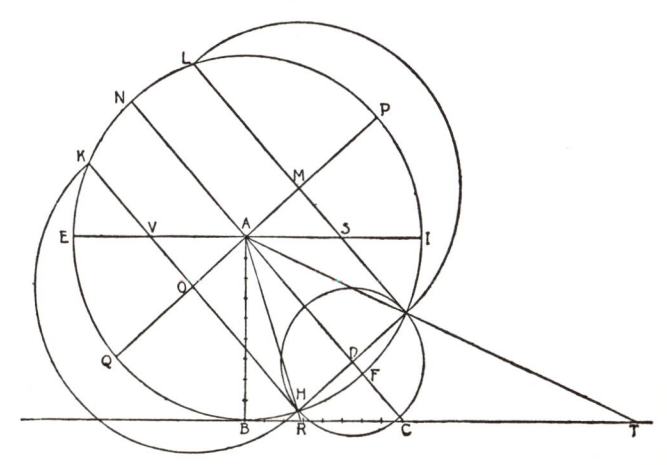

ference, and let a line be drawn through the centre, dividing the circle into two equal semicircles. This line is called by mathematicians the horizon.

4. Then, take a fifteenth part of the entire circumference, and, placing the centre of the compasses on the circumference at the point where the equinoctial ray cuts it at the letter F, mark off the points G and H on the right and left. Then lines must be drawn from these (and the centre) to the line of the plane at the points T and R, and thus, one will represent the ray of the sun in winter, and the other the ray in summer. Opposite E will be the point I, where the line drawn through the centre at the point A cuts the circumference; opposite G and H will be the points L and K; and opposite C, F, and A will be the point N.

5. Then, diameters are to be drawn from G to L and from H to K. The upper will denote the summer and the lower the winter portion. These diameters are to be divided equally in the middle at the points M and O, and those centres marked; then, through

these marks and the centre A, draw a line extending to the two sides of the circumference at the points P and Q. This will be a line perpendicular to the equinoctial ray, and it is called in mathematical figures the axis. From these same centres open the compasses to the ends of the diameters, and describe semicircles, one of which will be for summer and the other for winter.

6. Then, at the points at which the parallel lines cut the line called the horizon, the letter S is to be on the right and the letter V on the left, and from the extremity of the semicircle, at the point G, draw a line parallel to the axis, extending to the lefthand semicircle at the point H. This parallel line is called the Logotomus. Then, centre the compasses at the point where the equinoctial ray cuts that line, at the letter D, and open them to the point where the summer ray cuts the circumference at the letter H. From the equinoctial centre, with a radius extending to the summer ray, describe the circumference of the circle of the months, which is called Menaeus. Thus we shall have the figure of the analemma.

7. This having been drawn and completed, the scheme of hours is next to be drawn on the baseplates from the analemma, according to the winter lines, or those of summer, or the equinoxes, or the months, and thus many different kinds of dials may be laid down and drawn by this ingenious method. But the result of all these shapes and designs is in one respect the same: namely, the days of the equinoxes and of the winter and summer solstices are always divided into twelve equal parts. Omitting details, therefore, — not for fear of the trouble, but lest I should prove tiresome by writing too much, — I will state by whom the different classes and designs of dials have been invented. For I cannot invent new kinds myself at this late day, nor do I think that I ought to display the inventions of others as my own. Hence, I will mention those that have come down to us, and by whom they were invented.

CHAPTER VIII

SUNDIALS AND WATER CLOCKS

1. The semicircular form, hollowed out of a square block, and cut under to correspond to the polar altitude, is said to have been invented by Berosus the Chaldean; the Scaphe or Hemisphere, by Aristarchus of Samos, as well as the disc on a plane surface; the Arachne, by the astronomer Eudoxus or, as some say, by Apollonius; the Plinthium or Lacunar, like the one placed in the Circus Flaminius, by Scopinas of Syracuse; the πρὸς τὰ ἱστορούμενα, by Parmenio; the πρὸς πᾶν κλῖμα, by Theodosius and Andreas; the Pelecinum, by Patrocles; the Cone, by Dionysodorus; the Quiver, by Apollonius. The men whose names are written above, as well as many others, have invented and left us other kinds: as, for instance, the Conarachne, the Conical Plinthium, and the Antiborean. Many have also left us written directions for making dials of these kinds for travellers, which can be hung up. Whoever wishes to find their baseplates, can easily do so from the books of these writers, provided only he understands the figure of the analemma.

2. Methods of making water clocks have been investigated by the same writers, and first of all by Ctesibius the Alexandrian, who also discovered the natural pressure of the air and pneumatic principles. It is worth while for students to know how these discoveries came about. Ctesibius, born at Alexandria, was the son of a barber. Preëminent for natural ability and great industry, he is said to have amused himself with ingenious devices. For example, wishing to hang a mirror in his father's shop in such a way that, on being lowered and raised again, its weight should be raised by means of a concealed cord, he employed the following mechanical contrivance.

3. Under the roof-beam he fixed a wooden channel in which he arranged a block of pulleys. He carried the cord along the channel to the corner, where he set up some small piping. Into this a

leaden ball, attached to the cord, was made to descend. As the weight fell into the narrow limits of the pipe, it naturally compressed the enclosed air, and, as its fall was rapid, it forced the mass of compressed air through the outlet into the open air, thus producing a distinct sound by the concussion.

4. Hence, Ctesibius, observing that sounds and tones were produced by the contact between the free air and that which was forced from the pipe, made use of this principle in the construction of the first water organs. He also devised methods of raising water, automatic contrivances, and amusing things of many kinds, including among them the construction of water clocks. He began by making an orifice in a piece of gold, or by perforating a gem, because these substances are not worn by the action of water, and do not collect dirt so as to get stopped up.

5. A regular flow of water through the orifice raises an inverted bowl, called by mechanicians the "cork" or "drum." To this are attached a rack and a revolving drum, both fitted with teeth at regular intervals. These teeth, acting upon one another, induce a measured revolution and movement. Other racks and other drums, similarly toothed and subject to the same motion, give rise by their revolution to various kinds of motions, by which figures are moved, cones revolve, pebbles or eggs fall, trumpets sound, and other incidental effects take place.

6. The hours are marked in these clocks on a column or a pilaster, and a figure emerging from the bottom points to them with a rod throughout the whole day. Their decrease or increase in length with the different days and months, must be adjusted by inserting or withdrawing wedges. The shutoffs for regulating the water are constructed as follows. Two cones are made, one solid and the other hollow, turned on a lathe so that one will go into the other and fit it perfectly. A rod is used to loosen or to bring them together, thus causing the water to flow rapidly or slowly into the vessels. According to these rules, and by this mechanism, water clocks may be constructed for use in winter.

7. But if it proves that the shortening or lengthening of the

day is not in agreement with the insertion and removal of the wedges, because the wedges may very often cause errors, the following arrangement will have to be made. Let the hours be marked off transversely on the column from the analemma, and let the lines of the months also be marked upon the column. Then let the column be made to revolve, in such a way that, as it turns continuously towards the figure and the rod with which the emerging figure points to the hours, it may make the hours short or long according to the respective months.

8. There is also another kind of winter dial, called the Anaphoric and constructed in the following way. The hours, indicated by bronze rods in accordance with the figure of the analemma, radiate from a centre on the face. Circles are described upon it, marking the limits of the months. Behind these rods there is a drum, on which is drawn and painted the firmament with the circle of the signs. In drawing the figures of the twelve celestial signs, one is represented larger and the next smaller, proceeding from the centre. Into the back of the drum, in the middle, a revolving axis is inserted, and round that axis is wound a flexible bronze chain, at one end of which hangs the "cork" which is raised by the water, and at the other a counterpoise of sand, equal in weight to the "cork."

9. Hence, the sand sinks as the "cork" is raised by the water, and in sinking turns the axis, and the axis the drum. The revolution of this drum causes sometimes a larger and sometimes a smaller portion of the circle of the signs to indicate, during the revolutions, the proper length of the hours corresponding to their seasons. For in every one of the signs there are as many holes as the corresponding month has days, and a boss, which seems to be holding the representation of the sun on a dial, designates the spaces for the hours. This, as it is carried from hole to hole, completes the circuit of a full month.

10. Hence, just as the sun during his passage through the constellations makes the days and hours longer or shorter, so the boss on a dial, moving from point to point in a direction contrary

to that of the revolution of the drum in the middle, is carried day by day sometimes over wider and sometimes over narrower spaces, giving a representation of the hours and days within the limits of each month.

To manage the water so that it may flow regularly, we must proceed as follows.

11. Inside, behind the face of the dial, place a reservoir, and let the water run down into it through a pipe, and let it have a hole at the bottom. Fastened to it is a bronze drum with an opening through which the water flows into it from the reservoir. Enclosed in this drum there is a smaller one, the two being perfectly jointed together by tenon and socket, in such a way that the smaller drum revolves closely but easily in the larger, like a stopcock.

12. On the lip of the larger drum there are three hundred and sixty-five points, marked off at equal intervals. The rim of the smaller one has a tongue fixed on its circumference, with the tip directed towards those points; and also in this rim is a small opening, through which water runs into the drum and keeps the works going. The figures of the celestial signs being on the lip of the larger drum, and this drum being motionless, let the sign Cancer be drawn at the top, with Capricornus perpendicular to it at the bottom, Libra at the spectator's right, Aries at his left, and let the other signs be given places between them as they are seen in the heavens.

13. Hence, when the sun is in Capricornus, the tongue on the rim touches every day one of the points in Capricornus on the lip of the larger drum, and is perpendicular to the strong pressure of the running water. So the water is quickly driven through the opening in the rim to the inside of the vessel, which, receiving it and soon becoming full, shortens and diminishes the length of the days and hours. But when, owing to the daily revolution of the smaller drum, its tongue reaches the points in Aquarius, the opening will no longer be perpendicular, and the water must give up its vigorous flow and run in a slower stream. Thus, the less the

velocity with which the vessel receives the water, the more the length of the days is increased.

14. Then the opening in the rim passes from point to point in Aquarius and Pisces, as though going upstairs, and when it reaches the end of the first eighth of Aries, the fall of the water is of medium strength, indicating the equinoctial hours. From Aries the opening passes, with the revolution of the drum, through Taurus and Gemini to the highest point at the end of the first eighth of Cancer, and when it reaches that point, the power diminishes, and hence, with the slower flow, its delay lengthens the days in the sign Cancer, producing the hours of the summer solstice. From Cancer it begins to decline, and during its return it passes through Leo and Virgo to the points at the end of the first eighth of Libra, gradually shortening and diminishing the length of the hours, until it comes to the points in Libra, where it makes the hours equinoctial once more.

15. Finally, the opening comes down more rapidly through Scorpio and Sagittarius, and on its return from its revolution to the end of the first eighth of Capricornus, the velocity of the stream renews once more the short hours of the winter solstice.

The rules and forms of construction employed in designing dials have now been described as well as I could. It remains to give an account of machines and their principles. In order to make my treatise on architecture complete, I will begin to write on this subject in the following book.

BOOK X

BOOK X

INTRODUCTION

1. In the famous and important Greek city of Ephesus there is said to be an ancient ancestral law, the terms of which are severe, but its justice is not inequitable. When an architect accepts the charge of a public work, he has to promise what the cost of it will be. His estimate is handed to the magistrate, and his property is pledged as security until the work is done. When it is finished, if the outlay agrees with his statement, he is complimented by decrees and marks of honour. If no more than a fourth has to be added to his estimate, it is furnished by the treasury and no penalty is inflicted. But when more than one fourth has to be spent in addition on the work, the money required to finish it is taken from his property.

2. Would to God that this were also a law of the Roman people, not merely for public, but also for private buildings. For the ignorant would no longer run riot with impunity, but men who are well qualified by an exact scientific training would unquestionably adopt the profession of architecture. Gentlemen would not be misled into limitless and prodigal expenditure, even to ejectments from their estates, and the architects themselves could be forced, by fear of the penalty, to be more careful in calculating and stating the limit of expense, so that gentlemen would procure their buildings for that which they had expected, or by adding only a little more. It is true that men who can afford to devote four hundred thousand to a work may hold on, if they have to add another hundred thousand, from the pleasure which the hope of finishing it gives them; but if they are loaded with a fifty per cent increase, or with an even greater expense, they lose hope, sacrifice what they have already spent, and are compelled to leave off, broken in fortune and in spirit.

3. This fault appears not only in the matter of buildings, but also in the shows given by magistrates, whether of gladiators in the forum or of plays on the stage. Here neither delay nor postponement is permissible, but the necessities of the case require that everything should be ready at a fixed time, — the seats for the audience, the awning drawn over them, and whatever, in accordance with the customs of the stage, is provided by machinery to please the eye of the people. These matters require careful thought and planning by a well trained intellect; for none of them can be accomplished without machinery, and without hard study skilfully applied in various ways.

4. Therefore, since such are our traditions and established practices, it is obviously fitting that the plans should be worked out carefully, and with the greatest attention, before the structures are begun. Consequently, as we have no law or customary practice to compel this, and as every year both praetors and aediles have to provide machinery for the festivals, I have thought it not out of place, Emperor, since I have treated of buildings in the earlier books, to set forth and teach in this, which forms the final conclusion of my treatise, the principles which govern machines.

CHAPTER I

MACHINES AND IMPLEMENTS

1. A MACHINE is a combination of timbers fastened together, chiefly efficacious in moving great weights. Such a machine is set in motion on scientific principles in circular rounds, which the Greeks call κυκλικὴ κίνησις· There is, however, a class intended for climbing, termed in Greek ἀκροβατικόν, another worked by air, which with them is called πνευματικόν, and a third for hoisting; this the Greeks named βαρουλκός. In the climbing class are machines so disposed that one can safely climb up high, by means of timbers set up on end and connected by crossbeams, in order to view operations. In the pneumatic class, air is forced by pressure to produce sounds and tones as in an ὄργανον.

2. In the hoisting class, heavy weights are removed by machines which raise them up and set them in position. The climbing machine displays no scientific principle, but merely a spirit of daring. It is held together by dowels and crossbeams and twisted lashings and supporting props. A machine that gets its motive power by pneumatic pressure will produce pretty effects by scientific refinements. But the hoisting machine has opportunities for usefulness which are greater and full of grandeur, and it is of the highest efficacy when used with intelligence.

3. Some of these act on the principle of the μηχανή, others on that of the ὄργανον. The difference between "machines" and "engines" is obviously this, that machines need more workmen and greater power to make them take effect, as for instance ballistae and the beams of presses. Engines, on the other hand, accomplish their purpose at the intelligent touch of a single workman, as the scorpio or anisocycli when they are turned. Therefore engines, as well as machines, are, in principle, practical necessities, without which nothing can be unattended with difficulties.

4. All machinery is derived from nature, and is founded on the teaching and instruction of the revolution of the firmament. Let us but consider the connected revolutions of the sun, the moon, and the five planets, without the revolution of which, due to mechanism, we should not have had the alternation of day and night, nor the ripening of fruits. Thus, when our ancestors had seen that this was so, they took their models from nature, and by imitating them were led on by divine facts, until they perfected the contrivances which are so serviceable in our life. Some things, with a view to greater convenience, they worked out by means of machines and their revolutions, others by means of engines, and so, whatever they found to be useful for investigations, for the arts, and for established practices, they took care to improve step by step on scientific principles.

5. Let us take first a necessary invention, such as clothing, and see how the combination of warp and woof on the loom, which does its work on the principle of an engine, not only protects the body by covering it, but also gives it honourable apparel. We should not have had food in abundance unless yokes and ploughs for oxen, and for all draught animals, had been invented. If there had been no provision of windlasses, pressbeams, and levers for presses, we could not have had the shining oil, nor the fruit of the vine to give us pleasure, and these things could not be transported on land without the invention of the mechanism of carts or waggons, nor on the sea without that of ships.

6. The discovery of the method of testing weights by steelyards and balances saves us from fraud, by introducing honest practices into life. There are also innumerable ways of employing machinery about which it seems unnecessary to speak, since they are at hand every day; such as mills, blacksmiths' bellows, carriages, gigs, turning lathes, and other things which are habitually used as general conveniences. Hence, we shall begin by explaining those that rarely come to hand, so that they may be understood.

CHAPTER II

HOISTING MACHINES

1. First we shall treat of those machines which are of necessity made ready when temples and public buildings are to be constructed. Two timbers are provided, strong enough for the weight of the load. They are fastened together at the upper end by a bolt, then spread apart at the bottom, and so set up, being kept upright by ropes attached at the upper ends and fixed at intervals all round. At the top is fastened a block, which some call a "rechamus." In the block two sheaves are enclosed, turning on axles. The traction rope is carried over the sheave at the top, then let fall and passed round a sheave in a block below. Then it is brought back to a sheave at the bottom of the upper block, and so it goes down to the lower block, where it is fastened through a hole in that block. The other end of the rope is brought back and down between the legs of the machine.

2. Socket-pieces are nailed to the hinder faces of the squared timbers at the point where they are spread apart, and the ends of the windlass are inserted into them so that the axles may turn freely. Close to each end of the windlass are two holes, so adjusted that handspikes can be fitted into them. To the bottom of the lower block are fastened shears made of iron, whose prongs are brought to bear upon the stones, which have holes bored in them. When one end of the rope is fastened to the windlass, and the latter is turned round by working the handspikes, the rope winds round the windlass, gets taut, and thus it raises the load to the proper height and to its place in the work.

3. This kind of machinery, revolving with three sheaves, is called a trispast. When there are two sheaves turning in the block beneath and three in the upper, the machine is termed a pentaspast. But if we have to furnish machines for heavier loads, we must use timbers of greater length and thickness, providing them with correspondingly large bolts at the top, and windlasses

turning at the bottom. When these are ready, let forestays be attached and left lying slack in front; let the backstays be carried over the shoulders of the machine to some distance, and, if there is nothing to which they can be fastened, sloping piles should be driven, the ground rammed down all round to fix them firmly, and the ropes made fast to them.

4. A block should then be attached by a stout cord to the top of the machine, and from that point a rope should be carried to a pile, and to a block tied to the pile. Let the rope be put in round the sheave of this block, and brought back to the block that is fastened at the top of the machine. Round its sheave the rope should be passed, and then should go down from the top, and back to the windlass, which is at the bottom of the machine, and there be fastened. The windlass is now to be turned by means of the handspikes, and it will raise the machine of itself without danger. Thus, a machine of the larger kind will be set in position, with its ropes in their places about it, and its stays attached to the piles. Its blocks and traction ropes are arranged as described above.

5. But if the loads of material for the work are still more colossal in size and weight, we shall not entrust them to a windlass, but set in an axle-tree, held by sockets as the windlass was, and carrying on its centre a large drum, which some term a wheel, but the Greeks call it ἀμφίεσις or περιθήκιον.

6. And the blocks in such machines are not arranged in the same, but in a different manner; for the rows of sheaves in them are doubled, both at the bottom and at the top. The traction rope is passed through a hole in the lower block, in such a way that the two ends of the rope are of equal length when it is stretched out, and both portions are held there at the lower block by a cord which is passed round them and lashed so that they cannot come out either to the right or the left. Then the ends of the rope are brought up into the block at the top from the outside, and passed down over its lower sheaves, and so return to the bottom, and are passed from the inside to the sheaves in the lowest block, and

then are brought up on the right and left, and return to the top and round the highest set of sheaves.

7. Passing over these from the outside, they are then carried to the right and left of the drum on the axle-tree, and are tied there so as to stay fast. Then another rope is wound round the drum and carried to a capstan, and when that is turned, it turns the drum and the axle-tree, the ropes get taut as they wind round regularly, and thus they raise the loads smoothly and with no danger. But if a larger drum is placed either in the middle or at one side, without any capstan, men can tread in it and accomplish the work more expeditiously.

8. There is also another kind of machine, ingenious enough and easy to use with speed, but only experts can work with it. It consists of a single timber, which is set up and held in place by stays on four sides. Two cheeks are nailed on below the stays, a block is fastened by ropes above the cheeks, and a straight piece of wood about two feet long, six digits wide, and four digits thick, is put under the block. The blocks used have each three rows of sheaves side by side. Hence three traction ropes are fastened at the top of the machine. Then they are brought to the block at the bottom, and passed from the inside round the sheaves that are nearest the top of it. Then they are brought back to the upper block, and passed inwards from outside round the sheaves nearest the bottom.

9. On coming down to the block at the bottom, they are carried round its second row of sheaves from the inside to the outside, and brought back to the second row at the top, passing round it and returning to the bottom; then from the bottom they are carried to the summit, where they pass round the highest row of sheaves, and then return to the bottom of the machine. At the foot of the machine a third block is attached. The Greeks call it ἐπάγων, but our people "artemon." This block fastened at the foot of the machine has three sheaves in it, round which the ropes are passed and then delivered to men to pull. Thus, three rows of men, pulling without a capstan, can quickly raise the load to the top.

10. This kind of machine is called a polyspast, because of the many revolving sheaves to which its dexterity and despatch are due. There is also this advantage in the erection of only a single timber, that by previously inclining it to the right or left as much as one wishes, the load can be set down at one side.

All these kinds of machinery described above are, in their principles, suited not only to the purposes mentioned, but also to the loading and unloading of ships, some kinds being set upright, and others placed horizontally on revolving platforms. On the same principle, ships can be hauled ashore by means of arrangements of ropes and blocks used on the ground, without setting up timbers.

11. It may also not be out of place to explain the ingenious procedure of Chersiphron. Desiring to convey the shafts for the temple of Diana at Ephesus from the stone quarries, and not trusting to carts, lest their wheels should be engulfed on account of the great weights of the load and the softness of the roads in the plain, he tried the following plan. Using four-inch timbers, he joined two of them, each as long as the shaft, with two crosspieces set between them, dovetailing all together, and then leaded iron gudgeons shaped like dovetails into the ends of the shafts, as dowels are leaded, and in the woodwork he fixed rings to contain the pivots, and fastened wooden cheeks to the ends. The pivots, being enclosed in the rings, turned freely. So, when yokes of oxen began to draw the four-inch frame, they made the shaft revolve constantly, turning it by means of the pivots and rings.

12. When they had thus transported all the shafts, and it became necessary to transport the architraves, Chersiphron's son Metagenes extended the same principle from the transportation of the shafts to the bringing down of the architraves. He made wheels, each about twelve feet in diameter, and enclosed the ends of the architraves in the wheels. In the ends he fixed pivots and rings in the same way. So when the four-inch frames were drawn by oxen, the wheels turned on the pivots enclosed in the rings, and the architraves, which were enclosed like axles in

the wheels, soon reached the building, in the same way as the shafts. The rollers used for smoothing the walks in palaestrae will serve as an example of this method. But it could not have been employed unless the distance had been short; for it is not more than eight miles from the stone-quarries to the temple, and there is no hill, but an uninterrupted plain.

13. In our own times, however, when the pedestal of the colossal Apollo in his temple had cracked with age, they were afraid that the statue would fall and be broken, and so they contracted for the cutting of a pedestal from the same quarries. The contract was taken by one Paconius. This pedestal was twelve feet long, eight feet wide, and six feet high. Paconius, with confident pride, did not transport it by the method of Metagenes, but determined to make a machine of a different sort, though on the same principle.

14. He made wheels of about fifteen feet in diameter, and in these wheels he enclosed the ends of the stone; then he fastened two-inch crossbars from wheel to wheel round the stone, encompassing it, so that there was an interval of not more than one foot between bar and bar. Then he coiled a rope round the bars, yoked up his oxen, and began to draw on the rope. Consequently as it uncoiled, it did indeed cause the wheels to turn, but it could not draw them in a line straight along the road, but kept swerving out to one side. Hence it was necessary to draw the machine back again. Thus, by this drawing to and fro, Paconius got into such financial embarrassment that he became insolvent.

15. I will digress a bit and explain how these stone-quarries were discovered. Pixodorus was a shepherd who lived in that vicinity. When the people of Ephesus were planning to build the temple of Diana in marble, and debating whether to get the marble from Paros, Proconnesus, Heraclea, or Thasos, Pixodorus drove out his sheep and was feeding his flock in that very spot. Then two rams ran at each other, and, each passing the other, one of them, after his charge, struck his horns against a

rock, from which a fragment of extremely white colour was dislodged. So it is said that Pixodorus left his sheep in the mountains and ran down to Ephesus carrying the fragment, since that very thing was the question of the moment. Therefore they immediately decreed honours to him and changed his name, so that instead of Pixodorus he should be called Evangelus. And to this day the chief magistrate goes out to that very spot every month and offers sacrifice to him, and if he does not, he is punished.

CHAPTER III

THE ELEMENTS OF MOTION

1. I HAVE briefly set forth what I thought necessary about the principles of hoisting machines. In them two different things, unlike each other, work together, as elements of their motion and power, to produce these effects. One of them is the right line, which the Greeks term εὐθεῖα; the other is the circle, which the Greeks call κυκλωτή; but in point of fact, neither rectilinear without circular motion, nor revolutions, without rectilinear motion, can accomplish the raising of loads. I will explain this, so that it may be understood.

2. As centres, axles are inserted into the sheaves, and these are fastened in the blocks; a rope carried over the sheaves, drawn straight down, and fastened to a windlass, causes the load to move upward from its place as the handspikes are turned. The pivots of this windlass, lying as centres in right lines in its socket-pieces, and the handspikes inserted in its holes, make the load rise when the ends of the windlass revolve in a circle like a lathe. Just so, when an iron lever is applied to a weight which a great many hands cannot move, with the fulcrum, which the Greeks call ὑπομόχλιον, lying as a centre in a right line under the lever, and with the tongue of the lever placed under the weight, one man's strength, bearing down upon the head of it, heaves up the weight.

3. For, as the shorter fore part of the lever goes under the weight from the fulcrum that forms the centre, the head of it, which is farther away from that centre, on being depressed, is made to describe a circular movement, and thus by pressure brings to an equilibrium the weight of a very great load by means of a few hands. Again, if the tongue of an iron lever is placed under a weight, and its head is not pushed down, but, on the contrary, is heaved up, the tongue, supported on the surface of the ground, will treat that as the weight, and the edge of the weight itself as the fulcrum. Thus, not so easily as by pushing down, but by motion in the opposite direction, the weight of the load will nevertheless be raised. If, therefore, the tongue of a lever lying on a fulcrum goes too far under the weight, and its head exerts its pressure too near the centre, it will not be able to elevate the weight, nor can it do so unless, as described above, the length of the lever is brought to equilibrium by the depression of its head.

4. This may be seen from the balances that we call steelyards. When the handle is set as a centre close to the end from which the scale hangs, and the counterpoise is moved along towards the other arm of the beam, shifting from point to point as it goes farther or even reaches the extremity, a small and inferior weight becomes equal to a very heavy object that is being weighed, on account of the equilibrium that is due to the levelling of the beam. Thus, as it withdraws from the centre, a small and comparatively light counterpoise, slowly turning the scale, makes a greater amount of weight rise gently upwards from below.

5. So, too, the pilot of the biggest merchantman, grasping the steering oar by its handle, which the Greeks call οἴαξ, and with one hand bringing it to the turning point, according to the rules of his art, by pressure about a centre, can turn the ship, although she may be laden with a very large or even enormous burden of merchandise and provisions. And when her sails are set only halfway up the mast, a ship cannot run quickly; but when the yard is hoisted to the top, she makes much quicker progress, because then the sails get the wind, not when they are

too close to the heel of the mast, which represents the centre, but when they have moved farther away from it to the top.

6. As a lever thrust under a weight is harder to manage, and does not put forth its strength, if the pressure is exerted at the centre, but easily raises the weight when the extreme end of it is pushed down, so sails that are only halfway up have less effect, but when they get farther away from the centre, and are hoisted to the very top of the mast, the pressure at the top forces the ship to make greater progress, though the wind is no stronger but just the same. Again, take the case of oars, which are fastened to the tholes by loops, — when they are pushed forward and drawn back by the hand, if the ends of the blades are at some distance from the centre, the oars foam with the waves of the sea and drive the ship forward in a straight line with a mighty impulse, while her prow cuts through the rare water.

7. And when the heaviest burdens are carried on poles by four or six porters at a time, they find the centres of balance at the very middle of the poles, so that, by distributing the dead weight of the burden according to a definitely proportioned division, each labourer may have an equal share to carry on his neck. For the poles, from which the straps for the burden of the four porters hang, are marked off at their centres by nails, to prevent the straps from slipping to one side. If they shift beyond the mark at the centre, they weigh heavily upon the place to which they have come nearer, like the weight of a steelyard when it moves from the point of equilibrium towards the end of the weighing apparatus.

8. In the same way, oxen have an equal draught when their yoke is adjusted at its middle by the yokestrap to the pole. But when their strength is not the same, and the stronger outdoes the other, the strap is shifted so as to make one side of the yoke longer, which helps the weaker ox. Thus, in the case of both poles and yokes, when the straps are not fastened at the middle, but at one side, the farther the strap moves from the middle, the shorter it makes one side, and the longer the other. So, if both

ends are carried round in circles, using as a centre the point to which the strap has been brought, the longer end will describe a larger, and the shorter end a smaller circle.

9. Just as smaller wheels move harder and with greater difficulty than larger ones, so, in the case of the poles and yokes, the parts where the interval from centre to end is less, bear down hard upon the neck, but where the distance from the same centre is greater, they ease the burden both for draught and carriage. As in all these cases motion is obtained by means of right lines at the centre and by circles, so also farm waggons, travelling carriages, drums, mills, screws, scorpiones, ballistae, pressbeams, and all other machines, produce the results intended, on the same principles, by turning about a rectilinear axis and by the revolution of a circle.

CHAPTER IV

ENGINES FOR RAISING WATER

1. I SHALL now explain the making of the different kinds of engines which have been invented for raising water, and will first speak of the tympanum. Although it does not lift the water high, it raises a great quantity very quickly. An axle is fashioned on a lathe or with the compasses, its ends are shod with iron hoops, and it carries round its middle a tympanum made of boards joined together. It rests on posts which have pieces of iron on them under the ends of the axle. In the interior of this tympanum there are eight crosspieces set at intervals, extending from the axle to the circumference of the tympanum, and dividing the space in the tympanum into equal compartments.

2. Planks are nailed round the face of it, leaving six-inch apertures to admit the water. At one side of it there are also holes, like those of a dovecot, next to the axle, one for each compartment. After being smeared with pitch like a ship, the thing is turned by the tread of men, and raising the water by means of the apertures in the face of the tympanum, delivers it through the

holes next to the axle into a wooden trough set underneath, with a conduit joined to it. Thus, a large quantity of water is furnished for irrigation in gardens, or for supplying the needs of saltworks.

3. But when it has to be raised higher, the same principle will be modified as follows. A wheel on an axle is to be made, large enough to reach the necessary height. All round the circumference of the wheel there will be cubical boxes, made tight with pitch and wax. So, when the wheel is turned by treading, the boxes, carried up full and again returning to the bottom, will of themselves discharge into the reservoir what they have carried up.

4. But, if it has to be supplied to a place still more high, a double iron chain, which will reach the surface when let down, is passed round the axle of the same wheel, with bronze buckets attached to it, each holding about six pints. The turning of the wheel, winding the chain round the axle, will carry the buckets to the top, and as they pass above the axle they must tip over and deliver into the reservoir what they have carried up.

CHAPTER V

WATER WHEELS AND WATER MILLS

1. WHEELS on the principles that have been described above are also constructed in rivers. Round their faces floatboards are fixed, which, on being struck by the current of the river, make the wheel turn as they move, and thus, by raising the water in the boxes and bringing it to the top, they accomplish the necessary work through being turned by the mere impulse of the river, without any treading on the part of workmen.

2. Water mills are turned on the same principle. Everything is the same in them, except that a drum with teeth is fixed into one end of the axle. It is set vertically on its edge, and turns in the same plane with the wheel. Next to this larger drum there is a smaller one, also with teeth, but set horizontally, and this is

attached (to the millstone). Thus the teeth of the drum which is fixed to the axle make the teeth of the horizontal drum move, and cause the mill to turn. A hopper, hanging over this contrivance, supplies the mill with corn, and meal is produced by the same revolution.

CHAPTER VI

THE WATER SCREW

1. THERE is also the method of the screw, which raises a great quantity of water, but does not carry it as high as does the wheel. The method of constructing it is as follows. A beam is selected, the thickness of which in digits is equivalent to its length in feet.

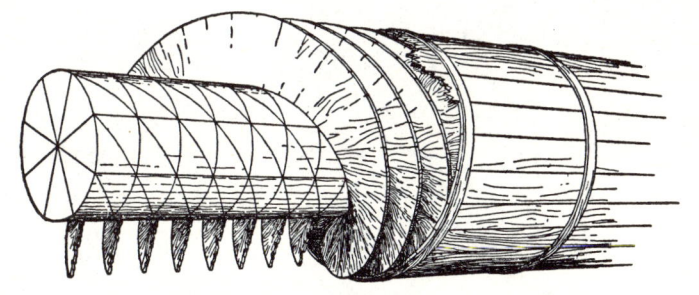

CONSTRUCTION OF THE WATER SCREW

This is made perfectly round. The ends are to be divided off on their circumference with the compass into eight parts, by quadrants and octants, and let the lines be so placed that, if the beam is laid in a horizontal position, the lines on the two ends may perfectly correspond with each other, and intervals of the size of one eighth part of the circumference of the beam may be laid off on the length of it. Then, placing the beam in a horizontal position, let perfectly straight lines be drawn from one end to the other. So the intervals will be equal in the directions both of the periphery and of the length. Where the lines are drawn along the length, the cutting circles will make intersections, and definite points at the intersections.

2. When these lines have been correctly drawn, a slender withe of willow, or a straight piece cut from the agnus castus tree, is taken, smeared with liquid pitch, and fastened at the first point of intersection. Then it is carried across obliquely to the succeeding

THE WATER SCREW
(From the edition of Vitruvius by Fra Giocondo, Venice, 1511)

intersections of longitudinal lines and circles, and as it advances, passing each of the points in due order and winding round, it is fastened at each intersection; and so, withdrawing from the first to the eighth point, it reaches and is fastened to the line to which its first part was fastened. Thus, it makes as much progress in its longitudinal advance to the eighth point as in its oblique advance over eight points. In the same manner, withes for the eight divisions of the diameter, fastened obliquely at the intersections on the entire longitudinal and peripheral surface, make spiral channels which naturally look just like those of a snail shell.

3. Other withes are fastened on the line of the first, and on these still others, all smeared with liquid pitch, and built up until the total diameter is equal to one eighth of the length. These are covered and surrounded with boards, fastened on to protect the spiral. Then these boards are soaked with pitch, and bound together with strips of iron, so that they may not be separated by the pressure of the water. The ends of the shaft are covered with iron. To the right and left of the screw are beams, with crosspieces fastening them together at both ends. In these crosspieces are holes sheathed with iron, and into them pivots are introduced, and thus the screw is turned by the treading of men.

4. It is to be set up at an inclination corresponding to that which is produced in drawing the Pythagorean right-angled triangle: that is, let its length be divided into five parts; let three of them denote the height of the head of the screw; thus the distance from the base of the perpendicular to the nozzle of the screw at the bottom will be equal to four of those parts. A figure showing how this ought to be, has been drawn at the end of the book, right on the back.

I have now described as clearly as I could, to make them better known, the principles on which wooden engines for raising water are constructed, and how they get their motion so that they may be of unlimited usefulness through their revolutions.

CHAPTER VII

THE PUMP OF CTESIBIUS

1. NEXT I must tell about the machine of Ctesibius, which raises water to a height. It is made of bronze, and has at the bottom a pair of cylinders set a little way apart, and there is a

pipe connected with each, the two running up, like the prongs of a fork, side by side to a vessel which is between the cylinders. In this vessel are valves, accurately fitting over the upper vents of the pipes, which stop up the ventholes, and keep what has been forced by pressure into the vessel from going down again.

2. Over the vessel a cowl is adjusted, like an inverted funnel, and fastened to the vessel by means of a wedge thrust through a staple, to prevent it from being lifted off by the pressure of the water that is forced in. On top of this a pipe is jointed, called the trumpet, which stands up vertically. Valves are inserted in the cylinders, beneath the lower vents of the pipes, and over the openings which are in the bottoms of the cylinders.

3. Pistons smoothly turned, rubbed with oil, and inserted from above into the cylinders, work with their rods and levers upon the air and water in the cylinders, and, as the valves stop up the openings, force and drive the water, by repeated pressure and expansion, through the vents of the pipes into the vessel, from which the cowl receives the inflated currents, and sends them up through the pipe at the top; and so water can be supplied for a fountain from a reservoir at a lower level.

4. This, however, is not the only apparatus which Ctesibius is said to have thought out, but many more of various kinds are shown by him to produce effects, borrowed from nature, by means of water pressure and compression of the air; as, for example, blackbirds singing by means of waterworks, and "angobatae," and figures that drink and move, and other things that are found to be pleasing to the eye and the ear.

5. Of these I have selected what I considered most useful and necessary, and have thought it best to speak in the preceding book about timepieces, and in this about the methods of raising water. The rest, which are not subservient to our needs, but to pleasure and amusement, may be found in the commentaries of Ctesibius himself by any who are interested in such refinements.

CHAPTER VIII

THE WATER ORGAN

1. With regard to water organs, however, I shall not fail with all possible brevity and precision to touch upon their principles, and to give a sufficient description of them. A wooden base is constructed, and on it is set an altar-shaped box made of bronze. Uprights, fastened together like ladders, are set up on the base, to the right and to the left (of the altar). They hold the bronze pump-cylinders, the moveable bottoms of which, carefully turned on a lathe, have iron elbows fastened to their centres and jointed to levers, and are wrapped in fleeces of wool. In the tops of the cylinders are openings, each about three digits in diameter. Close to these openings are bronze dolphins, mounted on joints and holding chains in their mouths, from which hang cymbal-shaped valves, let down under the openings in the cylinders.

2. Inside the altar, which holds the water, is a regulator shaped like an inverted funnel, under which there are cubes, each about three digits high, keeping a free space below between the lips of the regulator and the bottom of the altar. Tightly fixed on the neck of the regulator is the windchest, which supports the principal part of the contrivance, called in Greek the κανὼν μουσικός. Running longitudinally, there are four channels in it if it is a tetrachord; six, if it is a hexachord; eight, if it is an octachord.

3. Each of the channels has a cock in it, furnished with an iron handle. These handles, when turned, open ventholes from the windchest into the channels. From the channels to the canon there are vertical openings corresponding to ventholes in a board above, which board is termed πίναξ in Greek. Between this board and the canon are inserted sliders, pierced with holes to correspond, and rubbed with oil so that they can be easily moved and slid back into place again. They close the above-mentioned openings, and are called the plinths. Their going and coming now closes and now opens the holes.

4. These sliders have iron jacks fixed to them, and connected with the keys, and the keys, when touched, make the sliders move regularly. To the upper surface of the openings in the board, where the wind finds egress from the channels, rings are soldered, and into them the reeds of all the organ pipes are inserted. From the cylinders there are connecting pipes attached to the neck of the regulator, and directed towards the ventholes in the windchest. In the pipes are valves, turned on a lathe, and set (where the pipes are connected with the cylinders). When the windchest has received the air, these valves will stop up the openings, and prevent the wind from coming back again.

5. So, when the levers are raised, the elbows draw down the bottoms of the cylinders as far as they can go; and the dolphins, which are mounted on joints, let the cymbals fall into the cylinders, thus filling the interiors with air. Then the elbows, raising the bottoms within the cylinders by repeated and violent blows, and stopping the openings above by means of the cymbals, compress the air which is enclosed in the cylinders, and force it into the pipes, through which it runs into the regulator, and through its neck into the windchest. With a stronger motion of the levers, the air is still more compressed, streams through the apertures of the cocks, and fills the channels with wind.

6. So, when the keys, touched by the hand, drive the sliders forward and draw them back regularly, alternately stopping and opening the holes, they produce resonant sounds in a great variety of melodies conforming to the laws of music.

With my best efforts I have striven to set forth an obscure subject clearly in writing, but the theory of it is not easy, nor readily understood by all, save only those who have had some practice in things of this kind. If anybody has failed to understand it, he will certainly find, when he comes to know the thing itself, that it is carefully and exquisitely contrived in all respects.

CHAPTER IX

THE HODOMETER

1. THE drift of our treatise now turns to a useful invention of the greatest ingenuity, transmitted by our predecessors, which enables us, while sitting in a carriage on the road or sailing by sea, to know how many miles of a journey we have accomplished. This will be possible as follows. Let the wheels of the carriage be each four feet in diameter, so that if a wheel has a mark made upon it, and begins to move forward from that mark in making its revolution on the surface of the road, it will have covered the definite distance of twelve and a half feet on reaching that mark at which it began to revolve.

2. Having provided such wheels, let a drum with a single tooth projecting beyond the face of its circumference be firmly fastened to the inner side of the hub of the wheel. Then, above this, let a case be firmly fastened to the body of the carriage, containing a revolving drum set on edge and mounted on an axle; on the face of the drum there are four hundred teeth, placed at equal intervals, and engaging the tooth of the drum below. The upper drum has, moreover, one tooth fixed to its side and standing out farther than the other teeth.

3. Then, above, let there be a horizontal drum, similarly toothed and contained in another case, with its teeth engaging the tooth fixed to the side of the second drum, and let as many holes be made in this (third) drum as will correspond to the number of miles — more or less, it does not matter — that a carriage can go in a day's journey. Let a small round stone be placed in every one of these holes, and in the receptacle or case containing that drum let one hole be made, with a small pipe attached, through which, when they reach that point, the stones placed in the drum may fall one by one into a bronze vessel set underneath in the body of the carriage.

4. Thus, as the wheel in going forward carries with it the lowest

drum, and as the tooth of this at every revolution strikes against the teeth of the upper drum, and makes it move along, the result will be that the upper drum is carried round once for every four hundred revolutions of the lowest, and that the tooth fixed to its side pushes forward one tooth of the horizontal drum. Since, therefore, with four hundred revolutions of the lowest drum, the upper will revolve once, the progress made will be a distance of five thousand feet or one mile. Hence, every stone, making a ringing sound as it falls, will give warning that we have gone one mile. The number of stones gathered from beneath and counted, will show the number of miles in the day's journey.

5. On board ship, also, the same principles may be employed with a few changes. An axle is passed through the sides of the ship, with its ends projecting, and wheels are mounted on them, four feet in diameter, with projecting floatboards fastened round their faces and striking the water. The middle of the axle in the middle of the ship carries a drum with one tooth projecting beyond its circumference. Here a case is placed containing a drum with four hundred teeth at regular intervals, engaging the tooth of the drum that is mounted on the axle, and having also one other tooth fixed to its side and projecting beyond its circumference.

6. Above, in another case fastened to the former, is a horizontal drum toothed in the same way, and with its teeth engaging the tooth fixed to the side of the drum that is set on edge, so that one of the teeth of the horizontal drum is struck at each revolution of that tooth, and the horizontal drum is thus made to revolve in a circle. Let holes be made in the horizontal drum, in which holes small round stones are to be placed. In the receptacle or case containing that drum, let one hole be opened with a small pipe attached, through which a stone, as soon as the obstruction is removed, falls with a ringing sound into a bronze vessel.

7. So, when a ship is making headway, whether under oars or under a gale of wind, the floatboards on the wheels will strike against the water and be driven violently back, thus turning the

wheels; and they, revolving, will move the axle, and the axle the drum, the tooth of which, as it goes round, strikes one of the teeth of the second drum at each revolution, and makes it turn a little. So, when the floatboards have caused the wheels to revolve four hundred times, this drum, having turned round once, will strike a tooth of the horizontal drum with the tooth that is fixed to its side. Hence, every time the turning of the horizontal drum brings a stone to a hole, it will let the stone out through the pipe. Thus by the sound and the number, the length of the voyage will be shown in miles.

I have described how to make things that may be provided for use and amusement in times that are peaceful and without fear.

CHAPTER X

CATAPULTS OR SCORPIONES

1. I SHALL next explain the symmetrical principles on which scorpiones and ballistae may be constructed, inventions devised for defence against danger, and in the interest of self-preservation.

The proportions of these engines are all computed from the given length of the arrow which the engine is intended to throw, and the size of the holes in the capitals, through which the twisted sinews that hold the arms are stretched, is one ninth of that length.

2. The height and breadth of the capital itself must then conform to the size of the holes. The boards at the top and bottom of the capital, which are called "peritreti," should be in thickness equal to one hole, and in breadth to one and three quarters, except at their extremities, where they equal one hole and a half. The sideposts on the right and left should be four holes high, excluding the tenons, and five twelfths of a hole thick; the tenons, half a hole. The distance from a sidepost to the hole is one quarter of a hole, and it is also one quarter of a hole from the hole to the post

in the middle. The breadth of the post in the middle is equal to one hole and one eighth, the thickness, to one hole.

3. The opening in the middle post, where the arrow is laid, is equal to one fourth of the hole. The four surrounding corners should have iron plates nailed to their sides and faces, or should be studded with bronze pins and nails. The pipe, called σῦριγξ in Greek, has a length of nineteen holes. The strips, which some term cheeks, nailed at the right and left of the pipe, have a length of nineteen holes and a height and thickness of one hole. Two other strips, enclosing the windlass, are nailed on to these, three holes long and half a hole in breadth. The cheek nailed on to them, named the "bench," or by some the "box," and made fast by means of dove-tailed tenons, is one hole thick and seven twelfths of a hole in height. The length of the windlass is equal to . . .[1] holes, the thickness of the windlass to three quarters of a hole.

4. The latch is seven twelfths of a hole in length and one quarter in thickness. So also its socket-piece. The trigger or handle is three holes in length and three quarters of a hole in breadth and thickness. The trough in the pipe is sixteen holes in length, one quarter of a hole in thickness, and three quarters in height. The base of the standard on the ground is equal to eight holes; the breadth of the standard where it is fastened into the plinth is three quarters of a hole, its thickness two thirds of a hole; the height of the standard up to the tenon is twelve holes, its breadth three quarters of a hole, and its thickness two thirds. It has three struts, each nine holes in length, half a hole in breadth, and five twelfths in thickness. The tenon is one hole in length, and the head of the standard one hole and a half in length.

5. The antefix has the breadth of a hole and one eighth, and the thickness of one hole. The smaller support, which is behind, termed in Greek ἀντίβασις, is eight holes long, three quarters of a hole broad, and two thirds thick. Its prop is twelve holes long,

[1] The dots here and in what follows, indicate lacunae in the manuscripts.

and has the same breadth and thickness as the smaller support just mentioned. Above the smaller support is its socket-piece, or what is called the cushion, two and a half holes long, one and a half high, and three quarters of a hole broad. The windlass cup is two and seven twelfths holes long, two thirds of a hole thick, and three quarters broad. The crosspieces with their tenons have the length of . . . holes, the breadth of three quarters, and the thickness of two thirds of a hole. The length of an arm is seven holes, its thickness at its base two thirds of a hole, and at its end one half a hole; its curvature is equal to two thirds of a hole.

6. These engines are constructed according to these proportions or with additions or diminutions. For, if the height of the capitals is greater than their width — when they are called "high-tensioned," — something should be taken from the arms, so that the more the tension is weakened by height of the capitals, the more the strength of the blow is increased by shortness of the arms. But if the capital is less high, — when the term "low-tensioned" is used, — the arms, on account of their strength, should be made a little longer, so that they may be drawn easily. Just as it takes four men to raise a load with a lever five feet long, and only two men to lift the same load with a ten-foot lever, so the longer the arms, the easier they are to draw, and the shorter, the harder.

I have now spoken of the principles applicable to the parts and proportions of catapults.

CHAPTER XI

BALLISTAE

1. BALLISTAE are constructed on varying principles to produce an identical result. Some are worked by handspikes and windlasses, some by blocks and pulleys, others by capstans, others again by means of drums. No ballista, however, is made without regard to the given amount of weight of the stone which the engine is intended to throw. Hence their principle is not easy

for everybody, but only for those who have knowledge of the geometrical principles employed in calculation and in multiplication.

2. For the holes made in the capitals through the openings of which are stretched the strings made of twisted hair, generally women's, or of sinew, are proportionate to the amount of weight in the stone which the ballista is intended to throw, and to the principle of mass, as in catapults the principle is that of the length of the arrow. Therefore, in order that those who do not understand geometry may be prepared beforehand, so as not to be delayed by having to think the matter out at a moment of peril in war, I will set forth what I myself know by experience can be depended upon, and what I have in part gathered from the rules of my teachers, and wherever Greek weights bear a relation to the measures, I shall reduce and explain them so that they will express the same corresponding relation in our weights.

3. A ballista intended to throw a two-pound stone will have a hole of five digits in its capital; four pounds, six digits, and six pounds, seven digits; ten pounds, eight digits; twenty pounds, ten digits; forty pounds, twelve and a half digits; sixty pounds, thirteen and a half digits; eighty pounds, fifteen and three quarters digits; one hundred pounds, one foot and one and a half digits; one hundred and twenty pounds, one foot and two digits; one hundred and forty pounds, one foot and three digits; one hundred and sixty pounds, one foot and a quarter; one hundred and eighty pounds, one foot and five digits; two hundred pounds, one foot and six digits; two hundred and forty pounds, one foot and seven digits; two hundred and eighty pounds, one foot and a half; three hundred and twenty pounds, one foot and nine digits; three hundred and sixty pounds, one foot and ten digits.

4. Having determined the size of the hole, design the "scutula," termed in Greek περίτρητος, . . . holes in length and two and one sixth in breadth. Bisect it by a line drawn diagonally from the angles, and after this bisecting bring together the outlines of the figure so that it may present a rhomboidal design, reducing it by one sixth of its length and one

fourth of its breadth at the (obtuse) angles. In the part composed by the curvatures into which the points of the angles run out, let the holes be situated, and let the breadth be reduced by one sixth; moreover, let the hole be longer than it is broad by the thickness of the bolt. After designing the scutula, let its outline be worked down to give it a gentle curvature.

5. It should be given the thickness of seven twelfths of a hole. The boxes are two holes (in height), one and three quarters in breadth, two thirds of a hole in thickness except the part that is inserted in the hole, and at the top one third of a hole in breadth. The sideposts are five holes and two thirds in length, their curvature half a hole, and their thickness thirty-seven forty-eighths of a hole. In the middle their breadth is increased as much as it was near the hole in the design, by the breadth and thickness of . . . hole; the height by one fourth of a hole.

6. The (inner) strip on the "table" has a length of eight holes, a breadth and thickness of half a hole. Its tenons are one hole and one sixth long, and one quarter of a hole in thickness. The curvature of this strip is three quarters of a hole. The outer strip has the same breadth and thickness (as the inner), but the length is given by the obtuse angle of the design and the breadth of the sidepost at its curvature. The upper strips are to be equal to the lower; the cross-pieces of the "table," one half of a hole.

7. The shafts of the "ladder" are thirteen holes in length, one hole in thickness; the space between them is one hole and a quarter in breadth, and one and one eighth in depth. Let the entire length of the ladder on its upper surface — which is the one adjoining the arms and fastened to the table — be divided into five parts. Of these let two parts be given to the member which the Greeks call the χελώνιον, its breadth being one and one sixth, its thickness one quarter, and its length eleven holes and one half; the claw projects half a hole and the "winging" three sixteenths of a hole. What is at the axis which is termed the . . . face . . . the crosspieces of three holes?

8. The breadth of the inner slips is one quarter of a hole; their

thickness one sixth. The coverjoint or lid of the chelonium is dovetailed into the shafts of the ladder, and is three sixteenths of a hole in breadth and one twelfth in thickness. The thickness of the square piece on the ladder is three sixteenths of a hole, ... the diameter of the round axle will be equal to that of the claw, but at the pivots seven sixteenths of a hole.

9. The stays are ... holes in length, one quarter of a hole in breadth at the bottom, and one sixth in thickness at the top. The base, termed ἐσχάρα, has the length of . . . holes, and the antibase of four holes; each is one hole in thickness and breadth. A supporter is jointed on, halfway up, one and one half holes in breadth and thickness. Its height bears no relation to the hole, but will be such as to be serviceable. The length of an arm is six holes, its thickness at the base two thirds of a hole, and at the end one half a hole.

I have now given those symmetrical proportions of ballistae and catapults which I thought most useful. But I shall not omit, so far as I can express it in writing, the method of stretching and tuning their strings of twisted sinew or hair.

CHAPTER XII

THE STRINGING AND TUNING OF CATAPULTS

1. BEAMS of very generous length are selected, and upon them are nailed socket-pieces in which windlasses are inserted. Midway along their length the beams are incised and cut away to form framings, and in these cuttings the capitals of the catapults are inserted, and prevented by wedges from moving when the stretching is going on. Then the bronze boxes are inserted into the capitals, and the little iron bolts, which the Greeks call ἐπιζυγίδες, are put in their places in the boxes.

2. Next, the loops of the strings are put through the holes in the capitals, and passed through to the other side; next, they are put upon the windlasses, and wound round them in order that

the strings, stretched out taut on them by means of the handspikes, on being struck by the hand, may respond with the same sound on both sides. Then they are wedged tightly into the holes so that they cannot slacken. So, in the same manner, they are passed through to the other side, and stretched taut on the windlasses by means of the handspikes until they give the same sound. Thus with tight wedging, catapults are tuned to the proper pitch by musical sense of hearing.

On these things I have said what I could. There is left for me, in the matter of sieges, to explain how generals can win victories and cities be defended, by means of machinery.

CHAPTER XIII

SIEGE MACHINES

1. It is related that the battering ram for sieges was originally invented as follows. The Carthaginians pitched their camp for the siege of Cadiz. They captured an outwork and attempted to destroy it. But having no iron implements for its destruction, they took a beam, and, raising it with their hands, and driving the end of it repeatedly against the top of the wall, they threw down the top courses of stones, and thus, step by step in regular order, they demolished the entire redoubt.

2. Afterwards a carpenter from Tyre, Bright by name and by nature, was led by this invention into setting up a mast from which he hung another crosswise like a steelyard, and so, by swinging it vigorously to and fro, he threw down the wall of Cadiz. Geras of Chalcedon was the first to make a wooden platform with wheels under it, upon which he constructed a framework of uprights and crosspieces, and within it he hung the ram, and covered it with oxhide for the better protection of the men who were stationed in the machine to batter the wall. As the machine made but slow progress, he first gave it the name of the tortoise of the ram.

3. These were the first steps then taken towards that kind of machinery, but afterwards, when Philip, the son of Amyntas, was besieging Byzantium, it was developed in many varieties and made handier by Polyidus the Thessalian. His pupils were Diades and Charias, who served with Alexander. Diades shows in his writings that he invented moveable towers, which he used also to take apart and carry round with the army, and likewise the borer, and the scaling machine, by means of which one can cross over to the wall on a level with the top of it, as well as the destroyer called the raven, or by others the crane.

4. He also employed the ram mounted on wheels, an account of which he left in his writings. As for the tower, he says that the smallest should be not less than sixty cubits in height and seventeen in breadth, but diminishing to one fifth less at the top; the uprights for the tower being nine inches at the bottom and half a foot at the top. Such a tower, he says, ought to be ten stories high, with windows in it on all sides.

5. His larger tower, he adds, was one hundred and twenty cubits high and twenty-three and one half cubits broad, diminishing like the other to one fifth less; the uprights, one foot at the bottom and six digits at the top. He made this large tower twenty stories high, each story having a gallery round it, three cubits wide. He covered the towers with rawhide to protect them from any kind of missile.

6. The tortoise of the battering ram was constructed in the same way. It had, however, a base of thirty cubits square, and a height, excluding the pediment, of thirteen cubits; the height of the pediment from its bed to its top was seven cubits. Issuing up and above the middle of the roof for not less than two cubits was a gable, and on this was reared a small tower four stories high, in which, on the top floor, scorpiones and catapults were set up, and on the lower floors a great quantity of water was stored, to put out any fire that might be thrown on the tortoise. Inside of this was set the machinery of the ram, termed in Greek κριοδόχη, in which was placed a roller, turned on a lathe, and the ram, be-

ing set on top of this, produced its great effects when swung to and fro by means of ropes. It was protected, like the tower, with rawhide.

7. He explained the principles of the borer as follows: that the machine itself resembled the tortoise, but that in the middle it had a pipe lying between upright walls, like the pipe usually found in catapults and ballistae, fifty cubits in length and one cubit in height, in which a windlass was set transversely. On the right and left, at the end of the pipe, were two blocks, by means of which the iron-pointed beam, which lay in the pipe, was moved. There were numerous rollers enclosed in the pipe itself under the beam, which made its movements quicker and stronger. Numerous arches were erected along the pipe above the beam which was in it, to hold up the rawhide in which this machine was enveloped.

8. He thought it needless to write about the raven, because he saw that the machine was of no value. With regard to the scaling machine, termed in Greek ἐπιβάθρα, and the naval contrivances which, as he wrote, could be used in boarding ships, I have observed that he merely promised with some earnestness to explain their principles, but that he has not done so.

I have set forth what was written by Diades on machines and their construction. I shall now set forth the methods which I have learned from my teachers, and which I myself believe to be useful.

CHAPTER XIV

THE TORTOISE

1. A TORTOISE intended for the filling of ditches, and thereby to make it possible to reach the wall, is to be made as follows. Let a base, termed in Greek ἐσχάρα, be constructed, with each of its sides twenty-one feet long, and with four crosspieces. Let these be held together by two others, two thirds of a foot thick and half a foot broad; let the crosspieces be about three feet and

a half apart, and beneath and in the spaces between them set the trees, termed in Greek ἁμαξόποδες, in which the axles of the wheels turn in iron hoops. Let the trees be provided with pivots, and also with holes through which levers are passed to make them turn, so that the tortoise can move forward or back or towards its right or left side, or if necessary obliquely, all by the turning of the trees.

2. Let two beams be laid on the base, projecting for six feet on each side, round the projections of which let two other beams be nailed, projecting seven feet beyond the former, and of the thickness and breadth prescribed in the case of the base. On this framework set up posts mortised into it, nine feet high exclusive of their tenons, one foot and a quarter square, and one foot and a half apart. Let the posts be tied together at the top by mortised beams. Over the beams let the rafters be set, tied one into another by means of tenons, and carried up twelve feet high. Over the rafters set the square beam by which the rafters are bound together.

3. Let the rafters themselves be held together by bridgings, and covered with boards, preferably of holm oak, or, this failing, of any other material which has the greatest strength, except pine or alder. For these woods are weak and easily catch fire. Over the boardings let there be placed wattles very closely woven of thin twigs as fresh as possible. Let the entire machine be covered with rawhide sewed together double and stuffed with seaweed or straw soaked in vinegar. In this way the blows of ballistae and the force of fires will be repelled by them.

CHAPTER XV

HEGETOR'S TORTOISE

1. THERE is also another kind of tortoise, which has all the other details as described above except the rafters, but it has round it a parapet and battlements of boards, and eaves sloping down-

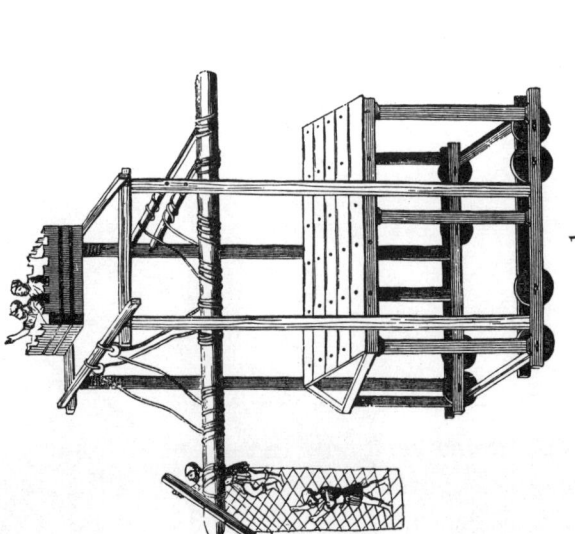

HEGETOR'S RAM AND TORTOISE

1. From a MS. of the sixteenth century (Wescher's *Poliorcétique des Grecs*).
2. From a model made by A. A. Howard.

wards, and is covered with boards and hides firmly fastened in place. Above this let clay kneaded with hair be spread to such a thickness that fire cannot injure the machine. These machines can, if need be, have eight wheels, should it be necessary to modify them with reference to the nature of the ground. Tortoises, however, which are intended for excavating, termed in Greek ὀρυκτίδες, have all the other details as described above, but their fronts are constructed like the angles of triangles, in order that when missiles are shot against them from a wall, they may receive the blows not squarely in front, but glancing from the sides, and those excavating within may be protected without danger.

2. It does not seem to me out of place to set forth the principles on which Hegetor of Byzantium constructed a tortoise. The length of its base was sixty-three feet, the breadth forty-two. The corner posts, four in number, which were set upon this framework, were made of two timbers each, and were thirty-six feet high, a foot and a quarter thick, and a foot and a half broad. The base had eight wheels by means of which it was moved about. The height of these wheels was six and three quarters feet, their thickness three feet. Thus constructed of three pieces of wood, united by alternate opposite dovetails and bound together by cold-drawn iron plates, they revolved in the trees or amaxopodes.

3. Likewise, on the plane of the crossbeams above the base, were erected posts eighteen feet high, three quarters of a foot broad, two thirds of a foot thick, and a foot and three quarters apart; above these, framed beams, a foot broad and three quarters of a foot thick, held the whole structure together; above this the rafters were raised, with an elevation of twelve feet; a beam set above the rafters united their joinings. They also had bridgings fastened transversely, and a flooring laid on them protected the parts beneath.

4. It had, moreover, a middle flooring on girts, where scorpiones and catapults were placed. There were set up, also, two framed

uprights forty-five feet long, a foot and a half in thickness, and three quarters of a foot in breadth, joined at the tops by a mortised crossbeam and by another, halfway up, mortised into the two shafts and tied in place by iron plates. Above this was set, between the shafts and the crossbeams, a block pierced on either side by sockets, and firmly fastened in place with clamps. In this block were two axles, turned on a lathe, and ropes fastened from them held the ram.

5. Over the head of these (ropes) which held the ram, was placed a parapet fitted out like a small tower, so that, without danger, two soldiers, standing in safety, could look out and report what the enemy were attempting. The entire ram had a length of one hundred and eighty feet, a breadth at the base of a foot and a quarter, and a thickness of a foot, tapering at the head to a breadth of a foot and a thickness of three quarters of a foot.

6. This ram, moreover, had a beak of hard iron such as ships of war usually have, and from the beak iron plates, four in number, about fifteen feet long, were fastened to the wood. From the head to the very heel of the beam were stretched cables, three in number and eight digits thick, fastened just as in a ship from stem to stern continuously, and these cables were bound with cross girdles a foot and a quarter apart. Over these the whole ram was wrapped with rawhide. The ends of the ropes from which the ram hung were made of fourfold chains of iron, and these chains were themselves wrapped in rawhide.

7. Likewise, the projecting end of the ram had a box framed and constructed of boards, in which was stretched a net made of rather large ropes, over the rough surfaces of which one easily reached the wall without the feet slipping. And this machine moved in six directions, forward (and backward), also to the right or left, and likewise it was elevated by extending it upwards and depressed by inclining it downwards. The machine could be elevated to a height sufficient to throw down a wall of about one hundred feet, and likewise in its thrust it covered a space from right to left of not less than one hundred feet. One

hundred men controlled it, though it had a weight of four thousand talents, which is four hundred and eighty thousand pounds.

CHAPTER XVI

MEASURES OF DEFENCE

1. With regard to scorpiones, catapults, and ballistae, likewise with regard to tortoises and towers, I have set forth, as seemed to me especially appropriate, both by whom they were invented and in what manner they should be constructed. But I have not considered it as necessary to describe ladders, cranes, and other things, the principles of which are simpler, for the soldiers usually construct these by themselves, nor can these very machines be useful in all places nor in the same way, since fortifications differ from each other, and so also the bravery of nations. For siege works against bold and venturesome men should be constructed on one plan, on another against cautious men, and on still another against the cowardly.

2. And so, if any one pays attention to these directions, and by selection adapts their various principles to a single structure, he will not be in need of further aids, but will be able, without hesitation, to design such machines as the circumstances or the situations demand. With regard to works of defence, it is not necessary to write, since the enemy do not construct their defences in conformity with our books, but their contrivances are frequently foiled, on the spur of the moment, by some shrewd, hastily conceived plan, without the aid of machines, as is said to have been the experience of the Rhodians.

3. For Diognetus was a Rhodian architect, to whom, as an honour, was granted out of the public treasury a fixed annual payment commensurate with the dignity of his art. At this time an architect from Aradus, Callias by name, coming to Rhodes, gave a public lecture, and showed a model of a wall, over which he set a machine on a revolving crane with which he seized an helepolis

as it approached the fortifications, and brought it inside the wall. The Rhodians, when they had seen this model, filled with admiration, took from Diognetus the yearly grant and transferred this honour to Callias.

4. Meanwhile, king Demetrius, who because of his stubborn courage was called Poliorcetes, making war on Rhodes, brought with him a famous Athenian architect named Epimachus. He constructed at enormous expense, with the utmost care and exertion, an helepolis one hundred and thirty-five feet high and sixty feet broad. He strengthened it with hair and rawhide so that it could withstand the blow of a stone weighing three hundred and sixty pounds shot from a ballista; the machine itself weighed three hundred and sixty thousand pounds. When Callias was asked by the Rhodians to construct a machine to resist this helepolis, and to bring it within the wall as he had promised, he said that it was impossible.

5. For not all things are practicable on identical principles, but there are some things which, when enlarged in imitation of small models, are effective, others cannot have models, but are constructed independently of them, while there are some which appear feasible in models, but when they have begun to increase in size are impracticable, as we can observe in the following instance. A half inch, inch, or inch and a half hole is bored with an auger, but if we should wish, in the same manner, to bore a hole a quarter of a foot in breadth, it is impracticable, while one of half a foot or more seems not even conceivable.

6. So too, in some models it is seen how they appear practicable on the smallest scale and likewise on a larger. And so the Rhodians, in the same manner, deceived by the same reasoning, inflicted injury and insult on Diognetus. Therefore, when they saw the enemy stubbornly hostile, slavery threatening them because of the machine which had been built to take the city, and that they must look forward to the destruction of their state, they fell at the feet of Diognetus, begging him to come to the aid of the fatherland. He at first refused.

7. But after free-born maidens and young men came with the priests to implore him, he promised to do it on condition that if he took the machine it should be his property. When these terms had been agreed upon, he pierced the wall in the place where the machine was going to approach it, and ordered all to bring forth from both public and private sources all the water, excrement, and filth, and to pour it in front of the wall through pipes projecting through this opening. After a great amount of water, filth, and excrement had been poured out during the night, on the next day the helepolis moving up, before it could reach the wall, came to a stop in the swamp made by the moisture, and could not be moved forwards, nor later even backwards. And so Demetrius, when he saw that he had been baffled by the wisdom of Diognetus, withdrew with his fleet.

8. Then the Rhodians, freed from the war by the cunning of Diognetus, thanked him publicly, and decorated him with all honours and distinctions. Diognetus brought that helepolis into the city, set it up in a public place, and put on it an inscription: "Diognetus out of the spoils of the enemy dedicated this gift to the people." Therefore, in works of defence, not merely machines, but, most of all, wise plans must be prepared.

9. Likewise at Chios, when the enemy had prepared storming bridges on their ships, the Chians, by night, carried out earth, sand, and stones into the sea before their walls. So, when the enemy, on the next day, tried to approach the walls, their ships grounded on the mound beneath the water, and could not approach the wall nor withdraw, but pierced with fire-darts were burned there. Again, when Apollonia was being besieged, and the enemy were thinking, by digging mines, to make their way within the walls without exciting suspicion, and this was reported by scouts to the people of Apollonia, they were much disturbed and alarmed by the news, and having no plans for defence, they lost courage, because they could not learn either the time or the definite place where the enemy would come out.

10. But at this time Trypho, the Alexandrine architect, was

there. He planned a number of countermines inside the wall, and extending them outside the wall beyond the range of arrows, hung up in all of them brazen vessels. The brazen vessels hanging in one of these mines, which was in front of a mine of the enemy, began to ring from the strokes of their iron tools. So from this it was ascertained where the enemy, pushing their mines, thought to enter. The line being thus found out, he prepared kettles of hot water, pitch, human excrement, and sand heated to a glow. Then, at night, he pierced a number of holes, and pouring the mixture suddenly through them, killed all the enemy who were engaged in this work.

11. In the same manner, when Marseilles was being besieged, and they were pushing forward more than thirty mines, the people of Marseilles, distrusting the entire moat in front of their wall, lowered it by digging it deeper. Thus all the mines found their outlet in the moat. In places where the moat could not be dug they constructed, within the walls, a basin of enormous length and breadth, like a fish pond, in front of the place where the mines were being pushed, and filled it from wells and from the port. And so, when the passages of the mine were suddenly opened, the immense mass of water let in undermined the supports, and all who were within were overpowered by the mass of water and the caving in of the mine.

12. Again, when a rampart was being prepared against the wall in front of them, and the place was heaped up with felled trees and works placed there, by shooting at it with the ballistae red-hot iron bolts they set the whole work on fire. And when a ram-tortoise had approached to batter down the wall, they let down a noose, and when they had caught the ram with it, winding it over a drum by turning a capstan, having raised the head of the ram, they did not allow the wall to be touched, and finally they destroyed the entire machine by glowing fire-darts and the blows of ballistae. Thus by such victory, not by machines but in opposition to the principle of machines, has the freedom of states been preserved by the cunning of architects.

Such principles of machines as I could make clear, and as I thought most serviceable for times of peace and of war, I have explained in this book. In the nine earlier books I have dealt with single topics and details, so that the entire work contains all the branches of architecture, set forth in ten books.

FINIS

SCAMILLI IMPARES (Book III, ch. 4)

No passage in Vitruvius has given rise to so much discussion or been the subject of such various interpretations as this phrase. The most reasonable explanation of its meaning seems to be that of Émile Burnouf, at one time Director of the French School at Athens, published in the *Revue Générale de l'Architecture* for 1875, as a note to a brief article of his on the explanation of the curves of Greek Doric buildings. This explanation was accepted by Professor Morgan, who called my attention to it in a note dated December 12, 1905. It has also quite recently been adopted by Professor Goodyear in his interesting book on *Greek Refinements*.

Burnouf would translate it *nivelettes inégales*, "unequal levellers." He states that in many parts of France in setting a long course of cut stone the masons make use of a simple device consisting of three pointed blocks of equal height used as levellers, of which two are placed one at each extremity of the course, while the third is used to level the stones, as they are successively set in place, by setting it upon the stone to be set and sighting across the other two levellers. If two "levellers" of equal height are used with a third of less height placed at the centre of the course, with perhaps others of intermediate height used at intermediate points, it would obviously be equally easy to set out a curved course, as, for instance, the curved stylobate of the Parthenon which rises about three inches in its length of one hundred feet. By a simple calculation any desired curve could be laid out in this way. The word *scamillus* is a diminutive of *scamnum*, a mounting-block or bench.

Practically the same explanation is given by G. Georges in a memoir submitted to the Sorbonne in April, 1875. Georges adds an interesting list, by no means complete, of the various explanations that have been offered at different times.

Philander (1522–1552). Projections of the stylobate or pedestals.
Barbaro (1556–1690). The same.
Bertano (1558). Swellings of the die of the stylobate or bosses in the stylobate or the frieze of the entablature.
Baldus (1612). Sub-plinths placed under the bases of the columns.
Perrault (1673–1684). Projection of the stylobate.
Polleni (1739). The same.
Galiani (1758–1790). Projection of the stylobate with hypothesis of embossments on the stylobates and the bases of the columns.
Tardieu and Coussin (1837) and Mauffras (1847). Projection of the stylobates.
Aurès (1865). Steps or offsets between the stylobate and the columns.

The list of Georges is wholly French and Italian.

Fra Giocondo's interpretation is indicated in our reproduction of the illustration in his edition of 1511.

Hoffer (1838) and afterwards Pennethorne (1846) and Penrose (1851) gave measurements showing the curvatures in the Parthenon and the temple of Theseus in Athens. Penrose and most writers who followed him supposed the "scamilli impares" to be projections or offsets on the stylobate required on account of the curves to bring the column into relation with the architraves above, and similar offsets of unequal or sloping form were supposed to be required above the abaci of the capitals, but such offsets, although sometimes existing, have no obvious connection with the passage in Vitruvius. C. Bötticher (1863) and more recently Durm have denied the original intention of the curves and ascribe them to settlement, a supposition which hardly accords with the observed facts. Reber, in the note on this passage in his translation of Vitruvius (1865), thinks the scamilli were sloping offsets on the stylobate to cause the inclination of the columns, but admits that nothing of the kind has been found in the remains so far examined. It may be added that this is at variance with the statement of the purpose of the scamilli which Vitruvius gives.

Assuming, as I think we must, that the horizontal curvature of the stylobate in such buildings as the Parthenon was intended and carefully planned, Burnouf's explanation fits the case precisely and makes this passage of Vitruvius straightforward and simple. This can be said of no other explanation, for all the others leave the passage obscure and more or less nonsensical. Durm's attempt to refer the passage to the case of the temple with a podium which has just been spoken of by Vitruvius is somewhat forced, or at least unnecessary. Clearly the passage refers to stylobates in general; but Reber also so translates and punctuates as to make the use of the "scamilli impares" refer only to the case of temples built in the Roman manner with the podium. His resulting explanation still leaves the passage obscure and unsatisfactory. One may finally refer to the ingenious but improbable explanation of Choisy, who translates it *echelons impairs*, and explains them as offsets arranged according to the odd numbers, *nombres impairs*, i.e., offsets varying at equal intervals in the proportion of 1, 3, 5, 7, 9, etc., and which he claims was applied also to the entasis of columns.

H. L. WARREN.

INDEX

INDEX

Abacus, 92, 106, 110, 122.
Ἄβατον, 56.
Abdera, 212, 269.
Acanthus pattern, origin of, 104.
Accius, 255.
Acoustics, of the site of a theatre, 153 f.
Acroteria, 96.
Aequians have springs which produce goitre, 239.
Aeruca (verdigris), 219.
Aeschylus, 198.
Aesculapius, proper site for temple of, 15; temple of, at Tralles, 198.
Aetna, 47.
Africa, 240.
Agatharcus, 198.
Agesistratus, 199.
Agger (river), 231.
Agnus castus (tree), 60 f., 296.
Ἀκροβατικόν, 283.
Alabanda, 212; temple of Apollo at, 78.
Alae, of house, 177; of temples, 120.
Albula (river), 233.
Alder, 61.
Alexander, 35 f., 195, 310.
Alexandria, 36, 196, 197, 218; length of shadow of gnomon at, 270.
Alexis (poet), 168.
Altars, 125 f.
Altino, 21.
Aluminous springs, 234.
Amiternum, stone quarries of, 49.
Ammon, 235.
Amphiprostyle, 75.
Amphithalamos, 186.
Amyntas, 310.
Analemma, 257; its applications, 270 ff.
Anaphoric dial, 275.
Anaxagoras, 195, 198, 225, 269.
Ancona, 63.
Andreas, 273.
Andromeda (constellation), 266.
Andron of Ephesus, 70.
Androne, 187.
Andronicus of Cyrrhus, 26.
Antae, 114, 120, 186; temple in antis, 75.
Antiborean (sun dial), 273.
Antimachides, 199.
Antiochus, 199.
Antipater, 238, 269.
Antistates, 199.
Apaturius, 212.
Apelles, 11.

Apollo, 69, 102, 103, 196; Panionion, 103, 255; colossal statue of, 289; temple of, at Alabanda, 78; at Miletus, 200; at Rome, 80; site of temple of, 80.
Apollonia, 235; siege of, 317 f.
Apollonius, 273.
Apollonius of Perga, 12.
Aqueducts, 244 ff.; Marcian, 232.
Aquileia, 21.
Arabia, 235, 237.
Arachne (sun dial), 273.
Aradus, 315.
Araeostyle temples, 78, 80; proportions of columns in, 84.
Aratus, 269.
Arcadia, 238.
Arcesius, 109, 198.
Arched substructures, 190.
Archer (constellation), 266.
Archimedes, 8, 12, 199, 243; detects a theft of gold by a contractor, 253 f.
Archinapolus (astrologer), 269.
Architecture, fundamental principles of, 13 ff.; departments of, 16 ff.
Architrave, 94, 288.
Archytas of Tarentum, 12, 199, 255.
Arcturus (star), 266.
Ardea, 233.
Arevanias, 54.
Arezzo, ancient wall of brick at, 53.
Argo (constellation), 268.
Argolis, precinct of Juno at, 102.
Argos, 54.
Ariobarzanes, 154.
Aristarchus, 11.
—— of Samos, 12, 263, 273.
Aristides, 241.
Aristippus, shipwreck of, 167.
Aristomenes of Thasos, 70.
Aristophanes, 168; grammaticus, 196.
Aristotle, 195, 251.
Aristoxenus, 11, 140, 145.
Armenian blue, 213, 217.
Ἁρπεδόναι (star group), 268.
Arrow (constellation), 266.
Arsenal, naval, at Peiraeus, 198.
Arsinoe, 103.
Artemisia, 55 f.
Artemon (Ἐπάγων), 287.
Asphalt, 235; asphaltic springs, 234; lake Asphaltitis, 235.
Ἄσπληνον, 20.
Assafoetida grown in Cyrene, 237.

INDEX

Astansoba (river), 231.
Astoboa (river), 231.
Astragals, 90.
Astrology, 269 ff.
Athens, 26, 40, 53, 78, 124, 199, 200, 234; colonnades at, 154; temple of Minerva at, 198; length of shadow of gnomon at, 257, 270.
Athos, Mt., 35.
Ἄτλαντες, 188.
Atlantides, 189.
Atlas, 188, 231.
Atrium, 185, 210; proportions of, 176 f.
Attalus, 53, 103, 195.
Attic doorways, 120.
Aurelius, Marcus, 3.
Aventine, 216.

Babylon, 24, 235.
Bacchus, proper site for temple of, 31; Ionic order appropriate to, 15; temple of, at Teos, 82, 109, 198.
Baiae, 46, 47.
Bakeries, 184.
Balance (constellation), 266.
Balconies in forum, 131.
Balearic Isles, 214, 240.
Ballistae, rules for making, 305 ff.
Bankers' offices, 131.
Barns, 184.
Βαρουλκός, 283.
Bases, Ionic, 90 ff.
Basilica, 132 ff.; of Vitruvius at Fano, 134 ff.
Bathrooms, 180; of farmhouse, 183.
Baths, 157 ff.
Beast (constellation), 268.
Bedrooms, 181.
Beech, 60.
Berosus, 262, 269, 273.
Bilberry, used to make purple, 220.
Bird (constellation), 266.
Black, 217 f.
Block (rechamus), 285 ff.
Blue, 218 f.
Body, proportions of, 72.
Boedas of Byzantium, 70.
Boeotia, 237.
Bolsena, lake of, 50.
Borer, principle of, 311.
Boscoreale, villa rustica at, 183.
Bowl (constellation), 268.
Breakwaters, 162 ff.
Brick, 42 ff.; test of, 57.
Bright (Pephrasmenos), inventor of battering ram, 309.
Bryaxis, 199.
Bucket-pump, 294.
Bug (river), 231.
Bull (constellation), 266.
Burnt-ochre, 218 f.

Buttresses, 190 f.
Byzantium, 310.

Cadiz, 309.
Caecuban (wine), 236.
Caesar, Julius, 62 f., 240.
Callaeschrus, 199.
Callias of Aradus, 315.
Callimachus (κατατηξίτεχνος), 104.
Callippus, 269.
Campania, 48, 64, 236, 238.
Campus Cornetus, 238.
Canon of water organ, 299.
Canopus (star), 268.
Capitals, Ionic, 92 ff.; Corinthian, 102, 104 f.; Doric, 110; of triglyphs, 112.
Capitol, hut of Romulus on, 40; temple on, 80.
Cappadocia, 235.
Carpion, 198.
Carthage, 235.
Caryae, 6 f.
Caryatides, 6 f.
Casius (town in Egypt), 235.
Cassiopea (constellation), 266.
Castor, temple of, 124.
Catacecaumenites (wine), 236.
Catapults, 303 ff.; stringing and tuning of, 308 f.
Cataract of Nile, 231.
Catheti, 92.
Caucasus, 231.
Cavaedium, 176 ff.
Cedar, 62.
Ceilings of baths, 158.
Cella, 114 ff., 120; of circular temple, 123.
Celtica, 231.
Censer (constellation), 267.
Centaur (constellation), 267.
Cepheus (constellation), 266.
Cephisus, 237.
Ceres, temple of 80, 200; site of temple of, 32.
Chalcedon, 309.
Chaldeans, 262.
Charias, 199, 310.
Charioteer (constellation), 266.
Χειρόκμητα of Democritus, 255.
Chersiphron, 78, 198, 200, 288.
Chion of Corinth, 70.
Chionides, 168.
Chios, 103, 197; siege of, 317.
Chorobates, levelling instrument, 242 f.
Chrobs, poisonous lake at, 237.
Chromatic mode, 140.
Cibdeli, 234.
Cicero, 256.
Cilbian country, 215.
Cilicia, 235.
Cinnabar, 215 ff.; adulteration of, 217.
Circular temples, 122 ff.

INDEX

Circumference of earth, 27 f.
Circumsonant sites of theatres (περιηχοῦντες), 153.
Circus, Flaminius, 124, 273; Maximus, 80.
Cisterns, 244 ff.
City, site of, 17 ff.; walls, 21 f.
Classification of temples, 75 ff., 78 ff.
Clazomenae, 103, 269.
Clearstock of fir, 60.
Climate determines the style of houses, 170.
Clitor, spring at, 239.
Colchis, 231.
Colline Gate, 75.
Colonnades, 131, 154, 155, 156 f., 160 f.
Colophon, 103, 269.
Colours, 214 ff.; natural, 214 f.; artificial, 217; manufactured from flowers, 220; how applied to stucco, 207.
Columbaria (ὀπαί), 108.
Columns, proportions of, in colonnades, 154; in forums, 132; in basilicas, 132; Corinthian, 102; diminution in top of, 84 f.; Ionic order, 90 ff.; arrangement of, 114.
Conarachne (sun dial), 273.
Concords in music, 142.
Concrete floors, 202.
Cone (sun dial), 273.
Conical Plinthium (sun dial), 273.
Consonancies in music, 142.
Consonant sites of theatres (συνηχοῦντες), 153.
Constellations, northern, 265 ff.; Southern, 267 ff.
Consumptives, resin of larch good for, 63.
Corinth, 145.
Corinthian cavaedium, 176.
Corinthian order, 15; origin of, 102 f.; proportions of, 106 f.; treatise on, by Arcesius, 198.
Cornelius, Gnaeus, 3.
Corona, 102, 107, 112.
Cos, island of, 269.
Cossutius, 200.
Courage dependent on climate, 173.
Counterforts, 190.
Courtyards, 183.
Crab (constellation), 268.
Crathis (river), 237.
Crete, 20, 62.
Creusa, 103.
Croesus, 195; house of, at Sardis, 53.
Cross-aisles in theatre, 138, 146; in Greek theatre, 151.
Crown (constellation), 266.
Ctesibius, 8, 199, 273 f.; pump of, 297 f.
Cube, properties of, 130.
Cubit equals six palms or twenty-four fingers, 74.
Cumae, 162.

Cunei in theatre, 146.
Cutiliae, 234.
Cyclades, 214.
Cydnus, 234.
Cymatium, 94, 110; Doric, 112.
Cypress, 59, 61.
Cyrene, 27, 237, 255.

Daphnis of Miletus, 200.
Darius, 195.
Decorations of walls, 209 f.
Defence, measures for, 315 ff.
Delos, problem enjoined upon, by Apollo, 255.
Delphi, Round Building at, 198.
Demetrius of Phalerum, 200.
Demetrius Poliorcetes, 316.
Demetrius (slave of Diana), 200.
Democles, 199.
Democritus, 42, 195, 251, 255, 269; his study of perspective, 198.
Demophilus, 199.
Denarius, 74.
Dentils, 94, 102, 108.
Departments of architecture, 16 f.
Diades, 199; inventor of siege machines, 310.
Dials arranged to show hours of varying length, 274 ff.
Diana, temple of Ionic order, 15, 78; temple of, at Ephesus, 78, 103, 198, 200, 288 f.; at Rome, 80, 124; at Magnesia, 78, 198; statue of, 62.
Diatonic mode, 140.
Diastyle temples, 78, 80; proportions of columns in, 84; Doric, 113.
Διάθυρα, 188.
Dichalca, 74.
Diesis, 140.
Diminution in top of column, 84, 110.
Dining rooms, proportions of, 179, 181, 186; Cyzicene, 186; winter, 209 f.
Dinocrates, 35 f.
Diognetus, Rhodian architect, 315 ff.
Diomede, 21.
Dionysodorus, 273.
Dioptra, 242.
Diphilus, 199.
Dipteral temple, 75, 78.
Displuviate cavaedium, 177.
Dissonant sites of theatres (κατηχοῦντες), 153.
Dnieper, 231.
Dog (constellation), 268.
Dolphin (constellation), 266.
Don (river), 231.
Doors, of temples, 118 f.; of dwellings, 178; in theatres, 146.
Doorways of temples, proportions of, 117 ff.
Doric order, 15; proportions of, 109 ff.; doorways, 117; temples of, 198.

326 INDEX

Dorus, 102.
Drachma, 74.
Dyer's weed, 220.
Dyris (river), 231.
Dyrrachium, 235.

Eagle (constellation), 266.
Echea (ἠχεῖα), 9, 143 ff.
Echinus, 93, 110, 122.
Economy, 16.
Education of the architect, 5 ff., 168 f.
Egypt, 214, 231, 235, 269.
Ἐκφορά, 90.
Elements (στοιχεῖα) and their proportions, 18 ff., 225.
Elephantis, 231.
Eleusis, 200.
Ἑλίκη, 267.
Elpias of Rhodes, 21.
Empedocles, 225.
Ἔμπλεκτον, 52.
Engines, 283; for raising water, 293 ff.
Enharmonic mode, 140.
Ennius, 255.
Ἔντασις of columns, 86.
Eolipiles, 25.
Ephesus, 103, 214, 215, 281; temple of Diana at, 78, 198, 200.
Epicharmus, 225.
Epicurus, 42, 167, 195.
Epimachus, 316.
Equestrian Fortune, temple of, 80.
Eratosthenes of Cyrene, 12, 27, 28, 255.
Erythrae, 103.
Ethiopia, 231, 235.
Etruria (Tuscany), 48, 64, 235.
Eucrates, 168.
Euctemon, 269.
Eudoxus, 269, 273.
Eumenes, colonnades of, 154.
Euphranor, 199.
Euphrates, 231.
Euripides, 225; buried in Macedonia, 238; "Phaethon" of, 261.
Eurythmy, 14.
Eustyle temples, 78, 80 f.; proportions of columns in, 84.
Exedrae, 160, 179, 186, 211.
Exposure, proper for rooms, 180 f.

Faberius, 216.
Falernian (wine), 236.
Fano, 63; basilica at, 134 ff.
Farmhouses, 183 f.
Fascia, 94; of Attic doorway, 120.
Fauces, their dimensions, 178.
Faunus temple on the Island of the Tiber, 75.
Femur (μηρός), 112.
Ferento, 50.
Fidenae, stone quarries at, 49.

Fir, qualities of, 60; highland and lowland, 64 f.
Fire, origin of, 38.
Fishes (constellation), 266.
Flaminius circus, 124.
Floors, 202 ff.; Greek method of making, 210; of baths, 157 f.
Flora, temple of Corinthian order, 15.
Flutes of columns, 96; Doric, 113.
Folds for sheep and goats, 184.
Fondi, 236.
Foot equals four palms, or sixteen fingers, 74.
Fortune, temple of Equestrian, 80; Three Fortunes, 75.
Forum, 131 ff.
Foundations of temples, 86 ff.; of houses, 189 ff.
Fresco painting, decadence of, 210 ff.
Frieze, 94, 123.
Fuficius (architect), 199.
Fulcrum (ὑπομόχλιον), 290.

Ganges, 231.
Γάνωσις, 217.
Gaul, 220, 231.
Geras, inventor of shed for battering ram, 309.
Gilding, 215.
Gnomon, 257; length of shadow at different places, 270.
Gnosus, 20, 200.
Gorgon's head (star group), 266.
Gortyna, 20.
Grain rooms, 184.
Greater Dog (constellation), 268.
Great Bear, 257; (ἄρκτος or ἑλίκη), 265.
Grecian Station, 56.
Greek houses, 185 ff.
Green chalk (θεοδοτεῖον), 214.
Grotta Rossa, stone quarries at, 49.
Guttae, 102, 110, 112.
Gynaeconitis, 186.
Gypsum not to be used for stucco work, 206.

Halicarnassus, 53, 54.
Harbinger of the Vintage (star), 265.
Harbours, 162 ff.
Harmonics, 139 ff.
Hegesias, 241.
He-Goat (constellation), 266.
Helepolis of Epimachus, 316 f.
Hellen, 102.
Hemisphere (sun dial), 273.
Heptabolus, lake, 231.
Heptagonus, lake, 231.
Heraclea, 289.
Heraclitus of Ephesus, 42, 225.
Hercules, Doric order appropriate to, 15; site of temple of, 31; cellae of temple of, 53; Pompey's temple of, 80.

INDEX

Hermodorus, temple of Jupiter Stator, 78.
Hermogenes, 109; temple of Diana by, 78; determined rules of symmetry for eustyle temples, 82.
Herodotus, 241.
Herring-bone pattern, 203.
Hierapolis, boiling springs at, 236.
Hiero, 253 *f.*
Hinge-stiles, 118.
Hipparchus, 269.
Hippocrates, 11.
Hodometer, 301 *ff.*
Hoisting machines, 285.
Homer, 197.
Hornbeam, 61.
Horse (constellation), 266.
Hostilius, Marcus, 21.
Hot springs, 232; healing properties of, 233 *f.*
Hours, how marked by clocks, 274.
House, origin of, 38 *f.*; early types of, 39 *f.*; style of, determined by climate, 170 *f.*
Hypaethral temple, 14, 75, 78.
Hypanis, 214, 236.
Hysginum, 220.

Ictinus, 198, 200.
Iliad and Odyssey, 197.
Ilium, 237.
Incertum opus, 51.
India, 231.
India ink, 217, 218.
Indigo, substitute for, 220.
Indus, 231.
Iollas, 238.
Ion, 103.
Ionic order, 15; proportions of, 90 *ff.*; doorways of, 118; temples of, 198, 200.
Isis, site of temple of, 31.
Ismuc, 240.
Isodomum, 52.
Isthmian games, 251.
Italy, 48, 53, 131, 145, 173, 214, 231, 239.

Jaffa, 235.
Jambs, proportions of, 117.
Juba, King, 240.
Julius, Caius, son of Masinissa, 240.
Juno, Ionic order appropriate to, 15; site for temple of, 31; precinct at Argolis, 102; Doric temple of, in Samos, 198.
Jupiter, temple of, 14, 199; site for temple of, 31; cellae of temple, 53; temple on Island of the Tiber, 75; altars of, 125.
Jupiter (planet), 258, 260, 261, 262.

Kids (constellation), 266.
Kitchen, 183.
Kneeler (constellation), 266.
Knotwood, 60.
Κυνόσουρα, 267.

Lacedaemonians, 7.
Laconicum, 159.
Lacunar (sun dial), 273.
Language, origin of, 38.
Larch, 62 *f.*
Larignum, 62, 63.
Law governing architects at Ephesus, 281.
Lead pipes poisonous, 247.
Lebedos, 103.
Lemnos, 214.
Leochares, 54, 199.
Leonidas, 199.
Lesbos, 25, 236.
Levelling instruments, 242 *f.*
Lever, explanation of, 290 *f.*
Libraries, 181, 186.
Licymnius, 212 *f.*
Lighting of rooms, how to test, 185.
Lime, 45 *f.*; slaking of, for stucco, 204.
Linden, 60.
Lintels, height of, 117.
Lion (constellation), 268.
Liparis (river), 235.
Little Dog (constellation), 268.
Liver examined to determine site of towns, 20.
Λογεῖον, scenic and thymelic, 151, dimensions of, 151.
Logotomus, 272.
Lucania, 237.
Lucretius, 256.
Lyncestus, acid springs of, 238.
Lyre (constellation), 267.
Lysippus, 69.

Macedonia, 217, 238.
Machines, 283 *ff.*; for defence, 315 *ff.*
Maeonia, wine of, 236.
Magi, 225.
Magnesia, 78, 214, 240; temple of Diana at, 198.
Malachite green, 213; where found, 217; substitute for, 220.
Mamertine (wine), 236.
Marble, powdered for stucco work, 206, 213 *f.*; where quarried, 289.
Marius' temple of Honour and Valour, 78.
Mars, temple should be Doric, 15; site of temple of, 31.
Mars (planet), 259 *f.*, 262.
Marseilles, siege of, 318.
Maurusia (Mauretania), 231.
Mausoleum, 54, 199.
Mausolus, 53 *ff.*
Mazaca, lake near, petrifies reeds, etc., 235.
Medicine, architect should know, 10.
Medulli have springs which produce goitre, 239.
Melampus, 199, 239.
Melas of Argos, 54.
Melas (river), 237.

Melassa, 54.
Melian white, 214.
Melite, 103.
Melos, 214.
Menaeus, 272.
Mercury, site of temple of, 31; temple of, 54.
Mercury (planet), 258, 259.
Meroë, 231.
Mesauloe, 187.
Metagenes, 198, 200, 288.
Metellus, portico of, 78.
Meto, 269.
Metopes ($\mu\epsilon\tau\delta\pi\eta$), 94, 108, 110; size of, 112; arrangement of, in Doric temples, 113.
Metrodorus, 241.
Miletus, 103, 200, 269.
Milo of Croton, 251.
Minerva, temple should be Doric, 15; site of temple, 31; temple at Sunium, 124; at Priene, 11, 198; at Athens, 198.
Minidius, Publius, 3.
Mithridates, 154.
Modes of music, 140 ff.
Moon, 258; phases of, 262 f.
Mortar, consistency of, for stucco work, 206 f.; of burnt brick, 209.
Motion, elements of, 290 ff.
Mouldings for stucco work, 206.
Mucius, C., temple of Honour and Valour, 78, 200.
Mummius, Lucius, 145.
Muses, 253; fountain of, 232.
Music useful to architect, 8.
Mutules, 102, 108; of Tuscan temples, 122.
Myager the Phocaean, 70.
Myron, 11, 69.
Mysia the "Burnt District," 47.
Mytilene, 25.
Myus, 103.

Nemean games, 251.
Neptune, spring of, 237.
Nexaris, 199.
Nile, 36, 231; temples on, should face the river, 117.
Nonacris, "Water of the Styx," 238.
Notes, names of, 141 f.
Number, perfect, 73 f.
Nymphodorus, 199.
Nymphs, temple of Corinthian order, 15.

Oak, 60; in floors, 202.
Obols, 74.
Ochre ($\mathring{\omega}\chi\rho\alpha$), 214.
Oeci, distinction between Corinthian and Egyptian, 179; Cyzicene, 180.
Oil room, 184.
Olympian games, 251.
'Oπaί, 108.

Opus incertum, 51; reticulatum, 51; Signinum, 247 f.
Orchestra, reserved for senators, 146; of Greek theatre, 151.
Order appropriate to temples, 15; origin of different orders, 102 ff.
Organ, water, 299 f.
"Οργανον, 283.
Orientation of streets, 24 ff.; of temples, 116 f.
Orion (constellation), 268.
Ornaments of the orders, 107 ff.
Orpiment ($\dot{\alpha}\rho\sigma\epsilon\nu\iota\kappa\dot{\sigma}\nu$), 214.
Ostrum, source of purple dye, 220.

Paconius, 289.
Paeonius of Ephesus, 200.
Palaestra, 159 ff.
Palla, stone quarries at, 49.
Panels of doors, 118.
Paphlagonia, intoxicating springs of, 239.
Παραδρομίδες, 188.
Paraetonium, 235; white, 214.
Parapet of theatre, dimensions of, 148.
Parmenio, 273.
Paros, 289.
Pastas, 186.
Patras, cellae of temple built of brick, 53.
Patrocles, 273.
Pausanias, son of Agesipolis, 7.
Peiraeus, 234; naval arsenal at, 198.
Peisistratus, 199.
Pelecinum (sun dial), 273.
Penne, 234.
Pentaspast (hoisting machine), 285.
Pergamus, 196.
Peripteral temple, 75 f.
Peristyle, 186; decorations of, 210 f.; proportions of, 179; Rhodian, 186.
Peritreti, 303 f.
Perseus (constellation), 266.
Persian Porch, 7.
Persians, statues of, 8 f.
Perspective, commentaries on by Agatharcus, Anaxagoras, and Democritus, 198.
Pesaro, 63.
Pharax of Ephesus, 70.
Phasis, 231.
Phidias, 69.
Philippus (physicist), 269.
Philip son of Amyntas, 310.
Philo, 198, 200; of Byzantium, 199.
Philolaus of Tarentum, 12.
Philosophy, why useful to architect, 8.
Phocaea, 103.
Phrygia, 236.
Phthia, 102.
Picenum, 49.
Picture galleries, 179, 186.
Piles, of alder, 61; olive, or oak, 88.
Πίναξ of water organ, 299.

INDEX

Pine, 61.
Pixodorus discovers marble near Ephesus, 289; his name changed to Evangelus, 290.
Planets, 257 ff.; their retrograde movement, 260 f.
Plataea, battle of, 7.
Plato, 195, 251; rule for doubling the square, 252.
Πλειάδες, 189.
Plinthium (sun dial), 273.
Πνευματικόν, 283.
Po, 231.
Podium of theatre, height of, 148.
Pollis, 199.
Πόλοι (pivots of heaven), 257.
Polus (star), 267.
Polycles of Ephesus, 70.
Polyclitus, 11, 69.
Polyidus, 199, 310.
Polyspast (hoisting machine), 288.
Pompeian pumice, 47.
Pompey, colonnades of, 154; temple of Hercules, 80.
Pontic wax, 216, 217.
Pontus, 214, 220, 231, 236.
Poplar, 60.
Pormus, 199.
Posidonius, 241.
Pothereus (river), 20.
Pozzolana, 46 f.
Praxiteles, 199.
Pressing room, 183 f.
Priene, 103; Temple of Minerva at, 11, 198.
Primordial substance, 42.
Prison, location of, 137.
Proconnesus, 289.
Pronaos, 114 ff., 120.
Proportions, 72, 174 f.; of circular temples, 123 f.; of colonnades, 154 f.; of columns and intercolumniations, 78 ff., 116; of the Corinthian order, 106 f.; of doorways of temples, 117 ff.; of Doric temples, 109 ff.; of the Ionic order, 90 ff.; of rooms, 176 ff.
Propriety, 14 ff.
Proscaenium of Greek theatre, 151.
Proserpine temple of Corinthian order, 15; temple of, 200.
Πρὸς πᾶν κλῖμα (sun dial), 273.
Πρὸς τὰ ἱστορούμενα (sun dial), 273.
Prostas, 186.
Prostyle, 75.
Proteus, daughters of, 239.
Prothyra, 188.
Protropum (wine), 236.
Προτρυγητής (star), 265.
Pseudisodomum, 52.
Pseudodipteral temple, 75, 78, 82.
Pseudoperipteral temples, 125.
Pteroma, 82, 114, 125.
Ptolemy, 196, 197; Philadelphus, 197.

Public buildings, sites of, 31 f.
Pump of Ctesibius, 297 f.
Purple, 213, 219; substitutes for, 220 f.
Puzzuoli, 218.
Pycnostyle temples, 78 f.; proportions of columns in, 84.
Pyrrus, 199.
Pythagoras, 42, 130, 225, 251, 269; right triangle of, 252 f.
Pytheos, 11, 109, 198, 199.
Pythian games, 251.

Quarries of Grotta Rosa, Palla, Fidenae, Campania, Umbria, Picenum, Tivoli, Amiternum, Venetia, Tarquinii, Lake of Bolsena, Ferento, 49, 50.
Quicksilver, 215 ff.
Quirinus, temple of, 78.
Quiver (sun dial), 273.

Rainwater, 229 ff.
Ram, battering, 309 f.; Hegetor's, 314 f.
Ram (constellation), 266.
Raven (constellation), 268.
Raven, a machine of no value, 310 f.
Ravenna, 21, 61, 63.
Reduction of columns, 114.
Refraction explained, 175.
Resin, soot of, used to make black, 218.
Resonant sites of theatres (ἀντηχοῦντες), 153.
Retaining walls, 190 f.
Reticulatum opus, 51.
Retrogression of planets, 261.
Rhine, 231.
Rhodes, 55 f., 167, 219, 220; length of shadow of gnomon at, 270; siege of, 316 f.
Rhone, 231.
River (constellation), 268.
Rivers rise in the north, 231.
Rome, 63, 64, 78, 80, 145, 217; site of, determined by divine intelligence, 174; length of shadow of gnomon at, 270.
Romulus, hut of, 40.
Roofs, of mud, 39 f.; timbers of, 107; of Tuscan temples, 122; of circular temples, 124.
Rooms, proportions of, 176 ff.; proper exposure for, 180 f.; should be suited to station of the owner, 181 f.
Round Building at Delphi, 198.

Salmacis, spring of, 54.
Salpia in Apulia, 21.
Sambuca illustrates effect of climate on voice, 171.
Samos, 12, 103, 263, 269, 273; Doric temple of Juno in, 198.
Sand, 44 f., 48.
Sandarach, 214; made from white lead, 219.
Sardis, 53.
Sarnacus, 199.

INDEX

Saturn (planet), 260, 261, 262.
Satyrus, 199.
Scaena of theatre, 146; dimensions of, 148; scheme of, 150; decorations of, 150; of theatre at Tralles, 212.
Scale, musical, 141.
Scaling machine, 311.
Scamilli impares, 89, 155, 320.
Scaphe (sun dial), 273.
Scopas, 199.
Scopinas, 12, 273.
Scorpion (constellation), 266.
Scorpiones, rules for making, 303 ff.
Scotia, 90, 112.
Scutula of ballistae, 306 f.
Seats in theatre, dimensions of, 148.
Selinusian chalk (ἰσάτις), 220.
Semiramis, 235.
Senate house, location of, 137.
Septentriones (She-Bears), 267.
Septimius, P., 199.
Serapis, site of temple of, 31.
Serpent (constellation), 266.
Serpent-holder (constellation), 266.
Sesterce, 74.
She-Goat (constellation), 266.
Ship, motion of, explained, 291.
Shipyards, 164.
Sicily, 236.
Siege machines, 309 ff.
Signinum work, 247 f.
Signs of the Zodiac, 258; sun's course through, 264 f.; shown on dials, 276 f.
Silanion, 199.
Silenus, on the proportions of Doric structures, 198.
Simae (ἐπαιετίδες), 96, 108.
Sinope, 214.
Smyrna, 197, 214; Stratoniceum at, 154.
Snake (constellation), 268.
Socrates, 69, 70, 195.
Soli, 235.
Soracte, stone quarries of, 49.
Sounding vessels in the theatre, 143 ff.
Southern Fish (constellation), 267.
Spain, 214; cinnabar mines of, 217.
Sparta, paintings on brick walls at, 53.
Spica (star), 265.
Stables, 184, 186.
Statonia, 50.
Steelyard, description of, 291.
Steps of temples odd in number, 88.
Stereobates, 88.
Stone, 48, 49 f.
Stratoniceum, 154.
Streets, directions of, 24.
Stucco, 204 ff.; in damp places, 208 ff.
Stucco-workers, Greek, 208.
Stylobates, 88.
Substructures of houses, 189 ff.
Sulphur springs, 233 f.

Sun, 258 f.; course of, through the twelve signs, 264 f.
Sundials, 273 ff.; how designed, 270 ff.
Sunium, temple of Pallas at, 124.
Susa, spring at, 240.
Syene, 231.
Symmetry, 14; in temples and in the human body, 72 f.; modifications to suit site, 174 ff.
Syracuse, 273.
Syria, 231, 235, 237.
Systyle temples, 78 f.; proportions of columns in, 84; Doric, 113.

Tablinum, proportions of, 178.
Tarentum, 12, 255; length of shadow of gnomon at, 270.
Tarquinii, 50.
Tarsus, 234, 240.
Teano, acid springs of, 238.
Telamones, 188.
Teleas of Athens, 70.
Τέλειον (perfect number), 73 f.
Tempering of iron, 18.
Temples, classification of, 75 ff.; circular, 122 ff.; Corinthian, 102 f.; Doric, 109 ff.; Ionic, 90 ff.; Tuscan, 120; foundations of, 86 ff.; orientation of, 116 f.; proportion of columns of, 78 ff.; sites of, 31 f.; Aesculapius, 15, 198; Apollo, 31, 78, 80, 200; Bacchus, 15, 31, 82, 109, 198; Castor, 124; Ceres, 32, 80, 200; Diana, 15, 78, 80, 103, 124, 198, 200, 288 f.; Equestrian Fortune, 80; Faunus, 75; Flora, 15; Three Fortunes, 75; Hercules, 15, 31, 53, 80; Isis, 31; Juno, 15, 31, 198; Jupiter, 14, 31, 53, 75, 199; Honour and Valour, 78, 200; Mars, 15, 31; Mercury, 31, 54; Minerva, 11, 15, 31, 124, 198; Nymphs, 15; Proserpine, 15, 200; Quirinus, 78; Serapis, 31; Vejovis, 124; Venus, 15, 31, 54; Vulcan, 31.
Teos, 103; temple of Bacchus at, 82, 198.
Terracina, 236, 237.
Testudinate cavaedium, 177.
Tetrachords, 140 ff.
Tetrastyle cavaedium, 176.
Thalamos, 186.
Thales, 42, 195, 225, 269.
Thasos, 289.
Theatre, 137 ff.; site of, 137; foundations of, 138 f.; entrances to, 138, 148; plan of Roman, 146 ff.; plan of Greek, 151 ff.; sounding vessels in, 143 f.; acoustics of site of, 153 ff.
Thebes in Egypt, 231.
Themistocles, colonnade of, 154.
Theo of Magnesia, 70.
Theocydes, 199.
Theodorus, 198.
Theodorus the Phocian, 198.

INDEX

Theodosius, 273.
Theodotus, 214.
Theophrastus, 167, 241.
Thessaly, 237.
Thrace, 237.
Θυρωρεῖον, 186.
Tiber, 231.
Tigris, 231.
Timaeus, 241.
Timavo, 231.
Timber, 58 ff.
Timotheus, 54, 199.
Tivoli, 233; stone quarries of, 49.
Tortoise, 311 ff.; of battering ram, 310; Hegetor's, 312 ff.
Torus, 90.
Towers, construction of, 22 f.; dimensions of moveable, 310.
Tralles, 212; palace of brick at, 53; colonnades at, 154; temple of Aesculapius at, 198.
Treasury, location of, 137.
Trichalca, 74.
Triglyphs, origin of, 107 ff.; arrangement of, 109 f., 113; size of, 112.
Trispast (hoisting machine), 285.
Τροχίλος (scotia), 90.
Troezen, 54, 234.
Troy, 195, 211, 237.
Trypho, Alexandrine architect, 317 f.
Tufa, its qualities, 49.
Tuscan, cavaedium, 176; temples, 120 f.
Twins (constellation), 266.
Tyana, 235.
Tympanum, 96, 122; water tympanum, 293.
Tyre, 309.

Ulysses, 211.
Universe, definition of, 257.

Varro, M. Terentius, 199, 256.
Vaultings, 205 ff.
Vejovis, temple of, 124.
Velian country, acid springs of, 238.
Venter (κοιλία), 245.
Venus, Corinthian order appropriate to, 15; site of temple of, 31; temple of, 54.
Venus (planet), 259.
Verdigris, 219.
Vergiliae, 189.
Vermilion, 213, 215; preparation of, 216.
Vesta, altar of, 125.
Vestorius, 218.
Vesuvius, 46, 47.
Via Campana, 238.
Vinegar a solvent of rocks, 239.
Violets used for purple colour, 220.

Virgin (constellation), 265.
Vitruvius, education, 13, 168; personal appearance, 36; method of writing, 197 ff.; military service, 3; his basilica at Fano, 134 ff.
Voice, defined, 138 f.; pitch of, determined by climate, 171.
Volutes, 93.
Voussoirs, 190.
Vulcan, site of temple of, 31.

Walks, how to be constructed, 156; serve practical purpose, 156.
Walls, material for, 24; methods of building, 51 ff., 56; of brick are durable, 53; of rubble, 53.
Warden (constellation), 265.
Water (constellation), 268.
Water, 225 ff.; indispensable, 226; how to find, 227 ff.; properties of, 232 ff.; tests of good, 242; methods of conducting, 244 ff.
Water clocks, 273 ff.
Waterman (constellation), 266.
Water organ, 299 f.
Water pipes, 244 ff.
Water screw, 295 ff.
Water wheels, 286 f.
Wattle and daub, 57 f.
Weather prognostics, 269 ff.
Wells, 244 ff.
Whale (constellation), 267.
Wheel (tread mill), 286 f.
White lead, 219, 238 f.
Willow, 60.
Winds, names and number of, 26 ff.; diagrams of, 29 f.; orientation of cities with reference to, 24 ff.
Wine, given its flavour by soil and water, 236; lees used to make black, 218.
Wine rooms, 184.

Xanthus, 237.
Xenia, 187.
Xenophanes, 195, 269.
Ξυστός, 161, 188.
Xuthus, 103.
Xysta (παραδρομίδες), 161, 188.

Yellow ochre, 220.

Zacynthus, 235.
Zama, 240.
Zea, spring at, 239 f.
Zeno, 195.
Zodiac, 257 ff.
Zoilus (Homeromastix), 197.

CATALOG OF DOVER BOOKS

CATALOG OF DOVER BOOKS

Philosophy, Religion

GUIDE TO PHILOSOPHY, C. E. M. Joad. A modern classic which examines many crucial problems which man has pondered through the ages: Does free will exist? Is there plan in the universe? How do we know and validate our knowledge? Such opposed solutions as subjective idealism and realism, chance and teleology, vitalism and logical positivism, are evaluated and the contributions of the great philosophers from the Greeks to moderns like Russell, Whitehead, and others, are considered in the context of each problem. "The finest introduction," BOSTON TRANSCRIPT. Index. Classified bibliography. 592pp. 5⅜ x 8.
T297 Paperbound $2.00

HISTORY OF ANCIENT PHILOSOPHY, W. Windelband. One of the clearest, most accurate comprehensive surveys of Greek and Roman philosophy. Discusses ancient philosophy in general, intellectual life in Greece in the 7th and 6th centuries B.C., Thales, Anaximander, Anaximenes, Heraclitus, the Eleatics, Empedocles, Anaxagoras, Leucippus, the Pythagoreans, the Sophists, Socrates, Democritus (20 pages), Plato (50 pages), Aristotle (70 pages), the Peripatetics, Stoics, Epicureans, Sceptics, Neo-platonists, Christian Apologists, etc. 2nd German edition translated by H. E. Cushman. xv + 393pp. 5⅜ x 8.
T357 Paperbound $1.75

ILLUSTRATIONS OF THE HISTORY OF MEDIEVAL THOUGHT AND LEARNING, R. L. Poole. Basic analysis of the thought and lives of the leading philosophers and ecclesiastics from the 8th to the 14th century—Abailard, Ockham, Wycliffe, Marsiglio of Padua, and many other great thinkers who carried the torch of Western culture and learning through the "Dark Ages": political, religious, and metaphysical views. Long a standard work for scholars and one of the best introductions to medieval thought for beginners. Index. 10 Appendices. xiii + 327pp. 5⅜ x 8.
T674 Paperbound $1.85

PHILOSOPHY AND CIVILIZATION IN THE MIDDLE AGES, M. de Wulf. This semi-popular survey covers aspects of medieval intellectual life such as religion, philosophy, science, the arts, etc. It also covers feudalism vs. Catholicism, rise of the universities, mendicant orders, monastic centers, and similar topics. Unabridged. Bibliography. Index. viii + 320pp. 5⅜ x 8.
T284 Paperbound $1.75

AN INTRODUCTION TO SCHOLASTIC PHILOSOPHY, Prof. M. de Wulf. Formerly entitled SCHOLASTICISM OLD AND NEW, this volume examines the central scholastic tradition from St. Anselm, Albertus Magnus, Thomas Aquinas, up to Suarez in the 17th century. The relation of scholasticism to ancient and medieval philosophy and science in general is clear and easily followed. The second part of the book considers the modern revival of scholasticism, the Louvain position, relations with Kantianism and Positivism. Unabridged. xvi + 271pp. 5⅜ x 8.
T296 Clothbound $3.50
T283 Paperbound $1.75

A HISTORY OF MODERN PHILOSOPHY, H. Höffding. An exceptionally clear and detailed coverage of western philosophy from the Renaissance to the end of the 19th century. Major and minor men such as Pomponazzi, Bodin, Boehme, Telesius, Bruno, Copernicus, da Vinci, Kepler, Galileo, Bacon, Descartes, Hobbes, Spinoza, Leibniz, Wolff, Locke, Newton, Berkeley, Hume, Erasmus, Montesquieu, Voltaire, Diderot, Rousseau, Lessing, Kant, Herder, Fichte, Schelling, Hegel, Schopenhauer, Comte, Mill, Darwin, Spencer, Hartmann, Lange, and many others, are discussed in terms of theory of knowledge, logic, cosmology, and psychology. Index. 2 volumes, total of 1159pp. 5⅜ x 8.
T117 Vol. 1, Paperbound $2.00
T118 Vol. 2, Paperbound $2.00

ARISTOTLE, A. E. Taylor. A brilliant, searching non-technical account of Aristotle and his thought written by a foremost Platonist. It covers the life and works of Aristotle; classification of the sciences; logic; first philosophy; matter and form; causes; motion and eternity; God; physics; metaphysics; and similar topics. Bibliography. New Index compiled for this edition. 128pp. 5⅜ x 8.
T280 Paperbound $1.00

THE SYSTEM OF THOMAS AQUINAS, M. de Wulf. Leading Neo-Thomist, one of founders of University of Louvain, gives concise exposition to central doctrines of Aquinas, as a means toward determining his value to modern philosophy. religion. Formerly "Medieval Philosophy Illustrated from the System of Thomas Aquinas." Trans. by E. Messenger. Introduction. 151pp. 5⅜ x 8.
T568 Paperbound $1.25

THE PHILOSOPHICAL WORKS OF DESCARTES. The definitive English edition of all the major philosophical works and letters of René Descartes. All of his revolutionary insights, from his famous "Cogito ergo sum" to his detailed account of contemporary science and his astonishingly fruitful concept that all phenomena of the universe (except mind) could be reduced to clear laws by the use of mathematics. An excellent source for the thought of men like Hobbes, Arnauld, Gassendi, etc., who were Descarte's contemporaries. Translated by E. S. Haldane and G. Ross. Introductory notes. Index. Total of 842pp. 5⅜ x 8.
T71 Vol. 1, Paperbound $2.00
T72 Vol. 2, Paperbound $2.00

CATALOG OF DOVER BOOKS

THE CHIEF WORKS OF SPINOZA. An unabridged reprint of the famous Bohn edition containing all of Spinoza's most important works: Vol. I: The Theologico-Political Treatise and the Political Treatise. Vol. II: On The Improvement Of Understanding, The Ethics, Selected Letters. Profound and enduring ideas on God, the universe, pantheism, society, religion, the state, democracy, the mind, emotions, freedom and the nature of man, which influenced Goethe, Hegel, Schelling, Coleridge, Whitehead, and many others. Introduction. 2 volumes. 826pp. 5⅜ x 8.
T249 Vol. I, Paperbound **$1.50**
T250 Vol. II, Paperbound **$1.50**

LEIBNIZ, H. W. Carr. Most stimulating middle-level coverage of basic philosophical thought of Leibniz. Easily understood discussion, analysis of major works: "Theodicy," "Principles of Nature and Grace," Monadology"; Leibniz's influence; intellectual growth; correspondence; disputes with Bayle, Malebranche, Newton; importance of his thought today, with reinterpretation in modern terminology. "Power and mastery," London Times. Bibliography. Index. 226pp. 5⅜ x 8.
T624 Paperbound **$1.35**

AN ESSAY CONCERNING HUMAN UNDERSTANDING, John Locke. Edited by A. C. Fraser. Unabridged reprinting of definitive edition; only complete edition of "Essay" in print. Marginal analyses of almost every paragraph; hundreds of footnotes; authoritative 140-page biographical, critical, historical prolegomena. Indexes. 1170pp. 5⅜ x 8.
T530 Vol. 1 (Books 1, 2) Paperbound **$2.25**
T531 Vol. 2 (Books 3, 4) Paperbound **$2.25**
2 volume set **$4.50**

THE PHILOSOPHY OF HISTORY, G. W. F. Hegel. One of the great classics of western thought which reveals Hegel's basic principle: that history is not chance but a rational process, the realization of the Spirit of Freedom. Ranges from the oriental cultures of subjective thought to the classical subjective cultures, to the modern absolute synthesis where spiritual and secular may be reconciled. Translation and introduction by J. Sibree. Introduction by C. Hegel. Special introduction for this edition by Prof. Carl Friedrich. xxxix + 447pp. 5⅜ x 8.
T112 Paperbound **$1.85**

THE PHILOSOPHY OF HEGEL, W. T. Stace. The first detailed analysis of Hegel's thought in English, this is especially valuable since so many of Hegel's works are out of print. Dr. Stace examines Hegel's debt to Greek idealists and the 18th century and then proceeds to a careful description and analysis of Hegel's first principles, categories, reason, dialectic method, his logic, philosophy of nature and spirit, etc. Index. Special 14 x 20 chart of Hegelian system. x + 526pp. 5⅜ x 8.
T254 Paperbound **$2.00**

THE WILL TO BELIEVE and HUMAN IMMORTALITY, W. James. Two complete books bound as one. THE WILL TO BELIEVE discusses the interrelations of belief, will, and intellect in man; chance vs. determinism, free will vs. determinism, free will vs. fate, pluralism vs. monism; the philosophies of Hegel and Spencer, and more. HUMAN IMMORTALITY examines the question of survival after death and develops an unusual and powerful argument for immortality. Two prefaces. Index. Total of 429pp. 5⅜ x 8.
T291 Paperbound **$1.65**

THE WORLD AND THE INDIVIDUAL, Josiah Royce. Only major effort by an American philosopher to interpret nature of things in systematic, comprehensive manner. Royce's formulation of an absolute voluntarism remains one of the original and profound solutions to the problems involved. Part one, 4 Historical Conceptions of Being, inquires into first principles, true meaning and place of individuality. Part two, Nature, Man, and the Moral Order, is application of first principles to problems concerning religion, evil, moral order. Introduction by J. E. Smith, Yale Univ. Index. 1070pp. 5⅜ x 8.
T561 Vol. 1 Paperbound **$2.25**
T562 Vol. 2 Paperbound **$2.25**
the set **$4.50**

THE PHILOSOPHICAL WRITINGS OF PEIRCE, edited by J. Buchler. This book (formerly THE PHILOSOPHY OF PEIRCE) is a carefully integrated exposition of Peirce's complete system composed of selections from his own work. Symbolic logic, scientific method, theory of signs, pragmatism, epistemology, chance, cosmology, ethics, and many other topics are treated by one of the greatest philosophers of modern times. This is the only inexpensive compilation of his key ideas. xvi + 386pp. 5⅜ x 8.
T217 Paperbound **$1.95**

EXPERIENCE AND NATURE, John Dewey. An enlarged, revised edition of the Paul Carus lectures which Dewey delivered in 1925. It covers Dewey's basic formulation of the problem of knowledge, with a full discussion of other systems, and a detailing of his own concepts of the relationship of external world, mind, and knowledge. Starts with a thorough examination of the philosophical method; examines the interrelationship of experience and nature; analyzes experience on basis of empirical naturalism, the formulation of law, role of language and social factors in knowledge; etc. Dewey's treatment of central problems in philosophy is profound but extremely easy to follow. ix + 448pp. 5⅜ x 8.
T471 Paperbound **$1.85**

CATALOG OF DOVER BOOKS

MIND AND THE WORLD-ORDER, C. I. Lewis. Building upon the work of Peirce, James, and Dewey, Professor Lewis outlines a theory of knowledge in terms of "conceptual pragmatism." Dividing truth into abstract mathematical certainty and empirical truth, the author demonstrates that the traditional understanding of the a priori must be abandoned. Detailed analyses of philosophy, metaphysics, method, the "given" in experience, knowledge of objects, nature of the a priori, experience and order, and many others. Appendices. xiv + 446pp. 5⅜ x 8.
T359 Paperbound **$1.95**

SCEPTICISM AND ANIMAL FAITH, G. Santayana. To eliminate difficulties in the traditional theory of knowledge, Santayana distinguishes between the independent existence of objects and the essence our mind attributes to them. Scepticism is thereby established as a form of belief, and animal faith is shown to be a necessary condition of knowledge. Belief, classical idealism, intuition, memory, symbols, literary psychology, and much more, discussed with unusual clarity and depth. Index. xii + 314pp. 5⅜ x 8.
T236 Paperbound **$1.50**

LANGUAGE AND MYTH, E. Cassirer. Analyzing the non-rational thought processes which go to make up culture, Cassirer demonstrates that beneath both language and myth there lies a dominant unconscious "grammar" of experience whose categories and canons are not those of logical thought. His analyses of seemingly diverse phenomena such as Indian metaphysics, the Melanesian "mana," the Naturphilosophie of Schelling, modern poetry, etc., are profound without being pedantic. Introduction and translation by Susanne Langer. Index. x + 103pp. 5⅜ x 8.
T51 Paperbound **$1.25**

SUBSTANCE AND FUNCTION, EINSTEIN'S THEORY OF RELATIVITY, E. Cassirer. In this double-volume, Cassirer develops a philosophy of the exact sciences that is historically sound, philosophically mature, and scientifically impeccable. Such topics as the concept of number, space and geometry, non-Euclidean geometry, traditional logic and scientific method, mechanism and motion, energy, relational concepts, degrees of objectivity, the ego, Einstein's relativity, and many others are treated in detail. Authorized translation by W. C. and M. C. Swabey. xii + 465pp. 5⅜ x 8.
T50 Paperbound **$2.00**

*THE ANALYSIS OF MATTER, Bertrand Russell. A classic which has retained its importance in understanding the relation between modern physical theory and human perception. Logical analysis of physics, prerelativity physics, causality, scientific inference, Weyl's theory, tensors, invariants and physical interpretations, periodicity, and much more is treated with Russell's usual brilliance. "Masterly piece of clear thinking and clear writing," NATION AND ATHENAEUM. "Most thorough treatment of the subject," THE NATION. Introduction. Index. 8 figures. viii + 408pp. 5⅜ x 8.
231 Paperbound **$1.95**

CONCEPTUAL THINKING (A LOGICAL INQUIRY), S. Körner. Discusses origin, use of general concepts on which language is based, and the light they shed on basic philosophical questions. Rigorously examines how different concepts are related; how they are linked to experience; problems of the field of contact between exact logical, mathematical, and scientific concepts, and the inexactness of everyday experience (studied at length). This work elaborates many new approaches to the traditional problems of philosophy—epistemology, value theories, metaphysics, aesthetics, morality. "Rare originality . . . brings a new rigour into philosophical argument," Philosophical Quarterly. New corrected second edition. Index. vii + 301pp. 5⅜ x 8
T516 Paperbound **$1.75**

INTRODUCTION TO SYMBOLIC LOGIC, S. Langer. No special knowledge of math required — probably the clearest book ever written on symbolic logic, suitable for the layman, general scientist, and philosopher. You start with simple symbols and advance to a knowledge of the Boole-Schroeder and Russell-Whitehead systems. Forms, logical structure, classes, the calculus of propositions, logic of the syllogism, etc., are all covered. "One of the clearest and simplest introductions," MATHEMATICS GAZETTE. Second enlarged, revised edition. 368pp. 5⅜ x 8.
S164 Paperbound **$1.75**

LANGUAGE, TRUTH AND LOGIC, A. J. Ayer. A clear, careful analysis of the basic ideas of Logical Positivism. Building on the work of Schlick, Russell, Carnap, and the Viennese School, Mr. Ayer develops a detailed exposition of the nature of philosophy, science, and metaphysics; the Self and the World; logic and common sense, and other philosophic concepts. An aid to clarity of thought as well as the first full-length development of Logical Positivism in English. Introduction by Bertrand Russell. Index. 160pp. 5⅜ x 8.
T10 Paperbound **$1.25**

ESSAYS IN EXPERIMENTAL LOGIC, J. Dewey. Based upon the theory that knowledge implies a judgment which in turn implies an inquiry, these papers consider the inquiry stage in terms of: the relationship of thought and subject matter, antecedents of thought, data and meanings. 3 papers examine Bertrand Russell's thought, while 2 others discuss pragmatism and a final essay presents a new theory of the logic of values. Index. viii + 444pp. 5⅜ x 8.
T73 Paperbound **$1.95**

TRAGIC SENSE OF LIFE, M. de Unamuno. The acknowledged masterpiece of one of Spain's most influential thinkers. Between the despair at the inevitable death of man and all his works and the desire for something better, Unamuno finds that "saving incertitude" that alone can console us. This dynamic appraisal of man's faith in God and in himself has been called "a masterpiece" by the ENCYCLOPAEDIA BRITANNICA. xxx + 332pp. 5⅜ x 8.
T257 Paperbound **$1.95**

CATALOG OF DOVER BOOKS

THE SENSE OF BEAUTY, G. Santayana. A revelation of the beauty of language as well as an important philosophic treatise, this work studies the "why, when, and how beauty appears, what conditions an object must fulfill to be beautiful, what elements of our nature make us sensible of beauty, and what the relation is between the constitution of the object and the excitement of our susceptibility." "It is doubtful if a better treatment of the subject has since been published," PEABODY JOURNAL. Index. ix + 275pp. 5⅜ x 8.
T238 Paperbound $1.00

THE IDEA OF PROGRESS, J. B. Bury. Practically unknown before the Reformation, the idea of progress has since become one of the central concepts of western civilization. Prof. Bury analyzes its evolution in the thought of Greece, Rome, the Middle Ages, the Renaissance, to its flowering in all branches of science, religion, philosophy, industry, art, and literature, during and following the 16th century. Introduction by Charles Beard. Index. xl + 357pp. 5⅜ x 8.
T40 Paperbound $1.95

HISTORY OF DOGMA, A. Harnack. Adolph Harnack, who died in 1930, was perhaps the greatest Church historian of all time. In this epoch-making history, which has never been surpassed in comprehensiveness and wealth of learning, he traces the development of the authoritative Christian doctrinal system from its first crystallization in the 4th century down through the Reformation, including also a brief survey of the later developments through the Infallibility decree of 1870. He reveals the enormous influence of Greek thought on the early Fathers, and discusses such topics as the Apologists, the great councils, Manichaeism, the historical position of Augustine, the medieval opposition to indulgences, the rise of Protestantism, the relations of Luther's doctrines with modern tendencies of thought, and much more. "Monumental work; still the most valuable history of dogma . . . luminous analysis of the problems . . . abounds in suggestion and stimulus and can be neglected by no one who desires to understand the history of thought in this most important field," Dutcher's Guide to Historical Literature. Translated by Neil Buchanan. Index. Unabridged reprint in 4 volumes. Vol I: Beginnings to the Gnostics and Marcion. Vol II & III: 2nd century to the 4th century Fathers. Vol IV & V: 4th century Councils to the Carlovingian Renaissance. Vol VI & VII: Period of Clugny (c. 1000) to the Reformation, and after. Total of cii + 2407pp. 5⅜ x 8.
T904 Vol I Paperbound $2.50
T905 Vol II & III Paperbound $2.50
T906 Vol IV & V Paperbound $2.50
T907 Vol VI & VII Paperbound $2.50
The set $10.00

THE GUIDE FOR THE PERPLEXED, Maimonides. One of the great philosophical works of all time and a necessity for everyone interested in the philosophy of the Middle Ages in the Jewish, Christian, and Moslem traditions. Maimonides develops a common meeting-point for the Old Testament and the Aristotelian thought which pervaded the medieval world. His ideas and methods predate such scholastics as Aquinas and Scotus and throw light on the entire problem of philosophy or science vs. religion. 2nd revised edition. Complete unabridged Friedländer translation. 55 page introduction to Maimonides's life, period, etc., with an important summary of the GUIDE. Index. lix + 414pp. 5⅜ x 8. T351 Paperbound $1.85

ASTROLOGY AND RELIGION AMONG THE GREEKS AND ROMANS, Franz Cumont. How astrology developed, spread, and took hold of superior intellects; from ancient Babylonia through Rome of the fourth century A.D. You see astrology as the base of a learned theology, the influence of the Neo-Pythagoreans, forms of oriental mysteries, the devotion of the emperors to the sun cult (such as the Sol Invictus of Aurelian), and much more. The second part deals with conceptions of the world as formed by astrology, the theology bound up with them, and moral and eschatological ideas. Introduction. Index. 128pp. 5⅜ x 8.
T581 Paperbound $1.35

AFTER LIFE IN ROMAN PAGANISM, Franz Cumont. Deepest thoughts, beliefs of epoch between republican period and fall of Roman paganism. Contemporary settings, hidden lore, sources in Greek, Hebrew, Egyptian, prehistoric thought. Secret teachings of mystery religions, Hermetic writings, the gnosis, Pythagoreans, Orphism; sacrifices, nether world, immortality; Hades, problem of violent death, death of children; reincarnation, ecstacy, purification; etc. Introduction. Index. 239pp. 5⅜ x 8.
T573 Paperbound $1.35

History, Political Science, Americana

THE POLITICAL THOUGHT OF PLATO AND ARISTOTLE, E. Barker. One of the clearest and most accurate expositions of the corpus of Greek political thought. This standard source contains exhaustive analyses of the "Republic" and other Platonic dialogues and Aristotle's "Politics" and "Ethics," and discusses the origin of these ideas in Greece, contributions of other Greek theorists, and modifications of Greek ideas by thinkers from Aquinas to Hegel. "Must" reading for anyone interested in the history of Western thought. Index. Chronological Table of Events. 2 Appendixes. xxiv + 560pp. 5⅜ x 8.
T521 Paperbound $1.85

CATALOG OF DOVER BOOKS

THE ANCIENT GREEK HISTORIANS, J. B. Bury. This well known, easily read work covers the entire field of classical historians from the early writers to Herodotus, Thucydides, Xenophon, through Poseidonius and such Romans as Tacitus, Cato, Caesar, Livy. Scores of writers are studied biographically, in style, sources, accuracy, structure, historical concepts, and influences. Recent discoveries such as the Oxyrhincus papyri are referred to, as well as such great scholars as Nissen, Gomperz, Cornford, etc. "Totally unblemished by pedantry." Outlook. "The best account in English," Dutcher, A Guide to Historical Lit. Bibliography, Index. x + 281pp. 5⅜ x 8.
T397 Paperbound **$1.50**

HISTORY OF THE LATER ROMAN EMPIRE, J. B. Bury. This standard work by the leading Byzantine scholar of our time discusses the later Roman and early Byzantine empires from 395 A.D. through the death of Justinian in 565, in their political, social, cultural, theological, and military aspects. Contemporary documents are quoted in full, making this the most complete reconstruction of the period and a fit successor to Gibbon's "Decline and Fall." "Most unlikely that it will ever be superseded," Glanville Downey, Dumbarton Oaks Research Lib. Geneological tables. 5 maps. Bibliography. Index. 2 volumes total of 965pp. 5⅜ x 8.
T398, 399 Two volume set, Paperbound **$4.00**

A HISTORY OF ANCIENT GEOGRAPHY, E. H. Bunbury. Standard study, in English, of ancient geography; never equalled for scope, detail. First full account of history of geography from Greeks' first world picture based on mariners, through Ptolemy. Discusses every important map, discovery, figure, travel, expedition, war, conjecture, narrative, bearing on subject. Chapters on Homeric geography, Herodotus, Alexander expedition, Strabo, Pliny, Ptolemy, would stand alone as exhaustive monographs. Includes minor geographers, men not usually regarded in this context: Hecataeus, Pytheas, Hipparchus, Artemidorus, Marinus of Tyre, etc. Uses information gleaned from military campaigns such as Punic Wars, Hannibal's passage of Alps, campaigns of Lucullus, Pompey, Caesar's wars, the Trojan War. New introduction by W. H. Stahl, Brooklyn College. Bibliography. Index. 20 maps. 1426pp. 5⅜ x 8.
T570-1, clothbound, 2-volume set **$12.50**

THE EYES OF DISCOVERY, J. Bakeless. A vivid reconstruction of how unspoiled America appeared to the first white men. Authentic and enlightening accounts of Hudson's landing in New York, Coronado's trek through the Southwest; scores of explorers, settlers, trappers, soldiers. America's pristine flora, fauna, and Indians in every region and state in fresh and unusual new aspects. "A fascinating view of what the land was like before the first highway went through," Time. 68 contemporary illustrations, 39 newly added in this edition. Index. Bibliography. x + 500pp. 5⅜ x 8.
T761 Paperbound **$2.00**

AUDUBON AND HIS JOURNALS, J. J. Audubon. A collection of fascinating accounts of Europe and America in the early 1800's through Audubon's own eyes. Includes the Missouri River Journals —an eventful trip through America's untouched heartland, the Labrador Journals, the European Journals, the famous "Episodes", and other rare Audubon material, including the descriptive chapters from the original letterpress edition of the "Ornithological Studies", omitted in all later editions. Indispensable for ornithologists, naturalists, and all lovers of Americana and adventure. 70-page biography by Audubon's granddaughter. 38 illustrations. Index. Total of 1106pp. 5⅜ x 8.
T675 Vol I Paperbound **$2.00**
T676 Vol II Paperbound **$2.00**
The set **$4.00**

TRAVELS OF WILLIAM BARTRAM, edited by Mark Van Doren. The first inexpensive illustrated edition of one of the 18th century's most delightful books is an excellent source of first-hand material on American geography, anthropology, and natural history. Many descriptions of early Indian tribes are our only source of information on them prior to the infiltration of the white man. "The mind of a scientist with the soul of a poet," John Livingston Lowes. 13 original illustrations and maps. Edited with an introduction by Mark Van Doren. 448pp. 5⅜ x 8.
T13 Paperbound **$2.00**

GARRETS AND PRETENDERS: A HISTORY OF BOHEMIANISM IN AMERICA, A. Parry. The colorful and fantastic history of American Bohemianism from Poe to Kerouac. This is the only complete record of hoboes, cranks, starving poets, and suicides. Here are Pfaff, Whitman, Crane, Bierce, Pound, and many others. New chapters by the author and by H. T. Moore bring this thorough and well-documented history down to the Beatniks. "An excellent account," N. Y. Times. Scores of cartoons, drawings, and caricatures. Bibliography. Index. xxviii + 421pp. 5⅜ x 8⅜.
T708 Paperbound **$1.95**

POLITICAL PARTIES, Robert Michels. Classic of social science, reference point for all later work, deals with nature of leadership in social organization on government and trade union levels. Probing tendency of oligarchy to replace democracy, it studies need for leadership, desire for organization, psychological motivations, vested interests, hero worship, reaction of leaders to power, press relations, many other aspects. Trans. by E. & C. Paul. Introduction. 447pp. 5⅜ x 8.
T569 Paperbound **$2.00**

THE EXPLORATION OF THE COLORADO RIVER AND ITS CANYONS, J. W. Powell. The thrilling first-hand account of the expedition that filled in the last white space on the map of the United States. Rapids, famine, hostile Indians, and mutiny are among the perils encountered as the unknown Colorado Valley reveals its secrets. This is the only uncut version of Major Powell's classic of exploration that has been printed in the last 60 years. Includes later reflections and subsequent expedition. 250 illustrations, new map. 400pp. 5⅝ x 8⅜.
T94 Paperbound **$2.00**

CATALOG OF DOVER BOOKS

FARES, PLEASE! by J. A. Miller. Authoritative, comprehensive, and entertaining history of local public transit from its inception to its most recent developments: trolleys, horsecars, streetcars, buses, elevateds, subways, along with monorails, "road-railers," and a host of other extraordinary vehicles. Here are all the flamboyant personalities involved, the vehement arguments, the unusual information, and all the nostalgia. "Interesting facts brought into especially vivid life," N. Y. Times. New preface. 152 illustrations, 4 new. Bibliography. xix + 204pp. 5⅜ x 8. T671 Paperbound **$1.50**

GARDNER'S PHOTOGRAPHIC SKETCH BOOK OF THE CIVIL WAR, Alexander Gardner. The first published collection of Civil War photographs, by one of the two or three most famous photographers of the era, outstandingly reproduced from the original positives. Scenes of crucial battles: Appomattox, Manassas, Mechanicsville, Bull Run, Yorktown, Fredericksburg, etc. Gettysburg immediately after retirement of forces. Battle ruins at Richmond, Petersburg, Gaines'Mill. Prisons, arsenals, a slave pen, fortifications, headquarters, pontoon bridges, soldiers, a field hospital. A unique glimpse into the realities of one of the bloodiest wars in history, with an introductory text to each picture by Gardner himself. Until this edition, there were only five known copies in libraries, and fewer in private hands, one of which sold at auction in 1952 for $425. Introduction by E. F. Bleiler. 100 full page 7 x 10 photographs (original size). 224pp. 8½ x 10¾. T476 Clothbound **$6.00**

Art, History of Art, Graphic Arts, Handcrafts

ART STUDENTS' ANATOMY, E. J. Farris. Outstanding art anatomy that uses chiefly living objects for its illustrations. 71 photos of undraped man, woman, and child are accompanied by carefully labeled matching sketches to illustrate the skeletal system, articulations and movements, bony landmarks, the muscular system, skin, fasciae, fat, etc. 9 x-ray photos show movement of joints. Undraped models are shown in such actions as serving in tennis, drawing a bow in archery, playing football, dancing, preparing to spring and to dive. Also discussed and illustrated are proportions, age and sex differences, the anatomy of the smile, etc. 8 plates by the great early 18th century anatomic illustrator Siegfried Albinus are also included. Glossary. 158 figures, 7 in color. x + 159pp. 5⅝ x 8⅜. T744 Paperbound **$1.45**

AN ATLAS OF ANATOMY FOR ARTISTS, F Schider. A new 3rd edition of this standard text enlarged by 52 new illustrations of hands, anatomical studies by Cloquet, and expressive life studies of the body by Barcsay. 189 clear detailed plates offer you precise information of impeccable accuracy. 29 plates show all aspects of the skeleton, with closeups of special areas, while 54 full-page plates, mostly in two colors, give human musculature as seen from four different points of view, with cutaways for important portions of the body. 14 full-page plates provide photographs of hand forms, eyelids, female breasts, and indicate the location of muscles upon models. 59 additional plates show how great artists of the past utilized human anatomy. They reproduce sketches and finished work by such artists as Michelangelo, Leonardo da Vinci, Goya, and 15 others. This is a lifetime reference work which will be one of the most important books in any artist's library. "The standard reference tool," AMERICAN LIBRARY ASSOCIATION. "Excellent," AMERICAN ARTIST. Third enlarged edition. 189 plates, 647 illustrations. xxvi + 192pp. 7⅞ x 10⅝. T241 Clothbound **$6.00**

AN ATLAS OF ANIMAL ANATOMY FOR ARTISTS, W. Ellenberger, H. Baum, H. Dittrich. The largest, richest animal anatomy for artists available in English. 99 detailed anatomical plates of such animals as the horse, dog, cat, lion, deer, seal, kangaroo, flying squirrel, cow, bull, goat, monkey, hare, and bat. Surface features are clearly indicated, while progressive beneath-the-skin pictures show musculature, tendons, and bone structure. Rest and action are exhibited in terms of musculature and skeletal structure and detailed cross-sections are given for heads and important features. The animals chosen are representative of specific families so that a study of these anatomies will provide knowledge of hundreds of related species. "Highly recommended as one of the very few books on the subject worthy of being used as an authoritative guide," DESIGN. "Gives a fundamental knowledge," AMERICAN ARTIST. Second revised, enlarged edition with new plates from Cuvier, Stubbs, etc. 288 illustrations. 153pp. 11⅜ x 9. T82 Clothbound **$6.00**

THE HUMAN FIGURE IN MOTION, Eadweard Muybridge. The largest selection in print of Muybridge's famous high-speed action photos of the human figure in motion. 4789 photographs illustrate 162 different actions: men, women, children—mostly undraped—are shown walking, running, carrying various objects, sitting, lying down, climbing, throwing, arising, and performing over 150 other actions. Some actions are shown in as many as 150 photographs each. All in all there are more than 500 action strips in this enormous volume, series shots taken at shutter speeds of as high as 1/6000th of a second! These are not posed shots, but true stopped motion. They show bone and muscle in situations that the human eye is not fast enough to capture. Earlier, smaller editions of these prints have brought $40 and more on the out-of-print market. "A must for artists," ART IN FOCUS. "An unparalleled dictionary of action for all artists," AMERICAN ARTIST. 390 full-page plates, with 4789 photographs. Printed on heavy glossy stock. Reinforced binding with headbands. 7⅞ x 10⅝.
T204 Clothbound **$10.00**

CATALOG OF DOVER BOOKS

ANIMALS IN MOTION, Eadweard Muybridge. This is the largest collection of animal action photos in print. 34 different animals (horses, mules, oxen, goats, camels, pigs, cats, guanacos, lions, gnus, deer, monkeys, eagles—and 21 others) in 132 characteristic actions. The horse alone is shown in more than 40 different actions. All 3919 photographs are taken in series at speeds up to 1/6000th of a second. The secrets of leg motion, spinal patterns, head movements, strains and contortions shown nowhere else are captured. You will see exactly how a lion sets his foot down; how an elephant's knees are like a human's—and how they differ; the position of a kangaroo's legs in mid-leap; how an ostrich's head bobs; details of the flight of birds—and thousands of facets of motion only the fastest cameras can catch. Photographed from domestic animals and animals in the Philadelphia zoo, it contains neither semiposed artificial shots nor distorted telephoto shots taken under adverse conditions. Artists, biologists, decorators, cartoonists, will find this book indispensable for understanding animals in motion. "A really marvelous series of plates," NATURE (London). "The dry plate's most spectacular early use was by Eadweard Muybridge," LIFE. 3919 photographs; 380 full pages of plates. 440pp. Printed on heavy glossy paper. Deluxe binding with headbands. 7⅞ x 10⅝.
T203 Clothbound **$10.00**

THE HUMAN FIGURE, J. H. Vanderpoel. Every important artistic element of the human figure is pointed out in minutely detailed word descriptions in this classic text and illustrated as well in 430 pencil and charcoal drawings. Thus the text of this book directs your attention to all the characteristic features and subtle differences of the male and female (adults, children, and aged persons), as though a master artist were telling you what to look for at each stage. 2nd edition, revised and enlarged by George Bridgman. Foreword. 430 illustrations. 143pp. 6⅛ x 9¼.
T432 Paperbound **$1.45**

ANIMAL DRAWING: ANATOMY AND ACTION FOR ARTISTS, C. R. Knight. The author and illustrator of this work was "the most distinguished painter of animal life." This extensive course in animal drawing discusses musculature, bone structure, animal psychology, movements, habits, habitats. Innumerable tips on proportions, light and shadow play, coloring, hair formation, feather arrangement, scales, how anmials lie down, animal expressions, etc., from great apes to birds. Pointers on avoiding gracelessness in horses, deer; on introducing proper power and bulk to heavier animals; on giving proper grace and subtle expression to members of the cat family. Originally titled "Animal Anatomy and Psychology for the Artist and Layman." Over 123 illustrations. 149pp. 8¼ x 10½.
T426 Paperbound **$2.00**

PRINCIPLES OF ART HISTORY, H. Wölfflin. Analyzing such terms as "baroque," "classic," "neoclassic," "primitive," "picturesque," and 164 different works by artists like Botticelli, van Cleve, Dürer, Hobbema, Holbein, Hals, Rembrandt, Titian, Brueghel, Vermeer, and many others, the author establishes the classifications of art history and style on a firm, concrete basis. This classic of art criticism shows what really occurred between the 14th century primitives and the sophistication of the 18th century in terms of basic attitudes and philosophies. "A remarkable lesson in the art of seeing," SAT. REV. OF LITERATURE. Translated from the 7th German edition. 150 illustrations. 254pp. 6⅛ x 9¼.
T276 Paperbound **$2.00**

THE MATERIALS AND TECHNIQUES OF MEDIEVAL PAINTING, D. V. Thompson. Based on years of study of medieval manuscripts and laboratory analysis of medieval paintings, this book discusses carriers and grounds, binding media, pigments, metals used in painting, etc. Considers relative merits of painting al fresco and al secco, the procession of coloring materials burnishing, and many other matters. Preface by Bernard Berenson. Index. 239pp. 5⅜ x 8.
T327 Paperbound **$1.85**

THE CRAFTSMAN'S HANDBOOK, Cennino Cennini. This is considered the finest English translation of IL LIBRO DELL' ARTE, a 15th century Florentine introduction to art technique. It is both fascinating reading and a wonderful mirror of another culture for artists, art students, historians, social scientists, or anyone interested in details of life some 500 years ago. While it is not an exact recipe book, it gives directions for such matters as tinting papers, gilding stone, preparation of various hues of black, and many other useful but nearly forgotten facets of the painter's art. As a human document reflecting the ideas of a practising medieval artist it is particularly important. 4 illustrations. xxvii + 142pp. D. V. Thompson translator. 6⅛ x 9¼.
T54 Paperbound **$1.25**

VASARI ON TECHNIQUE, G. Vasari. Pupil of Michelangelo and outstanding biographer of the Renaissance artists, Vasari also wrote this priceless treatise on the technical methods of the painters, architects, and sculptors of his day. This is the only English translation of this practical, informative, and highly readable work. Scholars, artists, and general readers will welcome these authentic discussions of marble statues, bronze, casting, fresco painting, oil painting, engraving, stained glass, rustic fountains and grottoes, etc. Introduction and notes by G. B. Brown. Index. 18 plates, 11 figures. xxiv + 328pp. 5⅜ x 8.
T717 Paperbound **$2.00**

HAWTHORNE ON PAINTING. A vivid recreation, from students' notes, of instruction by Charles W. Hawthorne, given for over 31 years at his famous Cape Cod School of Art. Divided into sections on the outdoor model, still life, landscape, the indoor model, and water color, each section begins with a concise essay, followed by epigrammatic comments on color, form, seeing, etc. Not a formal course, but comments of a great teacher-painter on specific student works, which will solve problems in your own painting and understanding of art. "An excellent introduction for laymen and students alike," Time. Introduction. 100pp. 5⅜ x 8.
T653 Paperbound **$1.00**

CATALOG OF DOVER BOOKS

METHODS AND MATERIALS OF PAINTING OF THE GREAT SCHOOLS AND MASTERS, C. L. Eastlake. A vast, complete, and authentic reconstruction of the secret techniques of the masters of painting, collected from hundreds of forgotten manuscripts by the eminent President of the British Royal Academy: Greek, Roman, and medieval techniques; fresco and tempera; varnishes and encaustics; the secrets of Leonardo, Van Eyck, Raphael, and many others. Art historians, students, teachers, critics, and laymen will gain new insights into the creation of the great masterpieces; while artists and craftsmen will have a treasury of valuable techniques. Index. Two volume set. Total of 1025pp. 5⅜ x 8.
T718 Paperbound **$2.00**
T719 Paperbound **$2.00**
The set **$4.00**

AFRICAN SCULPTURE, Ladislas Segy. First publication of a new book by the author of critically acclaimed AFRICAN SCULPTURE SPEAKS. It contains 163 full page plates illustrating masks, fertility figures, ceremonial objects, etc., representing the culture of 50 tribes of West and Central Africa. Over 85% of these works of art have never been illustrated before, and each is an authentic and fascinating tribal artifact. A 34 page introduction explains the anthropological, psychological, and artistic values of African sculpture. "Mr. Segy is one of its top authorities," NEW YORKER. 164 full-page photographic plates. Bibliography. 244pp. 6 x 9.
T396 Paperbound **$2.00**

PRIMITIVE ART, Franz Boas. This authoritative and exhaustive work by a great American anthropologist covers the entire gamut of primitive art. Pottery, leatherwork, metal work, stone work, wood, basketry, are treated in detail. Theories of primitive art, historical depth in art history, technical virtuosity, unconscious levels of patterning, symbolism, styles, literature, music, dance, etc. A must book for the interested layman, the anthropologist, artist, handicrafter (hundreds of unusual motifs), and the historian. Over 900 illustrations (50 ceramic vessels, 12 totem poles, etc.). 376pp. 5⅜ x 8.
T25 Paperbound **$1.95**

DESIGN MOTIFS OF ANCIENT MEXICO, J. Enciso. This unique collection of pre-Columbian stamps for textiles and pottery contains 766 superb designs from Aztec, Olmec, Totonac, Maya, and Toltec origins. Plumed serpents, calendrical elements, wind gods, animals, flowers, demons, dancers, monsters, abstract ornament, and other designs. More than 90% of these illustrations are completely unobtainable elsewhere. Use this work to bring new barbaric beauty into your crafts or drawing. Originally $17.50. Printed in three colors. 766 illustrations, thousands of motifs. 192pp. 7⅞ x 10¾.
T84 Paperbound **$1.85**

DECORATIVE ART OF THE SOUTHWEST INDIANS, D. S. Sides. A magnificent album of authentic designs (both pre- and post-Conquest) from the pottery, textiles, and basketry of the Navaho, Hopi, Mohave, Santo Domingo, and over 20 other Southwestern groups. Designs include birds, clouds, butterflies, quadrupeds, geometric forms, etc. A valuable book for folklorists, and a treasury for artists, designers, advertisers, and craftsmen, who may use without payment or permission any of the vigorous, colorful, and strongly rhythmic designs. Aesthetic and archeological notes. 50 plates. Bibliography of over 50 items.
T139 Paperbound **$1.00**

PAINTING IN THE FAR EAST, Laurence Binyon. Excellent introduction by one of greatest authorities on subject studies 1500 years of oriental art (China, Japan; also Tibet, Persia), over 250 painters. Examines works, schools, influence of Wu Tao-tzu, Kanaoka, Toba Sojo, Masanobu, Okio, etc.; early traditions; Kamakura epoch; the Great Decorators; T'ang Dynasty; Matabei, beginnings of genre; Japanese woodcut, color print; much more, all chronological, in cultural context. 42 photos. Bibliography. 317pp. 6 x 9¼.
T520 Paperbound **$2.00**

ON THE LAWS OF JAPANESE PAINTING, H. Bowie. This unusual book, based on 9 years of profound study-experience in the Late Kano art of Japan, remains the most authentic guide in English to the spirit and technique of Japanese painting. A wealth of interesting and useful data on control of the brush; practise exercises; manufacture of ink, brushes, colors; the use of various lines and dots to express moods. It is the best possible substitute for a series of lessons from a great oriental master. 66 plates with 220 illustrations. Index. xv + 177pp. 6⅛ x 9¼.
T30 Paperbound **$1.95**

JAPANESE HOMES AND THEIR SURROUNDINGS, E. S. Morse. Every aspect of the purely traditional Japanese home, from general plan and major structural features to ceremonial and traditional appointments—tatami, hibachi, shoji, tokonoma, etc. The most exhaustive discussion in English, this book is equally honored for its strikingly modern conception of architecture. First published in 1886, before the contamination of the Japanese traditions, it preserves the authentic features of an ideal of construction that is steadily gaining devotees in the Western world. 307 illustrations by the author. Index. Glossary. xxxvi + 372pp. 5⅝ x 8⅜.
T746 Paperbound **$2.00**

FOUNDATIONS OF MODERN ART, A. Ozenfant. An illuminating discussion by a great artist of the interrelationship of all forms of human creativity, from painting to science, writing to religion. The creative process is explored in all facets of art, from paleolithic cave painting to modern French painting and architecture, and the great universals of art are isolated. Expressing its countless insights in aphorisms accompanied by carefully selected illustrations, this book is itself an embodiment in prose of the creative process. Enlarged by 4 new chapters. 226 illustrations. 368pp. 6⅛ x 9¼.
T215 Paperbound **$1.95**

CATALOG OF DOVER BOOKS

BYZANTINE ART AND ARCHAEOLOGY, O. M. Dalton. Still the most thorough work in English—both in breadth and in depth—on the astounding multiplicity of Byzantine art forms throughout Europe, North Africa, and Western Asia from the 4th to the 15th century. Analyzes hundreds of individual pieces from over 160 public and private museums, libraries, and collections all over the world. Full treatment of Byzantine sculpture, painting, mosaic, jewelry, textiles, etc., including historical development, symbolism, and aesthetics. Chapters on iconography and ornament. Indispensable for study of Christian symbolism and medieval art. 457 illustrations, many full-page. Bibliography of over 2500 references. 4 Indexes. xx + 727pp. 6⅛ x 9¼. T776 Clothbound **$7.50**

METALWORK AND ENAMELLING, H. Maryon. This is probably the best book ever written on the subject. Prepared by Herbert Maryon, F.S.A., of the British Museum, it tells everything necessary for home manufacture of jewelry, rings, ear pendants, bowls, and dozens of other objects. Clearly written chapters provide precise information on such topics as materials, tools, soldering, filigree, setting stones, raising patterns, spinning metal, repoussé work, hinges and joints, metal inlaying, damascening, overlaying, niello, Japanese alloys, enamelling, cloisonné, painted enamels, casting, polishing coloring, assaying, and dozens of other techniques. This is the next best thing to apprenticeship to a master metalworker. 363 photographs and figures. 374pp. 5½ x 8½. T183 Clothbound **$8.00**

SILK SCREEN TECHNIQUES, J. I. Biegeleisen, Max A. Cohn. A complete-to-the-last-detail copiously illustrated home course in this fast growing modern art form. Full directions for building silk screen out of inexpensive materials; explanations of five basic methods of stencil preparation—paper, blockout, tusche, film, photographic—and effects possible: light and shade, washes, dry brush, oil paint type impastos, gouaches, pastels. Detailed coverage of multicolor printing, illustrated by proofs showing the stages of a 4 color print. Special section on common difficulties. 149 illustrations, 8 in color. Sources of supply. xiv + 187pp. 6⅛ x 9¼. T433 Paperbound **$1.55**

A HANDBOOK OF WEAVES, G. H. Oelsner. Now back in print! Probably the most complete book of weaves ever printed, fully explained, differentiated, and illustrated. Includes plain weaves; irregular, double-stitched, and filling satins; derivative, basket, and rib weaves; steep, undulating, broken, offset, corkscrew, interlocking, herringbone, and fancy twills; honeycomb, lace, and crepe weaves; tricot, matelassé, and montagnac weaves; and much more. Translated and revised by S. S. Dale, with supplement on the analysis of weaves and fabrics. 1875 illustrations. vii + 402pp. 6 x 9¼. T209 Clothbound **$5.00**

THE STANDARD BOOK OF QUILT MAKING AND COLLECTING, Marguerite Ickis. A complete easy-to-follow guide with all the information you need to make beautiful, useful quilts. How to plan, design, cut, sew, appliqué, avoid sewing problems, use rag bag, make borders, tuft, every other aspect. Over 100 traditional quilts shown, including over 40 full-size patterns. No better book on the market. Index. 483 illus. 1 color plate. 287pp. 6¾ x 9½. T582 Paperbound **$2.00**

DESIGN FOR ARTISTS AND CRAFTSMEN, L. Wolchonok. The most thorough course ever prepared on the creation of art motifs and designs. It teaches you to create your own designs out of things around you — from geometric patterns, plants, birds, animals, humans, landscapes, and man-made objects. It leads you step by step through the creation of more than 1300 designs, and shows you how to create design that is fresh, well-founded, and original. Mr. Wolchonok, whose text is used by scores of art schools, shows you how the same idea can be developed into many different forms, ranging from near representationalism to the most advanced forms of abstraction. The material in this book is entirely new, and combines full awareness of traditional design with the work of such men as Miro, Léger, Picasso, Moore, and others. 113 detailed exercises, with instruction hints, diagrams, and details to enable you to apply Wolchonok's methods to your own work. "A great contribution to the field of design and crafts," N. Y. SOCIETY OF CRAFTSMEN. More than 1300 illustrations. xv + 207pp. 7⅞ x 10¾. T274 Clothbound **$4.95**

BASIC BOOKBINDING, A. W. Lewis. Enables the beginner and the expert to apply the latest and most simplified techniques to rebinding old favorites and binding new paperback books. Complete lists of all necessary materials and guides to the selection of proper tools, paper, glue, boards, cloth, leather, or sheepskin covering fabrics, lettering inks and pigments, etc. You are shown how to collate a book, sew it, back it, trim it, make boards and attach them in easy step-by-step stages. Author's preface. 261 illustrations with appendix. Index. xi + 144pp. 5⅜ x 8. T169 Paperbound **$1.35**

THE UNIVERSAL PENMAN, George Bickham. This beautiful book, which first appeared in 1743, is the largest collection of calligraphic specimens, flourishes, alphabets, and calligraphic illustrations ever published. 212 full-page plates are drawn from the work of such 18th century masters of English roundhand as Dove, Champion, Bland, and 20 others. They contain 22 complete alphabets, over 2,000 flourishes, and 122 illustrations, each drawn with a stylistic grace impossible to describe. This book is invaluable to anyone interested in the beauties of calligraphy, or to any artist, hobbyist, or craftsman who wishes to use the very best ornamental handwriting and flourishes for decorative purposes. Commercial artists, advertising artists, have found it unexcelled as a source of material suggesting quality. "An essential part of any art library, and a book of permanent value," AMERICAN ARTIST. 212 plates. 224pp. 9 x 13¾. T20 Clothbound **$10.00**

CATALOG OF DOVER BOOKS

LETTERING AND ALPHABETS, J. A. Cavanagh. This unabridged reissue of LETTERING offers a full discussion, analysis, illustration of 89 basic hand lettering styles — styles derived from Caslons, Bodonis, Garamonds, Gothic, Black Letter, Oriental, and many others. Upper and lower cases, numerals and common signs pictured. Hundreds of technical hints on make-up, construction, artistic validity, strokes, pens, brushes, white areas, etc. May be reproduced without permission! 89 complete alphabets; 72 lettered specimens. 121pp. 9¾ x 8.
T53 Paperbound **$1.25**

DECORATIVE ALPHABETS AND INITIALS, ed. by Alexander Nesbitt. No payment, no permission to reproduce any one of these 3924 different letters, covering 1000 years. Crisp, clear letters all in line, from Anglo-Saxon mss., Luebeck Cathedral, 15th century Augsburg; the work of Dürer, Holbein, Cresci; Beardsley, Rossing Wadsworth, John Moylin, etc. Every imaginable style. 91 complete alphabets. 123 full-page plates. 192pp. 7¾ x 10¾.
T544 Paperbound **$2.25**

THREE CLASSICS OF ITALIAN CALLIGRAPHY, edited by Oscar Ogg. Here, combined in a single volume, are complete reproductions of three famous calligraphic works written by the greatest writing masters of the Renaissance: Arrighi's OPERINA and IL MODO, Tagliente's LO PRESENTE LIBRO, and Palatino's LIBRO NUOVO. These books present more than 200 complete alphabets and thousands of lettered specimens. The basic hand is Papal Chancery, but scores of other alphabets are also given: European and Asiatic local alphabets, foliated and art alphabets, scrolls, cartouches, borders, etc. Text is in Italian. Introduction. 245 plates. x + 272pp. 6⅛ x 9¼.
T212 Paperbound **$2.25**

CALLIGRAPHY, J. G. Schwandner. One of the legendary books in the graphic arts, copies of which brought $500 each on the rare book market, now reprinted for the first time in over 200 years. A beautiful plate book of graceful calligraphy, and an inexhaustible source of first rate material, copyright free, for artists, art directors, craftsmen, commercial artists, etc. More than 300 ornamental initials forming 12 complete alphabets, over 150 ornate frames and panels, over 200 flourishes, over 75 calligraphic pictures including a temple, cherubs, cocks, dodos, stags, chamois, foliated lions, greyhounds, etc. Thousand of calligraphic elements to be used for suggestions of quality, sophistication, antiquity, and sheer beauty. Historical introduction. 158 full-page plates. 368pp. 9 x 13.
T475 Clothbound **$10.00**

THE HISTORY AND TECHNIQUES OF LETTERING, A. Nesbitt. The only thorough inexpensive history of letter forms from the point of view of the artist. Mr. Nesbitt covers every major development in lettering from the ancient Egyptians to the present and illustrates each development with a complete alphabet. Such masters as Baskerville, Bell, Bodoni, Caslon, Koch, Kilian, Morris, Garamont, Jenson, and dozens of others are analyzed in terms of artistry and historical development. The author also presents a 65 page practical course in lettering, besides the full historical text. 89 complete alphabets; 165 additional lettered specimens. xvii + 300pp. 5⅜ x 8.
T427 Paperbound **$2.00**

FOOT-HIGH LETTERS: A GUIDE TO LETTERING (A PRACTICAL SYLLABUS FOR TEACHERS), M. Price. A complete alphabet of Classic Roman letters, each a foot high, each on a separate 16 x 22 plate—perfect for use in lettering classes. In addition to an accompanying description, each plate also contains 9 two-inch-high forms of letter in various type faces, such as "Caslon," "Empire," "Onyx," and "Neuland," illustrating the many possible derivations from the standard classical forms. One plate contains 21 additional forms of the letter A. The fully illustrated 16-page syllabus by Mr. Price, formerly of the Pratt Institute and the Rhode Island School of Design, contains dozens of useful suggestions for student and teacher alike. An indispensable teaching aid. Extensively revised. 16-page syllabus and 30 plates in slip cover, 16 x 22.
T239 Clothbound **$6.00**

THE STYLES OF ORNAMENT, Alexander Speltz. Largest collection of ornaments in print— 3765 illustrations of prehistoric, Lombard, Gothic, Frank, Romanesque, Mohammedan, Renaissance, Polish, Swiss, Rococo, Sheraton, Empire, U. S. Colonial, etc., ornament. Gargoyles, dragons, columns, necklaces, urns, friezes, furniture, buildings, keyholes, tapestries, fantastic animals, armor, religious objects, much more, all in line. Reproduce any one free. Index. Bibliography. 400 plates. 656pp. 5⅝ x 8⅜.
T557 Paperbound **$2.25**

THE BOOK OF SIGNS, Rudolf Koch. Formerly $20 to $25 on the out-of-print market, now only $1.00 in this unabridged new edition! 493 symbols from ancient manuscripts, medieval cathedrals, coins, catacombs, pottery, etc. Crosses, monograms of Roman emperors, astrological, chemical, botanical, runes, housemarks, and 7 other categories. Invaluable for handicraft workers, illustrators, scholars, etc., this material may be reproduced without permission. 493 illustrations by Fritz Kredel. 104pp. 6½ x 9¼.
T162 Paperbound **$1.00**

HANDBOOK OF DESIGNS AND DEVICES, C. P. Hornung. This unique book is indispensable to the designer, commercial artist, and hobbyist. It is not a text-book but a working collection of 1836 basic designs and variations, carefully reproduced, which may be used without permission. Variations of circle, line, band, triangle, square, cross, diamond, swastika, pentagon, octagon, hexagon, star, scroll, interlacement, shields, etc. Supplementary notes on the background and symbolism of the figures. "A necessity to every designer who would be original without having to labor heavily," ARTIST AND ADVERTISER. 204 plates. 240pp. 5⅜ x 8.
T125 Paperbound **$1.90**

CATALOG OF DOVER BOOKS

A HANDBOOK OF EARLY ADVERTISING ART, C. P. Hornung. The largest collection of copyright-free early advertising art ever compiled. Vol. I contains some 2,000 illustrations of agricultural devices, animals, old automobiles, birds, buildings, Christmas decorations (with 7 Santa Clauses by Nast), allegorical figures, fire engines, horses and vehicles, Indians, portraits, sailing ships, trains, sports, trade cuts — and 30 other categories! Vol. II, devoted to typography, has over 4000 specimens: 600 different Roman, Gothic, Barnum, Old English faces; 630 ornamental type faces; 1115 initials, hundreds of scrolls, flourishes, etc. This third edition is enlarged by 78 additional plates containing all new material. "A remarkable collection," PRINTERS' INK. "A rich contribution to the history of American design," GRAPHIS. Volume I, Pictorial. Over 2000 illustrations. xiv + 242pp. 9 x 12. T122 Clothbound **$10.00**
Volume II, Typographical. Over 4000 specimens. vii + 312pp. 9 x 12. T123 Clothbound **$10.00**
Two volume set, T121 Clothbound, only **$18.50**

THE 100 GREATEST ADVERTISEMENTS, WHO WROTE THEM AND WHAT THEY DID, J. L. Watkins. 100 (plus 13 added for this edition) of most successful ads ever to appear. "Do You Make These Mistakes in English," "They laughed when I sat down," "A Hog Can Cross the Country," "The Man in the Hathaway Shirt," over 100 more ads that changed habits of a nation, gave new expressions to the language, built reputations. Also salient facts behind ads, often in words of their creators. "Useful . . . valuable . . . enlightening," Printers' Ink. 2nd revised edition. Introduction. Foreword by Raymond Rubicam. Index. 130 illustrations. 252pp. 7¾ x 10¾.
T540 Paperbound **$2.25**

*   *   *

THE DIDEROT PICTORIAL ENCYCLOPEDIA OF TRADES AND INDUSTRY, MANUFACTURING AND THE TECHNICAL ARTS IN PLATES SELECTED FROM "L'ENCYCLOPEDIE OU DICTIONNAIRE RAISONNE DES SCIENCES, DES ARTS, ET DES METIERS" OF DENIS DIDEROT, edited with text by C. Gillispie. The first modern selection of plates from the high point of 18th century French engraving, Diderot's famous Encyclopedia. Over 2000 illustrations on 485 full page plates, most of them original size, illustrating the trades and industries of one of the most fascinating periods of modern history, 18th century France. These magnificent engravings provide an invaluable source of fresh, copyright-free material to artists and illustrators, a lively and accurate social document to students of cultures, an outstanding find to the lover of fine engravings. The plates teem with life, with men, women, and children performing all of the thousands of operations necessary to the trades before and during the early stages of the industrial revolution. Plates are in sequence, and show general operations, closeups of difficult operations, and details of complex machinery. Such important and interesting trades and industries are illustrated as sowing, harvesting, beekeeping, cheesemaking, operating windmills, milling flour, charcoal burning, tobacco processing, indigo, fishing, arts of war, salt extraction, mining, smelting iron, casting iron steel, extracting mercury, zinc, sulphur, copper, etc., slating, tinning, silverplating, gilding, making gunpowder, cannons, bells, shoeing horses, tanning, papermaking, printing, dying, and more than 40 other categories. Besides being a work of remarkable beauty and skill, this is also one of the largest collections of working figures in print. 920pp. 9 x 12. Heavy library cloth. T421 Two volume set **$18.50**

*   *   *

THE HANDBOOK OF PLANT AND FLORAL ORNAMENT, R. G. Hatton. One of the truly great collections of plant drawings for reproduction: 1200 different figures of flowering or fruiting plants—line drawings that will reproduce excellently. Selected from superb woodcuts and copperplate engravings appearing mostly in 16th and 17th century herbals including the fabulously rare "Kreuter Büch (Bock), Cruijde Boeck (Dodoens), etc. Plants classified according to botanical groups. Also excellent reading for anyone interested in home gardening or any phase of horticulture. Formerly "The Craftsman's Plant-Book: or Figures of Plants." Introductions. Over 1200 illustrations. Index. 548pp. 6⅛ x 9¼. T649 Paperbound **$2.98**

HANDBOOK OF ORNAMENT, F. S. Meyer. One of the largest collections of copyright-free traditional art in print. It contains over 3300 line cuts from Greek, Roman, Medieval, Islamic, Renaissance, Baroque, 18th and 19th century sources. 180 plates illustrate elements of design with networks, Gothic tracery, geometric elements, flower and animal motifs, etc., while 100 plates illustrate decorative objects: chairs, thrones, daises, cabinets, crowns, weapons, utensils, vases, jewelry, armor, heraldry, bottles, altars, and scores of other objects. Indispensable for artists, illustrators, designers, handicrafters, etc. Full text. 3300 illustrations. xiv + 548pp. 5⅜ x 8.
T302 Paperbound **$2.25**

SHAKER FURNITURE, E. D. Andrews and F. Andrews. The most illuminating study on what many scholars consider the best examples of functional furniture ever made. Includes the history of the sect and the development of Shaker style. The 48 magnificent plates show tables, chairs, cupboards, chests, boxes, desks, beds, woodenware, and much more, and are accompanied by detailed commentary. For all antique collectors and dealers, designers and decorators, historians and folklorists. "Distinguished in scholarship, in pictorial illumination, and in all the essentials of fine book making," Antiques. 3 Appendixes. Bibliography. Index. 192pp. 7⅞ x 10¾.
T679 Paperbound **$2.00**

CATALOG OF DOVER BOOKS

STIEGEL GLASS, F. W. Hunter. Acclaimed and treasured by librarians, collectors, dealers and manufacturers, this volume is a clear and entertaining account of the life, early experiments, and final achievements in early American glassware of "Baron" Stiegel. An 18th century German adventurer and industrialist, Stiegel founded an empire and produced much of the most highly esteemed early American glassware. His career and varied glassware is set forth in great detail by Mr. Hunter and a new introduction by Helen McKearin provides details revealed by later research. "This pioneer work is reprinted in an edition even more beautiful than the original," ANTIQUES DEALER. "Well worth reading," MARYLAND HISTORICAL MAGAZINE. Introduction. 171 illustrations; 12 in full color. xxii + 338pp. 7⅞ x 10¾.
T128 Clothbound **$10.00**

PINE FURNITURE OF EARLY NEW ENGLAND, R. H. Kettell. A rich understanding of one of America's most original folk arts that collectors of antiques, interior decorators, craftsmen, woodworkers, and everyone interested in American history and art will find fascinating and immensely useful. 413 illustrations of more than 300 chairs, benches, racks, beds, cupboards, mirrors, shelves, tables, and other furniture will show all the simple beauty and character of early New England furniture. 55 detailed drawings carefully analyze outstanding pieces. "With its rich store of illustrations, this book emphasizes the individuality and varied design of early American pine furniture. It should be welcomed," ANTIQUES. 413 illustrations and 55 working drawings. 475. 8 x 10¾.
T145 Clothbound **$10.00**

VITRUVIUS: TEN BOOKS ON ARCHITECTURE. Book by 1st century Roman architect, engineer, is oldest, most influential work on architecture in existence; for hundreds of years his specific instructions were followed all over the world, by such men as Bramante, Michelangelo, Palladio, etc., and are reflected in major buildings. He describes classic principles of symmetry, harmony; design of treasury, prison, etc.; methods of durability; much more. He wrote in a fascinating manner, and often digressed to give interesting sidelights, making this volume appealing reading even to the non-professional. Standard English translation, by Prof. M. H. Morgan, Harvard U. Index. 6 illus. 334pp. 5⅜ x 8.
T645 Paperbound **$2.00**

THE BROWN DECADES, Lewis Mumford. In this now classic study of the arts in America, Lewis Mumford resurrects the "buried renaissance" of the post-Civil War period. He demonstrates that it contained the seeds of a new integrity and power and documents his study with detailed accounts of the founding of modern architecture in the work of Sullivan, Richardson, Root, Roebling; landscape development of Marsh, Olmstead, and Eliot; the graphic arts of Homer, Eakins, and Ryder. 2nd revised enlarged edition. Bibliography. 12 illustrations. Index. xiv + 266pp. 5⅜ x 8.
T200 Paperbound **$1.65**

STICKS AND STONES, Lewis Mumford. A survey of the forces that have conditioned American architecture and altered its forms. The author discusses the medieval tradition in early New England villages; the Renaissance influence which developed with the rise of the merchant class; the classical influence of Jefferson's time; the "Mechanicsvilles" of Poe's generation; the Brown Decades; the philosophy of the Imperial facade; and finally the modern machine age. "A truly remarkable book," SAT. REV. OF LITERATURE. 2nd revised edition. 21 illustrations. xvii + 228pp. 5⅜ x 8.
T202 Paperbound **$1.60**

THE AUTOBIOGRAPHY OF AN IDEA, Louis Sullivan. The pioneer architect whom Frank Lloyd Wright called "the master" reveals an acute sensitivity to social forces and values in this passionately honest account. He records the crystallization of his opinions and theories, the growth of his organic theory of architecture that still influences American designers and architects, contemporary ideas, etc. This volume contains the first appearance of 34 full-page plates of his finest architecture. Unabridged reissue of 1924 edition. New introduction by R. M. Line. Index. xiv + 335pp. 5⅜ x 8.
T281 Paperbound **$1.85**

THE DRAWINGS OF HEINRICH KLEY. The first uncut republication of both of Kley's devastating sketchbooks, which first appeared in pre-World War I Germany. One of the greatest cartoonists and social satirists of modern times, his exuberant and iconoclastic fantasy and his extraordinary technique place him in the great tradition of Bosch, Breughel, and Goya, while his subject matter has all the immediacy and tension of our century. 200 drawings. viii + 128pp. 7¾ x 10¾.
T24 Paperbound **$1.85**

Miscellaneous

THE COMPLETE KANO JIU-JITSU (JUDO), H. I. Hancock and K. Higashi. Most comprehensive guide to judo, referred to as outstanding work by Encyclopaedia Britannica. Complete authentic Japanese system of 160 holds and throws, including the most spectacular, fully illustrated with 487 photos. Full text explains leverage, weight centers, pressure points, special tricks, etc.; shows how to protect yourself from almost any manner of attack though your attacker may have the initial advantage of strength and surprise. This authentic Kano system should not be confused with the many American imitations. xii + 500pp. 5⅜ x 8.
T639 Paperbound **$2.00**

CATALOG OF DOVER BOOKS

THE MEMOIRS OF JACQUES CASANOVA. Splendid self-revelation by history's most engaging scoundrel—utterly dishonest with women and money, yet highly intelligent and observant. Here are all the famous duels, scandals, amours, banishments, thefts, treacheries, and imprisonments all over Europe: a life lived to the fullest and recounted with gusto in one of the greatest autobiographies of all time. What is more, these Memoirs are also one of the most trustworthy and valuable documents we have on the society and culture of the extravagant 18th century. Here are Voltaire, Louis XV, Catherine the Great, cardinals, castrati, pimps, and pawnbrokers—an entire glittering civilization unfolding before you with an unparalleled sense of actuality. Translated by Arthur Machen. Edited by F. A. Blossom. Introduction by Arthur Symons. Illustrated by Rockwell Kent. Total of xlviii + 2216pp. 5⅜ x 8.

T338 Vol I Paperbound **$2.00**
T339 Vol II Paperbound **$2.00**
T340 Vol III Paperbound **$2.00**
The set **$6.00**

BARNUM'S OWN STORY, P. T. Barnum. The astonishingly frank and gratifyingly well-written autobiography of the master showman and pioneer publicity man reveals the truth about his early career, his famous hoaxes (such as the Fejee Mermaid and the Woolly Horse), his amazing commercial ventures, his fling in politics, his feuds and friendships, his failures and surprising comebacks. A vast panorama of 19th century America's mores, amusements, and vitality. 66 new illustrations in this edition. xii + 500pp. 5⅜ x 8.
T764 Paperbound **$1.65**

THE STORY OF THE TITANIC AS TOLD BY ITS SURVIVORS, ed. by Jack Winocour. Most significant accounts of most overpowering naval disaster of modern times: all 4 authors were survivors. Includes 2 full-length, unabridged books: "The Loss of the S.S. Titanic," by Laurence Beesley, "The Truth about the Titanic," by Col. Archibald Gracie; 6 pertinent chapters from "Titanic and Other Ships," autobiography of only officer to survive, Second Officer Charles Lightoller; and a short, dramatic account by the Titanic's wireless operator, Harold Bride. 26 illus. 368pp. 5⅜ x 8.
T610 Paperbound **$1.50**

THE PHYSIOLOGY OF TASTE, Jean Anthelme Brillat-Savarin. Humorous, satirical, witty, and personal classic on joys of food and drink by 18th century French politician, litterateur. Treats the science of gastronomy, erotic value of truffles, Parisian restaurants, drinking contests; gives recipes for tunny omelette, pheasant, Swiss fondue, etc. Only modern translation of original French edition. Introduction. 41 illus. 346pp. 5⅝ x 8⅜.
T591 Paperbound **$1.50**

THE ART OF THE STORY-TELLER, M. L. Shedlock. This classic in the field of effective storytelling is regarded by librarians, story-tellers, and educators as the finest and most lucid book on the subject. The author considers the nature of the story, the difficulties of communicating stories to children, the artifices used in story-telling, how to obtain and maintain the effect of the story, and, of extreme importance, the elements to seek and those to avoid in selecting material. A 99 page selection of Miss Shedlock's most effective stories and an extensive bibliography of further material by Eulalie Steinmetz enhance the book's usefulness. xxi + 320pp. 5⅜ x 8.
T635 Paperbound **$1.50**

CREATIVE POWER: THE EDUCATION OF YOUTH IN THE CREATIVE ARTS, Hughes Mearns. In first printing considered revolutionary in its dynamic, progressive approach to teaching the creative arts; now accepted as one of the most effective and valuable approaches yet formulated. Based on the belief that every child has something to contribute, it provides in a stimulating manner invaluable and inspired teaching insights, to stimulate children's latent powers of creative expression in drama, poetry, music, writing, etc. Mearns's methods were developed in his famous experimental classes in creative education at the Lincoln School of Teachers College, Columbia Univ. Named one of the 20 foremost books on education in recent times by National Education Association. New enlarged revised 2nd edition. Introduction. 272pp. 5⅜ x 8.
T490 Paperbound **$1.50**

FREE AND INEXPENSIVE EDUCATIONAL AIDS, T. J. Pepe, Superintendent of Schools, Southbury, Connecticut. An up-to-date listing of over 1500 booklets, films, charts, etc. 5% costs less than 25¢; 1% costs more; 94% is yours for the asking. Use this material privately, or in schools from elementary to college, for discussion, vocational guidance, projects. 59 categories include health, trucking, textiles, language, weather, the blood, office practice, wild life, atomic energy, other important topics. Each item described according to contents, number of pages or running time, level. All material is educationally sound, and without political or company bias. 1st publication. Extensive index. xii + 289pp. 5⅜ x 8.
T663 Paperbound **$1.35**

THE WORLD'S GREAT SPEECHES, edited by **Lewis Copeland** and **Lawrence Lamm.** 255 speeches ranging over scores of topic and moods (including a special section of "Informal Speeches") and a fine collection of historically important speeches of the U.S.A. and other western hemisphere countries), present the greatest speakers of all time from Pericles of Athens to Churchill, Roosevelt, and Dylan Thomas. Invaluable as a guide to speakers, fascinating as history both past and contemporary, much material here is available elsewhere only with great difficulty. 3 indices: Topic, Author, Nation. xx + 745pp. 5⅜ x 8. T376 Paperbound **$2.49**

CATALOG OF DOVER BOOKS

THE ROMANCE OF WORDS, E. Weekley. An entertaining collection of unusual word-histories that tracks down for the general reader the origins of more than 2000 common words and phrases in English (including British and American slang): discoveries often surprising, often humorous, that help trace vast chains of commerce in products and ideas. There are Arabic trade words, cowboy words, origins of family names, phonetic accidents, curious wanderings, folk-etymologies, etc. Index. xiii + 210pp. 5⅜ x 8.   T710 Paperbound **$1.25**

PHRASE AND WORD ORIGINS: A STUDY OF FAMILIAR EXPRESSIONS, A. H. Holt. One of the most entertaining books on the unexpected origins and colorful histories of words and phrases, based on sound scholarship, but written primarily for the layman. Over 1200 phrases and 1000 separate words are covered, with many quotations, and the results of the most modern linguistic and historical researches. "A right jolly book Mr. Holt has made," N. Y. Times. v + 254pp. 5⅜ x 8.   T758 Paperbound **$1.35**

AMATEUR WINE MAKING, S. M. Tritton. Now, with only modest equipment and no prior knowledge, you can make your own fine table wines. A practical handbook, this covers every type of grape wine, as well as fruit, flower, herb, vegetable, and cereal wines, and many kinds of mead, cider, and beer. Every question you might have is answered, and there is a valuable discussion of what can go wrong at various stages along the way. Special supplement of yeasts and American sources of supply. 13 tables. 32 illustrations. Glossary. Index. 239pp. 5½ x 8½.   T514 Clothbound **$4.00**

SAILING ALONE AROUND THE WORLD. Captain Joshua Slocum. A great modern classic in a convenient inexpensive edition. Captain Slocum's account of his single-handed voyage around the world in a 34 foot boat which he rebuilt himself. A nearly unparalleled feat of seamanship told with vigor, wit, imagination, and great descriptive power. "A nautical equivalent of Thoreau's account," Van Wyck Brooks. 67 illustrations. 308pp. 5⅜ x 8.
T326 Paperbound **$1.00**

TREASURY OF THE WORLD'S COINS, Fred Reinfeld. The finest general introduction to numismatics, non-technical, thorough, always fascinating. Coins of Greece, Rome, modern countries of every continent, primitive societies, such oddities as the 50 lb. stone money of Yap, the nail coinage of New England; all mirror man's economy, customs, religion, politics, philosophy, and art. An entertaining, absorbing study, and a novel view of history. Over 750 illustrations. Table of value of coins illustrated. List of U.S. coin clubs. Bibliographical material. Index. 224pp. 6½ x 9¼.   T457 Paperbound **$1.75**

HOAXES, C. D. MacDougall. Shows how art, science, history, journalism can be perverted for private purposes. Hours of delightful entertainment and a work of scholarly value, this often shocking book tells of the deliberate creation of nonsense news, the Cardiff giant, Shakespeare forgeries, the Loch Ness monster, Biblical frauds, political schemes, literary hoaxers like Chatterton, Ossian, the disumbrationist school of painting, the lady in black at Valentino's tomb, and over 250 others. It will probably reveal the truth about a few things you've believed, and help you spot more readily the editorial "gander" and planted publicity release. "A stupendous collection . . . and shrewd analysis." New Yorker. New revised edition. 54 photographs. Index. 320pp. 5⅜ x 8.   T465 Paperbound **$1.75**

A HISTORY OF THE WARFARE OF SCIENCE WITH THEOLOGY IN CHRISTENDOM, A. D. White. Most thorough account ever written of the great religious-scientific battles shows gradual victory of science over ignorant, harmful beliefs. Attacks on theory of evolution; attacks on Galileo; great medieval plagues caused by belief in devil-origin of disease; attacks on Franklin's experiments with electricity; the witches of Salem; scores more that will amaze you. Author, co-founder and first president of Cornell U., writes with vast scholarly background, but in clear, readable prose. Acclaimed as classic effort in America to do away with superstition. Index. Total of 928pp. 5⅜ x 8.   T608 Vol I Paperbound **$1.85**
T609 Vol II Paperbound **$1.85**

Dover publishes books on art, music, philosophy, literature, languages, history, social sciences, psychology, handcrafts, orientalia, puzzles and entertainments, chess, pets and gardens, books explaining science, intermediate and higher mathematics mathematical physics, engineering, biological sciences, earth sciences, classics of science, etc. Write to:

Dept. catrr.
Dover Publications, Inc.
180 Varick Street, N. Y. 14, N. Y.